Lewis Ward Mudge

Songs of Praise

With Tunes

Lewis Ward Mudge

Songs of Praise
With Tunes

ISBN/EAN: 9783337020767

Printed in Europe, USA, Canada, Australia, Japan

Cover: Foto ©Thomas Meinert / pixelio.de

More available books at **www.hansebooks.com**

FOR SOCIAL AND SABBATH WORSHIP

Songs of Praise

WITH TUNES

COMPILED AND EDITED

BY

LEWIS WARD MUDGE

Copyright 1889, by

A. S. BARNES & CO

NEW YORK AND CHICAGO

SONGS OF PRAISE SERIES.

SONGS OF PRAISE.—*A companion, not an abridgment of*

I. Carmina Sanctorum:

A SELECTION OF

HYMNS AND SONGS OF PRAISE, WITH TUNES,

EDITED BY

ROSWELL D. HITCHCOCK, ZACHARY EDDY,
LEWIS WARD MUDGE.

746 Hymns, 452 Tunes, 48 Chants, 21 Doxologies, 7 Separate Indexes, 447 pp. Quarto. Two Editions of Hymns without Music.

II. The People's Praise Book;

OR,

CARMINA SANCTORUM, BAPTIST EDITION,

EDITED BY

HENRY M. SANDERS, GEORGE A. LORIMER,

With the Editors of the Carmina.

PREFACE.

SONGS OF PRAISE has been carefully prepared with one aim in view—to furnish a book of sacred song adapted to the needs of Churches and Christian Associations in social worship. Many of its hymns are also in the larger collection, the Carmina Sanctorum, and in such cases the same tunes will be found, in almost every instance, at the same opening. Many hymns, however, have been added, especially such as are adapted to seasons of religious interest, and such as emphasize Christian aspirations and the activities of the Christian life. The musical adaptations also have been carefully studied to meet the requirements of social worship.

The same thoroughness of editing which is a marked feature of the Carmina Sanctorum will be found to characterize this book, and the copious indexes will, it is hoped, not only aid in ready reference, but also enhance the literary value of the book.

Copyright music or hymns must not be taken from this volume, for the sake of publication, without the permission of those who own the same.

LEWIS W. MUDGE.

CONTENTS.

	HYMNS.	PAGES.
OPENING AND CLOSING HYMNS	1–32	5–15
MORNING AND EVENING	33–60	16–27
THE LORD'S DAY	61–67	28–30
PRAISE TO GOD	68–96	31–41
THE LORD JESUS CHRIST	97–144	42–61
THE HOLY SPIRIT	145–170	62–69
THE HOLY SCRIPTURES	171–177	70–72
SALVATION OFFERED	178–211	73–88
SALVATION SOUGHT AND FOUND	212–257	89–107
GRACE MAGNIFIED	258–295	108–123
PILGRIM SONGS	296–310	124–130
WARFARE AND VICTORY	311–328	131–136
THE CHRISTIAN LIFE	329–403	137–163
THE LORD'S SUPPER	404–422	164–171
THE COMMUNION OF SAINTS	423–430	172–173
HYMNS FOR CHILDREN	431–436	174–175
MISSIONS	437–469	176–187
LIFE AND DEATH	470–477	188–190
HEAVEN	478–488	191–194
TIMES AND SEASONS	489–503	195–200
DOXOLOGIES		201–202
ALPHABETICAL INDEX OF TUNES		203–205
METRICAL INDEX OF TUNES		206–208
INDEX OF AUTHORS		209–212
INDEX OF COMPOSERS		213–215
INDEX OF SCRIPTURE TEXTS		216–220
INDEX OF SUBJECTS		221–233
INDEX OF FIRST LINES		234–239

SONGS OF PRAISE.

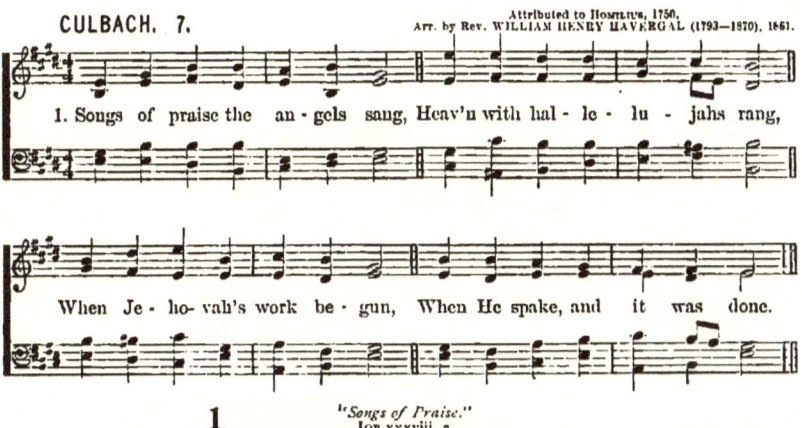

CULBACH. 7.
Attributed to HOMILIUS, 1750.
Arr. by Rev. WILLIAM HENRY HAVERGAL (1793—1870). 1861.

1. Songs of praise the an-gels sang, Heav'n with hal-le-lu-jahs rang,
When Je-ho-vah's work be-gun, When He spake, and it was done.

1 "*Songs of Praise.*"
   JOB xxxviii. 7.

2 Songs of praise awoke the morn,
  When the Prince of Peace was born;
  Songs of praise arose, when He
  Captive led captivity.

3 Heaven and earth must pass away,
  Songs of praise shall crown that day;
  God will make new heavens, new earth,
  Songs of praise shall hail their birth.

4 Saints below, with heart and voice,
  Still in songs of praise rejoice;
  Learning here, by faith and love,
  Songs of praise to sing above.

5 Borne upon their latest breath,
  Songs of praise shall conquer death;
  Then, amidst eternal joy,
  Songs of praise their powers employ.
              James Montgomery (1771—1854), 1819, 1853. Ab.

OPENING HYMNS.

ROCKINGHAM. L. M.
LOWELL MASON, (1792—1872), 1832.

1. Come, dear-est Lord, de-scend and dwell, By faith and love, in ev-'ry breast;
Then shall we know, and taste, and feel, The joys that can-not be ex-prest.

2 *The love of God shed abroad in the heart.*
Rom. iii. 16.

2 Come, fill our hearts with inward strength;
Make our enlarged souls possess,
And learn the height and breadth and length
Of Thine immeasurable grace. [length

3 Now to the God, whose power can do
More than our thoughts or wishes know,
Be everlasting honors done,
By all the church, thro' Christ, His Son.
Rev. Isaac Watts (1674—1748), 1709.

3 *Delight in Worship.*

1 Far from my thoughts, vain world, be gone;
Let my religious hours alone;
Fain would mine eyes my Saviour see;
I wait a visit, Lord, from Thee.

2 My heart grows warm with holy fire,
And kindles with a pure desire;
Come, my dear Jesus, from above,
And feed my soul with heavenly love.

3 Blest Jesus, what delicious fare,
How sweet Thine entertainments are:
Never did angels taste above
Redeeming grace, and dying love.

4 Hail, great Immanuel, all-divine,
In Thee Thy Father's glories shine:
Thou brightest, sweetest, fairest One,
That eyes have seen, or angels known.
Rev. Isaac Watts, 1709. Ab.

4 *Retirement and Meditation.*
Titus ii. 12.

1 My God, permit me not to be
A stranger to myself and Thee;
Amidst a thousand thoughts I rove,
Forgetful of my highest Love.

2 Call me away from flesh and sense,
One sovereign word can draw me thence
I would obey the voice divine,
And all inferior joys resign.

3 Be earth, with all her scenes, withdrawn:
Let noise and vanity be gone;
In secret silence of the mind
My heaven, and there my God, I find.
Rev. Isaac Watts, 1709. Ab

5 *"Where two or three."*
Matt. xviii. 20.

1 "Where two or three, with sweet accord
Obedient to their sovereign Lord,
Meet to recount His acts of grace,
And offer solemn prayer and praise;

2 "There," says the Saviour, "will I be,
Amid this little company;
To them unveil My smiling face,
And shed My glories round the place."

3 We meet at Thy command, dear Lord,
Relying on Thy faithful word:
Now send Thy Spirit from above,
Now fill our hearts with heavenly love.
Rev. Samuel Stennett, (1727—1795.) 1778.

MELCOMBE. L. M.
SAMUEL WEBBE (1740—1816.)

OPENING HYMNS.

ST. ALKMUND. L. M.   Arr. fr. Ancient Melody.

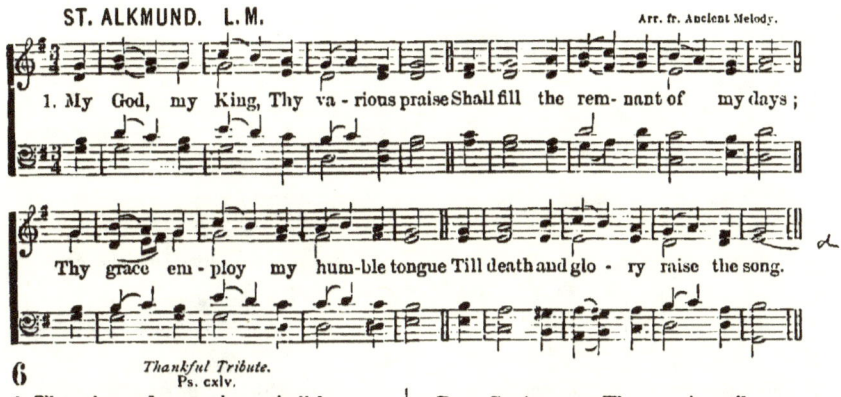

1. My God, my King, Thy va-rious praise Shall fill the rem-nant of my days;
Thy grace em-ploy my hum-ble tongue Till death and glo-ry raise the song.

6   *Thankful Tribute.*
Ps. cxlv.

2 The wings of every hour shall bear
Some thankful tribute to Thine ear,
And every setting sun shall see
New works of duty done for Thee.

3 But who can speak Thy wondrous deeds?
Thy greatness all our thoughts exceeds:
Vast and unsearchable Thy ways;
Vast and immortal be Thy praise.
                    Rev. Isaac Watts, 1709. Ab

7   *"Gate of Heaven."*
Gen. xxviii. 17.

1 How sweet to leave the world awhile,
And seek the presence of our Lord;

Dear Saviour, on Thy people smile,
And come, according to Thy word.

2 From busy scenes we now retreat,
That we may here converse with Thee:
Ah, Lord, behold us at Thy feet:
Let this the "gate of Heaven" be.

3 "Chief of ten thousand!" now appear,
That we by faith may see Thy face:
O speak, that we Thy voice may hear,
And let Thy presence fill this place.
                Rev. Thomas Kelly (1769-1855), 1809.

GILEAD. L. M.   Arr. from ETIENNE HENRI MEHUL (1763–1817), 1807.

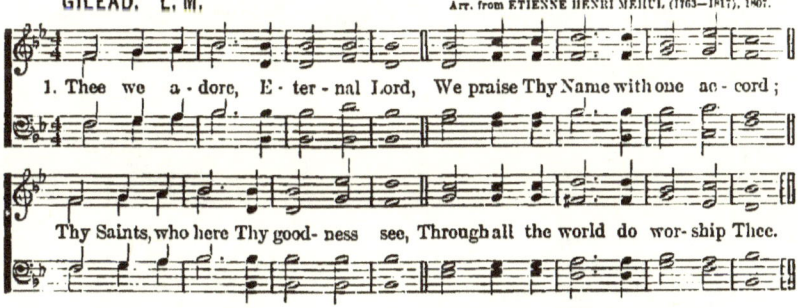

1. Thee we a-dore, E-ter-nal Lord, We praise Thy Name with one ac-cord;
Thy Saints, who here Thy good-ness see, Through all the world do wor-ship Thee.

8   *"Te Deum Laudamus."*

2 To Thee aloud all Angels cry,
The Heaven and all the Powers on high:
Thee, Holy, Holy, Holy King,
Lord God of Hosts, they ever sing.

3 The Apostles join the glorious throng;
The Prophets swell th' immortal song;

The Martyrs' noble army raise
Eternal anthems to Thy praise.

4 From day to day, O Lord, do we
Highly exalt and honor Thee:
Thy Name we worship and adore,
World without end, for evermore.
       Rev. Thomas Cotterill (1779—1823), 1819. Ab. and Alt.

OPENING AND CLOSING.

RIVAULX. L. M. Rev. JOHN BACCHUS DYKES (1823—1876). 1874.

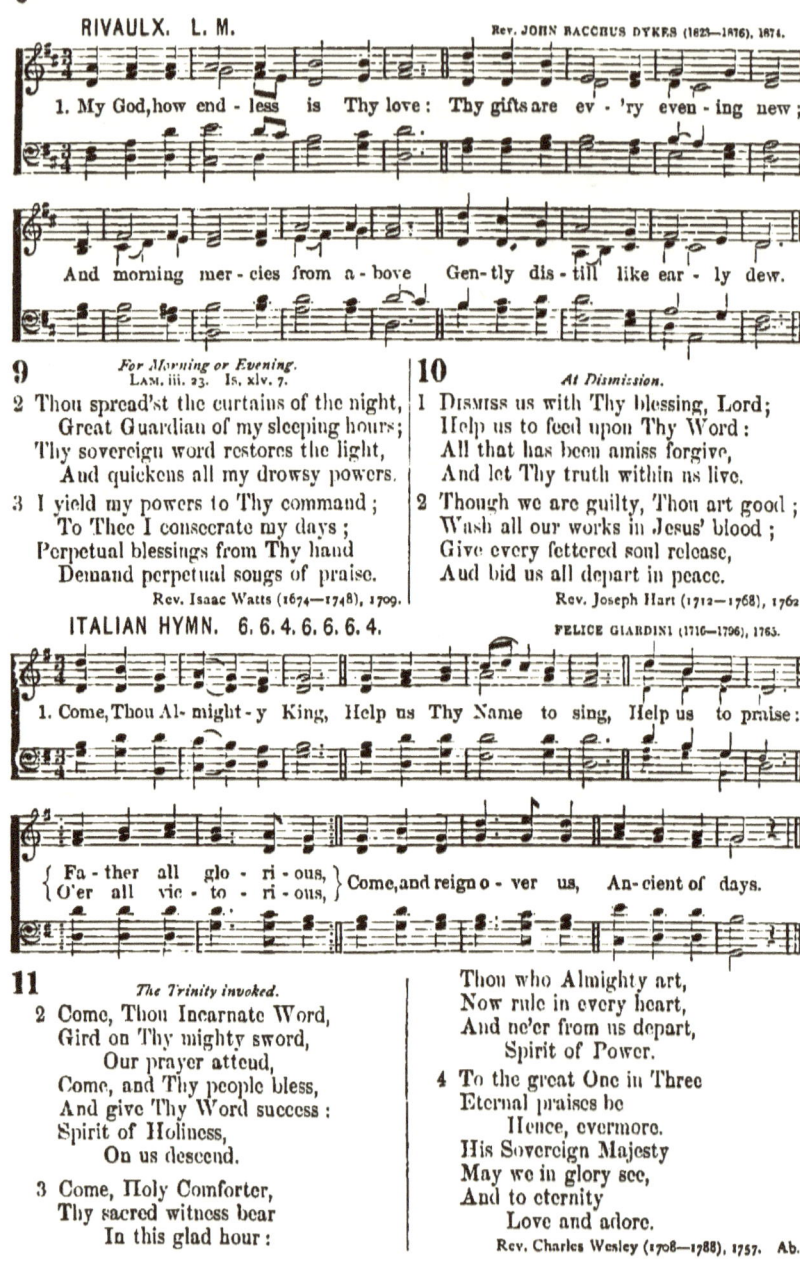

1. My God, how end-less is Thy love: Thy gifts are ev-'ry even-ing new; And morning mer-cies from a-bove Gen-tly dis-till like ear-ly dew.

9 *For Morning or Evening.*
LAM. iii. 23. Is. xlv. 7.

2 Thou spread'st the curtains of the night,
   Great Guardian of my sleeping hours;
   Thy sovereign word restores the light,
   And quickens all my drowsy powers.

3 I yield my powers to Thy command;
   To Thee I consecrate my days;
   Perpetual blessings from Thy hand
   Demand perpetual songs of praise.

        Rev. Isaac Watts (1674—1748), 1709.

10 *At Dismission.*

1 Dismiss us with Thy blessing, Lord;
  Help us to feed upon Thy Word:
  All that has been amiss forgive,
  And let Thy truth within us live.

2 Though we are guilty, Thou art good;
  Wash all our works in Jesus' blood;
  Give every fettered soul release,
  And bid us all depart in peace.

        Rev. Joseph Hart (1712—1768), 1762.

ITALIAN HYMN. 6. 6. 4. 6. 6. 6. 4. FELICE GIARDINI (1716—1796), 1763.

1. Come, Thou Al-might-y King, Help us Thy Name to sing, Help us to praise: Fa-ther all glo-ri-ous, O'er all vic-to-ri-ous, Come, and reign o-ver us, An-cient of days.

11 *The Trinity invoked.*

2 Come, Thou Incarnate Word,
  Gird on Thy mighty sword,
    Our prayer attend,
  Come, and Thy people bless,
  And give Thy Word success:
    Spirit of Holiness,
      On us descend.

3 Come, Holy Comforter,
  Thy sacred witness bear
    In this glad hour:
  Thou who Almighty art,
  Now rule in every heart,
  And ne'er from us depart,
    Spirit of Power.

4 To the great One in Three
  Eternal praises be
    Hence, evermore.
  His Sovereign Majesty
  May we in glory see,
  And to eternity
    Love and adore.

    Rev. Charles Wesley (1708—1788), 1757. Ab.

OPENING HYMNS.

12 *Praise to Jesus!*

1 Come, all ye saints of God,
Wide through the earth abroad
Spread Jesus' fame;
Tell what His love has done;
Trust in His Name alone;
Shout to His lofty throne,
"Worthy the Lamb!"

2 Hence, gloomy doubts and fears;
Dry up your mournful tears;
Join our glad theme;

8. 4.

Beauty for ashes bring;
Strike each melodious string,
Join heart and voice to sing,
"Worthy the Lamb!"

3 Hark how the choirs above,
Filled with the Saviour's love
Dwell on His Name;
There too may we be found,
With light and glory crowned,
While all the heavens resound,
"Worthy the Lamb!"

Rev. James Boden (1757—1841), 1801. Sl. alt,

ST. RAPHAEL. 8. 7. 4.

EDWARD JOHN HOPKINS (1818—),

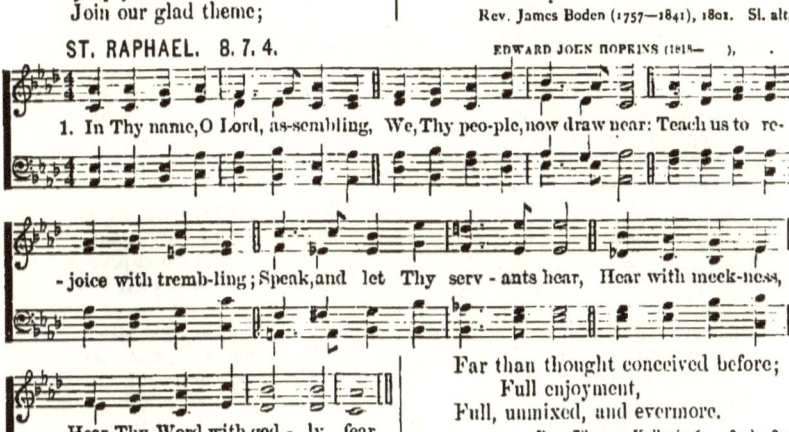

1. In Thy name, O Lord, as-sembling, We, Thy peo-ple, now draw near: Teach us to re-joice with trem-bling; Speak, and let Thy serv-ants hear, Hear with meek-ness, Hear Thy Word with god-ly fear.

13 *"Speak, for Thy servant heareth."*
1 Sam. iii, 10.

2 While our days on earth are lengthened,
May we give them, Lord, to Thee;
Cheered by hope, and daily strengthened,
May we run, nor weary be,
Till Thy glory
Without clouds in Heaven we see.

3 There in worship purer, sweeter,
Thee Thy people shall adore;
Tasting of enjoyment greater

Far than thought conceived before;
Full enjoyment,
Full, unmixed, and evermore.

Rev. Thomas Kelly (1769—1855), 1815.

14 *Dismission.*

1 Lord, dismiss us with Thy blessing,
Fill our hearts with joy and peace;
Let us now, Thy love possessing,
Triumph in redeeming grace:
O refresh us,
Traveling through this wilderness.

2 Thanks we give, and adoration,
For Thy Gospel's joyful sound:
May the fruits of Thy salvation
In our hearts and lives abound;
May Thy presence
With us evermore be found.

Rev. John Fawcett (1739—1817), 1774. Ah.

GREENVILLE. 8. 7. 4.

JEAN JACQUES ROUSSEAU (1712—1778), 1750.
D.C.

OPENING AND CLOSING.

GLEBE FIELD. 7.
Rev. JOHN BACCHUS DYKES (1823–1876), 1874.

1. Lord, we come be-fore Thee now, At Thy feet we humbly bow; O do not our suit disdain. Shall we seek Thee, Lord, in vain?

15 *Seeking after God.*
JER. xxix. 13.

2 Lord, on Thee our souls depend,
In compassion, now descend;
Fill our hearts with Thy rich grace,
Tune our lips to sing Thy praise.

3 In Thine own appointed way,
Now we seek Thee, here we stay :
Lord, we know not how to go,
Till a blessing Thou bestow.

4 Send some message from Thy Word,
That may joy and peace afford :
Let Thy Spirit now impart
Full salvation to each heart.
Rev. William Hammond (—1783), 1745. Ab.

16 *God's Omniscience.*

1 They who seek the throne of grace
Find that throne in every place ;
If we live a life of prayer,
God is present everywhere.

2 In our sickness and our health,
In our want, or in our wealth,
If we look to God in prayer,
God is present everywhere.

3 When our earthly comforts fail,
When the foes of life prevail,
'Tis the time for earnest prayer;
God is present everywhere.

4 Then, my soul, in every strait,
To thy Father come, and wait ;
He will answer every prayer :
God is present everywhere.
Oliver Holden (1765–1844), 1793. Alt.

FERRIER. 7.
Rev. JOHN BACCHUS DYKES, 1861.

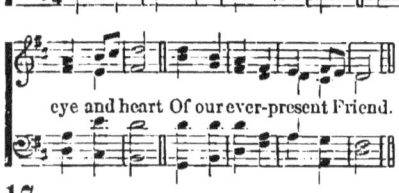

1. For a sea-son called to part, Let us now ourselves commend To the gracious eye and heart Of our ever-present Friend.

17 *Parting Hymn.*

2 Jesus, hear our humble prayer ;
Tender Shepherd of Thy sheep,
Let Thy mercy and Thy care
All our souls in safety keep.

3 In Thy strength may we be strong,
Sweeten every cross and pain ;

Give us, if we live, ere long
Here to meet in peace again.
Rev. John Newton (1725—1807), 1776. Ab.

18 *"Part in Peace."*

1 Part in peace, Christ's life was peace ;
Let us live our life in Him :
Part in peace, Christ's death was peace
Let us die our death in Him.

2 Part in peace, Christ promise gave
Of a life beyond the grave,
Where all mortal partings cease :
Brethren, sisters, part in peace.
Mrs. Sarah Flower Adams (1805—1848), 1841. Alt.

OPENING AND CLOSING.

SEYMOUR. 7. CARL MARIA von WEBER (1786—1826), 1826.
Arr. by HENRY WELLINGTON GREATOREX (1811—1858), 1849.

1. Come my soul, thy suit pre-pare, Je-sus loves to answer pray'r; Thou art com-ing to a King, Large petitions with Thee bring.

Let me live a life of faith,
Let me die Thy people's death.
Rev. John Newton, 1779. Ab.

19 *Asking of God.*
1 KINGS iii. 5.

2 With my burden I begin,
Lord, remove this load of sin;
Let Thy blood, for sinners spilt,
Set my conscience free from guilt.
3 Lord, I come to Thee for rest,
Take possession of my breast;
There Thy blood-bought right maintain,
And without a rival reign.
4 Show me what I have to do,
Every hour my strength renew;

20 *Evening Prayer.*
1 Thou, from whom we never part,
Thou, whose love is everywhere,
Thou, who seest every heart,
Listen to our evening prayer.
2 Father, fill our hearts with love,
Love unfailing, full and free;
Love that no alarm can move,
Love that ever rests on Thee.
3 Heavenly Father, through the night,
Keep us safe from every ill;
Cheerful as the morning light,
May we wake to do Thy will.
Mrs. Eliza Lee Follen (1787—1860).

HOLLEY. 7. GEORGE HEWS (1806—1873), 1835.

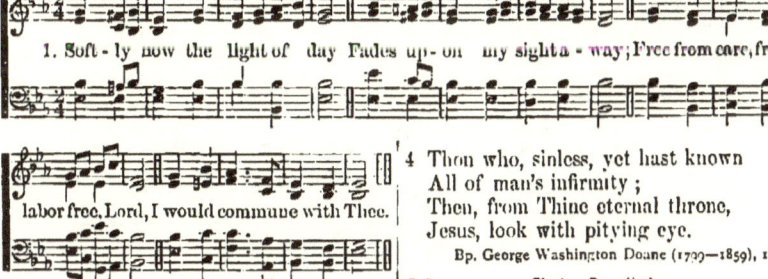

1. Soft-ly now the light of day Fades up-on my sight a-way; Free from care, from labor free, Lord, I would commune with Thee.

21 *The fading Light.*
2 Thou, whose all-pervading eye
Naught escapes, without, within,
Pardon each infirmity,
Open fault, and secret sin.
3 Soon, for me, the light of day
Shall forever pass away:
Then, from sin and sorrow free,
Take me, Lord, to dwell with Thee.

4 Thou who, sinless, yet hast known
All of man's infirmity;
Then, from Thine eternal throne,
Jesus, look with pitying eye.
Bp. George Washington Doane (1799—1859), 1824.

22 *Closing Benediction.*
HEB. xiii. 20, 24.
1 Now may He who from the dead
Brought the Shepherd of the sheep,
Jesus Christ, our King and Head,
All our souls in safety keep.
2 May He teach us to fulfil
What is pleasing in His sight;
Perfect us in all His will,
And preserve us day and night.
Rev. John Newton, 1779. Ab.

OPENING HYMNS.

SHIRLAND. S. M.   SAMUEL STANLEY (1767–1822), 1805.

1. Come, we that love the Lord, And let our joys be known: Join in a song of sweet ac-cord, And thus sur-round the Throne.

23 *Glory begun.*

2 Let those refuse to sing
   That never knew our God;
But favorites of the heavenly King
   May speak their joys abroad.

3 The men of grace have found
   Glory begun below;
Celestial fruits on earthly ground
   From faith and hope may grow.

4 The hill of Zion yields
   A thousand sacred sweets
Before we reach the heavenly fields,
   Or walk the golden streets.

5 Then let our songs abound,
   And every tear be dry;
We're marching thro' Immanuel's ground
   To fairer worlds on high.
       Rev. Isaac Watts (1674–1748), 1709. Ab.

24 *Importunity in Prayer.*
    Luke xviii. 1–7.

1 Our Lord, who knows full well
   The heart of every saint,
Invites us all our griefs to tell,
   To pray, and never faint.

2 He bows His gracious ear,
   We never plead in vain;
Yet we must wait till He appear,
   And pray, and pray again.

3 Jesus, the Lord, will hear
   His chosen when they cry;
And though He may a while forbear,
   He'll help them from on high.

4 Then let us earnest be,
   And never faint in prayer;
He loves our importunity,
   And makes our cause His care.
       Rev. John Newton (1725–1807), 1779. Ab. and alt.

THATCHER. S. M.   Arr. from GEORGE FREDERICK HANDEL (1685–1759), 1732.

1. Our Heavenly Fa-ther calls, And Christ in-vites us near; With both our friendship shall be sweet, And our communion dear.

25 *Communion with God and Christ.*
   1 John i. 3.

2 God pities all my griefs;
   He pardons every day;
Almighty to protect my soul,
   And wise to guide my way.

3 Jesus, my living Head,
   We bless Thy faithful care;
Mine Advocate before the throne,
   And my Forerunner there.

4 Here fix, my roving heart,
   Here wait, my warmest love,
Till the communion be complete,
   In nobler scenes above.
       Rev. Philip Doddridge (1702–1751), 1755. Ab.

OPENING HYMNS.

MORNINGTON. S. M.
GARRET COLLEY WELLESLEY (1735—1781), 1760.
Arr. by LOWELL MASON (1792—1872), 1822.

1. Behold the throne of grace! The promise calls me near; There Jesus shows a smiling face, And waits to answer prayer.

26   *"Ask what I shall give thee."*
     1 Kings iii. 5.

2 My soul, ask what thou wilt,
   Thou canst not be too bold ;
Since His own blood for thee He spilt,
   What else can He withhold.

3 Thine image, Lord, bestow,
   Thy presence and Thy love ;
I ask to serve Thee here below,
   And reign with Thee above.

4 Teach me to live by faith,
   Conform my will to Thine,
Let me victorious be in death,
   And then in glory shine.
           Rev. John Newton, 1779. Ab.

27   *"Pray without ceasing."*
     1 Thess. v. 17.

1 PRAY, without ceasing, pray,
   Your Captain gives the word :
His summons cheerfully obey,
   And call upon the Lord.

2 To God your every want
   In instant prayer display ;
Pray always ; pray; and never faint ;
   Pray, without ceasing, pray.

3 From strength to strength go on ;
   Wrestle, and fight, and pray ;
Tread all the powers of darkness down,
   And win the well-fought day.

4 Still let the Spirit cry,
   In all His soldiers—"Come,"
Till Christ the Lord descends from high,
   And takes the conquerors home.
       Rev. Charles Wesley (1708—1788), 1749. Ab.

DIX. 7. 6l.
CONRAD KOCHER (1786—1872), 1838.
Arr. by WILLIAM HENRY MONK (1823—), 1861.

1. { God of mercy, God of grace, Show the brightness of Thy face;
    Shine upon us, Saviour, shine, Fill Thy Church with light divine;}
And Thy saving health extend Unto earth's remotest end.

28   *"God of Mercy, God of Grace."*
     Ps. lxvii.

2 Let the people praise Thee, Lord,
Be by all that live adored :
Let the nations shout and sing
Glory to their Saviour-King ;
At Thy feet their tribute pay,
And Thy holy will obey.

3 Let the people praise Thee, Lord,
Earth shall then her fruits afford :
God to man His blessing give,
Man to God devoted live ;
All below, and all above,
One in joy, and light, and love.
       Rev. Henry Francis Lyte (1793—1847), 1834.

OPENING HYMNS.

RETREAT. L. M. THOMAS HASTINGS (1784—1872), 1840.

1. From ev - 'ry stormy wind that blows, From ev - 'ry swelling tide of woes, There is a calm, a sure re-treat: 'Tis found be-neath the mer - cy seat.

29 *The Mercy-seat.*

2 There is a place where Jesus sheds
  The oil of gladness on our heads;
  A place than all besides more sweet:
  It is the blood-bought mercy-seat.

3 There is a spot where spirits blend,
  Where friend holds fellowship with friend;

4 There, there, on eagle wings we soar,
  And time and sense seem all no more;
  And Heaven comes down our souls to greet,
  And glory crowns the mercy-seat. [greet,
    Rev. Hugh Stowell (1799—1865), 1831. Ab.

ALMSGIVING. 8. 8. 8. 4. Rev. JOHN BACCHUS DYKES (1823—1876),

1. My God, is a - ny hour so sweet, From blush of morn to evening star, As that which calls me to Thy feet, The hour of pray'r?

30 *The Hour of Prayer.*
    Phil. iv. 6, 7.

2 Blest is that tranquil hour of morn,
  And blest that solemn hour of eve,
  When, on the wings of prayer upborne,
  The world I leave.

3 Then is my strength by Thee renewed;
  Then are my sins by Thee forgiven;
  Then dost Thou cheer my solitude
  With hopes of heaven.

4 No words can tell what sweet relief
  Here for my every want I find;

  What strength for warfare, balm for
  What peace of mind.   [grief,

5 Hushed is each doubt, gone every fear;
  My spirit seems in heaven to stay;
  And e'en the penitential tear
  Is wiped away.

6 Lord, till I reach that blissful shore,
  No privilege so dear shall be
  As thus my inmost soul to pour
  In prayer to Thee.
    Miss Charlotte Elliott (1789—1871), 1834.

OPENING HYMNS.

BELMONT. C. M. SAMUEL WEBBE (1740—1816).

1. Pray'r is the soul's sin-cere de-sire, Ut-tered or un-ex-pressed, The mo-tion of a hid-den fire That trem-bles in the breast.

31 *Prayer.*

2 Prayer is the burden of a sigh,
  The falling of a tear,
  The upward glancing of an eye,
  When none but God is near.

3 Prayer is the contrite sinner's voice
  Returning from his ways,
  While angels in their songs rejoice,
  And cry, "Behold, he prays!"

4 Prayer is the Christian's vital breath,
  The Christian's native air,
  His watchword at the gates of death;
  He enters Heaven with prayer.

5 O Thou, by whom we come to God,
  The Life, the Truth, the Way,
  The path of prayer Thyself hast trod:
  Lord, teach us how to pray.

  James Montgomery (1771—1854), 1819, 1853. Ab.

WOODSTOCK. C. M. DEODATUS DUTTON, Jr., 1829.

1. I love to steal a-while a-way From ev-'ry cumbering care, And spend the hours of set-ting day In hum-ble, grate-ful pray'r.

32 *Evening Twilight.*

2 I love, in solitude, to shed
  The penitential tear;
  And all His promises to plead
  Where none but God can hear.

3 I love to think on mercies past,
  And future good implore;
  And all my cares and sorrows cast
  On Him whom I adore.

4 I love, by faith, to take a view
  Of brighter scenes in Heaven;
  The prospect doth my strength renew,
  While here by tempests driven.

5 Thus, when life's toilsome day is o'er,
  May its departing ray
  Be calm as this impressive hour,
  And lead to endless day.

  Mrs. Phœbe Hinsdale Brown (1783—1861), 1824. Ab. and alt.

MORNING AND EVENING.

EVENING HYMN. L. M. THOMAS TALLIS (1529—1585), 1565.

1. A-wake, my soul, and with the sun Thy dai-ly stage of du-ty run; Shake off dull sloth, and joy-ful rise To pay thy morn-ing sac-ri-fice.

33   *Morning Hymn.*

2 All praise to Thee who safe hast kept,
And hast refreshed me whilst I slept;
Grant, Lord, when I from death shall
    I may of endless life partake.   [wake,

3 Lord, I my vows to Thee renew:
Disperse my sins as morning dew;
Guide my first springs of thought and will,
And with Thyself my spirit fill.

4 Direct, control, suggest this day,
All I design, or do, or say;
That all my powers, with all their might,
In Thy sole glory may unite.
      Bp. Thomas Ken (1637—1711), 1697, 1709. Ab.

34   *Evening Hymn.*

1 All praise to Thee, my God, this night,
For all the blessings of the light:
Keep me, O keep me, King of kings,
Beneath Thine own almighty wings.

2 Forgive me, Lord, for Thy dear Son,
The ill that I this day have done;
That with the world, myself, and Thee,
I, ere I sleep, at peace may be.

3 Teach me to live, that I may dread
The grave as little as my bed;
To die, that this vile body may
Rise glorious at the awful day.

4 O may my soul on Thee repose,
And may sweet sleep my eyelids close;
Sleep, that shall me more vigorous make,
To serve my God when I awake.
      Bp. Thomas Ken. 1697, 1709. Ab.

35   *"Splendor paternæ gloriæ"*

1 O JESUS, Lord of light and grace,
Thou brightness of the Father's face,
Thou Fountain of eternal light,
Whose beams disperse the shades of night.

2 Come holy Sun of heavenly love,
Come in Thy radiance from above,
And to our inward hearts convey
The Holy Spirit's cloudless ray.

3 May He our actions deign to bless,
And loose the bonds of wickedness;
From sudden falls our feet defend,
And guide us safely to the end.

4 O hallowed thus be every day;
Let meekness be our morning ray,
Our faith like noontide splendor glow,
Our souls the twilight never know.
      Ambrose of Milan (140—397).
Tr. by Rev. John Chandler (1806—1876), 1837. Ab. and alt.

36   *An Evening Hymn.*

1 Great God, to Thee my evening song,
  With humble gratitude I raise;
O let Thy mercy tune my tongue,
  And fill my heart with lively praise.

2 My days, unclouded as they pass,
  And every gently rolling hour,
Are monuments of wondrous grace,
  And witness to Thy love and power

3 Seal my forgiveness in the blood
  Of Jesus; His dear name alone
I plead for pardon, gracious God,
  And kind acceptance at Thy throne.
      Miss Anne Steele (1717—1778), 1760. Ab.

HURSLEY. L. M.

1. Sun of my soul, Thou Saviour dear,
It is not night if Thou be near:
O may no earth-born cloud arise
To hide Thee from Thy servant's eyes.

37 *"Abide with us."* Luke xxiv. 29.

2 When the soft dews of kindly sleep
My wearied eyelids gently steep,
Be my last thought, how sweet to rest
Forever on my Saviour's breast.

3 Abide with me from morn till eve,
For without Thee I cannot live;
Abide with me when night is nigh,
For without Thee I dare not die.

4 If some poor wandering child of Thine
Have spurned, to-day, the voice divine;

Now, Lord, the gracious work begin;
Let him no more lie down in sin.

5 Watch by the sick; enrich the poor
With blessings from Thy boundless store;
Be every mourner's sleep to-night,
Like infant's slumbers, pure and light.

6 Come near and bless us when we wake,
Ere through the world our way we take;
Till in the ocean of Thy love,
We lose ourselves in heaven above.

Rev. John Keble (1792—1866), 1827. Ab.

HUMILITY. L. M.

SAMUEL PARKMAN TUCKERMAN (1819—),

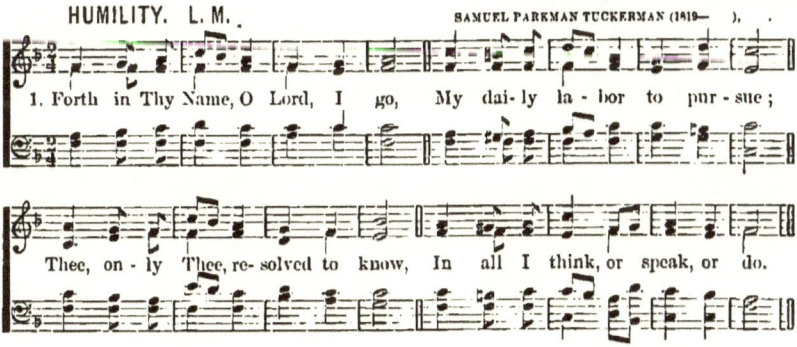

1. Forth in Thy Name, O Lord, I go,
My daily labor to pursue;
Thee, only Thee, resolved to know,
In all I think, or speak, or do.

38 *Before Work.*

2 The task Thy wisdom hath assigned
O let me cheerfully fulfil;
In all my works Thy presence find,
And prove Thy good and perfect will.

3 Thee may I set at my right hand,
Whose eyes my inmost substance see;

And labor on at Thy command,
And offer all my works to Thee.

4 Give me to bear Thine easy yoke,
And every moment watch and pray;
And still to things eternal look,
And hasten to Thy glorious day.

Rev. Charles Wesley (1708—1788), 1749. Ab. and alt.

EVENING.

STOCKWELL. 8, 7.
Rev. DARIUS ELIOT JONES (1815–1881), 1847.

1. Sav-iour, breathe an eve-ning bless-ing, Ere re-pose our spir-its seal;
Sin and want we come con-fess-ing, Thou canst save, and Thou canst heal.

39 *Evening Blessing.*

2 Though destruction walk around us,
 Though the arrow past us fly,
Angel-guards from Thee surround us,
 We are safe, if Thou art nigh.

3 Though the night be dark and dreary,
 Darkness cannot hide from Thee;
 Thou art He who, never weary,
 Watchest where Thy people be.

4 Should swift death this night o'ertake us,
 And our couch become our tomb,
May the morn in Heaven awake us,
 Clad in light and deathless bloom.
 James Edmeston (1791–1867), 1820.

STUTTGARD. 8, 7.
Arr. from JOHANN GEORG CHRISTIAN STÖRL (1676–1743).

1. Tar-ry with me, O my Sav-iour, For the day is pass-ing by;
See, the shades of eve-ning gath-er, And the night is draw-ing nigh.

40 *Evening Shadows.*

2 Deeper, deeper grow the shadows,
 Paler now the glowing west;
Swift the night of death advances;
 Shall it be the night of rest?

3 Feeble, trembling, fainting, dying,
 Lord, I cast myself on Thee;
Tarry with me through the darkness;
 While I sleep, still watch by me.

4 Tarry with me, O my Saviour;
 Lay my head upon Thy breast
Till the morning, then awake me:
 Morning of eternal rest.
 Mrs. Caroline Sprague Smith (1827–   ), 1855. Ab.

41 *Benediction.*
 2 Cor. xiii. 14.

1 MAY the grace of Christ our Saviour,
 And the Father's boundless love,
With the Holy Spirit's favor,
 Rest upon us from above.

2 Thus may we abide in union
 With each other and the Lord,
And possess, in sweet communion,
 Joys which earth cannot afford.
 Rev. John Newton (1725–1807).

EVENING.

WESTMINSTER. 8.7.   JOSEPH PERRY HOLBROOK (1822—).

1. Hear my pray'r, O Heav-'nly Fa-ther, Ere I lay me down to sleep:
Bid Thine an-gels, pure and ho-ly, Round my bed their vig-il keep.

42   *An Evening Prayer.*

2 Great my sins are, but Thy mercy
Far outweighs them every one;
Down before Thy cross I cast them,
Trusting in Thy help alone.

3 Keep me, through this night of peril,
Underneath its boundless shade;
Take me to Thy rest, I pray Thee,
When my pilgrimage is made.

4 Pardon all my past transgressions;
Give me strength for days to come:
Guide and guard me with Thy blessing,
Till Thine angels bid me home.
         Miss Harriet Parr, 1856. Ab. and Sl. alt.

BATTY. 8.7.   Arr. from German.

1. Vain-ly through night's weary hours, Keep we watch, lest foes a-larm;
Vain our bul-warks, and our tow-ers, But for God's pro-tect-ing arm.

43   *Our Need of God.*
         Ps. cxxvii.

2 Vain were all our toil and labor,
Did not God that labor bless;
Vain, without His grace and favor,
Every talent we possess.

3 Vainer still the hope of Heaven,
That on human strength relies;
But to him shall help be given,
Who in humble faith applies.

4 Seek we, then, the Lord's Anointed;
He will grant us peace and rest;
Ne'er was suppliant disappointed,
Who thro' Christ his prayer addressed.
         Miss Harriet Auber (1773—1862), 1829.

44   *Doxology.*

1 Praise the God of our salvation;
Praise the Father's boundless love;
Praise the Lamb, our expiation;
Praise the Spirit from above:

2 Author of the new creation,
Him by whom our spirits live;
Undivided adoration
To the one Jehovah give.
         Josiah Conder (1789—1855).

EVENING.

LAUS MATUTINA. 11.10.
JOHN STAINER (1840–), 1872.

1. Now, when the dusky shades of night re-treat-ing Be-fore the sun's red ban-ner swift-ly flee; Now, when the ter-rors of the dark are fleet-ing, O Lord, we lift our thank-ful hearts to Thee.

45 *Walking in the Light of the Lord.*
Is. ii. 5.

2 Look from the height of heaven, and send to cheer us
Thy light and truth, and guide us onward still;
Still let Thy mercy, as of old, be near us,
And lead us safely to Thy holy hill.

3 So, when that morn of endless light is waking,
And shades of evil from its splendors flee,
Safe may we rise, this earth's dark vale forsaking,
Through all the long bright day to dwell with Thee.

Hedge & Huntington's Hymns for the Church of Christ, 1853.

RENOVATION. S. M.
JOHANN NEPOMUK HUMMEL (1778–1837).

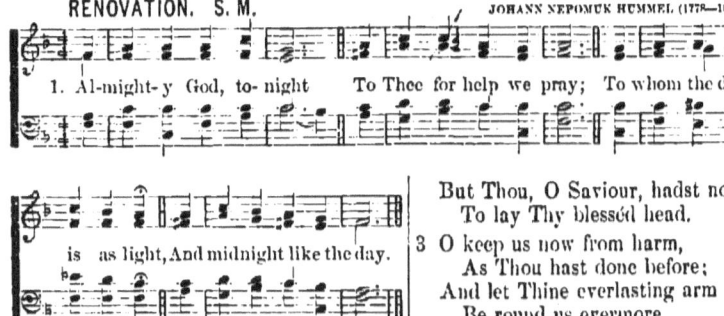

1. Al-might-y God, to-night To Thee for help we pray; To whom the darkness is as light, And midnight like the day.

46 *"Hath not where to lay His Head."*
Luke ix. 58.

2 Thy tender love and care
Prepares our peaceful bed;
But Thou, O Saviour, hadst not where
To lay Thy blessèd head.

3 O keep us now from harm,
As Thou hast done before;
And let Thine everlasting arm
Be round us evermore.

4 Let holy angels stand
About us every night,
Until they bear us to the land
Of everlasting light.

Rev. John Mason Neale (1818–1866), 1842. Ab.

EVENING.

YOAKLEY. L. M. 61. WILLIAM YOAKLEY, 1820.

1. { Sweet Sav - iour, bless us ere we go; Thy word in - to our minds instill; }
   { And make our lukewarm hearts to glow With low - ly love and fer-vent will. }

Thro' life's long day and death's dark night, O gen - tle Je - sus be our light.

47 "*The Lord is my Light.*"
Ps. xxvii. 1.

2 The day is done, its hours have run;
  And Thou hast taken count of all—
  The scanty triumphs grace hath won,
  The broken vow, the frequent fall.
  Through life's long day and death's dark night,
  O gentle Jesus, be our light.

3 Grant us, dear Lord, from evil ways
  True absolution and release;
  And bless us, more than in past days,
  With purity and inward peace.
  Through life's long day and death's dark night,
  O gentle Jesus, be our light.

4 Do more than pardon; give us joy,
  Sweet fear, and sober liberty,
  And loving hearts without alloy,
  That only long to be like Thee.
  Through life's long day and death's dark night,
  O gentle Jesus, be our light.

5 For all we love, the poor, the sad,
  The sinful, unto Thee we call;
  O let Thy mercy make us glad;
  Thou art our Jesus and our All.
  Through life's long day and death's dark night,
  O gentle Jesus, be our light.

Rev. Frederick William Faber (1814—1863), 1849. Ab.

MERRIAL. 6. 5. JOSEPH BARNBY (1838—), 1868.

1. Now the day is o - ver, Night is draw- ing nigh, Shad- ows of the eve - ning Steal a - cross the sky.

Steal a - cross the sky.

48 *The Day is over.*

2 Jesus, give the weary
  Calm and sweet repose;
  With Thy tenderest blessing
  May our eyelids close.

3 Grant to little children
  Visions bright of Thee;
  Guard the sailors tossing
  On the deep blue sea.

4 Through the long night-watches,
  May Thine angels spread
  Their white wings above me,
  Watching round my bed.

5 When the morning wakens,
  Then may I arise,
  Pure and fresh and sinless
  In Thy holy eyes.

Rev. Sabine Baring-Gould (1834—), 1865. Ab.

EVENING AND MORNING.

FLEMMING. 11, 11, 11, 5. FRIEDRICH FERDINAND FLEMMING (1778—1813), 1810.

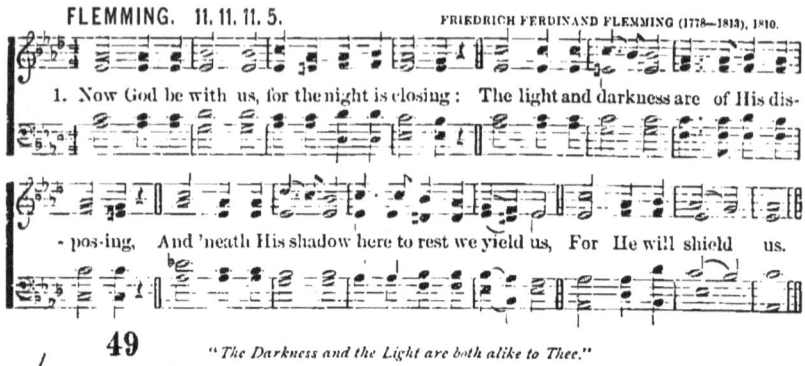

1. Now God be with us, for the night is closing: The light and darkness are of His dis-posing, And 'neath His shadow here to rest we yield us, For He will shield us.

49 *"The Darkness and the Light are both alike to Thee."*

2 Let evil thoughts and spirits flee before us;
Till morning cometh, watch, O Master, o'er us;
In soul and body Thou from harm defend us,
Thine angels send us.

3 We have no refuge; none on earth to aid us,
Save Thee, O Father, who Thine own hast made us;
But Thy dear presence will not leave them lonely
Who seek Thee only.

4 Father, Thy Name be praised, Thy Kingdom given,
Thy will be done on earth as 'tis in Heaven,
Keep us in life, forgive our sins, deliver
Us now and ever.

"Bohemian Brethern Collection," 1531.
Tr. by Miss Catherine Winkworth (1827—1878), 1863. Ab.

INNOCENTS. 7. Ascribed to THEOBALD, King of Navarre (1201—1253).

1. As the sun doth dai-ly rise, Brightening all the morn-ing skies, So to Thee with one ac-cord Lift we up our hearts, O Lord.

50 *"Matutinus altiora."*

2 Be our Guard in sin and strife;
Be the Leader of our life;
While we daily search Thy Word,
Wisdom true impart, O Lord.

3 When the sun withdraws his light,
When we seek our beds at night,

Thou, by sleepless hosts adored,
Hear the prayer of faith, O Lord.

4 Praise we, with the heavenly host,
Father, Son, and Holy Ghost;
Thee would we with one accord
Praise and magnify, O Lord.

King Alfred of England (849—901).
Tr. by Earl Horatio Nelson (1823—), 1864. Ab.

EVENING.

ANGELUS. L. M.
GEORG JOSEPHI, 1657.

1. At even, ere the sun was set, The sick, O Lord, a-round Thee lay; O in what divers pains they met, O with what joy they went a-way.

51 *Evening Prayer for Healing.*
Mark i. 32.

2 Once more 'tis eventide, and we,
Oppressed with various ills, draw near:
What if Thy form we cannot see?
We know and feel that Thou art here.

3 O Saviour Christ, our woes dispel,
For some are sick, and some are sad,
And some have never loved Thee well,
And some have lost the love they had.

4 And none, O Lord, have perfect rest,
For none are wholly free from sin;

And they who fain would serve Thee best,
Are conscious most of wrong within.

5 O Saviour Christ, Thou too art Man;
Thou hast been troubled, tempted, tried;
Thy kind but searching glance can scan,
The very wounds that shame would hide;

6 Thy touch has still its ancient power,
No word from Thee can fruitless fall;
Hear in this solemn evening hour,
And in Thy mercy heal us all.

Rev. Henry Twells (1823—), 1868. Ab.

HAZELWOOD. 6, 6, 4, 6, 6, 6, 4.
EDWARD JOHN HOPKINS (1818—).

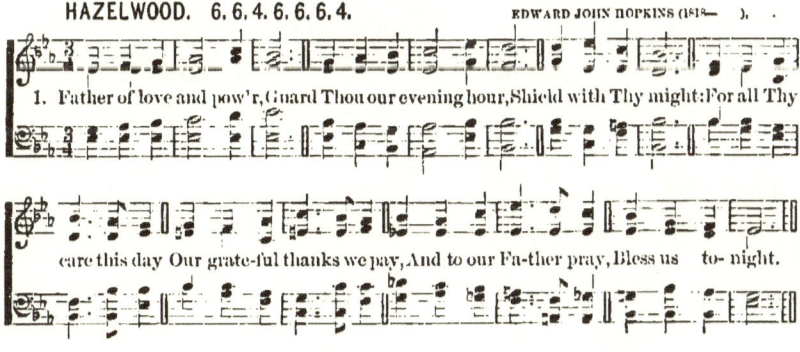

1. Father of love and pow'r, Guard Thou our evening hour, Shield with Thy might: For all Thy care this day Our grateful thanks we pay, And to our Father pray, Bless us to-night.

52 *Evening Prayer.*

2 Jesus Immanuel,
Come in Thy love to dwell
In hearts contrite:
For many sins we grieve,
But we Thy grace receive,
And in Thy word believe;
Bless us to-night.

3 Spirit of truth and love,
Life-giving, holy Dove,
Shed forth Thy light:
Heal every sinner's smart,
Still every throbbing heart,
And Thine own peace impart;
Bless us to-night.'

George Rawson (1807—1885), 1853.

MORNING.

CAPETOWN. 7.7.7.5. — FRIEDRICH FILITZ (1804—1860), 1847.

1. Three in One, and One in Three, Rul-er of the earth and sea,
Hear us, while we lift to Thee Ho-ly chant and psalm.

53 *"Three in One, and One in Three."*
2 Light of lights, with morning shine:
Lift on us Thy light divine;
And let charity benign
Breathe on us her balm.

3 Light of lights, when falls the even,
Let it close on sin forgiven;

Fold us in the peace of heaven,
Shed a holy calm.

4 Three in One, and One in Three,
Dimly here we worship Thee:
With the saints hereafter we
Hope to bear a palm.
Rev. Gilbert Rorison (1821—1869), 1859. Alt.

SABBATH. 7. 6 1. — LOWELL MASON (1792—1872), 1824.

1. Safe-ly through another week, God has brought us on our way; Let us now a blessing seek, Wait-ing in His courts to-day: Day of all the week the best, Emblem of e-ter-nal rest, Day of all the week the best, Emblem of e-ter-nal rest.

54 *"Safely through another Week."*
2 While we pray for pardoning grace,
Through the dear Redeemer's Name,
Show Thy reconciléd face,
Take away our sin and shame;
From our worldly cares set free,
May we rest this day in Thee.

3 Here we come Thy Name to praise;
May we feel Thy presence near:
May Thy glory meet our eyes,

While we in Thy house appear:
Here afford us, Lord, a taste
Of our everlasting feast.

4 May Thy Gospel's joyful sound
Conquer sinners, comfort saints;
Make the fruits of grace abound,
Bring relief for all complaints;
Thus may all our Sabbaths prove,
Till we join the Church above.
Rev. John Newton (1725—1807), 1774.

HALLE. 7. 61. Arr. from PETER RITTER (1760—1846), 1792.

1. Fa-ther, by Thy love and power, Comes a-gain the even-ing hour;
   Light has van-ished, la-bors cease, Wea-ry crea-tures rest in peace:
   We to Thee our-selves re-sign, Let our lat-est thoughts be Thine.

55 *Evening Hymn.*

2 Saviour, to Thy Father bear
This our feeble evening prayer;
Thou hast seen how oft to-day
We, like sheep, have gone astray;
Blessed Saviour, we, through Thee,
Pray that we may pardoned be.

3 Holy Spirit, Breath of balm,
Fall on us in evening's calm;
Yet awhile, before we sleep,
We with Thee will vigil keep.
Melt our spirits, mould our will,
Soften, strengthen, comfort still.

4 Blessed Trinity, be near
Through the hours of darkness drear;
Father, Son, and Holy Ghost,
Round us set th' angelic host,
Till the flood of morning rays
Wake us to a song of praise.
Prof. Joseph Anstice (1808—1836), 1836. Ab. and alt.

56 *Evening Hymn.*

1 Now from labor and from care
    Evening hours have set me free,
  In the work of praise and prayer,
    Lord, I would converse with Thee:
  O behold me from above,
  Fill me with a Saviour's love.

2 Sin and sorrow, guilt and woe
    Wither all my earthly joys;
  Naught can charm me here below,

But my Saviour's melting voice:
Lord, forgive, Thy grace restore,
Make me Thine forevermore.

3 For the blessings of this day,
    For the mercies of this hour,
  For the Gospel's cheering ray,
    For the Spirit's quickening power,
  Grateful notes to Thee I raise:
  O accept the song of praise.
    Thomas Hastings (1784—1872), 1831.

57 *Morning Prayer.*

1 In this calm impressive hour,
    Let my prayer ascend on high;
  God of mercy, God of power,
    Hear me, when to Thee I cry;
  Hear me from Thy lofty throne,
  For the sake of Christ, Thy Son.

2 With the morning's early ray,
    While the shades of night depart,
  Let Thy beams of light convey
    Joy and gladness to my heart:
  Now o'er all my steps preside,
  And for all my wants provide.

3 O what joy that word affords,
    "Thou shalt reign o'er all the earth;"
  King of kings, and Lord of lords,
    Send Thy Gospel-heralds forth:
  Now begin Thy boundless sway.
  Usher in the glorious day.
    Thomas Hastings, 1831.

MORNING.

ELLERS. 10.   EDWARD JOHN HOPKINS (1818—), 1866.

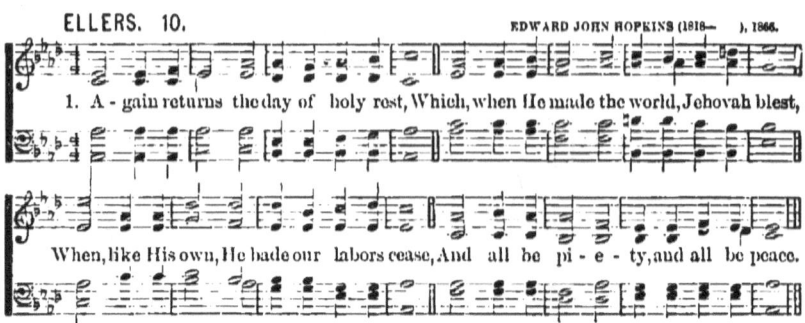

1. A - gain returns the day of holy rest, Which, when He made the world, Jehovah blest, When, like His own, He bade our labors cease, And all be pi - e - ty, and all be peace.

58   *"The Day of holy Rest."*

2 Let us devote this consecrated day
To learn His will, and all we learn obey;
So shall He hear, when fervently we raise
Our supplications and our songs of praise.

3 Father of Heaven, in whom our hopes confide,
Whose power defends us, and whose precepts guide,
In life our Guardian, and in death our Friend,
Glory supreme be Thine, till time shall end.
Rev. William Mason (1725—1797), 1811.

PAX DEI. 10.   Rev. JOHN BACCHUS DYKES (1823—1876).

1. Sav - iour, a - gain to Thy dear Name we raise, With one ac - cord, our part - ing hymn of praise; We rise to bless Thee ere our wor - ship cease, Then, low - ly kneel-ing, wait Thy word of peace.

59   *"The Word of Peace."*

2 Grant us Thy peace upon our homeward way;
With Thee began, with Thee shall end the day;
Guard Thou the lips from sin, the hearts from shame,
That in this house have called upon Thy Name.

EVENING. 27

3 Grant us Thy peace, Lord, through the coming night,
Turn Thou for us its darkness into light;
From harm and danger keep Thy children free:
Darkness and light are both alike to Thee.

4 Grant us Thy peace throughout our earthly life,
Our balm in sorrow, and our stay in strife;
Then, when Thy voice shall bid our conflict cease,
Call us, O Lord, to Thine eternal peace.

Rev. John Ellerton (1826—), 1868.

EVENTIDE. 10.   WILLIAM HENRY MONK (1823—), 1861.

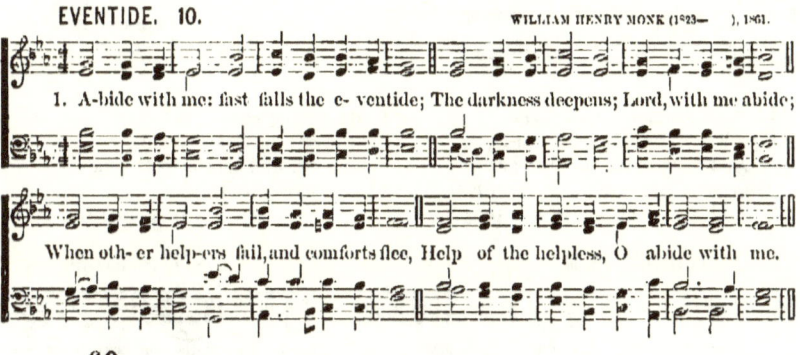

1. A-bide with me: fast falls the e-ventide; The darkness deepens; Lord, with me abide;
When oth-er helpers fail, and comforts flee, Help of the helpless, O abide with me.

60   *"Fast falls the Eventide."*

2 Swift to its close ebbs out life's little day;
Earth's joys grow dim, its glories pass away;
Change and decay in all around I see;
O Thou, who changest not, abide with me.

3 I need Thy presence every passing hour:
What but Thy grace can foil the tempter's power?
Who like Thyself my guide and stay can be?
Through cloud and sunshine, O abide with me.

4 I fear no foe, with Thee at hand to bless;
Ills have no weight, and tears no bitterness;
Where is death's sting? where, grave, thy victory?
I triumph still, if Thou abide with me.

5 Hold Thou Thy cross before my closing eyes;
Shine through the gloom and point me to the skies;
Heaven's morning breaks, and earth's vain shadows flee;
In life, in death, O Lord, abide with me.

Rev. Henry Francis Lyte (1793—1847), 1847. Ab.

DOXOLOGY.

All praise and glory to the Father be
And Son and Spirit, undivided Three,
As hath been alway, shall be, and is now,
To Thee, O God, the everlasting Thou.

Bp. Edward Henry Bickersteth (1825—), 1870.

THE LORD'S DAY.

LISBON. S. M.   DANIEL READ (1757–1836), 1785.

1. Welcome, sweet day of rest, That saw the Lord a-rise: Welcome to this re-viving breast, And these rejoicing eyes.

61   *The Lord's Day welcomed.*

2 The King Himself comes near,
   And feasts His saints to-day;
Here we may sit, and see Him here,
   And love, and praise, and pray.

3 One day amidst the place
   Where my dear God hath been,
Is sweeter than ten thousand days
   Of pleasure and of sin.

4 My willing soul would stay
   In such a frame as this,
And sit, and sing herself away
   To everlasting bliss.
        Rev. Isaac Watts (1674—1748), 1707. Sl. alt.

WATCHMAN. S. M.   JAMES LEACH (1762–1797), 1798.

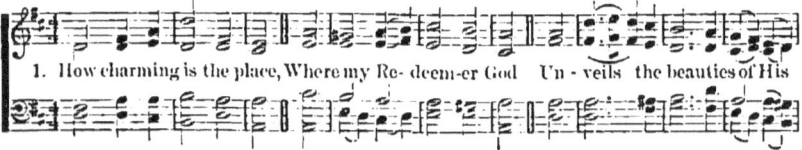

1. How charming is the place, Where my Redeemer God Un-veils the beauties of His face, And sheds His love abroad.

62   *Our Redeemer worshipped.*

2 Here, on the Mercy-seat,
   With radiant glory crowned,
Our joyful eyes behold Him sit,
   And smile on all around.

3 To Him their prayers and cries,
   Each humble soul presents:
He listens to their broken sighs,
   And grants them all their wants

4 To them His sovereign will
   He graciously imparts;
And in return accepts, with smiles,
   The tribute of their hearts.

5 Give me, O Lord, a place
   Within Thy blest abode,
Among the children of Thy grace,
   The servants of my God.
        Rev. Samuel Stennett (1727—1795), 1787. Ab.

63   *Sabbath Praise.*

1 This is the glorious day
   That our Redeemer made:
Let us rejoice, and sing, and pray,
   Let all the Church be glad.

2 Hosanna to the King
   Of David's royal blood:
Bless Him, ye saints, He comes to bring
   Salvation from your God.

3 We bless Thy holy Word,
   Which all this grace displays;
And offer on Thine altar, Lord,
   Our sacrifice and praise.
        Rev. Isaac Watts, 1719. Ab.

THE LORD'S DAY. 29

MENDEBRAS. 7. 6. D. German Melody. Arr. by LOWELL MASON (1792—1872), 1839.

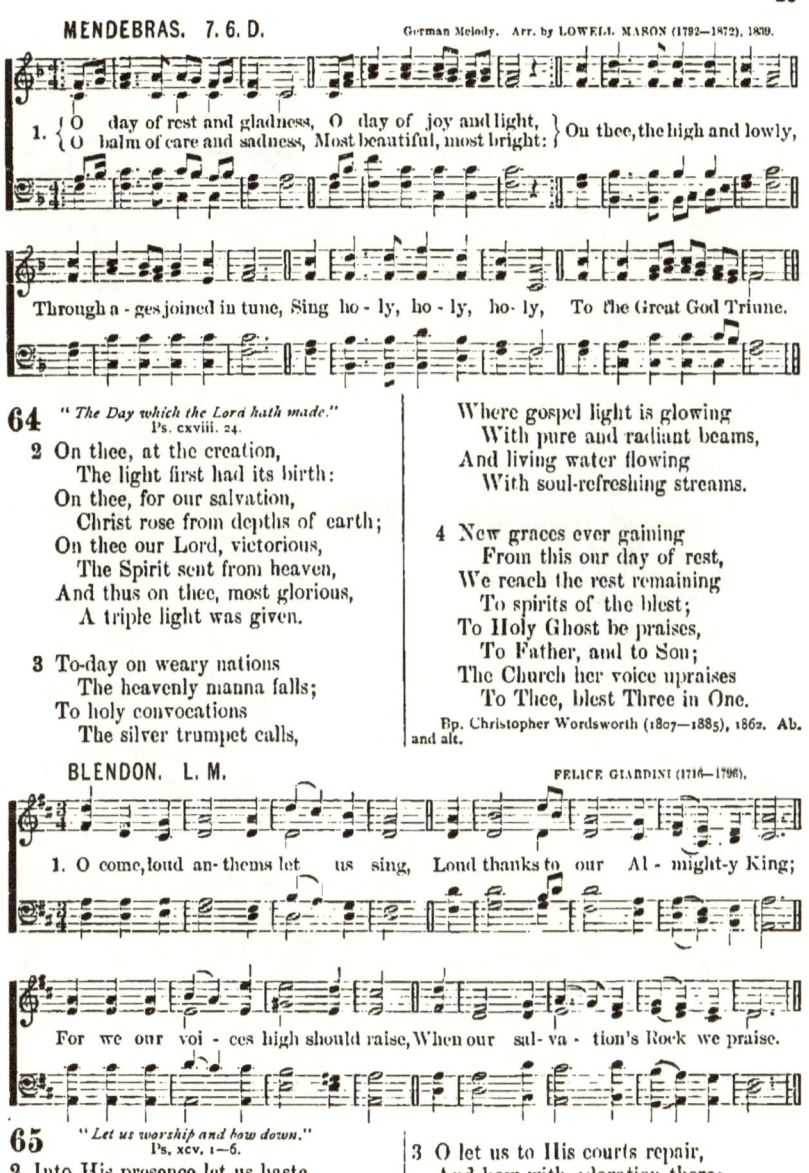

1. { O day of rest and gladness, O day of joy and light, }
   { O balm of care and sadness, Most beautiful, most bright: } On thee, the high and lowly,
   Through ages joined in tune, Sing ho-ly, ho-ly, ho-ly, To the Great God Triune.

64 *"The Day which the Lord hath made."*
Ps. cxviii. 24.

2 On thee, at the creation,
    The light first had its birth:
  On thee, for our salvation,
    Christ rose from depths of earth;
  On thee our Lord, victorious,
    The Spirit sent from heaven,
  And thus on thee, most glorious,
    A triple light was given.

3 To-day on weary nations
    The heavenly manna falls;
  To holy convocations
    The silver trumpet calls,

Where gospel light is glowing
  With pure and radiant beams,
And living water flowing
  With soul-refreshing streams.

4 New graces ever gaining
    From this our day of rest,
  We reach the rest remaining
    To spirits of the blest;
  To Holy Ghost be praises,
    To Father, and to Son;
  The Church her voice upraises
    To Thee, blest Three in One.
      Bp. Christopher Wordsworth (1807—1885), 1862. Ab.
      and alt.

BLENDON. L. M. FELICE GIARDINI (1716—1796).

1. O come, loud anthems let us sing, Loud thanks to our Almighty King;
   For we our voices high should raise, When our salvation's Rock we praise.

65 *"Let us worship and bow down."*
Ps. xcv. 1—6.

2 Into His presence let us haste,
  To thank Him for His favors past;
  To Him address, in joyful songs,
  The praise that to His name belongs.

3 O let us to His courts repair,
  And bow with adoration there:
  Down on our knees devoutly all
  Before the Lord our Maker fall.
          Tate and Brady, 1696. Ab.

THE LORD'S DAY.

ARMAGH. C.M.
JAMES TURLE (1802—1882).

1. Blest day of God, most calm, most bright, The first and best of days: The toil-er's rest, the saint's de-light, A day of joy and praise.

66 *"Most calm, most bright."*

2 My Saviour's face did make thee shine
His rising did thee raise;
This made thee heavenly and divine
Beyond all other days.

3 The first-fruits do a blessing prove
To all the sheaves behind;
And they, that do a Sabbath love,
A happy week shall find.

4 My Lord on thee His Name did fix,
Which makes thee rich and gay;
Amid His golden candlesticks
My Saviour walks this day.

5 This day must I 'fore God appear,
For, Lord, this day is Thine:
O let me spend it in Thy fear,
The day shall then be mine.

Rev. John Mason (1634—1694), 1683. Alt.

WARWICK. C.M.
SAMUEL STANLEY (1767—1822), 1800.

1. Lord, in the morn-ing Thou shalt hear My voice as-cend-ing high; To Thee will I di-rect my pray'r, To Thee lift up mine eye:

67 *The Lord's Day Morning."*
Ps. v.

2 Up to the hills, where Christ is gone
To plead for all His saints,
Presenting, at His Father's throne,
Our songs and our complaints.

3 Thou art a God, before whose sight
The wicked shall not stand;
Sinners shall ne'er be Thy delight,
Nor dwell at Thy right hand.

4 But to Thy house will I resort,
To taste Thy mercies there;
I will frequent Thy holy court,
And worship in Thy fear.

5 O may Thy Spirit guide my feet
In ways of righteousness;
Make every path of duty straight,
And plain before my face.

Rev. Isaac Watts (1674—1748), 1719. Ab.

PRAISE TO GOD.

TREVES. 7. 7. 7. 5. Arr. by HENRY JOHN GAUNTLETT (1805—1876), 1872.

1. God of pity, God of grace; When we humbly seek Thy face, Bend from heav'n Thy

dwelling place: Hear, forgive, and save.

From our burden set us free:
Hear, forgive, and save.
Mrs. Eliza Fanny Morris (1821—), 1857. Ab.

68
"Hear and Save."

2 When Thy love our hearts shall fill,
And we long to do Thy will,
Turning to Thy holy hill:
   Lord, accept and save.

3 Should we wander from Thy fold,
And our love to Thee grow cold,
With a pitying eye behold:
   Lord, forgive and save.

4 Should the hand of sorrow press,
Earthly care and want distress,
May our souls Thy peace possess:
   Jesus, hear and save.

5 And whate'er our cry may be,
When we lift our hearts to Thee,

69
"Light at Evening Time."

1 HOLY Father, cheer our way
With Thy love's perpetual ray;
Grant us, ev'ry closing day,
   Light at evening time.

2 Holy Saviour, calm our fears,
When earth's brightness disappears;
Grant us, in our later years,
   Light at evening time.

3 Holy Spirit, be Thou nigh,
When in mortal pains we lie;
Grant us, as we come to die,
   Light at evening time.

4 Holy blessèd Trinity
Darkness is not dark with Thee;
Those Thou keepest always see
   Light at evening time.
Rev. Richard Hayes Robinson (1842—),

RATHBUN. 8. 7. ITHAMAR CONKEY (1815—1867), 1847.

1. God is Love; His mercy brightens All the path in which we rove;
Bliss He wakes, and woe He lightens: God is wisdom, God is love.

70
God is Love.
1 John iv. 8.

2 Chance and change are busy ever;
Man decays, and ages move;
But His mercy waneth never;
   God is wisdom, God is love.

3 E'en the hour that darkest seemeth
Will His changeless goodness prove;

From the mist His brightness streameth:
   God is wisdom, God is love.

4 He with earthly cares entwineth
Hope and comfort from above;
Everywhere His glory shineth:
   God is wisdom, God is love.
Sir John Bowring (1792—1872), 1825.

THE ETERNAL GOD.

TRURO. L. M.   CHARLES BURNEY (1726—1814), 1769.

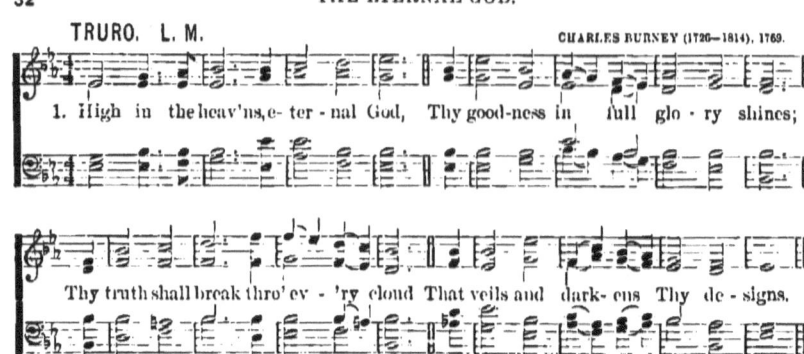

1. High in the heav'ns, e-ter-nal God, Thy good-ness in full glo-ry shines;
Thy truth shall break thro' ev-'ry cloud That veils and dark-ens Thy de-signs.

71   *Providence and Grace.*
      Ps. xxxvi. 5—9.

2 Forever firm Thy justice stands,
   As mountains their foundations keep;
   Wise are the wonders of Thy hands;
   Thy judgments are a mighty deep.

3 My God, how excellent Thy grace,
   Whence all our hope and comfort springs;
   The sons of Adam in distress
   Fly to the shadow of Thy wings.

4 Life, like a fountain rich and free,
   Springs from the presence of my Lord;
   And in Thy light our souls shall see
   The glories promised in Thy Word.
           Rev. Isaac Watts (1674—1748), 1719. Ab.

72   *"Bless the Lord."*
      Ps. ciii.

1 Bless, O my soul, the Living God,
   Call home thy thoughts that rove abroad;
   Let all the powers within me join
   In work and worship so divine.

2 Bless, O my soul, the God of grace;
   His favors claim thy highest praise;
   Why should the wonders He hath wrought
   Be lost in silence and forgot?

3 'Tis He, my soul, that sent His Son
   To die for crimes which thou hast done;
   He owns the ransom, and forgives
   The hourly follies of our lives.

4 Let the whole earth His power confess;
   Let the whole earth adore His grace:
   The Gentile with the Jew shall join
   In work and worship so divine.
           Rev. Isaac Watts, 1719. Ab.

OLD HUNDREDTH. L. M.   LOUIS BOURGEOIS, 1551.

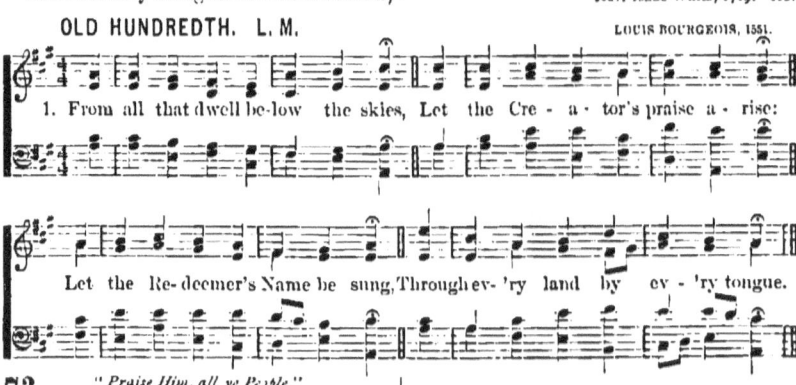

1. From all that dwell be-low the skies, Let the Cre-a-tor's praise a-rise:
Let the Re-deemer's Name be sung, Through ev-'ry land by ev-'ry tongue.

73   *"Praise Him, all ye People."*
      Ps. cxvii.

2 Eternal are Thy mercies, Lord;
   Eternal truth attends Thy Word;
   Thy praise shall sound from shore to shore
   Till suns shall rise and set no more.
           Rev. Isaac Watts, 1719

MISSIONARY CHANT. L. M.
HENRICH CHRISTOPHER ZEUNER (1795—1857), 1832.

1. Prais-es to Him, whose love has given, In Christ, His Son, the life of Heaven;
Who for our dark-ness gives us light, And turns to day our deep-est night.

74 *God Triune praised.*

2 Praises to Him, in grace who came,
To bear our woe, and sin, and shame;
Who lived to die, who died to rise,
The God-accepted sacrifice.

3 Praises to Him, who sheds abroad
Within our hearts the love of God;
The Spirit of all truth and peace,
Fountain of joy and holiness!

4 To Father, Son, and Spirit now
The hands we lift, the knees we bow;
To Thee, Jehovah, thus we raise
The sinner's endless song of praise.
<small>Rev. Horatius Bonar (1808—), 1861. Ab. and alt.</small>

75 *"Whose Love profound."*

1 FATHER of heaven, whose love profound
A ransom for our souls hath found,
Before Thy throne we sinners bend:
To us Thy pardoning love extend.

2 Almighty Son, Incarnate Word,
Our Prophet, Priest, Redeemer, Lord,
Before Thy throne we sinners bend:
To us Thy saving grace extend.

3 Eternal Spirit, by whose breath
The soul is raised from sin and death,
Before Thy throne we sinners bend:
To us Thy quickening power extend.

4 Jehovah, Father, Spirit, Son,
Mysterious Godhead, Three in One,
Before Thy throne we sinners bend:
Grace, pardon, life, to us extend.
<small>Edward Cooper (1770—1833), 1805.</small>

RUSSIAN HYMN. L. M.
ALEXIS FEODOROVITCH LVOFF (1799—1870), 1833.

1. Give to our God im-mor-tal praise; Mer-cy and truth are all His ways:
Won-ders of grace to God be-long; Re-peat His mer-cies in your song.

76 *Wonders of Creation and Grace. Ps. cxxxvi.*

2 He built the earth, He spread the sky,
And fixed the starry lights on high:
Wonders of grace to God belong;
Repeat His mercies in your song.

3 He sent His Son with power to save,
From guilt, and darkness, and the grave;
Wonders of grace to God belong;
Repeat His mercies in your song.

4 Thro' this vain world He guides our feet,
And leads us to His heavenly seat:
His mercies ever shall endure,
When this vain world shall be no more.
<small>Rev. Isaac Watts, 1719. Ab.</small>

THE ETERNAL GOD.

MAJESTY. L. M.   FRANCIS JOSEPH HAYDN (1732—1809). 1798.

1. Je-ho-vah reigns; His throne is high, His robes are light and ma-jes-ty;
His glo-ry shines with beams so bright, No mor-tal can sus-tain the sight.

77   *The Divine Perfections.*

2 His terrors keep the world in awe,
His justice guards His holy law,
His love reveals a smiling face,
His truth and promise seal the grace.

3 Through all His works His wisdom shines,
And baffles Satan's deep designs;
His power is sovereign to fulfil
The noblest counsels of His will.

4 And will the glorious Lord descend
To be my Father and my Friend?
Then let my songs with angels join;
Heaven is secure, if God be mine.
                    Rev. Isaac Watts (1674—1748), 1709.

WARE. L. M.   GEORGE KINGSLEY (1811—1864), 1853.

1. Now to the Lord a no-ble song! A-wake, my soul, a-wake, my tongue.
Ho-san-na to the eternal Name, And all His boundless love pro-claim.

78   *Grace Magnified.*

2 See where it shines in Jesus' face,
The brightest image of His grace;
God, in the person of His Son,
Hath all His mightiest works outdone.

3 Grace, 'tis a sweet, a charming theme:
My thoughts rejoice at Jesus' name:
Ye angels, dwell upon the sound:
Ye heavens, reflect it to the ground.

4 O, may I reach that happy place,
Where He unvails His lovely face,
Where all His beauties you behold,
And sing His name to harps of gold.
           Rev. Isaac Watts, 1709. Ab.

79   *The Majesty and Mercy of God.*
             Ps. lxviii.

1 KINGDOMS and thrones to God belong;
Crown Him, ye nations, in your song;
His wondrous names and powers rehearse;
His honors shall enrich your verse.

2 He shakes the heavens with loud alarms;
How terrible is God in arms!
In Israel are His mercies known,
Israel is His peculiar throne.

3 Proclaim Him King, pronounce Him blest;
He's your defence, your joy, your rest;
When terrors rise, and nations faint,
God is the strength of every saint.
           Rev. Isaac Watts, 1719.

TRIBUTE. 8.7.4. — Sir JOHN GOSS (1800—1880).

1. Praise, my soul, the King of heav-en; To His feet thy tribute bring; Ransomed, healed, restored, forgiven, Ev-er-more His prais-es sing: Al-le-lu-ia! Al-le-lu-ia! Praise the ev-er-last-ing King.

Slow to chide, and swift to bless:
Alleluia!
Glorious in His faithfulness.

3 Father-like, He tends and spares us,
Well our feeble frame He knows;
In His hands He gently bears us,
Rescues us from all our foes:
Alleluia!
Praise with us the God of grace.

Rev. Henry Francis Lyte (1793—1847), 1834. Ab. and alt.
Rev. Sir Henry Williams Baker (1821—1877), 1861.

80 *"Bless the Lord, O my Soul."* Ps. ciii.

2 Praise Him for His grace and favor
To our fathers in distress;
Praise Him still the same as ever,

AUSTRIAN HYMN. 8.7.4. — FRANCIS JOSEPH HAYDN (1732—1809), 1797.

1. Glo-ry be to God the Father, Glo-ry be to God the Son, Glo-ry be to God the Spir-it, Great Je-ho-vah, Three in One: Glo-ry, glo-ry, glo-ry, glo-ry, While e-ter-nal a-ges run!

Glory be to Him who bought us,
Made us kings with Him to reign:
Glory, Glory,
To the Lamb that once was slain!

3 Glory, blessing, praise eternal!
Thus the choir of angels sings;
Honor, riches, power, dominion!
Thus its praise creation brings:
Glory, Glory,
Glory to the King of kings.

Rev Horatius Bonar (1808—), 1856. Ab.

81 *Glory to God.* 1 Tim. i. 17.

2 Glory be to Him who loved us,
Washed us from each spot and stain;

DENNIS. S. M.

HANS GEORG NAEGELI (1773—1836), 1837.
Arr. by WILLIAM BATCHELDER BRADBURY (1816—1868), 1849.

1 O bless the Lord, my soul; Let all with- in me join, And aid my tongue to bless His

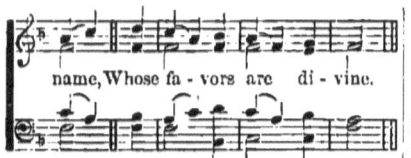

name, Whose fa- vors are di- vine.

But sent the world His truth and grace
By His belovéd Son.
Rev. Isaac Watts (1674—1748), 1719. Ab.

82 *Praise for temporal and spiritual Mercies.*
Ps. ciii. 1-7.

2 O bless the Lord, my soul,
Nor let His mercies lie
Forgotten in unthankfulness,
And without praises die.

3 'Tis He forgives thy sins,
'Tis He relieves thy pain,
'Tis He that heals thy sicknesses,
And makes thee young again.

4 He crowns thy life with love,
When ransomed from the grave;
He that redeemed my soul from hell,
Hath sovereign power to save.

5 His wondrous works and ways
He made by Moses known;

83 *Exhortation to Worship.*
Ps. xcv.

1 COME, sound His praise abroad,
And hymns of glory sing:
Jehovah is the sovereign God,
The universal king.

2 He formed the deeps unknown,
He gave the seas their bound;
The watery worlds are all His own,
And all the solid ground.

3 Come, worship at His throne,
Come, bow before the Lord,
We are His work, and not our own;
He formed us by His word.

4 To-day attend His voice,
Nor dare provoke His rod;
Come, like the people of His choice,
And own your gracious God.
Rev. Isaac Watts, 1719. Ab.

MONKLAND. 7.

Arr. by JOHN P. WILKES, 1861.

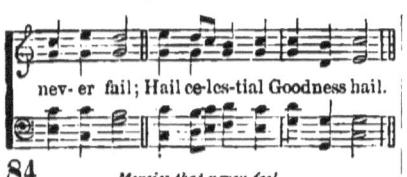

1. Ho- ly, ho- ly, ho- ly Lord, Be Thy glo-rious Name a-dored: Lord Thy mercies
nev- er fail; Hail ce-les-tial Goodness hail.

3 While on earth ordained to stay,
Guide our footsteps in Thy way,
Till we come to dwell with Thee,
Till we all Thy glory see.

84 *Mercies that never fail.*

2 Though unworthy, Lord, thine ear
Deign our humble songs to hear;
Purer praise we hope to bring,
When around Thy throne we sing.

4 Then with angel-harps, again
We will wake a nobler strain;
There, in joyful songs of praise,
Our triumphant voices raise.
Rev. Benjamin Williams, 1778. Ab.

FULTON. 7. WILLIAM BATCHELDER BRADBURY (1816—1868).

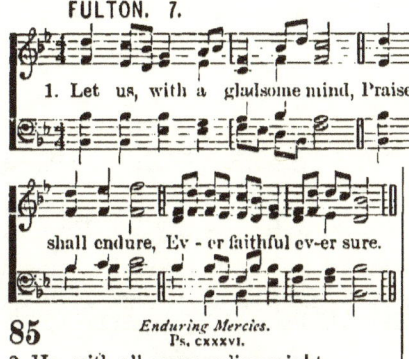

1. Let us, with a gladsome mind, Praise the Lord, for He is kind: For His mercies shall endure, Ev-er faithful ev-er sure.

2 All the holy angels cry,
Hail, thrice holy, God most High:
Lord of all the heavenly powers,
Be the same loud anthem ours.

3 God eternal, mighty King,
Unto Thee our praise we bring:
Seated on Thy judgment-throne,
Number us among Thine own.
Rev. James Elwin Millard (1821—), 1840. Ab. and alt.

85
Enduring Mercies.
Ps. cxxxvi.

2 He, with all-commanding might,
Filled the new-made world with light;
All things living He doth feed,
His full hand supplies their need.

3 He His chosen race did bless
In the wasteful wilderness;
He hath, with a piteous eye,
Looked upon our misery.

4 Let us therefore warble forth
His high majesty and worth:
For His mercies shall endure,
Ever faithful, ever sure.
John Milton (1608—1674), 1624. Ab. and alt.

86
"Te Deum laudamus."

1 God eternal, Lord of all,
Lowly at Thy feet we fall:
All the earth doth worship Thee,
We amidst the throng would be.

87
Thanks and Praise.
Ps. cvii; cxvii.

1 Thank and praise Jehovah's name
For His mercies, firm and sure,
From eternity the same,
To eternity endure.

2 Praise Him, ye who know His love,
Praise Him from the depths beneath
Praise Him in the heights above;
Praise your Maker, all that breathe.

3 For his truth and mercy stand,
Past, and present, and to be,
Like the years of His right hand,
Like His own eternity
James Montgomery (1771—1854), 1822. Ab.

SOLITUDE. 7. LEWIS THOMAS DOWNES (1827—), 1850.

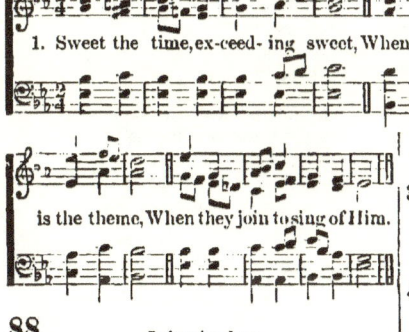

1. Sweet the time, ex-ceed-ing sweet, When the saints together meet; When the Saviour is the theme, When they join to sing of Him.

He beheld the world undone,
Loved the world and gave His Son.

3 Sing the Son's amazing love:
How He left the realms above,
Took our nature and our place,
Lived and died to save our race.

4 Sing we, too, the Spirit's love:
With our wretched hearts He strove,
Took the things of Christ, and showed
How to reach His blest abode
Rev. George Burder (1752—1832), 1779. Ab. and alt

88
Redeeming Love.

2 Sing we then eternal love,
Such as did the Father move:

BRADFORD. C. M. Arr. from GEORGE FREDERICK HANDEL (1685—1759), 1741.

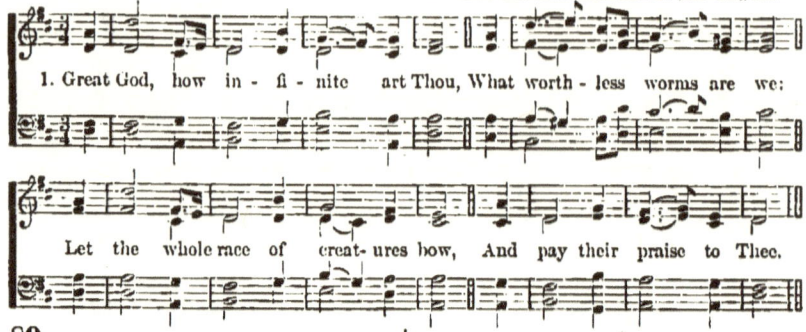

1. Great God, how in-fi-nite art Thou, What worth-less worms are we:
Let the whole race of creat-ures bow, And pay their praise to Thee.

89
God infinite and eternal.

2 Thy throne eternal ages stood,
   Ere seas or stars were made;
   Thou art the ever-living God,
   Were all the nations dead.

3 Eternity, with all its years,
   Stands present in Thy view;
   To Thee there's nothing old appears,
   Great God, there's nothing new.

4 Our lives thro' various scenes are drawn,
   And vexed with trifling cares;
   While Thine eternal thought moves on
   Thine undisturbed affairs.
   Rev. Isaac Watts (1674—1748), 1709. Ab.

90
God our Help, and Security.
Ps. xc.

1 O GOD, our help in ages past,
   Our hope for years to come;
   Our shelter from the stormy blast,
   And our eternal home:

2 Before the hills in order stood,
   Or earth received her frame,
   From everlasting Thou art God,
   To endless years the same.

3 A thousand ages, in Thy sight,
   Are like an evening gone;
   Short as the watch that ends the night,
   Before the rising sun.

4 Time, like an ever-rolling stream,
   Bears all its sons away;
   They fly, forgotten, as a dream
   Dies at the opening day.

5 O God, our help in ages past,
   Our hope for years to come,
   Be Thou our guard while troubles last,
   And our eternal home.
   Rev. Isaac Watts, 1719. Ab. and sl. alt.

91
Resignation to God's Will.

1 SINCE, all the varying scenes of time
   God's watchful eye surveys,
   O who so wise to choose our lot,
   Or to appoint our ways?

2 Good, when He gives, supremely good;
   Nor less when He denies;
   E'en crosses, from His sovereign hand,
   Are blessings in disguise.

3 Why should we doubt a Father's love,
   So constant and so kind?
   To His unerring gracious will
   Be every wish resigned.

4 In Thy fair book of life divine,
   My God, inscribe my name;
   There let it fill some humble place
   Beneath my Lord, the Lamb.
   Rev. James Hervey (1714—1758), 1746. Alt.

ST. ANN. C. M. WILLIAM CROFT (1677—1727), 1708.

HIS GOODNESS IN PROVIDENCE.

GENEVA. C. M. JOHN COLE (1774–1855), 1830.

1. When all Thy mercies, O my God, My rising soul surveys, Transported with the view, I'm lost In wonder, love, and praise.

92 *Mercies of God recounted.*

2 Unnumbered comforts to my soul
  Thy tender care bestowed,
  Before my infant heart conceived
  From whom those comforts flowed.

3 When worn with sickness, oft hast Thou
  With health renewed my face;
  And, when in sins and sorrows sunk,
  Revived my soul with grace.

4 Ten thousand thousand precious gifts
  My daily thanks employ;
  Nor is the least a cheerful heart
  That tastes those gifts with joy.

5 Through every period of my life
  Thy goodness I'll pursue;
  And after death, in distant worlds,
  The glorious theme renew.

6 Through all eternity to Thee
  A joyful song I'll raise;
  For O, eternity's too short
  To utter all Thy praise.

  Joseph Addison (1672–1719), 1712. Ab.

CHURCH. C. M. JOSEPH PERRY HOLBROOK (1822–).

1. Jehovah, God, Thy gracious pow'r On ev'ry hand we see; O may the blessings of each hour Lead all our thoughts to Thee.

93 *The constant Goodness of God.*
  Ps. cxxxix.

2 Thy power is in the ocean deeps,
  And reaches to the skies;
  Thine eye of mercy never sleeps,
  Thy goodness never dies.

3 From morn till noon, till latest eve,
  Thy hand, O God, we see;
  And all the blessings we receive,
  Proceed alone from Thee.

4 In all the changing scenes of time,
  On Thee our hopes depend;
  Through every age, in every clime,
  Our Father, and our Friend.

  Rev. John Thomson (1782–1818), 1810. Ab. and sl. alt.

LYONS. 5.5.5.6. D.　　　　　FRANCIS JOSEPH HAYDN (1732—1809), 1770.

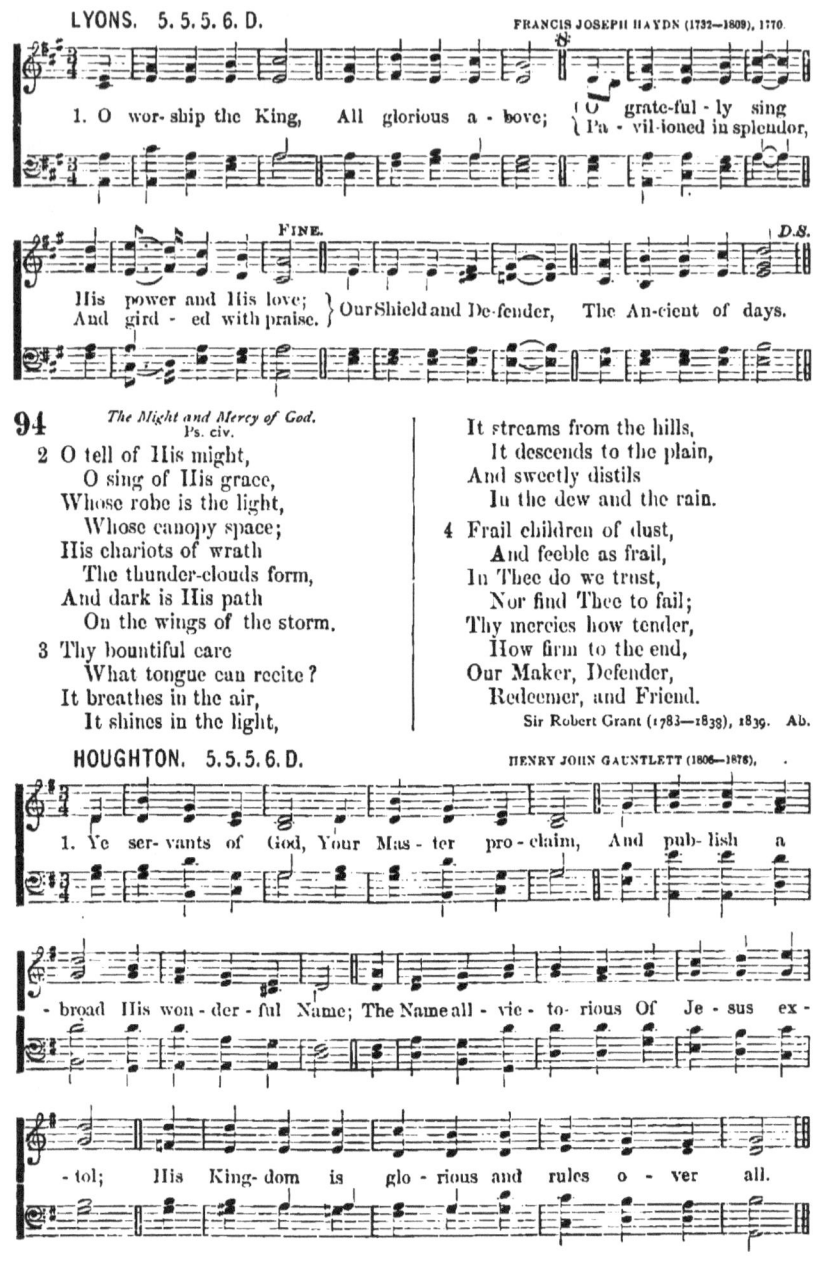

1. O wor-ship the King, All glorious a-bove; O grate-ful-ly sing
Pa-vil-ioned in splendor,
His power and His love;
And gird-ed with praise. Our Shield and De-fender, The An-cient of days.

94 *The Might and Mercy of God.*
Ps. civ.

2 O tell of His might,
O sing of His grace,
Whose robe is the light,
Whose canopy space;
His chariots of wrath
The thunder-clouds form,
And dark is His path
On the wings of the storm.

3 Thy bountiful care
What tongue can recite?
It breathes in the air,
It shines in the light,

It streams from the hills,
It descends to the plain,
And sweetly distils
In the dew and the rain.

4 Frail children of dust,
And feeble as frail,
In Thee do we trust,
Nor find Thee to fail;
Thy mercies how tender,
How firm to the end,
Our Maker, Defender,
Redeemer, and Friend.

Sir Robert Grant (1783—1839), 1839. Ab.

HOUGHTON. 5.5.5.6. D.　　　　　HENRY JOHN GAUNTLETT (1806—1876).

1. Ye ser-vants of God, Your Mas-ter pro-claim, And pub-lish a
-broad His won-der-ful Name; The Name all-vic-to-rious Of Je-sus ex-
-tol; His King-dom is glo-rious and rules o-ver all.

95

"Jesus, our King."

2 God ruleth on high,
    Almighty to save:
And still he is nigh,
    His presence we have.
The great congregation
    His triumph shall sing,
Ascribing salvation
    To Jesus, our King.

3 "Salvation to God,
    Who sits on the throne,"
Let all cry aloud,
    And honor the Son:
The praises of Jesus
    The angels proclaim,
Fall down on their faces,
    And worship the Lamb.

4 Then let us adore,
    And give Him His right,
All glory, and power,
    And wisdom and might;
All honor and blessing,
    With angels above,
And thanks never ceasing,
    And infinite love.

Rev. Charles Wesley (1708—1788), 1744. Ab.

CEYLON. 7. 6. D. SAMUEL REAY (1825—),

1. O God, the Rock of Ages, who evermore hast been, What time the tempest rages, Our dwelling place serene: Before Thy first creations, O Lord, the same as now, To endless generations, The everlasting Thou.

96

"The Rock of Ages."

2 Our years are like the shadows
    On sunny hills that lie,
Or grasses in the meadows
    That blossom but to die:
A sleep, a dream, a story,
    By strangers quickly told,
An unremaining glory
    Of things that soon are old.

3 O Thou who canst not slumber,
    Whose light grows never pale,
Teach us aright to number
    Our years before they fail.
On us Thy mercy lighten,
    On us Thy goodness rest,
And let Thy Spirit brighten
    The hearts Thyself hast blessed.

4 Lord, crown our faith's endeavor
    With beauty and with grace,
Till, clothed in light forever,
    We see Thee face to face:
A joy no language measures,
    A fountain brimming o'er,
An endless flow of pleasures,
    An ocean without shore.

Bp. Edward Henry Bickersteth (1825—), 1862.

REGENT SQUARE. 8, 7, 4. HENRY SMART (1812—1879), 1867.

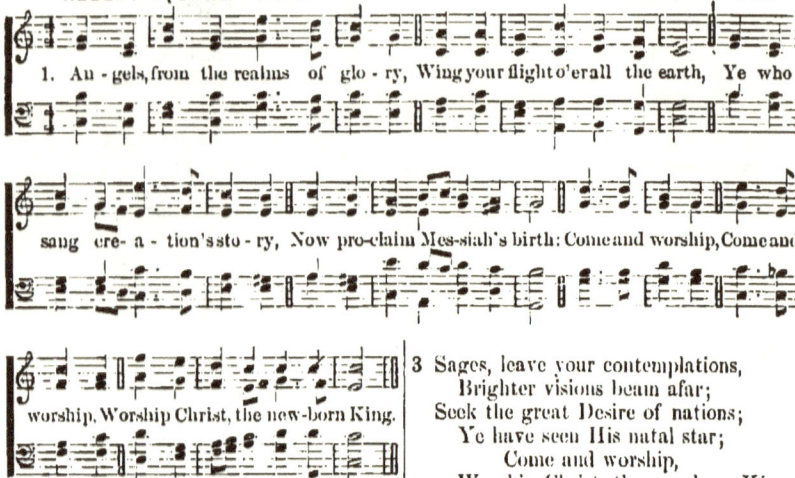

1. An-gels, from the realms of glo-ry, Wing your flight o'er all the earth, Ye who sang cre-a-tion's sto-ry, Now pro-claim Mes-si-ah's birth: Come and worship, Come and worship, Worship Christ, the new-born King.

97 *"Good Tidings of great Joy."*
Luke ii. 10.

2 Shepherds, in the field abiding,
   Watching o'er your flocks by night,
God with man is now residing;
   Yonder shines the infant light;
     Come and worship,
   Worship Christ, the new-born King.

3 Sages, leave your contemplations,
   Brighter visions beam afar;
Seek the great Desire of nations;
   Ye have seen His natal star;
     Come and worship,
   Worship Christ, the new-born King.

4 Saints before the altar bending,
   Watching long in hope and fear,
Suddenly the Lord, descending,
   In His temple shall appear:
     Come and worship,
   Worship Christ, the new-born King.
James Montgomery (1771—1854), 1825. Ab. and alt.

DIX. 7, 6 l. German. Arr. by WILLIAM HENRY MONK (1823—). 1868.

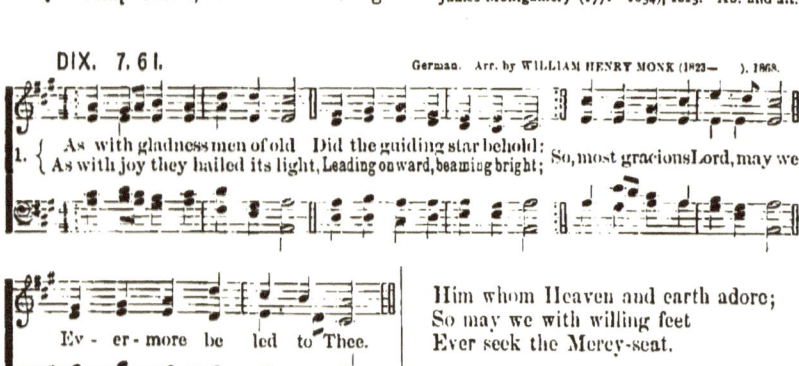

1. { As with gladness men of old Did the guiding star behold;
    As with joy they hailed its light, Leading onward, beaming bright; } So, most gracious Lord, may we Ev-er-more be led to Thee.

98 *"Leading onward."*
Matt. ii. 10.

2 As with joyful steps they sped
   To that lowly manger-bed,
There to bend the knee before
   Him whom Heaven and earth adore;
So may we with willing feet
Ever seek the Mercy-seat.

3 As they offered gifts most rare
   At that manger rude and bare;
So may we with holy joy,
   Pure, and free from sin's alloy,
All our costliest treasures bring,
Christ, to Thee, our heavenly King.

4 Holy Jesus, every day
  Keep us in the narrow way;
  And, when earthly things are past,
  Bring our ransomed souls at last
  Where they need no star to guide,
  Where no clouds Thy glory hide.

5 In the heavenly country bright,
  Need they no created light;
  Thou its Light, its Joy, its Crown,
  Thou its Sun, which goes not down:
  There forever may we sing
  Alleluias to our King.
      William Chatterton Dix (1837—   ), 1860.

WILMOT. 8.7.   CARL MARIA VON WEBER (1786—1826).

1. Hark! what mean those holy voi-ces, Sweetly sounding through the skies? Lo, th'angelic host rejoic-es; Heav'nly hallelujahs rise.

99   *"Those holy Voices."*

2 Listen to the wondrous story,
   Which they chant in hymns of joy:
  "Glory in the highest, glory,
   Glory be to God most high.

3 "Peace on earth, good-will from Heaven,
   Reaching far as man is found;
   Souls redeemed, and sins forgiven,
   Loud our golden harps shall sound.

4 "Christ is born, the great Anointed;
   Heaven and earth His glory sing:
   Glad receive whom God appointed
   For your Prophet, Priest, and King.

5 "Hasten, mortals, to adore Him;
   Learn His Name and taste His joy:
   Till in Heaven you sing before Him,
  "Glory be to God most high."
      Rev. John Cawood (1775—1852), 1819. Ab.

ANTIOCH. C.M.   From GEORGE FREDERICK HANDEL.   Arr. by LOWELL MASON (1792—1872), 1836.

1. Joy to the world, the Lord is come: Let earth receive her King; { Let ev-'ry heart pre-pare Him room, } And heav'n and nature sing, And heav'n and nature sing, And heav'n, And heav'n and nature sing.

And heav'n and nature sing, And heav'n and nature sing,

100   *"Joy to the World."*   Ps. xcviii.

2 Joy to the earth, the Saviour reigns:
   Let men their songs employ;
   While fields and floods, rocks, hills, and plains,
   Repeat the sounding joy.

3 No more let sins and sorrows grow,
   Nor thorns infest the ground:
   He comes to make His blessings flow
   Far as the curse is found.

4 He rules the world with truth and grace,
   And makes the nations prove
   The glories of His righteousness,
   And wonders of His love.
      Rev. Isaac Watts (1674—1748), 1709.

THE LORD JESUS CHRIST.

MANOAH. C. M.
FRANCIS JOSEPH HAYDN (1732—1809), 1801.
Arr. by HENRY WELLINGTON GREATOREX (1811—1858), 1851.

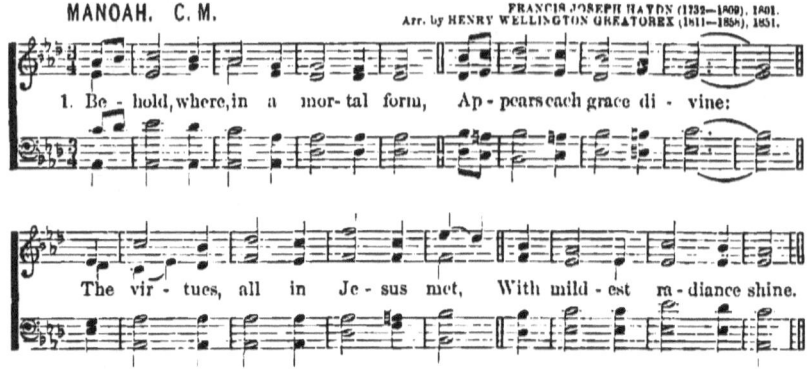

1. Behold, where, in a mortal form, Appears each grace divine: The virtues, all in Jesus met, With mildest radiance shine.

101 *"Who went about doing good."* Acts x. 38.

2 To spread the rays of heavenly light,
  To give the mourner joy,
  To preach glad tidings to the poor,
  Was His divine employ,

3 'Midst keen reproach, and cruel scorn,
  Patient and meek He stood;
  His foes, ungrateful, sought His life,
  He labored for their good.

4 To God He left His righteous cause,
  And still His task pursued;
  With humble prayer, and holy faith,
  His fainting strength renewed.

5 Be Christ our pattern and our guide,
  His image may we bear;
  O may we tread His holy steps,
  His joy and glory share.
  Prof. William Enfield (1741—1797), 1771. Ab. and alt.

102 *"Grace is poured into Thy Lips."* Ps. xlv. 2.

1 What grace, O Lord, and beauty shone
  Around Thy steps below:
  What patient love was seen in all
  Thy life and death of woe.

2 Forever on Thy burdened heart
  A weight of sorrow hung;
  Yet no ungentle, murmuring word
  Escaped Thy silent tongue.

3 O give us hearts to love like Thee,
  Like Thee, O Lord, to grieve
  Far more for others' sins, than all
  The wrongs that we receive.

4 One with Thyself, may every eye
  In us, Thy brethren, see
  The gentleness and grace that springs
  From union, Lord, with Thee.
  Sir Edward Denny (1796—   ), 1839. Ab.

ELIZABETHTOWN. C. M.
GEORGE KINGSLEY (1811—1884), 1838.

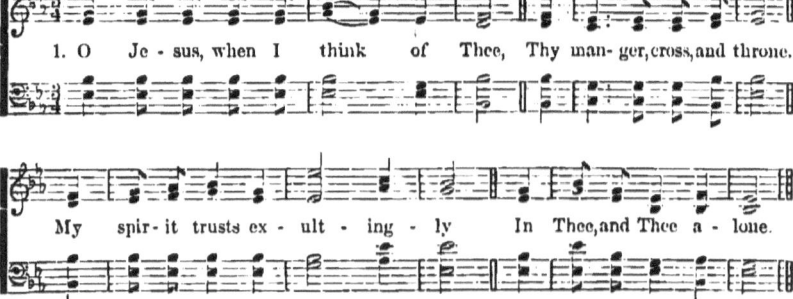

1. O Jesus, when I think of Thee, Thy manger, cross, and throne. My spirit trusts exultingly In Thee, and Thee alone.

103 *Trust in Christ.*

2 For me Thou didst become a man,
  For me didst weep and die;
  For me achieve Thy wondrous plan,
  For me ascend on high.

3 O let me share Thy holy birth,
  Thy faith, Thy death to sin,
  And, strong amidst the toils of earth
  My heavenly life begin.

4 Then shall I know what means the
    Triumphant of Saint Paul: [strain
  "To live is Christ, to die is gain;"
  "Christ is my All in all."

Rev. George Washington Bethune (1805—1862), 1847. Ab.

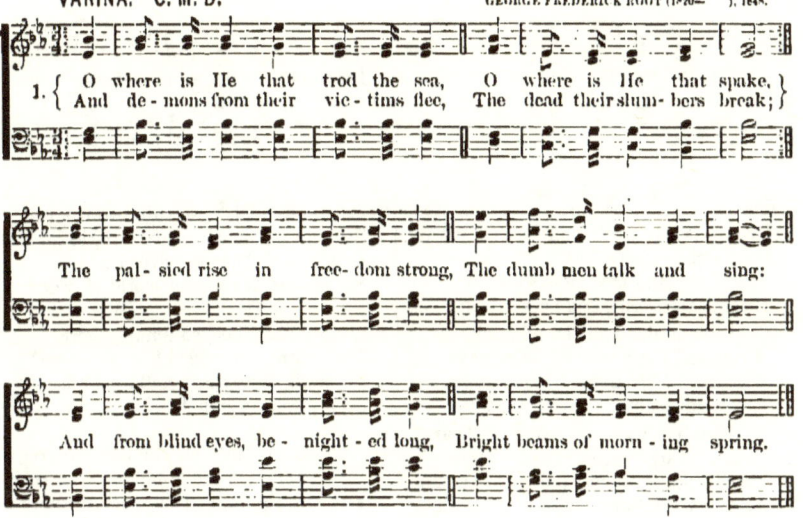

VARINA. C. M. D.   GEORGE FREDERICK ROOT (1820—). 1848.

1. { O where is He that trod the sea, O where is He that spake,
     And demons from their victims flee, The dead their slumbers break; }
   The palsied rise in freedom strong, The dumb men talk and sing:
   And from blind eyes, benighted long, Bright beams of morning spring.

104 "*O where is He that trod the Sea.*"

2 O where is He that trod the sea,
  'Tis only He can save;
  To thousands hungering wearily,
  A wondrous meal He gave:
  Full soon, with food celestial fed,
  Their mystic fare they take;
  'Twas springtide when He blest the bread,
  And harvest when He brake.

3 O where is He that trod the sea,
  My soul, the Lord is here:
  Let all thy fears be hushed in thee;
  To leap, to look, to hear,
  Be thine: thy needs He'll satisfy:
  Art thou diseased, or dumb?
  Or dost thou in thy hunger cry?
  "I come," said Christ, "I come."

Rev. Thomas Toke Lynch (1818—1871), 1855. Ab. and sl. alt.

105 *The Fellowship of Suffering.*

1 O Lord, when we the path retrace
  Which Thou on earth hast trod,
  To man Thy wondrous love and grace,
  Thy faithfulness to God:—
  Thy love, by man so sorely tried,
  Proved stronger than the grave;
  The very spear that pierced Thy side
  Drew forth the blood to save.

2 Unmoved by Satan's subtle wiles,
  Of suffering, shame, and loss,
  Thy path, uncheered by earthly smiles,
  Led only to the cross.
  Give us Thy meek, Thy lowly mind:
  We would obedient be;
  And all our rest and pleasure find
  In fellowship with Thee.

James George Deck (1802—), 1838. Ab.

THE LORD JESUS CHRIST.

HAMBURG. L. M.   Arr. by LOWELL MASON (1792—1872), 1825.

1. My dear Redeemer, and my Lord, I read my duty in Thy Word;
But in Thy life the law appears, Drawn out in living characters.

106   *Christ our Pattern.*
1 Pet. ii. 21.

2 Such was Thy truth, and such Thy zeal,
Such deference to Thy Father's will,
Such love, and meekness so divine,
I would transcribe and make them mine.

3 Cold mountains and the midnight air
Witnessed the fervor of Thy prayer;
The desert Thy temptations knew,
Thy conflict and Thy victory, too.

4 Be Thou my pattern; make me bear
More of Thy gracious image here;
Then God, the Judge, shall own my name
Amongst the followers of the Lamb.

Rev. Isaac Watts (1674—1748), 1709.

107   *The Meekness of Christ.*

1 How beauteous were the marks divine,
That in Thy meekness used to shine,
That lit Thy lonely pathway, trod
In wondrous love, O Son of God.

2 O who like Thee, so calm, so bright,
So pure, so made to live in light?
O who like Thee did ever go
So patient, through a world of woe?

3 O who like Thee, so humbly bore
The scorn, the scoffs of men, before?
So meek, forgiving, godlike, high,
So glorious in humility?

4 And death, that sets the prisoner free,
Was pang, and scoff, and scorn to Thee;
Yet love through all Thy torture glowed,
And mercy with Thy life-blood flowed.

5 O in Thy light be mine to go,
Illuming all my way of woe;
And give me ever, on the road,
To trace Thy footsteps, O my God.

Bp. Arthur Cleveland Coxe (1818—), 1840. Ab.

OLIVE'S BROW. L. M.   WILLIAM BATCHELDER BRADBURY (1816—1868), 1853.

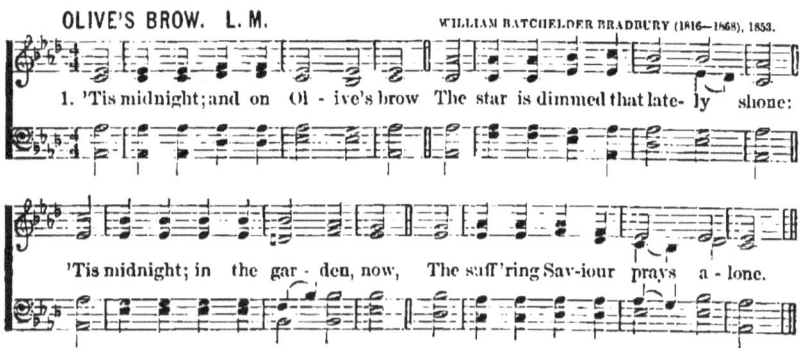

1. 'Tis midnight; and on Olive's brow The star is dimmed that lately shone:
'Tis midnight; in the garden, now, The suff'ring Saviour prays alone.

108 *Christ in Gethsemane.*

2 'Tis midnight; and from all removed,
 The Saviour wrestles lone with fears;
 E'en that disciple whom He loved
 Heeds not his Master's grief and tears.

3 'Tis midnight; and for others' guilt
 The Man of Sorrows weeps in blood;

Yet He that hath in anguish knelt
 Is not forsaken by His God.

4 'Tis midnight; and from ether-plains
 Is borne the song that angels know;
 Unheard by mortals are the strains
 That sweetly soothe the Saviour's woe.

Rev. William Bingham Tappan (1794—1849), 1822.

GETHSEMANE. 7.6 l.    RICHARD REDHEAD (1820—), 1853.

1. Go to dark Geth-sem-a-ne, Ye that feel the tempter's pow'r;
Your Re-deem-er's con-flict see; Watch with Him one bit-ter hour:
Turn not from His griefs a-way; Learn of Je-sus Christ to pray.

109 *Gethsemane.*

2 Follow to the judgment-hall,
 View the Lord of life arraigned;
 O the wormwood and the gall!
 O the pangs His soul sustained!
 Shun not suffering, shame, or loss;
 Learn of Him to bear the cross.

3 Calvary's mournful mountain climb;
 There, adoring at His feet,
 Mark that miracle of time,
 God's own sacrifice complete:
 "It is finished," hear the cry;
 Learn of Jesus Christ to die.

4 Early hasten to the tomb,
 Where they laid His breathless clay;
 All is solitude and gloom;
 Who hath taken Him away?
 Christ is risen; He meets our eyes;
 Saviour, teach us so to rise.

James Montgomery (1771—1854), 1822, 1853.

110 *"Venit a cælo Mediator alto."*

1 Zion's daughter, weep no more,
 Though thy troubled heart be sore:
 He of whom the psalmist sung,
 He who woke the prophet's tongue,
 Christ, the Mediator blest,
 Brings thee everlasting rest.

2 In a garden man became
 Heir of sin, and death, and shame:
 Jesus in a garden wins
 Life, and pardon for our sins;
 Through His hour of agony,
 Praying in Gethsemane.

3 There for us He intercedes;
 There with God the Father pleads;
 Willing there for us to drain
 To the dregs the cup of pain,
 That in everlasting day
 He may wipe our tears away.

Roman Breviary.
Tr. by Rev. Sir Henry Williams Baker (1821—1877), 1861. Ab.

AVON. C.M. HUGH WILSON (1764—1824), 1798.

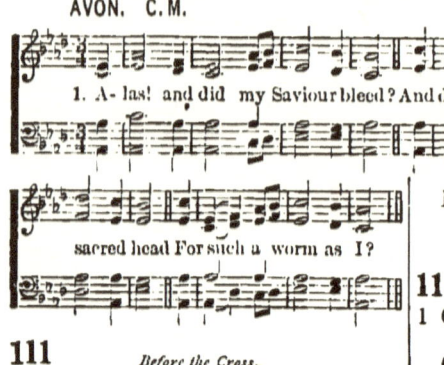

1. A-las! and did my Saviour bleed? And did my Sov'reign die? Would He devote that sacred head For such a worm as I?

Here, Lord, I give myself away;
'Tis all that I can do.
Rev. Isaac Watts (1674—1748), 1709. Ab.

111 *Before the Cross.*

2 Was it for crimes that I had done
He groaned upon the tree?
Amazing pity! grace unknown!
And love beyond degree!

3 Well might the sun in darkness hide,
And shut his glories in,
When God, the mighty Maker, died
For man the creature's sin.

4 Thus might I hide my blushing face,
While His dear cross appears:
Dissolve, my heart, in thankfulness,
And melt, mine eyes, to tears.

5 But drops of grief can ne'er repay
The debt of love I owe:

112 *Kneeling at the Cross.*

1 O Jesus, sweet the tears I shed,
While at Thy cross I kneel,
Gaze on Thy wounded, fainting head,
And all Thy sorrows feel.

2 'Twas for the sinful Thou didst die,
And I a sinner stand:
What love speaks from Thy dying eye,
And from each piercèd hand.

3 I know this cleansing blood of Thine
Was shed, dear Lord, for me:
For me, for all, O Grace divine,
Who look by faith on Thee.

4 O Christ of God, O spotless Lamb,
By love my soul is drawn;
Henceforth, for ever, Thine I am;
Here life and peace are born.
Rev. Ray Palmer (1808—1887), 1867. Ab.

ASHWELL. L.M. LOWELL MASON (1792—1872), 1842.

1. Lord Je-sus, when we stand a-far And gaze up-on Thy ho-ly cross, In love of Thee and scorn of self, O may we count the world as loss.

113 *Gazing upon the Cross.*

2 When we behold Thy bleeding wounds,
And the rough way that Thou hast trod,
Make us to hate the load of sin
That lay so heavy on our God.

3 Give us an ever-living faith
To gaze beyond the things we see;
And, in the mystery of Thy death,
Draw us and all men unto Thee.
Bp. William Walsham How (1823—   ), 1854. Ab.

DONCASTER. L. M.   EDWARD MILLER (1731—1807). 1787.

1. When I sur-vey the wondrous cross, On which the Prince of glo-ry died, My rich-est gain I count but loss, And pour contempt on all my pride.

114 *"The wondrous Cross."*

2 Forbid it, Lord, that I should boast,
Save in the death of Christ, my God:
All the vain things that charm me most,
I sacrifice them to His blood.

3 See, from His head, His hands, His feet,
Sorrow and love flow mingled down:

Did e'er such love and sorrow meet,
Or thorns compose so rich a crown?

4 Were the whole realm of nature mine,
That were a present far too small;
Love so amazing, so divine,
Demands my soul, my life, my all.

Rev. Isaac Watts (1674—1748), 1709. Ab.

BREST. 8. 7. 4.   LOWELL MASON (1792—1872), 1836.

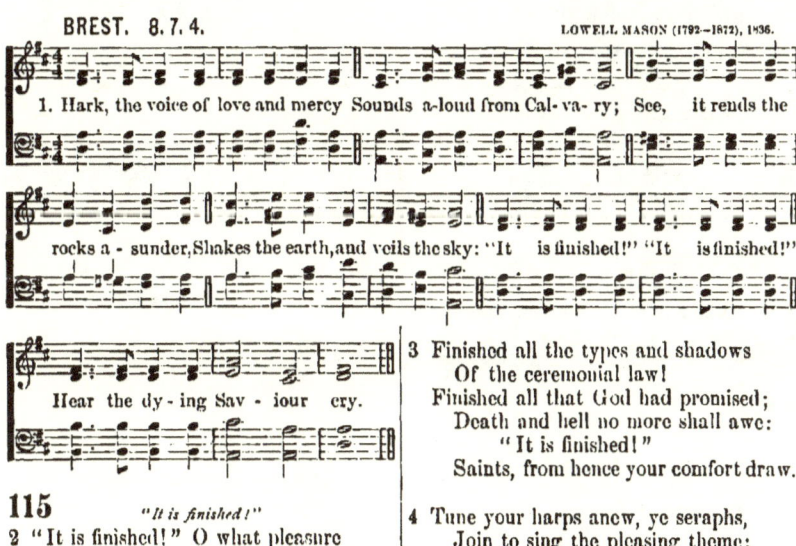

1. Hark, the voice of love and mercy Sounds a-loud from Cal-va-ry; See, it rends the rocks a-sunder, Shakes the earth, and veils the sky: "It is finished!" "It is finished!" Hear the dy-ing Sav-iour cry.

115 *"It is finished!"*

2 "It is finished!" O what pleasure
Do these charming words afford!
Heavenly blessings without measure
Flow to us from Christ, the Lord:
"It is finished!"
Saints, the dying words record.

3 Finished all the types and shadows
Of the ceremonial law!
Finished all that God had promised;
Death and hell no more shall awe:
"It is finished!"
Saints, from hence your comfort draw.

4 Tune your harps anew, ye seraphs,
Join to sing the pleasing theme;
All on earth and all in heaven,
Join to praise Immanuel's name:
Hallelujah!
Glory to the bleeding Lamb.

Rev. Jonathan Evans (1749—1809), 1787. Ab.

SHAWMUT. S. M.
Arr. by LOWELL MASON (1792–1872), 1832.

1. Not all the blood of beasts On Jewish altars slain, Could give the guilty conscience peace, Or wash away the stain.

116   *"The Heavenly Lamb."*

2 But Christ, the heavenly Lamb,
   Takes all our sins away;
  A sacrifice of nobler name,
   And richer blood, than they.

3 My faith would lay her hand
   On that dear head of Thine,
  While like a penitent I stand,
   And there confess my sin.

4 My soul looks back to see
   The burdens Thou didst bear,
  When hanging on the cursèd tree,
   And hopes her guilt was there.

5 Believing, we rejoice
   To see the curse remove;
  We bless the Lamb with cheerful voice,
   And sing His bleeding love.
          Rev. Isaac Watts (1674—1748), 1709.

ALDERSGATE. S. M.
Rev. Sir G. P. MERRICK.

1. O perfect life of love! All, all is finished now, All that He left His throne above To do for us below.

117   *The finished Work.*

2 No work is left undone
   Of all the Father willed;
  His toil, His sorrows, one by one,
   The Scriptures have fulfilled.

3 No pain that we can share
   But He has felt its smart;
  All forms of human grief and care
   Have pierced that tender heart.

4 And on His thorn-crowned head,
   And on His sinless soul,
  Our sins and all their guilt were laid,
   That He might make us whole.

5 In perfect love He dies;
   For me He dies, for me;
  O all-atoning sacrifice,
   I cling by faith to Thee.

6 In every time of need,
   Before the judgment-throne,
  Thy work, O Lamb of God, I'll plead,
   Thy merits, not my own.

7 Yet work, O Lord, in me,
   As Thou for me hast wrought;
  And let my love the answer be
   To grace Thy love has brought.
      Rev. Sir Henry Williams Baker (1821—1877).

HIS RESURRECTION.

MARCELLUS. 8 8. 8. 4. Arr. from GIOVANNI PIERLUIGI DA PALESTRINA (1524?—1594).

1. The strife is o'er, the battle done; The victory of life is won; The song of triumph has begun; Hallelujah!

118 *"Finita jam sunt proelia."*

2 The three sad days are quickly sped,
He rises glorious from the dead;
All glory to our risen Head;
   Hallelujah!

3 He closed the yawning gates of hell;
The bars from Heaven's high portals fell;
Let hymns of praise His triumphs tell.
   Hallelujah!

4 Lord, by the stripes which wounded Thee,
From death's dread sting Thy servants free,
That we may live and sing to Thee.
   Hallelujah!

Unknown Author of the 12th century.
Tr. by Rev. Francis Pott (1832—), 1860.

MIGDOL. L. M. LOWELL MASON, 1839.

1. "I know that my Redeemer lives:" What comfort this sweet sentence gives,
He lives, He lives, who once was dead, He lives, my ever-living Head.

119 *"He lives."*

2 He lives to bless me with His love,
He lives to plead for me above,
He lives my hungry soul to feed,
He lives to help in time of need.

3 He lives, my kind, my faithful Friend,
He lives and loves me to the end,
He lives, and while He lives I'll sing,
He lives, my Prophet, Priest, and King.

4 He lives, and grants me daily breath,
He lives, and I shall conquer death,
He lives my mansion to prepare,
He lives to bring me safely there.

Rev. Samuel Medley (1738—1799), 1789. Ab.

120 *Christ interceding.*
Heb. vii. 25.

1 He lives, the Great Redeemer lives,
What joy the blest assurance gives;
And now, before His Father, God,
Pleads the full merits of His blood.

2 In every dark, distressful hour;
When sin and Satan join their power,
Let this dear hope repel the dart,
That Jesus bears us on His heart

3 Great Advocate, Almighty Friend,
On Him our humble hopes depend;
Our cause can never, never fail,
For Jesus pleads, and must prevail.

Miss Anne Steele (1717—1778), 1760. Ab.

THE LORD JESUS CHRIST.

BROWN. C. M.   WILLIAM BATCHELDER BRADBURY (1816—1868), 1844.

1. The head that once was crown'd with thorns Is crown'd with glory now; A royal diadem adorns The mighty Victor's brow.

121   *"Perfect through Sufferings."* Heb. ii. 10.

2 The joy of all who dwell above,
    The joy of all below
To whom He manifests His love,
    And grants His Name to know.

3 They suffer with their Lord below,
    They reign with Him above;
Their profit and their joy to know
    The mystery of His love.

4 The cross He bore is life and health,
    Though shame and death to Him;
His people's hope, His people's wealth,
    Their everlasting theme.
        Rev. Thomas Kelly (1769—1855), 1820. Ab.

122   *"The universal Anthem."* Rev. v. 11—13.

1 Come, let us join our cheerful songs
    With angels round the throne;
Ten thousand thousand are their tongues,
    But all their joys are one.

2 "Worthy the Lamb that died," they cry,
    "To be exalted thus;"
"Worthy the Lamb," our lips reply
    "For He was slain for us."

3 Jesus is worthy to receive
    Honor and power divine;
And blessings, more than we can give,
    Be, Lord, forever Thine.
        Rev. Isaac Watts (1674—1748), 1709. Ab.

123   *"Our ascended Priest."*

1 Come, let us join in songs of praise
    To our ascended Priest;
He entered Heaven with all our names
    Deep graven on His breast.

2 Below He washed our guilt away,
    By His atoning blood;
Now He appears before the throne,
    And pleads our cause with God.

3 Clothed with our nature still, He knows
    The weakness of our frame,
And how to shield us from the foes
    Which He Himself o'ercame.

4 O may we ne'er forget His grace,
    Nor blush to wear His Name;
Still may our hearts hold fast His faith
    Our mouths His praise proclaim.
        Rev. Alexander Pirie (—1804), 1786. Ab. and sl. alt.

CHIMES. C. M.   LOWELL MASON (1792—1872),

NATIVITY. C. M.   HENRY LAHEE (1826—).

1. Behold the glories of the Lamb, Amidst His Father's throne:
Prepare new honors for His Name, And songs before unknown.

124 *To the Lamb that was slain.*
Rev. v. 6–12.

2 Let elders worship at His feet,
The church adore around,
With vials full of odors sweet,
And harps of sweeter sound.

3 Those are the prayers of all the saints,
And these the hymns they raise:
Jesus is kind to our complaints,
He loves to hear our praise

4 Now to the Lamb that once was slain,
Be endless blessings paid;
Salvation, glory, joy remain
Forever on Thy head.

5 Thou hast redeemed our souls with blood,
Hast set the prisoners free,
Hast made us kings and priests to God,
And we shall reign with Thee.
    Rev. Isaac Watts, 1709. Ab.

HOWARD. C. M.   SAMUEL HOWARD (1710—1782), 1760.

1. Come, let us lift our joyful eyes Up to the courts above,
And smile to see our Father there, Upon a throne of love.

125 *The Gates opened.*

2 Now we may bow before His feet,
And venture near the Lord:
No fiery cherub guards His seat,
Nor double flaming sword.

3 The peaceful gates of heavenly bliss
Are opened by the Son;

High let us raise our notes of praise,
And reach th'almighty throne.

4 To Thee ten thousand thanks we bring
Great Advocate on high;
And glory to th'eternal King,
Who lays His anger by.
    Rev. Isaac Watts, 1709. Ab. and sl. alt

AUTOMN. 8, 7. D. Spanish Melody.

1. Hail, Thou once despis-ed Jesus, Hail, Thou Gal-i-le-an King.
Thou didst suf-fer to re-lease us, Thou didst free sal-va-tion bring:
D.S. By Thy mer-its we find fa-vor; Life is giv-en through Thy Name.
Hail, Thou ag-o-niz-ing, Sav-iour, Bear-er of our sin and shame;

126 *"Enthroned in Glory."*

2 Paschal Lamb, by God appointed,
  All our sins on Thee were laid;
By almighty love anointed,
  Thou hast full atonement made:
All Thy people are forgiven
  Through the virtue of Thy blood;
Opened is the gate of Heaven,
  Peace is made 'twixt man and God.

3 Jesus, hail, enthroned in glory,
  There forever to abide;
All the heavenly hosts adore Thee,
  Seated at Thy Father's side.
There for sinners Thou art pleading;
  There Thou dost our place prepare;
Ever for us interceding
  Till in glory we appear.
    Rev. John Bakewell (1721—1819), 1760. Alt.
    Rev. Augustus Montague Toplady (1740—1778), 1776.

127 *"Thou art worthy."*
   (Second part of preceding Hymn.)

1 Worship, honor, power, and blessing,
  Thou art worthy to receive;
Loudest praises, without ceasing,
  Meet it is for us to give,
Help, ye bright angelic spirits,
  Bring your sweetest, noblest lays;
Help to sing our Saviour's merits,
  Help to chant Immanuel's praise.

2 Soon we shall, with those in glory,
  His transcendent grace relate;
Gladly sing th' amazing story
  Of His dying love so great:
In that blessèd contemplation
  We forevermore shall dwell,
Crowned with bliss and consolation,
  Such as none below can tell.
    Rev. John Bakewell, 1760. Alt.
    Rev. Augustus Montague Toplady, 1776.

128 *"On the right Hand of God."*
    1 Pet. iii, 22.

1 Christ, above all glory seated,
  King eternal, strong to save,
Dying, Thou hast death defeated,
  Buried, Thou hast spoiled the grave,
Thou art gone, where now is given,
  What no mortal might could gain:
On th' eternal throne of Heaven,
  In Thy Father's power to reign.

2 We, O Lord, with hearts adoring,
  Follow Thee above the sky:
Hear our prayers Thy grace imploring,
  Lift our souls to Thee on high.
So when Thou again in glory
  On the clouds of Heaven shalt shine,
We Thy flock shall stand before Thee,
  Owned forevermore as Thine.
    Bp. James Russell Woodford (1820—   ), 1863. Ab.

129 *"I am with you alway."* 8. 7. D.
 Matt. xxviii. 20.

1 Always with us, always with us,
  Words of cheer, and words of love,
 Thus the risen Saviour whispers,
  From His dwelling-place above.
 With us when the storm is sweeping,
  O'er our pathway dark and drear,
 Waking hope within our bosoms,
  Stilling every anxious fear.
2 With us in the lonely valley,
  When we cross the chilling stream;
 Lighting up the steps to glory
  Like the ancient prophet's dream.
 Always with us, always with us,
  Pilot on the surging main,
 Guiding to the distant haven,
  Where we shall be home again.
  Rev. Edwin Henry Nevin (1814—   ), 1858. Ab.

130 *Dismission.* 8. 7. D.

Lord, dismiss us with Thy blessing,
 Bid us now depart in peace;
Still on heavenly manna feeding,
 Let our faith and love increase:
Fill each breast with consolation;
 Up to Thee our hearts we raise;
When we reach our blissful station,
 Then we'll give Thee nobler praise.
  Rev. Robert Hawker (1753—1827), 1794.

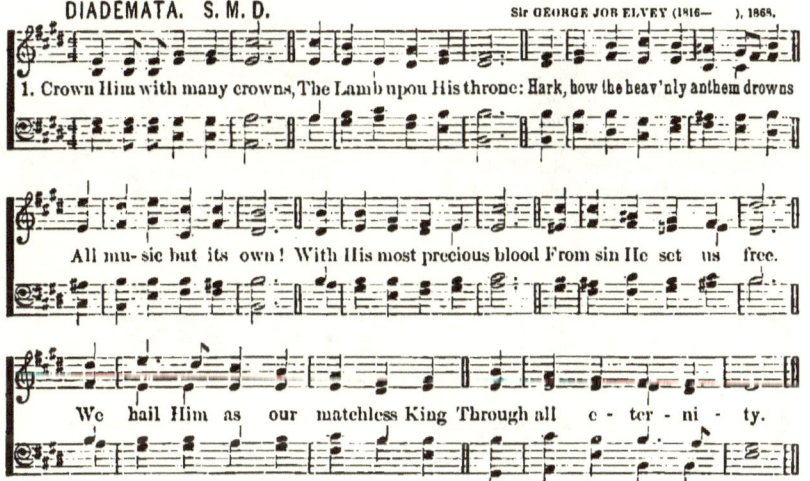

DIADEMATA. S. M. D.   Sir GEORGE JOB ELVEY (1816—   ), 1868.

1. Crown Him with many crowns, The Lamb upon His throne: Hark, how the heav'nly anthem drowns All mu-sic but its own! With His most precious blood From sin He set us free. We hail Him as our matchless King Through all e-ter-ni-ty.

131 *The Song of the Seraphs.*

2 Crown Him the Lord of love:
  Behold His hands and side,
 Rich wounds, yet visible above
  In beauty glorified:
 No angel in the sky
  Can fully bear that sight,
 But downward bends his burning eye
  At mysteries so bright.
3 Crown Him the Lord of peace,
  Whose power a sceptre sways,
 From pole to pole, that wars may cease,
  And all be prayer and praise.
 His reign shall know no end,
  And round His piercèd feet
 Fair flowers of Paradise extend
  Their fragrance ever sweet.
4 Crown Him the Lord of Heaven,
  One with the Father known,
 One with the Spirit through Him given
  From yonder radiant throne!
 To Thee be endless praise,
  For Thou for us hast died:
 Be Thou, O Lord, through endless days
  Adored and magnified.
  Matthew Bridges (1800—   ), 1848. Ab. and alt.

THE LORD JESUS CHRIST.

DORT. 6. 6. 4. 6. 6. 6. 4.   LOWELL MASON. (1792—1872), 1832.

1. Glory to God on high, Let praises fill the sky! Praise ye His Name. { Angels His Name adore, Who all our sorrows bore, And saints cry evermore, "Worthy the Lamb!"

132   *"Worthy the Lamb."*

2 All they around the throne
Cheerfully join in one,
  Praising His Name.
We who have felt His blood
Sealing our peace with God,
Spread His dear fame abroad:
  "Worthy the Lamb!"

3 Join all the human race,
Our Lord and God to bless;
  Praise ye His Name!
In Him we will rejoice,
Making a cheerful noise,
And say with heart and voice,
  "Worthy the Lamb!"

4 Though we must change our place,
Our souls shall never cease
  Praising His Name;
To Him we'll tribute bring,
Laud Him our gracious King,
And without ceasing sing,
  "Worthy the Lamb!"

          Rev. James Allen (1734—1804), 1761. Ab.

EDINA. 6. 5. D.   Sir HERBERT STANLEY OAKELEY (1830—),

1. At the Name of Jesus Ev-'ry knee shall bow, Ev-'ry tongue confess Him King of Glo-ry now; 'Tis the Father's pleas-ure We should call Him Lord, Who from the be-gin-ning Was the might-y Word.

133 *"At the Name of Jesus."*

2 Humbled for a season
  To receive a name
From the lips of sinners
  Unto whom He came;
Faithfully He bore it
  Spotless to the last;
Brought it back victorious,
  When from death He passed.

3 Name Him, brothers, name Him,
  With love strong as death,
But with awe and wonder,
  And with 'bated breath;
He is God the Saviour,
  He is Christ the Lord,
Ever to be worshipped,
  Trusted, and adored.

4 In your hearts enthrone Him;
  There let Him subdue
All that is not holy,
  All that is not true;
Crown Him as your Captain
  In temptation's hour;
Let His will enfold you
  In its light and power.

5 Brothers, this Lord Jesus
  Shall return again,
With His Father's glory,
  With His angel train;
For all wreaths of empire
  Meet upon His brow,
And our hearts confess Him
  King of glory now.

Miss Caroline M. Noel (—). Ab.

VICTORY. 8, 7, 4. HARRY HOBART BEADLE (1828—), 1854.

1. Look, ye saints, the sight is glorious, See "the Man of Sorrows" now;
From the fight returned victorious, Ev'ry knee to Him shall bow.
Crown Him, crown Him; Crowns become the Victor's brow.

134 *"He shall reign forever and ever."*
Rev. xi. 15.

2 Crown the Saviour, angels, crown Him:
  Rich the trophies Jesus brings:
In the seat of power enthrone Him,
  While the vault of Heaven rings:
Crown Him, crown Him;
  Crown the Saviour "King of kings."

3 Sinners in derision crowned Him,
  Mocking thus the Saviour's claim;
Saints and angels crowd around Him,
  Own His title, praise His Name:
Crown Him, crown Him;
  Spread abroad the Victor's fame.

4 Hark, those bursts of acclamation!
  Hark, those loud triumphant chords!
Jesus takes the highest station:
  O what joy the sight affords!
Crown Him, crown Him;
  "King of kings, and Lord of lords."

Rev. Thomas Kelly (1769—1855), 1809.

THE LORD JESUS CHRIST.

HEBER. C. M. — GEORGE KINGSLEY (1811—1884), 1838.

1. Thou art the Way: To Thee alone From sin and death we flee;
And he who would the Father seek, Must seek Him, Lord, by Thee.

135 *"The Way, the Truth, the Life."*
John xiv. 6.

2 Thou art the Truth: Thy word alone
True wisdom can impart;
Thou only canst inform the mind,
And purify the heart.

3 Thou art the Life: the rending tomb
Proclaims Thy conquering arm
And those who put their trust in Thee
Nor death, nor hell shall harm.

4 Thou art the Way, the Truth, the Life;
Grant us that Way to know,
That Truth to keep, that Life to win,
Whose joys eternal flow.
*Bp. George Washington Doane (1799—1859), 1824.

136 *Our double Kindred to Immanuel.*
1 Cor. xv. 47, 49.

1 O mean may seem this house of clay,
Yet 'twas the Lord's abode;
Our feet may mourn this thorny way,
Yet here Immanuel trod.

2 This fleshly robe the Lord did wear;
This watch the Lord did keep;
These burdens sore the Lord did bear;
These tears the Lord did weep.

3 O vale of tears no longer sad,
Wherein the Lord did dwell!
O happy robe of flesh that clad
Our own Immanuel!

4 But not this fleshly robe alone
Shall link us, Lord, to Thee;
Not only in the tear and groan
Shall the dear kindred be.

5 We shall be reckoned for Thine own,
Because Thy Heaven we share,
Because we sing around Thy throne,
And Thy bright raiment wear.

6 O mighty grace, our life to live,
To make our earth divine!
O mighty grace, Thy Heaven to give,
And lift our life to Thine!
Thomas Hornblower Gill (1819—), 1850. Ab.

137 *"Majestic Sweetness."*

1 Majestic sweetness sits enthroned
Upon the Saviour's brow;
His head with radiant glories crowned,
His lips with grace o'erflow.

2 No mortal can with Him compare
Among the sons of men;
Fairer is He than all the fair
That fill the heavenly train.

3 He saw me plunged in deep distress,
He flew to my relief;
For me He bore the shameful cross,
And carried all my grief.

4 To Him I owe my life and breath,
And all the joys I have;
He makes me triumph over death,
He saves me from the grave.

5 Since from His bounty I receive
Such proofs of love divine,
Had I a thousand hearts to give,
Lord, they should all be Thine.
Rev. Samuel Stennett (1727—1795), 1782. Ab.

138 *"The Incarnate Mystery."* C. M.
1 Cor. i. 22—29.

1 DEAREST of all the names above,
  My Jesus and my God,
Who can resist Thy heavenly love,
  Or trifle with Thy blood?

2 'Tis by the merits of Thy death
  The Father smiles again;
'Tis by Thine interceding breath
  The Spirit dwells with men.

3 Till God in human flesh I see,
  My thoughts no comfort find;
The holy, just, and sacred Three
  Are terrors to my mind.

4 But if Immanuel's face appear,
  My hope, my joy, begins:
His Name forbids my slavish fear;
  His grace removes my sins.

5 While Jews on their own law rely,
  And Greeks of wisdom boast,
I love th' incarnate Mystery,
  And there I fix my trust.

Rev. Isaac Watts (1674—1748), 1709.

CORONATION. C. M.

OLIVER HOLDEN (1765—1844), 1793.

1. All hail the pow'r of Jesus' Name! Let angels prostrate fall, Bring forth the royal diadem, And crown Him Lord of all, Bring forth the royal diadem, And crown Him Lord of all.

139 *"And crown Him Lord of all."*
Acts x. 36.

2 Ye seed of Israel's chosen race,
  Ye ransomed of the fall,
Hail Him, who saves you by His grace,
  And crown Him Lord of all.

3 Sinners, whose love can ne'er forget
  The wormwood and the gall,
Go, spread your trophies at His feet,
  And crown Him Lord of all.

4 Let every kindred, every tribe,
  On this terrestrial ball,
To Him all majesty ascribe,
  And crown Him Lord of all.

Rev. Edward Perronet (—1792), 1780. Ab and alt.

MILES LANE. C. M.

WILLIAM SHRUBSOLE (1758—1806), 1793.
Har. by Rev. JOHN BACCHUS DYKES (1823—1876), 1861.

1. All hail the pow'r of Jesus' Name! Let an-gels prostrate fall, Bring forth the royal diadem, And crown Him, crown Him, crown Him, crown Him Lord of all.

THE LORD JESUS CHRIST.

GROSTETE. L. M. HENRY WELLINGTON GREATOREX (1811—1858), 1849.

1. O Christ, our King, Creator, Lord, Saviour of all who trust Thy word,
To them who seek Thee ever near, Now to our praises bend Thine ear.

140 *"Rex Christe, factor omnium."*

2 Thou didst create the stars of night,
Yet Thou hast veiled in flesh Thy light;
Hast deigned a mortal form to wear,
A mortal's painful lot to bear.

3 When Thou didst hang upon the tree,
The quaking earth acknowledged Thee;
When Thou didst there yield up Thy breath,
The world grew dark as shades of death.

4 Now in the Father's glory high,
Great Conqueror, never more to die,
Us by Thy mighty power defend,
And reign through ages without end.

Gregory the Great (540—604),
Tr. by Rev. Ray Palmer (1808—1887), 1858. Ab.

141 *The enthroned High Priest.*

1 WHERE high the heavenly temple stands,
The house of God not made with hands,
A great High Priest our nature wears,
The Guardian of mankind appears.

2 He who for men their surety stood,
And poured on earth His precious blood,
Pursues in Heaven His mighty plan,
The Saviour and the Friend of man.

3 Though now ascended up on high,
He bends on earth a brother's eye;
Partaker of the human name,
He knows the weakness of our frame

4 Our fellow-sufferer yet retains
A fellow-feeling of our pains;
And still remembers in the skies
His tears, and agonies, and cries.

5 With boldness, therefore, at the throne,
Let us make all our sorrows known,
And ask the aid of heavenly power,
To help us in the evil hour.

Michael Bruce (1746—1767), 1781. Ab. and sl. alt

SAMSON. L. M. Arr. from GEORGE FREDERICK HANDEL (1685—1759), 1742.

1. Come, let us sing the song of songs, The saints in Heav'n began the strain,
The homage which to Christ belongs: "Worthy the Lamb, for He was slain."

142
"The song of Songs."

2 Slain to redeem us by His blood,
To cleanse from every sinful stain,
And make us kings and priests to God:
"Worthy the Lamb, for He was slain!"

3 To Him, enthroned by filial right,
All power in Heaven and earth proclaim,
Honor, and majesty, and might:
"Worthy the Lamb, for He was slain!"

4 Long as we live, and when we die,
And while in Heaven with Him we reign,
This song our song of songs shall be:
"Worthy the Lamb, for He was slain!"

James Montgomery (1771—1854), 1853. Ab. and alt.

143
Our Priest and King. L. M.

1 Now to the Lord, who makes us know
The wonders of His dying love,
Be humble honors paid below,
And strains of noble praise above.

2 'Twas He who cleansed our foulest sins,
And washed us in His precious blood;
'Tis He who makes us priests and kings,
And brings us rebels near to God.

3 To Jesus, our atoning Priest,
To Jesus, our eternal King,
Be everlasting power confest,
And every tongue His glory sing.

4 Behold, on flying clouds He comes,
And every eye shall see Him move;
Tho' with our sins we pierced Him once,
He now displays His pard'ning love.

Rev. Isaac Watts (1674—1748), 1719. Ab. and sl. alt.

SALISBURY. P. M.   RAVENSCROFT'S Whole Booke of Psalmes, 1621.

1. Salvation! O the joyful sound! 'Tis pleasure to our ears; A sovereign balm for every wound, A cordial for our fears. Glo-ry, honour, praise, and power, Be unto the Lamb for-ev-er! Je-sus Christ is our Re-deem-er; Hal-le-lu-jah! Hal-le-lu-jah! Hal-le-lu-jah! Praise ye the Lord.

144
The joyful sound.

2 Salvation! let the echo fly
The spacious earth around;
While all the armies of the sky
Conspire to raise the sound. REF.

3 Salvation! O Thou bleeding Lamb,
To Thee the praise belongs:
Salvation shall inspire our hearts,
And dwell upon our tongues. REF.

Rev. Isaac Watts, 1709. Ab.

THE HOLY SPIRIT.

WESLEY. 8.7.D.   JOHN ZUNDEL (1815—1882), 1870.

1. Love Di-vine, all love ex-cel-ling, Joy of Heav'n to earth come down; Fix in us Thy hum-ble dwelling, All Thy faith-ful mer-cies crown; Jesus, Thou art all compassion, Pure un-bound-ed love Thou art;

D.S.—Vis-it us with Thy sal-va-tion, En-ter ev-'ry trembling heart.

145   *"Love Divine."*

2 Breathe, O breathe, Thy loving Spirit
   Into every troubled breast;
Let us all in Thee inherit,
   Let us find that second rest;
Take away our power of sinning,
   Alpha and Omega be,
End of faith, as its beginning,
   Set our hearts at liberty.

3 Come, almighty to deliver,
   Let us all Thy life receive;
Suddenly return, and never,
   Never more Thy temples leave.
Thee we would be always blessing,
   Serve Thee as Thy hosts above,
Pray, and praise Thee without ceasing,
   Glory in Thy perfect love.

4 Finish then Thy new creation,
   Pure, and spotless let us be;
Let us see Thy great salvation
   Perfectly restored in Thee:
Changed from glory into glory,
   Till in Heaven we take our place,
Till we cast our crowns before Thee,
   Lost in wonder, love, and praise.

Rev. Charles Wesley (1708—1788), 1747. Sl. alt.

NEW HAVEN. 6.6.4.6.6.6.4.   THOMAS HASTINGS (1784—1872), 1833.

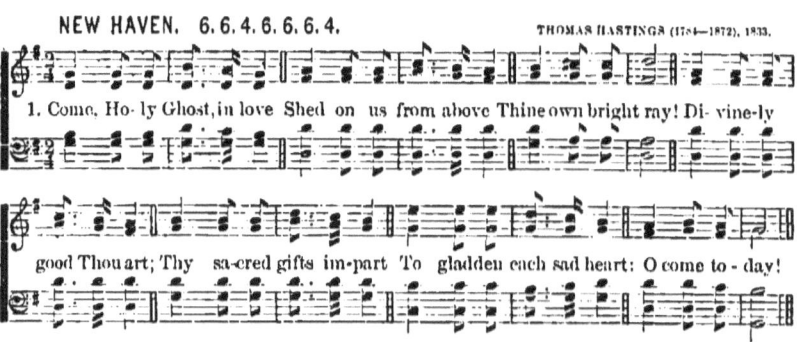

1. Come, Ho-ly Ghost, in love Shed on us from above Thine own bright ray! Di-vine-ly good Thou art; Thy sa-cred gifts im-part To gladden each sad heart: O come to-day!

146   *"Veni, Sancte Spiritus."*

2 Come, tenderest Friend, and best,
   Our most delightful Guest,
     With soothing power:
Rest, which the weary know,
Shade, 'mid the noontide glow,
Peace, when deep griefs o'erflow,
     Cheer us, this hour!

HIS OFFICE AND WORK.   63

3 Come, Light serene, and still
   Our inmost bosoms fill;
   Dwell in each breast;
   We know no dawn but Thine;
   Send forth Thy beams divine,
   On our dark souls to shine,
   And make us blest!

4 Come, all the faithful bless;
   Let all who Christ confess,
   His praise employ:
   Give virtue's rich reward;
   Victorious death accord,
   And, with our glorious Lord,
   Eternal joy!

   Hermannus Contractus? (1013—1054).
   Tr. by Rev. Ray Palmer (1808—1887), 1858.

ALLELUIA. 8. 8. 6. 8. 8. 6.   OTTO GOLDSCHMIDT (1829—).

1. To Him who for our sins was slain, To Him, for all His dy-ing pain.
Sing we Hal-le-lu-jah! To Him, the Lamb our sac-ri-fice, Who gave His soul our
ransom-price, Sing we Halle-lu - jah!

147
"To whom be glory."

2 To Him who died that we might die
   To sin, and live with Him on high,
      Sing we Hallelujah!
   To Him who rose that we might rise
   And reign with Him beyond the skies,
      Sing we Hallelujah!

3 To Him who now for us doth plead,
   And helpeth us in all our need,
      Sing we Hallelujah!
   To Him who doth prepare on high
   Our home in immortality,
      Sing we Hallelujah!

4 To Him be glory evermore!
   Ye heavenly hosts, your Lord adore,
      Sing we Hallelujah!
   To Father, Son, and Holy Ghost,
   One God most high, our joy and boast,
      Sing we Hallelujah!

   Arthur Tozer Russell (1851—   ).

148
Comforter Divine.

1 To Thee, O Comforter Divine,
   For all Thy grace and power benign,
      Sing we Hallelujah!
   To Thee, whose faithful love had place
   In God's great covenant of grace,
      Sing we Hallelujah!

2 To Thee, whose faithful voice doth win
   The wandering from the ways of sin,
      Sing we Hallelujah!
   To Thee, whose faithful power doth heal,
   Enlighten, sanctify, and seal,
      Sing we Hallelujah!

3 To Thee, whose faithful truth is shown
   By every promise made our own,
      Sing we Hallelujah!
   To Thee, our Teacher and our Friend,
   Our faithful Leader to the end,
      Sing we Hallelujah!

4 To Thee, by Jesus Christ sent down,
   Of all His gifts the sum and crown,
      Sing we Hallelujah!
   To Thee, who art with God the Son
   And God the Father ever One,
      Sing we Hallelujah!

   Miss Frances Ridley Havergal (1836—1879).

ELVET. C.M. — Rev. JOHN BACCHUS DYKES (1823—1876).

1. Why should the chil-dren of a King Go mourn-ing all their days? Great Com-fort-er, de-scend and bring Some to-kens of Thy grace.

149 *The witnessing and sealing Spirit.*
Rom. viii. 14, 16. Eph. 1. 13, 14.

2 Dost Thou not dwell in all the saints,
And seal the heirs of Heaven?
When wilt Thou banish my complaints
And show my sins forgiven?

3 Assure my conscience of her part
In the Redeemer's blood;
And bear Thy witness with my heart,
That I am born of God.

4 Thou art the earnest of His love,
The pledge of joys to come;
And Thy soft wings, celestial dove,
Will safe convey me home.

Rev. Isaac Watts (1674—1748), 1709.

AZMON. C.M. — CARL GOTTHILF GLÄSER (1784—1829), 1828.
Arr. by LOWELL MASON (1792—1872), 1839.

1. Come, Holy Spir-it, Heav-en-ly Dove, With all Thy quickening powers, Kin-dle a flame of sa-cred love In these cold hearts of ours.

150 *Breathing after the Holy Spirit.*

2 In vain we tune our formal songs,
In vain we strive to rise;
Hosannas languish on our tongues,
And our devotion dies.

3 Dear Lord, and shall we ever live
At this poor dying rate,
Our love so faint, so cold to Thee,
And Thine to us so great?

4 Come, Holy Spirit, Heavenly Dove,
With all thy quickening powers,
Come, shed abroad a Saviour's love,
And that shall kindle ours.

Rev. Isaac Watts, 1709. Ab.

151 *"O fons amoris, Spiritus."*

1 O Holy Spirit, Fount of love,
Blest source of gifts divine,
Kindle, we pray Thee, from above
The inmost souls of Thine.

2 Shed in each faithful heart abroad
Love that doth all excel;
That God in us, and we in God,
For evermore may dwell.

Prof. Charles Coffin (1676—1749), 1736. Ab.
Tr. by Miss Jane Elizabeth Leeson. 1864.

HIS WORSHIP AND PRAISE.

BOARDMAN. C. M.   LEWIS DEVEREUX. Arr. by GEORGE KINGSLEY (1811—1884). 1833.

1. My soul doth mag-ni-fy the Lord, My spir-it doth re-joice
In God my Sav-iour, and my God; I hear His joy-ful voice.

152   *"The Comforter is come."*

2 Down from above the blessèd Dove
  Is come into my breast,
To witness God's eternal love:
  This is my heavenly feast.

3 My God, my reconciled God,
  Creator of my peace:
Thee will I love, and praise, and sing,
  Till life and breath shall cease.
          Rev. John Mason (—1694), 1683. Ab.

153   *Prayer to the Spirit.*

1 Spirit Divine, attend our prayers,
  And make this house Thy home;
Descend with all Thy gracious powers,
  O come, Great Spirit, come!

2 Come as the light; to us reveal
  Our sinfulness and woe;
And lead us in those paths of life
  Where all the righteous go.

3 Come as the fire, and purge our hearts,
  Like sacrificial flame;
Let our whole soul an offering be
  To our Redeemer's Name.

4 Come as the wind, with rushing sound,
  With Pentecostal grace;
And make the great salvation known,
  Wide as the human race.
Rev. Andrew Reed (1787—1862), 1842. Ab. and sl. alt.

154   *The Spirit's Influences desired.*
          Acts x. 44.

1 Great Father of each perfect gift,
  Behold Thy servants wait;
With longing eyes and lifted hands,
  We flock around Thy gate.

2 O shed abroad that royal gift,
  Thy spirit from above,
To bless our eyes with sacred light,
  And fire our hearts with love.

3 Blest earnest of eternal joy,
  Declare our sins forgiven;
And bear, with energy divine,
  Our raptured thoughts to Heaven.

4 Pour down, O God, those copious showers,
  That earth its fruit may yield,
And change the barren wilderness
  To Carmel's flowery field.
Rev. Philip Doddridge (1702—1751), 1755. Ab. and sl. alt.

155   *The Promise fulfilled.*

1 Let songs of praises fill the sky:
  Christ, our ascended Lord,
Sends down His Spirit from on high,
  According to His word.

2 The Spirit, by His heavenly breath,
  New life creates within;
He quickens sinners from the death
  Of trespasses and sin.

3 The things of Christ the Spirit takes,
  And shows them unto men:
The fallen soul His temple makes,
  God's image stamps again.

4 Come, Holy Spirit, from above,
  With Thy celestial fire;
Come, and with flames of zeal and love,
  Our hearts and tongues inspire.
         Rev. Thomas Cotterill (1779—1823), 1819. Ab.

THE HOLY SPIRIT.

MERCY. 7.   Arr. from LOUIS MOREAU GOTTSCHALK (1829—1869), 1854.

[music: 1. Gra-cious Spir-it, Dove di-vine, Let Thy light within me shine; All my guilty fears remove, Fill me full of Heav'n and love.]

        Long has sin, without control,
        Held dominion o'er my soul.

3 Holy Ghost, with joy divine,
    Cheer this saddened heart of mine;
    Bid my many woes depart,
    Heal my wounded, bleeding heart.

4 Holy Spirit, all divine,
    Dwell within this heart of mine,
    Cast down every idol-throne;
    Reign supreme, and reign alone.
                Rev. Andrew Reed (1787—1862), 1843. Ab.

156   *Prayer for Peace and Rest.*
2 Speak Thy pardoning grace to me,
    Set the burdened sinner free,
    Lead me to the Lamb of God,
    Wash me in His precious blood.

3 Life and peace to me impart,
    Seal salvation on my heart,
    Breathe Thyself into my breast,
    Earnest of immortal rest.
                John Stocker, 1776. Ab.

158   *"Granted is the Saviour's Prayer."*
1 GRANTED is the Saviour's prayer,
    Sent the gracious Comforter,
    Promise of our parting Lord,
    Jesus, to His Heaven restored.

2 God, the everlasting God,
    Makes with mortals His abode;
    Whom the heavens cannot contain,
    He stoops down to dwell in man.

157   *Light, Power, Joy.*
1 HOLY Ghost, with light divine,
    Shine upon this heart of mine;
    Chase the shades of night away,
    Turn the darkness into day.

2 Holy Ghost, with power divine,
    Cleanse this guilty heart of mine;

3 Come, divine and peaceful Guest,
    Enter our devoted breast:
    Life divine in us renew,
    Thou the Gift and Giver, too!
        Rev. Charles Wesley (1708—1788), 1739. Ab. and alt.

PENTECOST. 7. 7. 7. 5.   Sir ARTHUR SULLIVAN (1842—).

[music: 1. Ho-ly Ghost, the In-fi-nite, Shine up-on our nature's night With Thy bless-ed in-ward light, Com-fort-er Di-vine!]

3 Like the dew, Thy peace distil:
    Guide, subdue our wayward will,
    Things of Christ unfolding still,
        Comforter Divine!

4 In us, for us, intercede,
    And with voiceless groaning plead
    Our unutterable need,
        Comforter Divine!

159   *"Holy Ghost, the Infinite."*
2 We are sinful, cleanse us, Lord;
    We are faint, Thy strength afford;
    Lost, until by Thee restored,
        Comforter Divine!

5 In us "Abba, Father," cry,
    Earnest of our bliss on high,
    Seal of immortality,
        Comforter Divine!
             George Rawson (1807—1885), 1853. Ab. and alt.

HIS INFLUENCE INVOKED. 67

HAYDN. S. M.   From FRANCIS JOSEPH HAYDN (1732—1809), 1801.

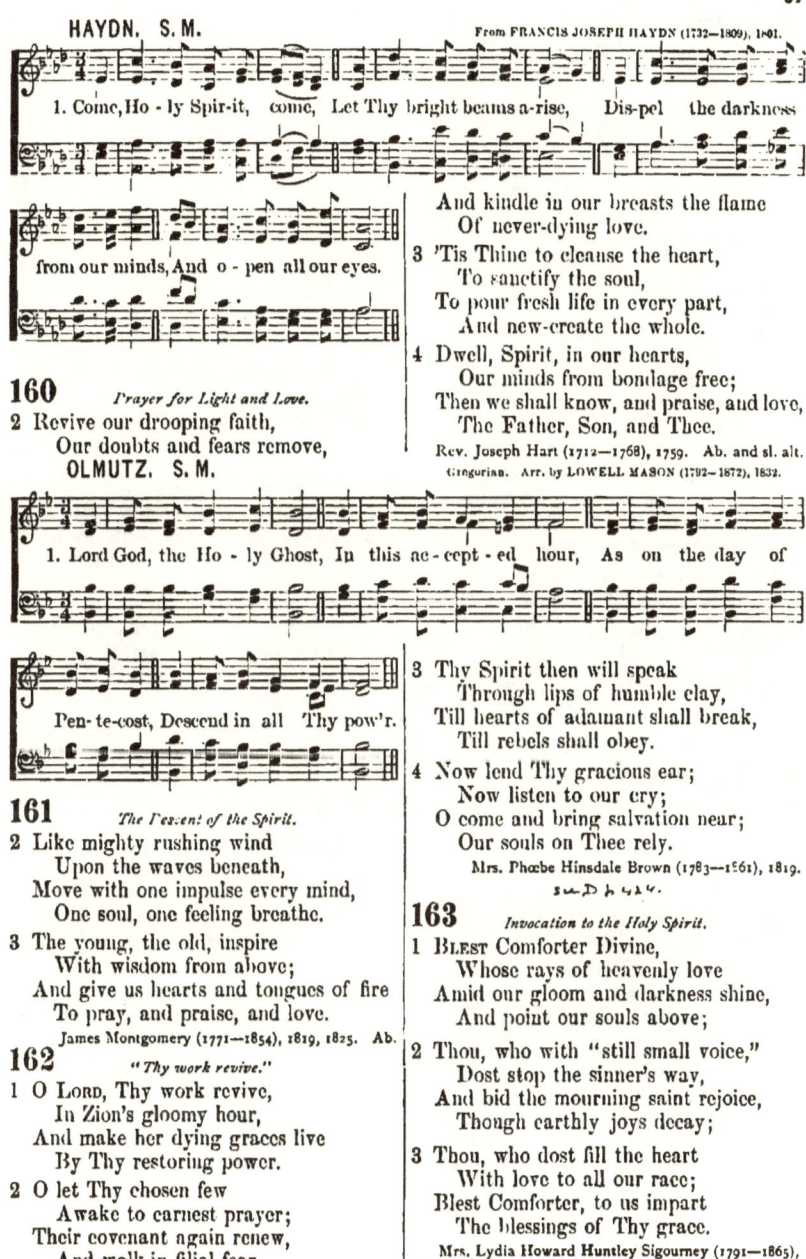

1. Come, Ho-ly Spir-it, come, Let Thy bright beams a-rise, Dis-pel the darkness from our minds, And o - pen all our eyes.

160   *Prayer for Light and Love.*

2 Revive our drooping faith,
   Our doubts and fears remove,
   And kindle in our breasts the flame
   Of never-dying love.

3 'Tis Thine to cleanse the heart,
   To sanctify the soul,
   To pour fresh life in every part,
   And new-create the whole.

4 Dwell, Spirit, in our hearts,
   Our minds from bondage free;
   Then we shall know, and praise, and love,
   The Father, Son, and Thee.
   Rev. Joseph Hart (1712—1768), 1759. Ab. and sl. alt.

OLMUTZ. S. M.   Gregorian. Arr. by LOWELL MASON (1792—1872), 1832.

1. Lord God, the Ho-ly Ghost, In this ac-cept-ed hour, As on the day of Pen-te-cost, Descend in all Thy pow'r.

161   *The Descent of the Spirit.*

2 Like mighty rushing wind
   Upon the waves beneath,
   Move with one impulse every mind,
   One soul, one feeling breathe.

3 The young, the old, inspire
   With wisdom from above;
   And give us hearts and tongues of fire
   To pray, and praise, and love.
   James Montgomery (1771—1854), 1819, 1825. Ab.

162   *"Thy work revive."*

1 O LORD, Thy work revive,
   In Zion's gloomy hour,
   And make her dying graces live
   By Thy restoring power.

2 O let Thy chosen few
   Awake to earnest prayer;
   Their covenant again renew,
   And walk in filial fear.

3 Thy Spirit then will speak
   Through lips of humble clay,
   Till hearts of adamant shall break,
   Till rebels shall obey.

4 Now lend Thy gracious ear;
   Now listen to our cry;
   O come and bring salvation near;
   Our souls on Thee rely.
   Mrs. Phœbe Hinsdale Brown (1783—1861), 1819.

163   *Invocation to the Holy Spirit.*

1 BLEST Comforter Divine,
   Whose rays of heavenly love
   Amid our gloom and darkness shine,
   And point our souls above;

2 Thou, who with "still small voice,"
   Dost stop the sinner's way,
   And bid the mourning saint rejoice,
   Though earthly joys decay;

3 Thou, who dost fill the heart
   With love to all our race;
   Blest Comforter, to us impart
   The blessings of Thy grace.
   Mrs. Lydia Howard Huntley Sigourney (1791—1865), 1824. Ab.

ERNAN. L. M. LOWELL MASON (1792-1872), 1850.

1. Come, O Creator Spirit blest, And in our souls take up Thy rest;
Come, with Thy grace and heav'nly aid, To fill the hearts which Thou hast made.

164 *"Veni, Creator Spiritus."*

2 Great Comforter, to Thee we cry;
O highest gift of God most high,
O Fount of life, O Fire of love,
And sweet anointing from above!

3 Kindle our senses from above,
And make our hearts o'erflow with love;
With patience firm, and virtue high,
The weakness of our flesh supply.

4 Far from us drive the foe we dread,
And grant us Thy true peace instead;
So shall we not, with Thee for Guide,
Turn from the path of life aside.

Rabanus Maurus (776—856),
Tr. by Rev. Edward Caswall (1814—1878), 1849. Ab.
and alt.

165 *"Come, Sacred Spirit!"* Ezek. xxxvi. 37.

1 Come, Sacred Spirit, from above,
And fill the coldest heart with love;
Soften to flesh the rugged stone,
And let Thy god-like power be known.

2 Speak Thou, and, from the haughtiest eyes,
Shall floods of pious sorrow rise;
While all their glowing souls are borne
To seek that grace, which now they scorn.

3 O let a holy flock await,
Numerous around Thy temple-gate,
Each pressing on with zeal to be
A living sacrifice to Thee.

Rev. Philip Doddridge (1702—1751), 1755. Ab

WAREHAM. L. M. WILLIAM KNAPP (1698—1768), 1738.

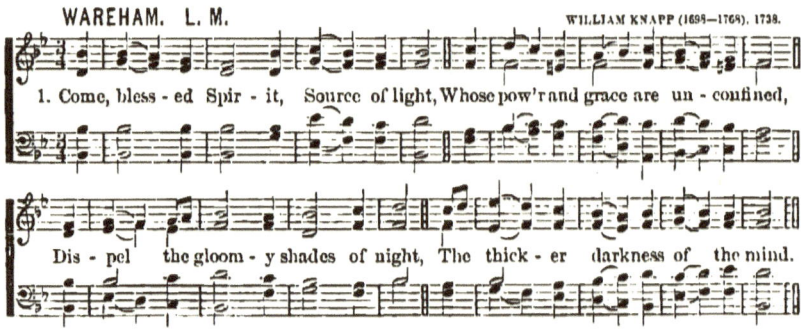

1. Come, blessed Spirit, Source of light, Whose pow'r and grace are unconfined,
Dispel the gloomy shades of night, The thicker darkness of the mind.

166 *Teachings of the Spirit.*

2 To mine illumined eyes display
  The glorious truths Thy word reveals;
  Cause me to run the heavenly way;
  The book unfold, and loose the seals.

3 Thine inward teachings make me know
  The mysteries of redeeming love,
  The vanity of things below,
  And excellence of things above.

4 While through this dubious maze I stray,
  Spread, like the sun, Thy beams abroad,
  To show the dangers of the way,
  And guide my feeble steps to God.

Rev. Benjamin Beddome (1717—1795), 1818.

167 *Prayer for Light and Guidance.* **L. M.**

1 Come, Holy Spirit, heavenly Dove,
With peace and healing from above;
Be Thou my Light, be Thou my Guide,
O'er every thought and step preside.

2 The light of truth to me display,
That I may know and choose my way;
Plant holy fear within my heart,
That I from God may ne'er depart.

3 Conduct me safe, conduct me far,
From every sin and hurtful snare;
Lead me to God, my final Rest,
In His enjoyment to be blest.

4 Lead me to holiness, the road
That I must take to dwell with God;
Lead me to Christ, the living Way,
Nor let me from His pastures stray.
Rev. Simon Browne (1680—1732), 1720. Ab. and alt.

168 *Prayer for Rest in God.* **L. M.**

1 Come, Holy Spirit, calm my mind,
And fit me to approach my God;
Remove each vain, each worldly thought,
And lead me to Thy blest abode.

2 Hast Thou imparted to my soul
A living spark of heavenly fire?

O kindle now the sacred flame;
Teach it to burn with pure desire.

3 A brighter faith and hope impart,
And let me now the Saviour see:
O soothe and cheer my burdened heart,
And bid my spirit rest in Thee.
John Stewart ( ), 1803.

169 *The Operations of the Spirit.* **L. M.**

1 Eternal Spirit, we confess
And sing the wonders of Thy grace;
Thy power conveys our blessings down
From God the Father and the Son.

2 Enlightened by Thy heavenly ray,
Our shades and darkness turn to day;
Thine inward teachings make us know
Our danger and our refuge, too.

3 Thy power and glory work within,
And break the chains of reigning sin;
Do our imperious lusts subdue,
And form our wretched hearts anew.

4 The troubled conscience knows Thy voice;
Thy cheering words awake our joys;
Thy words allay the stormy wind,
And calm the surges of the mind.
Rev. Isaac Watts (1674—1748), 1709.

ZEBULON. H. M.   LOWELL MASON. 1830.

1. O Thou that hear-est pray'r, Attend our humble cry; And
let Thy servants share Thy blessing from on high: (Omit.) We
plead the promise of Thy word; Grant us Thy Holy Spirit, Lord.

170 *The Spirit asked for.*

2 If earthly parents hear
Their children when they cry,
If they, with love sincere,
Their children's wants supply;
Much more wilt Thou Thy love display,
And answer when Thy children pray.

3 Our heavenly Father, Thou!
We, children of Thy grace:
O let Thy spirit now
Descend, and fill the place:
So shall we feel the heavenly flame,
And all unite to praise Thy name.

4 O send Thy Spirit down
On all the nations, Lord,
With great success to crown
The preaching of Thy word,
Till heathen lands shall own Thy sway,
And cast their idol-gods away.
John Burton Jr., (1803—), 1824. Ab.

THE HOLY SCRIPTURES.

CHESTERFIELD. C. M. Rev. THOMAS HAWEIS (1732—1820), 1792.

1. Fa-ther of mer-cies, in Thy Word What end-less glo-ry shines! For-ev-er be Thy name a-dored For these ce-les-tial lines.

171 *The Riches of God's Word.*
Ps. cxix.

2 Here may the wretched sons of want
Exhaustless riches find;
Riches above what earth can grant,
And lasting as the mind.

3 Here the Redeemer's welcome voice
Spreads heavenly peace around;
And life and everlasting joys
Attend the blissful sound.

4 O may these heavenly pages be
My ever dear delight;
And still new beauties may I see,
And still increasing light.

Miss Anne Steele (1717—1778), 1760. Ab.

BARNBY. C. M. JOSEPH BARNBY (1838—), 1856.

1. A glo-ry gilds the sa-cred page, Ma-jes-tic like the sun; It gives a light to ev-'ry age, It gives, but bor-rows none.

172 *"The Light and Glory of the Word."*
Ps. cxix. 130. 2 Cor. iv. 4.

2 The hand, that gave it, still supplies
The gracious light and heat;
Its truths upon the nations rise,
They rise, but never set.

3 Let everlasting thanks be Thine,
For such a bright display,
As makes a world of darkness shine
With beams of heavenly day.

4 My soul rejoices to pursue
The steps of Him I love,
Till glory breaks upon my view,
In brighter worlds above.

William Cowper (1731—1800), 1779. Ab.

173 *A Lamp, and a Light.*
Ps. cxix. 105. 2. Tim. iii. 16.

1 How precious is the book divine,
By inspiration given:
Bright as a lamp its doctrines shine,
To guide our souls to Heaven.

2 Its light, descending from above,
Our gloomy world to cheer,
Displays a Saviour's boundless love,
And brings His glories near.

THE HOLY SCRIPTURES.

3 It sweetly cheers our drooping hearts,
In this dark vale of tears;
Life, light, and joy it still imparts,
And quells our rising fears.

4 This lamp, thro' all the tedious night
Of life, shall guide our way,
Till we behold the clearer light
Of an eternal day.
Rev. John Fawcett (1739—1817), 1782. Ab.

MARLOW. C. M.   English Melody. Arr. by LOWELL MASON (1792—1872), 1834.

1. La-den with guilt, and full of fears, I fly to Thee, my Lord;
And not a glimpse of hope ap-pears, But in Thy writ-ten word.

174   *The Scriptures our only Help and Guide.*

2 This is the field where hidden lies
The pearl of price unknown:
That merchant is divinely wise,
Who makes the pearl his own.

3 This is the judge that ends the strife,
Where wit and reason fail;
My guide to everlasting life,
Through all this gloomy vale.

4 O may Thy counsels, mighty God,
My roving feet command;
Nor I forsake the happy road,
That leads to Thy right hand.
Rev. Isaac Watts (1674—1748), 1709. Ab.

DALLAS. 7.   From MARIA LUIGI CHERUBINI (1760—1842).

1. Ho-ly Bi-ble, book di-vine, Pre-cious treas-ure, thou art mine;
Mine to tell me whence I came, Mine to teach me what I am.

175   *"Holy Bible, Book Divine."*

2 Mine to chide me when I rove,
Mine to show a Saviour's love;
Mine art thou to guide my feet,
Mine to judge, condemn, acquit.

3 Mine to comfort in distress,
If the Holy Spirit bless;
Mine to show by living faith
Man can triumph over death.

4 Mine to tell of joys to come,
Light and life beyond the tomb;
Holy Bible, book divine,
Precious treasure, thou art mine.
John Burton (1773—1822), 1805. Alt.

UXBRIDGE. L. M.   LOWELL MASON. (1792—1872), 1830.

1. God, in the gos-pel of His Son, Makes His e-ter-nal coun-sels known:
Where love in all its glo-ry shines, And truth is drawn in fair-est lines.

176   *"God's Word our Guide."*

2 Here sinners, of a humble frame,
May taste His grace, and learn His Name;
May read, in characters of blood,
The wisdom, power, and grace of God.

3 Here faith reveals to mortal eyes
A brighter world beyond the skies;
Here shines the light which guides our way
From earth to realms of endless day.

4 O grant us grace, Almighty Lord,
To read and mark Thy holy Word;
Its truth with meekness to receive,
And by its holy precepts live.
      Rev. Benjamin Beddome (1717—1795), 1787. Ab. and alt.
      Rev. Thomas Cotterill (1779—1823), 1819. Ab.

177   *Thanks for the Gospel.*

1 Let everlasting glories crown
Thy head, my Saviour, and my Lord:
Thy hands have brought salvation down,
And writ the blessings in Thy Word.

2 In vain the trembling conscience seeks
Some solid ground to rest upon;
With long despair the spirit breaks,
Till we apply to Christ alone.

3 How well Thy blessèd truths agree,
How wise and holy Thy commands;
Thy promises, how firm they be,
How firm our hope and comfort stands!

4 Should all the forms that men devise
Assault my faith with treacherous art,
I'd call them vanity and lies,
And bind the Gospel to my heart.
      Rev. Isaac Watts (1674—1748), 1709. Ab.

TRUSTING. 7.   WILLIAM GUSTAVUS FISCHER (1835—   ). 1869.

1. I am com-ing to the cross; I am poor, and weak, and blind; I am count-ing
all but dross; I shall Thy sal-va-tion find,
Cho.—I am trust-ing, Lord, in Thee, Dear Lamb of Cal-va-ry; Humbly at Thy
cross I bow: Save me, Je-sus, save me now.

178   *At the Cross.*

2 Here I give my all to Thee,
Friends, and time, and earthly store;
Soul and body Thine to be,
Wholly Thine for evermore.—Cho.

3 In the promises I trust:
Now I feel the blood applied;
I am prostrate in the dust;
I with Christ am crucified.—Cho.
      Rev. William McDonald (1820—   ), 1869. Ab.

ABRIDGE. C. M.

Har. fr. ISAAC SMITH (1735—1809), 1770.

1. The Saviour calls, let ev-'ry ear
Attend the heav'n-ly sound;
Ye doubt-ing souls, dis-miss your fear,
Hope smiles re-viv-ing round.

179 *The Saviour calls."*
John vii. 37.

2 For every thirsty, longing heart,
Here streams of bounty flow,
And life, and health, and bliss impart,
To banish mortal woe.

3 Ye sinners, come, 'tis mercy's voice,
The gracious call obey;
Mercy invites to heavenly joys,
And can you yet delay?

4 Dear Saviour, draw reluctant hearts,
To Thee let sinners fly,
And take the bliss Thy love imparts,
And drink and never die.

Miss Anne Steele (1717—1778), 1760. 'Ab.

180 *"Without Money and without Price."*
Is. lv. 1, 2.

1 LET every mortal ear attend,
And every heart rejoice;
The trumpet of the gospel sounds,
With an inviting voice.

2 Ho, ye that pant for living streams,
And pine away and die,
Here you may quench your raging thirst
With springs that never dry.

3 Rivers of love and mercy here
In a rich ocean join;

Salvation in abundance flows,
Like floods of milk and wine.

4 The happy gates of gospel grace
Stand open night and day;
Lord, we are come to seek supplies,
And drive our wants away.

Rev. Isaac Watts (1674—1748), 1709.

181 *Born of God.*
John i. 13.

1 Nor all the outward forms on earth,
Nor rites that God has given,
Nor will of man, nor blood, nor birth,
Can raise a soul to heaven.

2 The sovereign will of God alone
Creates us heirs of grace;
Born in the image of His Son,
A new, peculiar race.

3 The Spirit, like some heavenly wind,
Breathes on the sons of flesh,
New-models all the carnal mind,
And forms the man afresh.

4 Our quickened souls awake and rise
From the long sleep of death;
On heavenly things we fix our eyes,
And praise employs our breath.

Rev. Isaac Watts 1709.

HUMMEL. C. M.

HEINRICH CHRISTOPHER ZEUNER (1795—1857), 1832.

THE GOSPEL.

ANGEL TOWER. 7. 6. D. — WILLIAM HENRY LONGHURST (1819—).

1. O Jesus, Thou art standing Outside the fast-clos'd door, In lowly patience waiting To pass the threshold o'er: Shame on us, Christian brethren, His Name and sign who bear, O shame, thrice shame upon us, To keep Him standing there!

182 *Standing at the Door.*

2 O Jesus, Thou art knocking:
And lo, that hand is scarred,
And thorns Thy brow encircle,
And tears Thy face have marred.
O love that passeth knowledge,
So patiently to wait!
O sin that hath no equal,
So fast to bar the gate!

3 O Jesus, Thou art pleading
In accents meek and low,
"I died for you, My children,
And will ye treat Me so?"
O Lord, with shame and sorrow
We open now the door:
Dear Saviour enter, enter,
And leave us never more.

Bp. William Walsham How (1823—), 1854.

COME UNTO ME. 7. 6. D. — Rev. JOHN BACCHUS DYKES (1823—1876), 1874.

1. "Come unto me, ye weary, And I will give you rest. O, blessed voice of Jesus, Which comes to hearts opprest! It tells of benediction, Of pardon, grace and peace, Of joy that hath no ending, Of love which cannot cease.

183 *"Come unto Me."*
Matt. xi. 28.

2 "Come unto Me, ye wanderers,
   And I will give you light."
O loving voice of Jesus,
   Which comes to cheer the night!
Our hearts were filled with sadness,
   And we had lost our way;
But morning brings us gladness,
   And songs, the break of day.

3 "Come unto Me, ye fainting,
   And I will give you life."
O cheering voice of Jesus,
   Which comes to end our strife!

The foe is stern and eager,
   The fight is fierce and long;
But Thou hast made us mighty,
   And stronger than the strong.

5 "And whosoever cometh,
   I will not cast him out."
O welcome voice of Jesus,
   Which drives away our doubt!
Which calls us, very sinners,
   Unworthy though we be
Of love so free and boundless,
   To come, dear Lord, to Thee!

              William Chatterton Dix (1837—), 1864.

BONAR. 7. 6. D.   JOSEPH BARNBY (1838—).

1. The King of glory standeth Beside that heart of sin, His mighty voice commandeth The raging waves within; The floods of deepest anguish Roll backward at His will, As o'er the storm ariseth His mandate, "Peace be still."

184 *Mighty to Save.*

2 At times with sudden glory,
   He speaks, and all is done;
Without one stroke of battle
   The victory is won:
While we with joy beholding,
   Can scarce believe it true,
That e'en our Kingly Jesus
   Can form such hearts anew.

3 But sometimes in the stillness,
   He gently draweth near,
And whispers words of welcome,
   Into the sinner's ear;

With anxious heart He waiteth
   The answer of His cry,
That oft repeated question,
   "O wherefore wilt thou die?"

4 O Christ, His love is mighty!
   Long suffering is His grace!
And glorious is the splendor
   That beameth from His face!
Our hearts up-leap in gladness
   When we behold that love,
As we go singing onward
   To dwell with Him above.

    Mrs. Charitie Lees Bancroft (1841—), 1860. Ab.

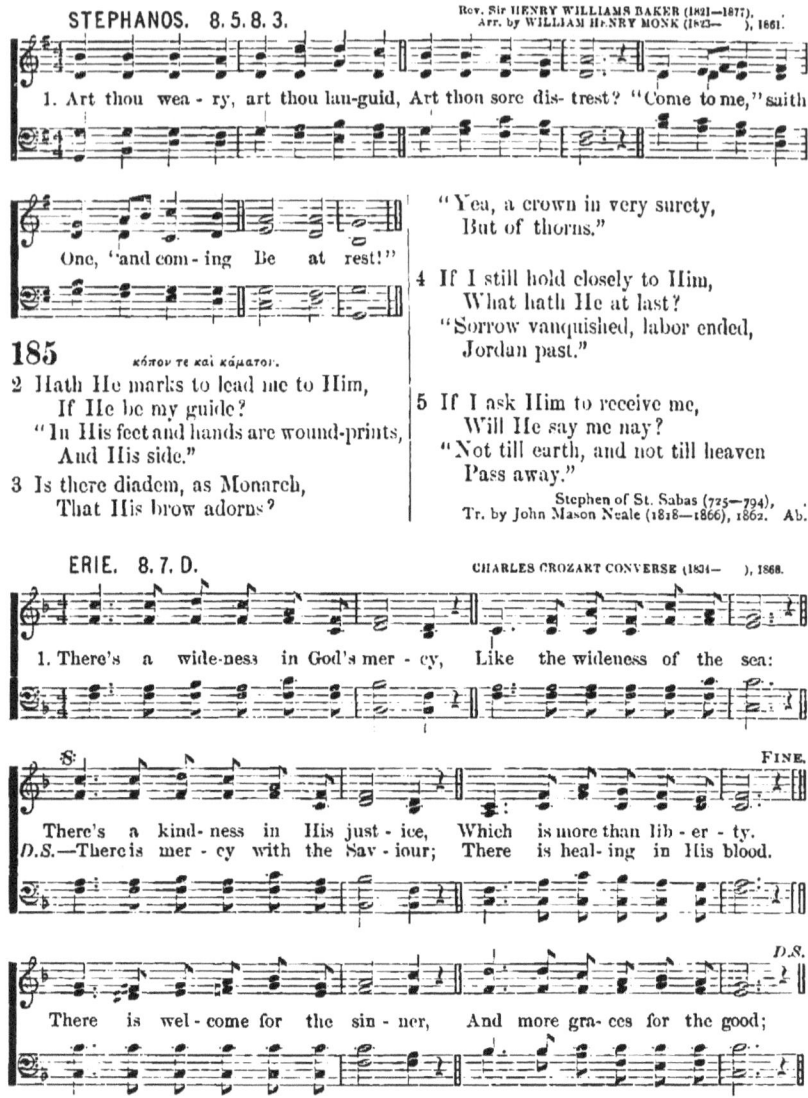

STEPHANOS. 8. 5. 8. 3. Rev. Sir HENRY WILLIAMS BAKER (1821—1877), Arr. by WILLIAM HENRY MONK (1823—), 1861.

1. Art thou wea-ry, art thou lan-guid, Art thou sore dis-trest? "Come to me," saith One, "and com-ing Be at rest!"

185 κόπον τε καὶ κάματον.

2 Hath He marks to lead me to Him,
  If He be my guide?
  "In His feet and hands are wound-prints,
  And His side."

3 Is there diadem, as Monarch,
  That His brow adorns?
  "Yea, a crown in very surety,
  But of thorns."

4 If I still hold closely to Him,
  What hath He at last?
  "Sorrow vanquished, labor ended,
  Jordan past."

5 If I ask Him to receive me,
  Will He say me nay?
  "Not till earth, and not till heaven
  Pass away."

Stephen of St. Sabas (725—794),
Tr. by John Mason Neale (1818—1866), 1862. Ab.

ERIE. 8. 7. D. CHARLES CROZART CONVERSE (1834—), 1868.

1. There's a wide-ness in God's mer-cy, Like the wideness of the sea:
There's a kind-ness in His just-ice, Which is more than lib-er-ty.
D.S.—There is mer-cy with the Sav-iour; There is heal-ing in His blood.

There is wel-come for the sin-ner, And more gra-ces for the good;

186 *Come to Jesus.*

2 There is plentiful redemption
  In the blood that has been shed;
  There is joy for all the members
  In the sorrows of the Head.

  If our love were but more simple
  We should take Him at His word;
  And our lives would be all sunshine
  In the sweetness of our Lord.

Rev. Frederick William Faber (1814—1863), 1849. Ab.

187 *"In Everything by Prayer."*
Phil. iv. 6.

1 What a Friend we have in Jesus,
   All our sins and griefs to bear!
  What a privilege to carry
   Everything to God in prayer!
  O what peace we often forfeit,
   O what needless pain we bear,
  All because we do not carry
   Everything to God in prayer!

2 Have we trials and temptation?
   Is there trouble anywhere?
  We should never be discouraged—
   Take it to the Lord in prayer.
  Can we find a friend so faithful,
   Who will all our sorrows share?
  Jesus knows our every weakness:
   Take it to the Lord in prayer.

3 Are we weak and heavy laden,
   Cumbered with a load of care?
  Precious Saviour, still our refuge!
   Take it to the Lord in prayer.
  Do thy friends despise, forsake thee?
   Take it to the Lord in prayer;
  In His arms He'll take and shield thee;
   Thou wilt find a solace there.

Joseph Scriven (1829—1886), 1855.

OLIPHANT. 8.7.4.

PIERRE-MARIE-FRANCOIS de SALES BAILLOT (1771—1842), 1830.
Arr. by LOWELL MASON (1792—1872), 1832.

1. Come, ye sin-ners, poor and wretched, Weak and wounded, sick and sore: Je-sus ready stands to save you, Full of pit-y, join'd with pow'r: He is a-ble, He is a-ble, He is will-ing, doubt no more, He is will-ing, doubt no more.

188 *"Come, and welcome."*

2 Let not conscience make you linger,
   Nor of fitness fondly dream;
  All the fitness He requireth
   Is to feel your need of Him:
     This He gives you;
   'Tis the Spirit's rising beam.

3 Come, ye weary, heavy-laden,
   Bruised and mangled by the fall;
  If you tarry till you're better,
   You will never come at all:
     Not the righteous,
   Sinners, Jesus came to call.

4 Lo, th' incarnate God, ascended,
   Pleads the merit of His blood:
  Venture on Him, venture wholly,
   Let no other trust intrude;
     None but Jesus
   Can do helpless sinners good.

Rev. Joseph Hart (1712—1768), 1759. Ab.

SALVATION OFFERED.

COME, YE DISCONSOLATE. 11. 10. Samuel Webbe (1740—1816), 1800.

1. Come, ye discon-solate, where'er ye languish, Come to the mercy-seat, fer-vent-ly kneel;
Here bring your wounded hearts, here tell your anguish, Earth has no sorrows that Heav'n cannot heal.

189   "*Come, ye disconsolate.*"

2 Joy of the desolate, Light of the straying,
   Hope of the penitent, fadeless and pure;
Here speaks the Comforter, tenderly saying,
   Earth has no sorrows that Heaven cannot cure.

3 Here see the Bread of Life, see waters flowing
   Forth from the throne of God, pure from above;
Come to the feast prepared, come, ever knowing
   Earth has no sorrows but Heaven can remove.

Thomas Moore (1779—1852), 1816, Vs. 1, 2. Alt.
Thomas Hastings (1784—1872), . V. 3.

ROSEFIELD. 7. 6 l. Rev. Cæsar Henri Abraham Malan (1787—1864), 1830.

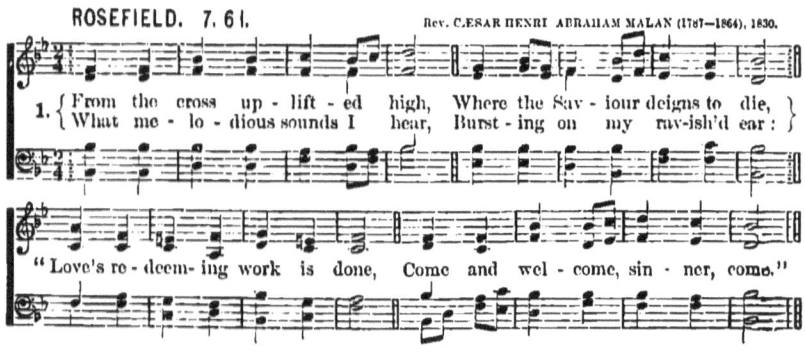

1. { From the cross up-lift-ed high, Where the Sav-iour deigns to die,
   { What me-lo-dious sounds I hear, Burst-ing on my rav-ish'd ear: }
"Love's re-deem-ing work is done, Come and wel-come, sin-ner, come."

190   "*Let him come unto Me.*"
      John vii. 37.

2 "Sprinkled now with blood the throne;
Why beneath thy burdens groan?
On My pierced body laid,
Justice owns the ransom paid;
Bow the knee, and kiss the Son,
Come and welcome, sinner, come.

3 "Spread for thee, the festal board
See with richest dainties stored;
To thy Father's bosom prest,

Yet again a child confest,
Never from His house to roam;
Come and welcome, sinner, come.

4 "Soon the days of life shall end,
Lo! I come, your Saviour, Friend,
Safe your spirits to convey
To the realms of endless day,
Up to My eternal home;
Come and welcome, sinner, come."

Rev. Thomas Haweis (1732—1820) 1792.

INVITATIONS AND WARNINGS.

GORTON. S. M.
Arr. from LUDWIG von BEETHOVEN (1770—1827)

1. The Spir-it, in our hearts, Is whisp'ring, "Sinner, come;" The Bride, the Church of Christ, proclaims To all His chil-dren, "come."

191 *"And the Spirit and the Bride say, Come."*
Rev. xvii. 17—20.

2 Let him that heareth, say
To all about him, "Come;"
Let him that thirsts for righteousness,
To Christ, the Fountain, come.

3 Yes, whosoever will,
O let him freely come,
And freely drink the stream of life:
'Tis Jesus bids him come.

4 Lo, Jesus, who invites,
Declares, "I quickly come;"
Lord, even so; I wait Thine hour;
Jesus, my Saviour, come.
Bp. Henry Ustick Onderdonk (1789—1858), 1826.

192 *"Behold the Ark of God."*
1 O CEASE, my wandering soul,
On restless wing to roam;
All the wide world, to either pole,
Has not for thee a home.

2 Behold the Ark of God,
Behold the open door;
Hasten to gain that dear abode,
And rove, my soul, no more.

3 There, safe thou shalt abide,
There, sweet shall be thy rest,
And every longing satisfied,
With full salvation blest.
Rev. William Augustus Muhlenburg (1796—1877), 1826. Ab.

193 *The Uncertainty of Life.*
James iv. 13—15.

1 TO-MORROW, Lord, is Thine,
Lodged in Thy sovereign hand·
And if its sun arise and shine,
It shines by Thy command.

2 Since on this winged hour,
Eternity is hung,
Waken, by Thine almighty power,
The aged and the young.

2 To Jesus may we fly,
Swift as the morning light,
Lest life's young golden beams should die
In sudden, endless night.
Rev. Philip Doddridge (1702—1751), 1755. Ab.

OLNEY. S. M.
LOWELL MASON (1792-1872), 1832.

1. Now is the accepted time, Now is the day of grace; Now, sinners, come without de-lay, And seek the Sav-iour's face.

194 *"Now is the accepted Time."*
2 Cor. vi. 2.

2 Now is the accepted time,
The Saviour calls to-day;

Pardon and peace He freely gives;
Then why should you delay?

3 Now is the accepted time,
The gospel bids you come;
And every promise in His word
Declares there yet is room.
John Dobell (1757—1840), 1806. Ab.

SALVATION OFFERED.

BERA. L.M. — JOHN EDGAR GOULD (1822–1875), 1849.

1. Re-turn, O wan-der-er, re-turn, And seek thine in-jured Fa-ther's face;
Those new desires that in thee burn, Were kindled by re-claim-ing grace.

195 *"Return!"* Jer. xxxi. 18–20.

2 Return, O wanderer, return,
And seek a Father's melting heart;
Whose pitying eyes thy grief discern,
Whose hand can heal thine inward smart.

3 Return, O wanderer, return,
He heard thy deep, repentant sigh,
He saw thy softened spirit mourn,
When no intruding ear was nigh.

4 Return, O wanderer, return,
Thy Saviour bids thy spirit live;
Go to His bleeding feet, and learn
How freely Jesus can forgive.

5 Return, O wanderer, return,
And wipe away the falling tear;
'Tis God who says, "No longer mourn,"
'Tis mercy's voice invites thee near.
Rev. William Bengo Collyer (1782–1854), 1812. Ab.

196 *No Hope after Death.*

1 While life prolongs its precious light,
Mercy is found and peace is given;
But soon, ah, soon approaching night
Shall blot out every hope of heaven.

2 Soon, borne on time's most rapid wing,
Shall death command you to the grave,
Before His bar your spirits bring,
And none be found to hear or save.

3 Now God invites, how blest the day!
How sweet the gospel's charming sound!
Come, sinners, haste, O haste away,
While yet a pardoning God is found.
Rev. Timothy Dwight (1752–1817), 1800. Ab.

ZEPHYR. L.M. — WILLIAM BATCHELDER BRADBURY (1816–1868), 1844.

1. Be-hold, a Stran-ger at the door: He gen-tly knocks, has knock'd be-fore;
Has wait-ed long, is wait-ing still: You treat no oth-er friend so ill.

197 *Christ knocking at the Door.* Cant. v. 2. Rev. iii. 20.

2 O lovely attitude! He stands
With melting heart, and laden hands:
O matchless kindness! and He shows
This matchless kindness to His foes.

THE GRACIOUS CALL.

3 Rise, touched with gratitude divine;
Turn out His enemy and thine,
That soul-destroying monster, Sin;
And let the heavenly Stranger in.

4 Admit Him, for the human breast
Ne'er entertained so kind a guest:
Admit Him, ere His anger burn;
His feet, departed, ne'er return!

Rev. Joseph Grigg (—1768), 1765. Ab. and alt.

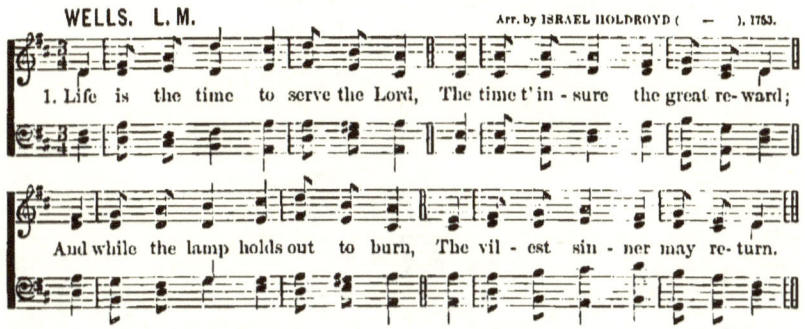

WELLS. L. M. Arr. by ISRAEL HOLDROYD (—), 1753.

1. Life is the time to serve the Lord, The time t' in-sure the great re-ward;
And while the lamp holds out to burn, The vil-est sin-ner may re-turn.

198 *This our only Probation.*
Eccl ix. 10.

2 Life is the hour that God has given
T' escape from hell and fly to heaven;
The day of grace, and mortals may
Secure the blessings of the day.

3 Then what my thoughts design to do,
My hands, with all your might pursue,

Since no device, nor work is found,
Nor faith, nor hope, beneath the ground.

4 There are no acts of pardon passed
In the cold grave to which we haste;
But darkness, death, and long despair
Reign in eternal silence there.

Rev. Isaac Watts (1674—1748), 1709. Ab.

TROYLAND. L. M. FRANCIS R. STATHAM (—),

1. Haste, traveller, haste! the night comes on, And many a shin-ing hour is gone;
The storm is gathering in the west, And thou art far from home and rest.

199 *The Day of Grace.*

2 O far from home thy footsteps stray;
Christ is the Life, and Christ the Way;
And Christ the Light; thy setting sun
Sinks ere thy morning is begun.

3 Awake, awake! pursue thy way
With steady course, while yet 'tis day;

While thou art sleeping on the ground,
Danger and darkness gather round.

4 Then linger not in all the plain,
Flee for thy life, the mountain gain;
Look not behind, make no delay,
O speed thee, speed thee on thy way.

Rev. William Bengo Collyer (—), 1812. Ab. and alt.

SALVATION OFFERED.

TO-DAY. 6, 4.   Arr. from LOWELL MASON (1792—1872), 1831.

1. To-day the Saviour calls: Ye wanderers, come; O ye benighted souls, Why longer roam.

200   *"To-Day."*

2 To-day the Saviour calls:
 O hear Him now;
 Within these sacred walls
 To Jesus bow.

3 To-day the Saviour calls:
 For refuge fly;
 The storm of justice falls,
 And death is nigh.

4 The Spirit calls to-day:
 Yield to His power;
 O grieve Him not away,
 'Tis mercy's hour.
      Rev. Samuel Francis Smith (1808—), 1831.
      Alt. by Thomas Hastings (1784—1872), 1831.

CYPRUS. 7.   Adap. from FELIX MENDELSSOHN BARTHOLDY (1809—1847).

1. Time is earnest, pass-ing by; Death is earnest drawing nigh: Sinner, wilt thou trifling be? Time and death ap-peal to thee.

201   *Life is earnest.*

2 Life is earnest: when 'tis o'er,
 Thou returnest nevermore;
 Soon to meet eternity,
 Wilt thou never serious be?

3 God is earnest: kneel and pray,
 Ere thy season pass away;
 Ere He set His judgment throne;
 Ere the day of grace be gone.

4 Christ is earnest, bids thee come;
 Paid, thy spirit's priceless sum;
 Wilt thou spurn the Saviour's love,
 Pleading with thee from above?

5 O be earnest, do not stay;
 Thou may'st perish e'en to-day.
 Rise, thou lost one, rise and flee;
 Lo! thy Saviour waits for thee.
      Rev. Sidney Dyer (1814—). Alt.

HORTON. 7.   XAVIER SCHNYDER von WARTENSEE (1786—1868), 1826.

1. Come, said Jesus' sacred voice, Come, and make My paths your choice; I will guide you to your home, Wear-y pilgrim, hither come.

202   *"The gracious Call."* Matt. xi. 28—30.

2 Thou who, houseless, sole, forlorn,
 Long hast borne the proud world's scorn,
 Long hast roamed the barren waste,
 Weary pilgrim, hither haste.

3 Hither come, for here is found
 Balm that flows for every wound,
 Peace that ever shall endure,
 Rest eternal, sacred, sure.
      Mrs. Anna Lætitia Barbauld (1743—1825) 1792. Ab. and alt.

INVITATION AND WARNING.

BLUMENTHAL. 7. D.   JACQUES BLUMENTHAL (1829—   ), 1847.

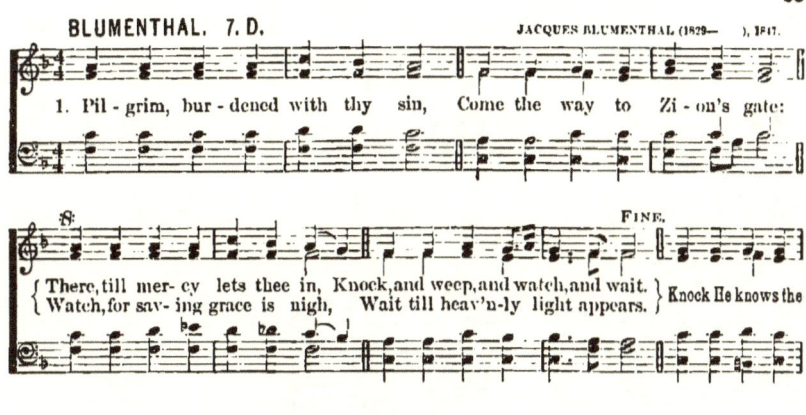

1. Pilgrim, burdened with thy sin, Come the way to Zion's gate:
{ There, till mercy lets thee in, Knock, and weep, and watch, and wait.
Watch, for saving grace is nigh, Wait till heav'nly light appears. } Knock He knows the sinner's cry; Weep, He loves the mourner's tears;

203
The Pilgrim welcomed.

2 Hark, it is the bridegroom's voice:
"Welcome, pilgrim, to thy rest!"
Now within the gate rejoice,
Safe, and sealed, and bought, and blest:
Safe, from all the lures of vice;
Sealed, by signs the chosen know;
Bought by love, and life the price;
  Blest, the mighty debt to owe.

3 Holy pilgrim, what for thee
In a world like this remain?
From thy guarded breast shall flee
Fear, and shame, and doubt, and pain;
Fear, the hope of Heaven shall fly;
Shame, from glory's view retire;
Doubt, in certain rapture die;
Pain, in endless bliss expire.

    Rev. George Crabbe (1754—1832), 1807. Ab.

204
"Why will ye die?"

1 Sinners, turn, why will ye die?
God, your Maker, asks you why;
God, who did your being give,
Made you with Himself to live;
He the fatal cause demands,
Asks the work of His own hands,
Why, ye thankless creatures, why
Will you cross His love, and die?

2 Sinners, turn, why will ye die?
God, your Saviour, asks you why;
God who did your souls retrieve,
Died Himself that ye might live:
Will you let Him die in vain?
Crucify your Lord again?
Why, ye ransomed sinners, why
Will you slight His grace, and die?

3 Sinners, turn, why will ye die?
God, the Spirit, asks you why;
He, who all your lives hath strove,
Wooed you to embrace His love:
Will you not His grace receive?
Will you still refuse to live?
Why, ye long-sought sinners, why
Will you grieve your God, and die?

    Rev. Charles Wesley (1708—1788), 1745. Ab.

MARTYN. 7. D.   SIMEON BUTLER MARSH (1798—1875), 1834.

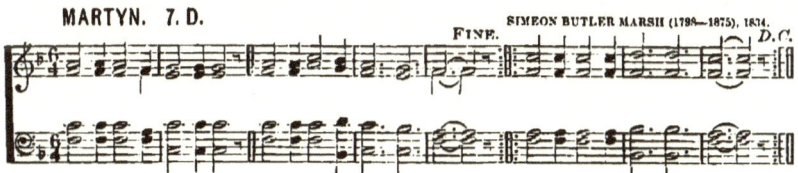

STOCKTON. H. M.

Arr. from old Church Melody.

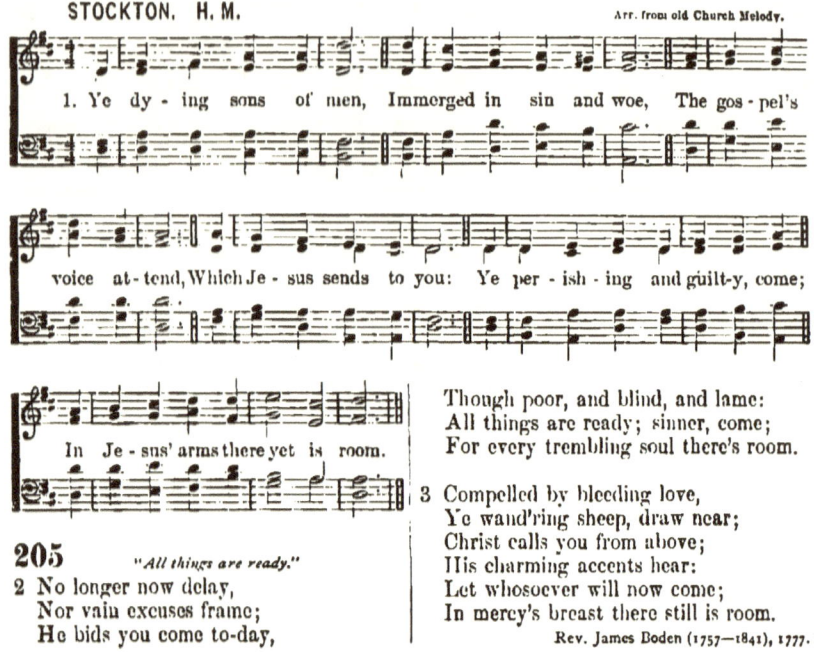

1. Ye dy-ing sons of men, Immerged in sin and woe, The gos-pel's voice at-tend, Which Je-sus sends to you: Ye per-ish-ing and guilt-y, come; In Je-sus' arms there yet is room.

Though poor, and blind, and lame:
All things are ready; sinner, come;
For every trembling soul there's room.

3 Compelled by bleeding love,
Ye wand'ring sheep, draw near;
Christ calls you from above;
His charming accents hear:
Let whosoever will now come;
In mercy's breast there still is room.

205 *"All things are ready."*

2 No longer now delay,
Nor vain excuses frame;
He bids you come to-day,

Rev. James Boden (1757—1841), 1777.

SERAPH. P. M.

Arr. by Rev. J. H. STOCKTON

1. The great Phy-si-cian now is near, The sympa-thiz-ing Je-sus: He speaks the drooping heart to cheer, O hear, the voice of Je-sus. Sweetest note in ser-aph song, Sweetest name on mor-tal tongue, Sweetest car-ol ev-er sung, Je-sus, bless-ed Je-sus.

206 *The Great Physician.*

2 Your many sins are all forgiven,
  O hear the voice of Jesus;
  Go on your way in peace to heaven,
  And wear a crown with Jesus.—Cho.

3 All glory to the dying Lamb!
  I now believe in Jesus;
  I love the blessed Saviour's name,
  I love the name of Jesus.—Cho.

4 His name dispels my guilt and fear,
  No other name but Jesus;
  O how my soul delights to hear
  The precious name of Jesus.—Cho.

5 And when to that bright world above,
  We rise to see our Jesus,
  We'll sing around the throne of love
  His name, the name of Jesus.—Cho.

  Rev. William Hunter (—), 1844. Ab.

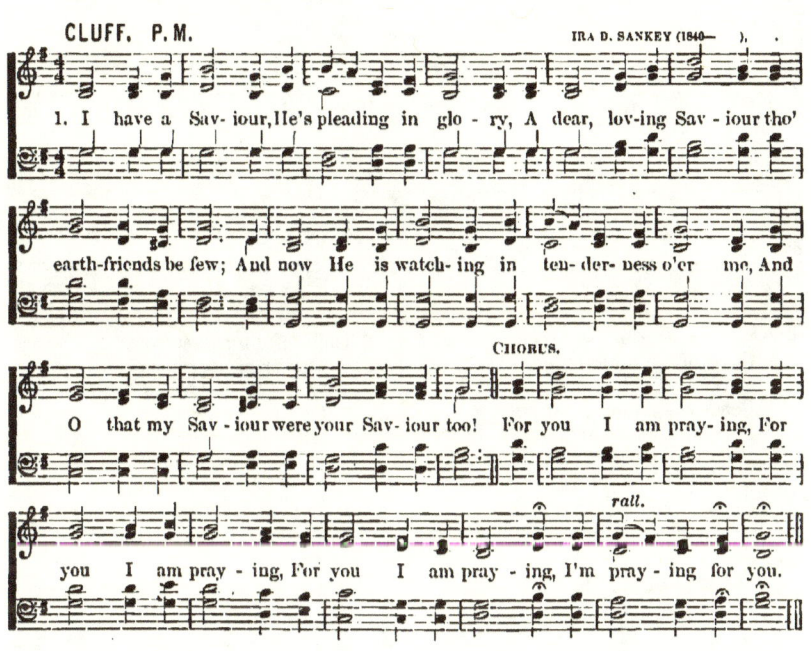

207 *Pleading with sinners.*

2 I have a Father: to me He has given
  A hope for eternity, blessed and true;
  And soon will He call me to meet Him in heaven,
  But O that He'd let me bring you with me too!—Cho.

3 I have a robe: 'tis resplendent in whiteness,
  Awaiting in glory my wondering view;
  O when I receive it all shining in brightness,
  Dear friend, could I see you receiving one too!—Cho.

4 I have a peace: it is calm as a river—
  A peace that the friends of this world never knew;
  My Saviour alone is its Author and Giver,
  And O could I know it was given to you!—Cho.

5 When Jesus has found you, tell others the story,
  That my loving Saviour is your Saviour too;
  Then pray that your Saviour may bring them to glory,
  And prayer will be answered—'twas answered for you!—Cho.

  S. O'Maley Cluff (—).

SALVATION OFFERED.

TARRING. P. M. — EDWARD JOHN HOPKINS (1818–), 1866.

1. Child of sin and sor-row, Filled with dis-may, Wait not for to-mor-row, Yield thee to-day: Heav'n bids thee come, While yet there's room. Child of sin and sor-row, Hear and o-bey.

208 *"Child of Sin and Sorrow."*

2 Child of sin and sorrow,
  Why wilt thou die?
Come while thou canst borrow
  Help from on high:
Grieve not that love
Which from above,
Child of sin and sorrow,
  Would bring thee nigh.

3 Child of sin and sorrow,
  Thy moments glide,
Like the flitting arrow,
  Or the rushing tide;
Ere time is o'er,
Heaven's grace implore;
Child of sin and sorrow,
  In Christ confide.

Thomas Hastings (1784–1872), 1832. Ab.

ST. REGULUS. 10. 10. 4. 6. — A. CROIL FALCONER (1850–), 1886.

1. "Yet there is room!" The Lamb's bright hall of song, With its fair glo-ry,

REFRAIN. *Slower.*

beck-ons thee a-long; Room, room, still room! O en-ter, en-ter now!

209 *"Yet there is room."*

2 Day is declining, and the sun is low;
  The shadows lengthen, light makes haste
    to go.—REF.

3 The bridal hall is filling for the feast;
  Pass in, pass in, and be the Bridegroom's
    guest.—REF.

THE GRACIOUS CALL.

4 It fills, it fills, that hall of jubilee:
   Make haste, make haste; 'tis not too full
       for thee.—Ref.
5 "Yet there is room!" Still open stands
       the gate,
   The gate of love; it is not yet too
       late.—Ref.
6 Pass in, pass in! The banquet is for thee;
   That cup of everlasting love is free.—Ref.

7 All heaven is there, all joy! Go in, go in;
   The angels beckon thee the prize to
       win.—Ref.
8 Louder and sweeter sounds the loving
       call;
   Come, lingerer, come; enter that festal
       hall!—Ref.

       Rev. Horatius Bonar (1808—).

INVITATION. P. M.   F. C. MAKER (1844—).

1. Come to the Saviour now! He gently calleth thee;
   In true repentance low, Before Him bend the knee. He waiteth
   to bestow Salvation, peace, and love, True joy on earth below,
   A home in heav'n above. Come, come, come!

210   *Come now, come all.*

2 Come to the Saviour now!
    Ye who have wandered far,
    Renew your solemn vow,
    For His by right you are.
  Come, like poor wandering sheep
    Returning to His fold;
  His arm will safely keep,
    His love will ne'er grow cold.
        Come, come, come!

3 Come to the Saviour, all!
    Whate'er your burden be;
  Hear now His loving call—
    "Cast all your care on me."
  Come, and for every grief
    In Jesus you will find
  A sure and safe relief,
    A loving Friend and kind.
        Come, come, come!

       John M. Wigner (—).

EXPOSTULATION. 11.   Rev. JOSIAH HOPKINS (1786–1862), 1830.

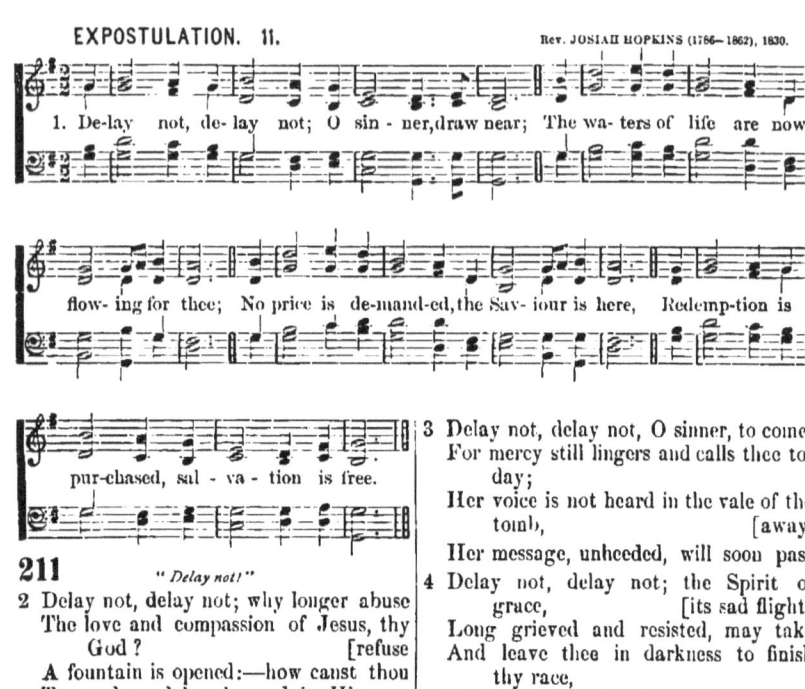

1. Delay not, delay not; O sinner, draw near; The waters of life are now flowing for thee; No price is demanded, the Saviour is here, Redemption is purchased, salvation is free.

211   *"Delay not!"*

2 Delay not, delay not; why longer abuse
The love and compassion of Jesus, thy
God?   [refuse
A fountain is opened:—how canst thou
To wash and be cleansed in His pardoning blood?

3 Delay not, delay not, O sinner, to come,
For mercy still lingers and calls thee today;
Her voice is not heard in the vale of the
tomb,   [away.
Her message, unheeded, will soon pass

4 Delay not, delay not; the Spirit of
grace,   [its sad flight;
Long grieved and resisted, may take
And leave thee in darkness to finish
thy race,
To sink in the vale of eternity's night.

Thomas Hastings (1784–1872), 1831.

EVEN ME. 8.7, 3.3.7.   Arr. by WILLIAM BATCHELDER BRADBURY (1816–1868), 1862.

{ Pass me not, O gracious Father, Sinful though my heart may be; }
{ Thou might's curse me, but the rather, Let thy mercy light on me, } Even me,

Even me, Let Thy mercy light on me.

212   *"Bless me, even me also."*
             Gen. xxvii. 34.

2 Pass me not, O tender Saviour,
Let me love and cling to Thee;
I am longing for Thy favor;
When Thou comest, call for me,
Even me.

3 Pass me not, O mighty Spirit,
Thou canst make the blind to see;
Witnesser of Jesus' merit,
Speak the word of power to me,
Even me.

4 Love of God, so pure and changeless,
Blood of God, so rich and free,
Grace of God, so strong and boundless,
Magnify them all in me,
Even me.

Mrs. Elizabeth Codner (—), 1861. Ab.

SALVATION SOUGHT AND FOUND.

MERIBAH. C. P. M.   LOWELL MASON (1792–1872), 1839.

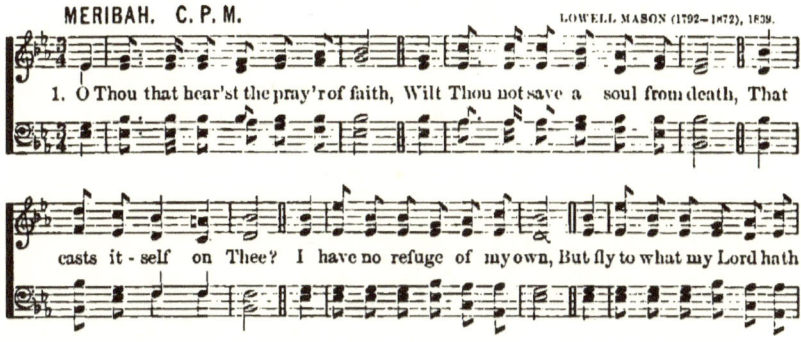

1. O Thou that hear'st the pray'r of faith, Wilt Thou not save a soul from death, That casts it-self on Thee? I have no refuge of my own, But fly to what my Lord hath done, And suffer'd once for me.

213   *The Prayer of Faith.*

2 Slain in the guilty sinner's stead,
His spotless righteousness I plead,
  And His availing blood:
Thy merit, Lord, my robe shall be,
Thy merit shall atone for me,
  And bring me near to God.

3 Then snatch me from eternal death,
The Spirit of adoption breathe,
  His consolations send:
By Him some word of life impart,
And sweetly whisper to my heart,
  "Thy Maker is thy Friend."

Rev. Augustus Montague Toplady (1740—1778), 1759. Ab.

ST. HELEN'S. 8, 5, 8, 3.   Sir ROBERT PRESCOTT STEWART (1825–   ), 1874.

I am trusting Thee, Lord Jesus, Trusting on-ly Thee; Trusting Thee for full sal-

-va-tion, Great and free.

214   *Trusting Jesus.*

2 I am trusting Thee for pardon;
  At Thy feet I bow,
For Thy grace and tender mercy,
  Trusting now.

3 I am trusting Thee for cleansing
  In the crimson flood;
Trusting Thee to make me holy
  By Thy blood.

4 I am trusting Thee to guide me,
  Thou alone shalt lead:
Every day and hour supplying
  All my need.

5 I am trusting Thee for power;
  Thine can never fail:
Words which Thou Thyself shalt give me
  Must prevail.

6 I am trusting Thee, Lord Jesus;
  Never let me fail:
I am trusting Thee for ever,
  And for all.

Miss Frances Ridley Havergal (1836—1879),

SALVATION SOUGHT AND FOUND.

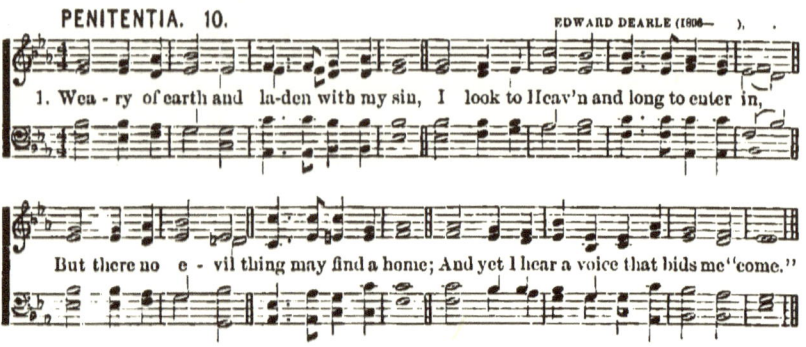

PENITENTIA. 10. EDWARD DEARLE (1806–).

1. Wea-ry of earth and la-den with my sin, I look to Heav'n and long to enter in, But there no e-vil thing may find a home; And yet I hear a voice that bids me "come."

215 *Sin Forgiven.*

2 So vile I am, how dare I hope to stand
In the pure glory of that holy land?
Before the whiteness of that throne appear?
Yet there are hands stretched out to draw me near;

3 It is the voice of Jesus that I hear;
His are the hands stretched out to draw me near,
And His the blood that can for all atone,
And set me faultless there before the throne.

4 'Twas He who found me on the deathly wild,
And made me heir of Heaven, the Father's child,
And day by day, whereby my soul may live,
Gives me His grace of pardon, and will give.

5 Yea, Thou wilt answer for me, Righteous Lord:
Thine all the merits, mine the great reward;
Thine the sharp thorns, and mine the golden crown;
Mine the life won, and Thine the life laid down.

Rev. Samuel John Stone (1839–), 1865. Ab.

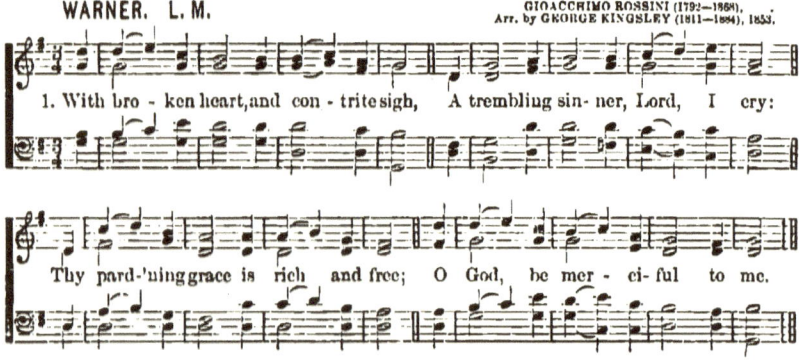

WARNER. L. M. GIOACCHIMO ROSSINI (1792–1868).
Arr. by GEORGE KINGSLEY (1811–1884), 1853.

1. With bro-ken heart, and con-trite sigh, A trembling sin-ner, Lord, I cry: Thy pard-'ning grace is rich and free; O God, be mer-ci-ful to me.

PENITENCE.

216 *The Prayer of the Publican.*
Luke xviii. 13.

2 I smite upon my troubled breast,
With deep and conscious guilt opprest,
Christ and His cross my only plea;
O God, be merciful to me.

3 Far off I stand with tearful eyes,
Nor dare uplift them to the skies;
But Thou dost all my anguish see;
O God, be merciful to me.

4 Nor alms, nor deeds that I have done,
Can for a single sin atone;
To Calvary alone I flee;
O God, be merciful to me.

5 And when, redeemed from sin and hell,
With all the ransomed throng I dwell,
My raptured song shall ever be,
God has been merciful to me.

Rev. Cornelius Elven (1797—   ), 1852.

LOUVAN. L. M.   VIRGIL CORYDON TAYLOR (1817—   ), 1847.

1. Show pit-y, Lord, O Lord, for-give; Let a re-pent-ing reb-el live: Are not Thy mer-cies large and free? May not a sin-ner trust in Thee?

217 *Pleading for Pardon.*
Ps. li.

2 O wash my soul from every sin,
And make my guilty conscience clean;
Here on my heart the burden lies,
And past offences pain mine eyes.

3 My lips with shame my sins confess,
Against Thy law, against Thy grace;
Lord, should Thy judgments grow severe,
I am condemned, but Thou art clear.

4 Yet save a trembling sinner, Lord,
Whose hope, still hovering round Thy Word,
Would light on some sweet promise there,
Some sure support against despair.

Rev. Isaac Watts (1674—1748), 1719. Ab.

218 *"Gott rufet noch."*

1 GOD calling yet! shall I not hear?
Earth's pleasures shall I still hold dear?
Shall life's swift passing years all fly,
And still my soul in slumber lie?

2 God calling yet! and shall He knock,
And I my heart the closer lock?
He still is waiting to receive,
And shall I dare His Spirit grieve?

3 God calling yet! and shall I give
No heed, but still in bondage live?
I wait, but He does not forsake;
He calls me still; my heart, awake!

4 God calling yet! I cannot stay;
My heart I yield without delay:
Vain world, farewell, from thee I part;
The voice of God hath reached my heart.

Gerhard Tersteegen (1697—1769), 1730.
Tr. by Miss Jane Borthwick (1813—   ) 1854. Ab. and alt.

219 *A contrite Heart.*
Ps. li.

1 A BROKEN heart, my God, my King,
Is all the sacrifice I bring;
The God of grace will ne'er despise
A broken heart for sacrifice.

2 My soul lies humbled in the dust,
And owns Thy dreadful sentence just;
Look down, O Lord, with pitying eye,
And save the soul condemned to die.

3 O may Thy love inspire my tongue!
Salvation shall be all my song;
And all my powers shall join to bless
The Lord, my strength and righteousness.

Rev. Isaac Watts, 1719. Ab. and alt.

SALVATION SOUGHT AND FOUND.

ST. MAURA. H. M. — Sir ARTHUR SULLIVAN (1842–), 1872.

1. I bring my sins to Thee, The sins I can- not count, That all may cleanséd be In Thy once o- pen'd fount. I bring them, Saviour, all to Thee; The bur-den is too great for me.

220 *"Lord, to whom shall we go?"* John vi. 68.

2 My heart to Thee I bring,
   The heart I cannot read—
   A faithless wandering thing,
   An evil heart indeed.
   I bring it, Saviour, now to Thee,
   That fixed and faithful it may be.

3 My life I bring to Thee,
   I would not be my own;
   O Saviour, let me be
   Thine ever, Thine alone.
   My heart, my life, my all I bring
   To Thee, My Saviour and my King!

   Miss Frances Ridley Havergal (1836–1879).

LENOX. H. M. — LEWIS EDSON (1784–1820), 1781.

1. A-rise, my soul, a-rise, Shake off thy guilt-y fears; The bleeding Sac- ri- fice In my be-half ap-pears; Be-fore the throne my Sure-ty stands, Be-fore the throne my Sure-ty stands, My name is writ-ten on His hands.

221   *"Behold the Man."*

2 He ever lives above,
   For me to intercede,
 His all-redeeming love,
   His precious blood, to plead;
 His blood atoned for all our race,
 And sprinkles now the throne of grace.

3 My God is reconciled,
   His pardoning voice I hear,
 He owns me for His child;
   I can no longer fear,
 With confidence I now draw nigh,
 And Father, Abba, Father, cry.

Rev. Charles Wesley (1708—1788), 1742. Ab.

BURNHAM. H. M.   WILLIAM CROFT (1677—1727), 1700.

1. Join all the glorious names Of wisdom, love, and pow'r,
That ever mortals knew, That angels ever bore: All
are too mean to speak His worth, Too mean to set my Saviour forth.

---

222   *Prophet, Priest, and King.*

2 Great Prophet of my God,
   My tongue would bless Thy Name;
 By Thee the joyful news
   Of our salvation came:
 The joyful news of sins forgiven,
 Of hell subdued, and peace with Heaven.

3 Jesus, my great High Priest,
   Offered His blood and died;
 My guilty conscience seeks
   No sacrifice beside:
 His powerful blood did once atone,
 And now it pleads before the throne.

4 My dear Almighty Lord,
   My Conqueror and my King,
 Thy sceptre and Thy sword,
   Thy reigning grace I sing:
 Thine is the power; behold, I sit,
 In willing bonds, beneath Thy feet.

Rev. Isaac Watts (1674—1748), 1709. Ab.

223   *"Wounded for our Transgressions."*
         Is. liii. 5.

1 Thy works, not mine, O Christ,
   Speak gladness to this heart;
 They tell me all is done;
   They bid my fear depart:
 To whom save Thee, who canst alone
 For sin atone, Lord, shall I flee?

2 Thy wounds, not mine, O Christ,
   Can heal my bruiséd soul;
 Thy stripes, not mine, contain
   The balm that makes me whole:
 To whom save Thee, who canst alone
 For sin atone, Lord, shall I flee?

3 Thy cross, not mine, O Christ,
   Has borne the awful load
 Of sins that none in Heaven
   Or earth could bear but God:
 To whom save Thee, who canst alone
 For sin atone, Lord, shall I flee?

4 Thy death, not mine, O Christ,
   Has paid the ransom due;
 Ten thousand deaths like mine
   Would have been all too few:
 To whom save Thee, who canst alone
 For sin atone, Lord, shall I flee?

Rev. Horatius Bonar (1808—), 1857. Ab.

SALVATION SOUGHT AND FOUND.

ST. LEONARD. C. M. HENRY SMART (1812—1879).

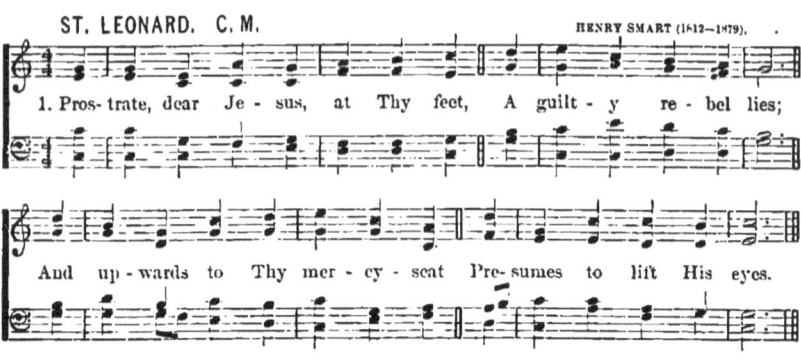

1. Pros-trate, dear Jesus, at Thy feet, A guilty rebel lies; And upwards to Thy mercy-seat Presumes to lift His eyes.

224 *At Christ's Feet.*

2 If tears of sorrow would suffice
   To pay the debt I owe,
 Tears should from both my weeping eyes
   In ceaseless torrents flow.

3 But no such sacrifice I plead
   To expiate my guilt;
 No tears but those which Thou hast shed,
   No blood but Thou hast spilt.

4 Think of Thy sorrows, dearest Lord,
   And all my sins forgive;
 Justice will well approve the word,
   That bids the sinner live,
      Rev. Samuel Stennett (1727—1795), 1787. Ab.

ST. JOHN. C. M. JAMES TURLE (1802—1882), 1862.

1. Ap-proach, my soul, the mercy-seat Where Jesus answers pray'r; There humbly fall before His feet, For none can perish there.

225 *Coming to Christ.*

2 Thy promise is my only plea,
   With this I venture nigh;
 Thou callest burdened souls to Thee,
   And such, O Lord, am I.

3 Bowed down beneath a load of sin,
   By Satan sorely prest,
 By war without, and fears within,
   I come to Thee for rest.

4 Be Thou my shield and hiding-place,
   That, sheltered near Thy side,
 I may my fierce accuser face,
   And tell him, Thou hast died.

5 O wondrous love, to bleed and die,
   To bear the cross and shame,
 That guilty sinners, such as I,
   Might plead Thy gracious Name.
      Rev. John Newton (1725—1807), 1779. Ab

COWPER. C. M.
LOWELL MASON (1792—1872), 1830.

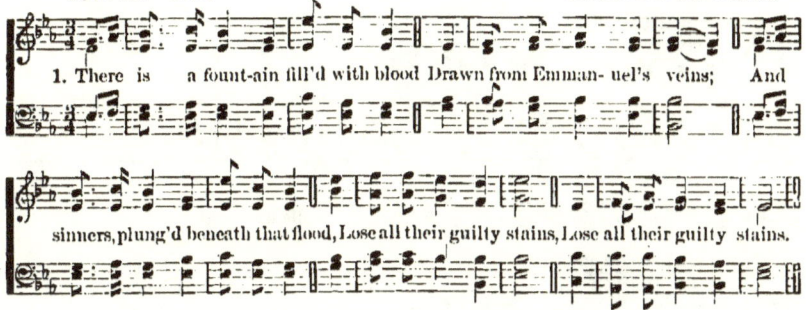

1. There is a fountain fill'd with blood Drawn from Emmanuel's veins; And sinners, plung'd beneath that flood, Lose all their guilty stains, Lose all their guilty stains.

226   *"A Fountain opened."* Zech. xiii. 1.

2 The dying thief rejoiced to see
   That fountain in his day;
And there have I, as vile as he,
   Washed all my sins away.

3 Dear dying Lamb, Thy precious blood
   Shall never lose its power,
Till all the ransomed Church of God
   Be saved, to sin no more.

4 E'er since, by faith, I saw the stream
   Thy flowing wounds supply,
Redeeming love has been my theme,
   And shall be till I die.

5 And when this feeble, stammering tongue
   Lies silent in the grave,
Then in a nobler, sweeter song,
   I'll sing Thy power to save.
      William Cowper (1731—1800), 1779. Ab. and alt.

227   *The Soul ruined.*

1 How sad our state by nature is!
   Our sin—how deep it stains!
And Satan holds our captive minds
   Fast in his slavish chains.

2 But there's a voice of sovereign grace,
   Sounds from the sacred Word;
"Ho! ye despairing sinners, come,
   And trust a pardoning Lord."

3 My soul obeys the almighty call,
   And runs to this relief;
I would believe Thy promise, Lord·
   O help my unbelief!

4 A guilty, weak, and helpless worm,
   On thy kind arms I fall;
Be thou my Strength and Righteousness,
   My Saviour and my All.
      Rev. Isaac Watts (1674—1748), 1709.

228   *"Remember me."*

1 JESUS, Thou art the sinner's Friend:
   As such I look to Thee;
Now, in the fulness of Thy love,
   O Lord, remember me.

2 Thou wondrous Advocate with God,
   I yield myself to Thee;
While Thou art sitting on Thy throne,
   Dear Lord, remember me.

3 Lord, I am guilty, I am vile,
   But Thy salvation's free;
Then in Thine all-abounding grace,
   Dear Lord, remember me.
      Rev. Richard Burnham (1749—1810), 1783. Ab.

COOLING. C. M.
ALONZO JUDSON ABBEY (1825—1887), 1868.

SALVATION SOUGHT AND FOUND.

DORRNANCE. 8, 7. ISAAC BAKER WOODBURY (1819–1858), 1850.

1. Take me, O my Father, take me, Take me, save me, through Thy Son, That which Thou wouldst have me

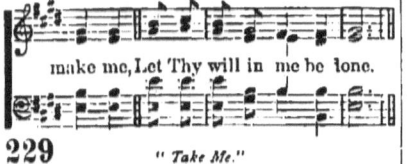

make me, Let Thy will in me be lone.

229 *"Take Me."*

2 Fruitless years with grief recalling,
　Humbly I confess my sin;
At Thy feet, O Father, falling,
　To Thy household take me in.

3 Freely now to Thee I proffer
　This relenting heart of mine:
Freely life and soul I offer,
　Gift unworthy love like Thine.

4 Once the world's Redeemer dying,
　Bore our sins upon the tree;
On that sacrifice relying,
　Now I look in hope to Thee.

5 Father, take me; all forgiving
　Fold me to Thy loving breast;
In Thy love for ever living,
　I must be for ever blest.
　　　Rev. Ray Palmer (1808–1887), 1865. Ab.

BARTIMEUS. 8, 7. STEPHEN JENKS (1772–1856), 1800.

1. Lord, I know Thy grace is nigh me, Though Thyself I cannot see; Je-sus, Master,

pass not by me; Son of David, pity me.

230 *"He received his sight."* Mark x. 51, 52.

2 While I sit in weary blindness,
　Longing for the blessed light,
Many taste Thy loving-kindness;
　"Lord, I would receive my sight."

3 I would see Thee and adore Thee,
　And Thy word the power can give;
Hear the sightless soul implore Thee:
　Let me see Thy face and live.

4 Ah, what touch is this that thrills me?
　What this burst of strange delight?
Lo, the rapturous vision fills me!
　This is Jesus! this is sight!

5 Room, ye saints that throng behind Him!
　Let me follow in the way;
I will teach the blind to find Him
　Who can turn their night to day.
　　　Rev. Hervey Doddridge Ganse (1822–), 1859.

231 *"Open, Lord, and let me in."*

1 At the door of mercy sighing
　With the burden of my sin,
Day and night my soul is crying,
　"Open, Lord, and let me in."

2 Waiting 'mid the darkness dreary,
　Stretching out my hands to Thee,
In the refuge for the weary
　Is there not a place for me?

3 Hark, what sounds my ear receiveth,
　Sweet as songs of seraphim!
He that in the Lord believeth
　Life eternal hath in Him.

4 At the outer door why staying?
　Nothing, soul, hast thou to pay:
Christ in love to thee is saying,
　"Weary child, come in to-day."
　　　Thomas MacKellar (1812–), 1872.

PLEADING FOR MERCY.

ALETTA. 7.   WILLIAM BATCHELDER BRADBURY (1816—1868), 1858.

1. Depth of mercy, can there be Mercy still reserv'd for me? Can my God His wrath forbear?

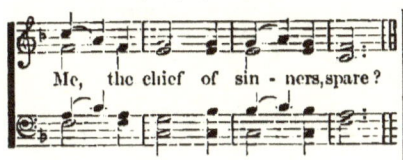

Me, the chief of sinners, spare?

232   *After a Relapse into Sin.*
          Heb. x. 29.

2 I have long withstood His grace,
Long provoked Him to His face;
Would not hearken to His calls;
Grieved Him by a thousand falls.

3 There for me the Saviour stands,
Shows His wounds, and spreads His
God is love: I know, I feel; [hands;
Jesus weeps, but loves me still.
       Rev. Charles Wesley (1708—1788), 1740. Ab.

233   *Rest in Christ.*

1 Jesus, full of truth and love,
We Thy kindest word obey,
Faithful let Thy mercies prove,
Take our load of guilt away.

2 Weary of this war within,
Weary of this endless strife,
Weary of ourselves and sin,
Weary of a wretched life;

3 Burdened with a world of grief,
Burdened with our sinful load,
Burdened with this unbelief,
Burdened with the wrath of God:

4 Lo, we come to Thee for ease,
True and gracious as Thou art;
Now our groaning soul release,
Write forgiveness on our heart.
       Rev. Charles Wesley, 1747. Ab. and alt.
       Rev. John Wesley (1703—1791), 1779.

234   *Looking to Jesus.*

1 Thou, who didst on Calvary bleed,
Thou, who dost for sinners plead,
Help me in my time of need,
Jesus, Saviour, hear my cry.

2 In my darkness and my grief,
With my heart of unbelief,
I, who am of sinners chief,
Jesus, lift to Thee mine eye.

3 Foes without and fears within,
With no plea Thy grace to win,
But that Thou canst save from sin,
Jesus, to Thy cross I fly.

4 There on Thee I cast my care,
There to Thee I raise my prayer,
Jesus, save me from despair,
Save me, save me, or I die.
     Rev. James Drummond Burns (1823—1864), 1858. Ab.

235   *Hear and save.*
        Prov. viii. 17.

1 Holy Father hear my cry;
Holy Saviour, bend Thine ear;
Holy Spirit, come Thou nigh:
Father, Saviour, Spirit, hear!

2 Father, save me from my sin;
Saviour, I Thy mercy crave;
Gracious Spirit, make me clear:
Father, Son, and Spirit save!

3 Father, let me taste Thy love;
Saviour, fill my soul with peace;
Spirit, come my heart to move:
Father, Son, and Spirit blest!

4 Father, Son, and Spirit Thou
One Jehovah, shed abroad
All Thy grace within me now;
Be my Father and my God.
       Rev. Horatius Bonar (1808—), 1857.

DIJON. 7.   German.

ROCK OF AGES. 7. 6 l.

Rev. JOHN BACCHUS DYKES (1823—1876), 1861.

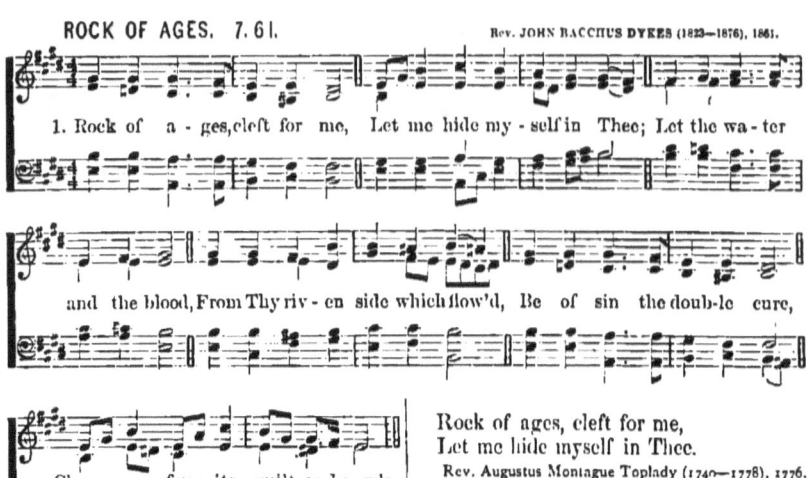

1. Rock of a-ges, cleft for me, Let me hide my-self in Thee; Let the wa-ter and the blood, From Thy riv-en side which flow'd, Be of sin the doub-le cure, Cleanse me from its guilt and pow'r.

Rock of ages, cleft for me,
Let me hide myself in Thee.

Rev. Augustus Montague Toplady (1740—1778), 1776. Sl. alt.

236 *"Rock of Ages."*

2 Not the labors of my hands
Can fulfil Thy law's demands;
Could my zeal no respite know,
Could my tears for ever flow,
All for sin could not atone;
Thou must save, and Thou alone.

3 Nothing in my hand I bring;
Simply to Thy cross I cling;
Naked, come to Thee for dress;
Helpless, look to Thee for grace;
Foul, I to the fountain fly;
Wash me, Saviour, or I die.

4 While I draw this fleeting breath,
When my eye-lids close in death,
When I soar to worlds unknown,
See Thee on Thy judgment-throne,

237 *"He hath borne our Griefs.."*
Is. liii. 4, 5, 12.

1 Surely Christ thy griefs hath borne;
Weeping soul, no longer mourn:
View Him bleeding on the tree:
Pouring out His life for thee:
There thy every sin He bore;
Weeping soul lament no more.

2 Weary sinner, keep thine eyes
On th' atoning sacrifice:
There th' incarnate Deity
Numbered with transgressors see;
There His Father's absence mourns,
Nailed and bruised, and crowned with thorns.

3 Cast Thy guilty soul on Him,
Find Him mighty to redeem;
At His feet thy burden lay,
Look thy doubts and cares away;
Now by faith the Son embrace,
Plead His promise, trust His grace.

Rev. Augustus Montague Toplady 1759, 1770. Ab.

TOPLADY. 7. 6 l.

THOMAS HASTINGS (1784—1872), 1830.
FINE. D.C.

SIN FORGIVEN.

GLASTONBURY. 7. 6 l. Rev. JOHN BACCHUS DYKES.

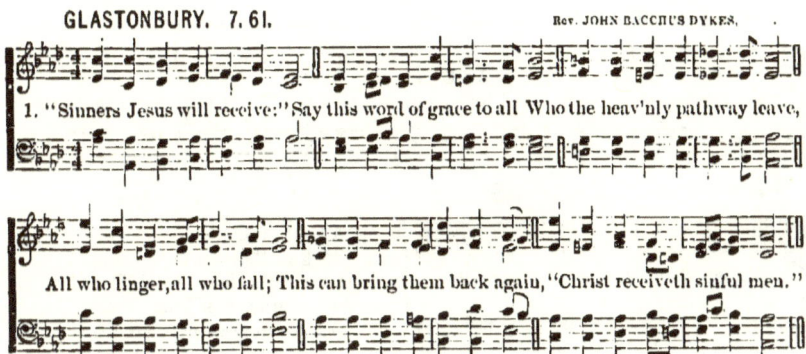

1. "Sinners Jesus will receive:" Say this word of grace to all Who the heav'nly pathway leave, All who linger, all who fall; This can bring them back again, "Christ receiveth sinful men."

238 *"This Man receiveth sinners."*

2 Shepherds seek their wandering sheep
O'er the mountains bleak and cold;
Jesus such a watch doth keep
O'er the lost ones of His fold,
Seeking them o'er moor and fen:
"Christ receiveth sinful men."

3 Sick and sorrowful and blind,
I, with all my sins, draw nigh;
O my Saviour, Thou canst find
Help for sinners such as I:
Speak that word of love again,
"Christ receiveth sinful men."

4 Yea, my soul is comforted;
For Thy blood hath washed away
All my sins, though crimson-red,
And I stand in white array,
Purged from every spot and stain:
"Christ receiveth sinful men."
Rev. Erdmann Neumeister (1671—1756).
Tr. Miss Emma Francis Bevan (1827—), . Ab.

239 *Before the Cross.*

1 Weary with my load of sin,
All diseased and faint within,
See me, Lord, Thy grace entreat,
See me prostrate at Thy feet:
Here before Thy Cross I lie,
Here I live or here I die.

2 I have tried and tried in vain
Many ways to ease my pain;
Now all other hope is past,
Only this is left at last:
Here before Thy Cross I lie,
Here I live and here I die.

3 If I perish, be it here
With the Friend of sinners near;
Lord, it is enough—I know
Never sinner perished so.
Here before Thy Cross I lie,
Here I cannot, cannot die.
Rev. George Wade Robinson (1838—1877).

GETHSEMANE. 7. 6 l. RICHARD REDHEAD (1820—), 1853.

SALVATION SOUGHT AND FOUND.

GREENWOOD. S. M.   JOSEPH EMERSON SWEETSER (1825—1873). 1849.

1. O where shall rest be found, Rest for the wear-y soul? 'Twere vain the ocean-depths to sound, Or pierce to ei-ther pole.

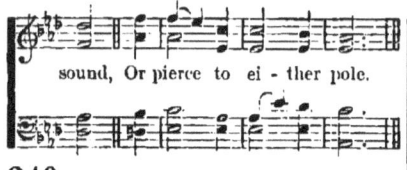

240   *The Issues of Life and Death.*

2 The world can never give
   The bliss for which we sigh;
'Tis not the whole of life to live,
   Nor all of death to die.

3 Beyond this vale of tears
   There is a life above,
Unmeasured by the flight of years;
   And all that life is love.

4 There is a death, whose pang
   Outlasts the fleeting breath:
O what eternal horrors hang
   Around the second death!

5 Lord God of truth and grace,
   Teach us that death to shun,
Lest we be banished from Thy face,
   And evermore undone.
    James Montgomery (1771—1854), 1819, 1853. Ab.

241   *" Out of the Depths."* Ps. cxxx.

1 OUT of the deep I call
   To Thee, O Lord, to Thee;
Before Thy throne of grace I fall;
   Be merciful to me.

2 Out of the deep I cry,
   The woful deep of sin,
Of evil done in days gone by,
   Of evil now within.

3 Out of the deep of fear,
   And dread of coming shame,
From morning watch till night is near.
   I plead the precious Name.
    Rev. Sir Henry Williams Baker (1821—1877), 1868. Ab.

STATE STREET. S. M.   JONATHAN CALL WOODMAN (1813—). 1844.

1. Did Christ o'er sin-ners weep, And shall our cheeks be dry? Let floods of pen-i-ten-tial grief Burst forth from ev-ery eye.

242   *Tears of Penitence.*

2 The Son of God in tears
   Angels with wonder see:
Be thou astonished, O my soul,
   He shed those tears for thee.

3 He wept that we might weep;
   Each sin demands a tear;

In Heaven alone no sin is found,
   And there's no weeping there.

4 Then tender be our hearts,
   Our eyes in sorrow dim,
Till every tear from every eye
   Is wiped away by Him.
    Rev. Benjamin Beddome (1717—1795), 1787. Vs. 1. 2. 3.
    Rev. Henry Francis Lyte (1793—1847), 1833   V. 4.

JESUS IS MINE.

OAK. 6. 4. 6. 4. 6. 6. 6. 4. LOWELL MASON (1792—1872), 1854.

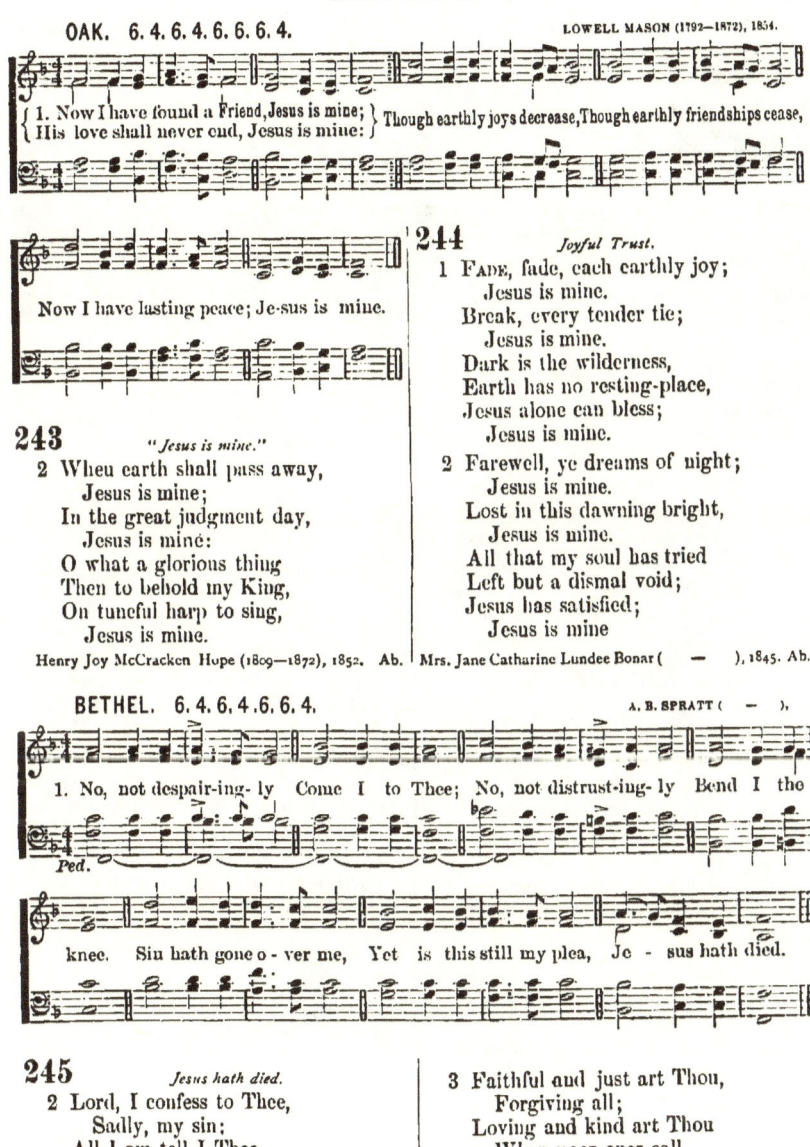

1. Now I have found a Friend, Jesus is mine;
   His love shall never end, Jesus is mine:
   Though earthly joys decrease, Though earthly friendships cease,
   Now I have lasting peace; Je-sus is mine.

243 *"Jesus is mine."*

2 When earth shall pass away,
   Jesus is mine;
   In the great judgment day,
   Jesus is mine:
   O what a glorious thing
   Then to behold my King,
   On tuneful harp to sing,
   Jesus is mine.

Henry Joy McCracken Hope (1809—1872), 1852. Ab.

244 *Joyful Trust.*

1 Fade, fade, each earthly joy;
   Jesus is mine.
   Break, every tender tie;
   Jesus is mine.
   Dark is the wilderness,
   Earth has no resting-place,
   Jesus alone can bless;
   Jesus is mine.

2 Farewell, ye dreams of night;
   Jesus is mine.
   Lost in this dawning bright,
   Jesus is mine.
   All that my soul has tried
   Left but a dismal void;
   Jesus has satisfied;
   Jesus is mine

Mrs. Jane Catharine Lundee Bonar (—), 1845. Ab.

BETHEL. 6. 4. 6. 4. 6. 6. 4. A. B. SPRATT (—),

1. No, not despair-ing-ly Come I to Thee; No, not distrust-ing-ly Bend I the
   knee. Sin hath gone o-ver me, Yet is this still my plea, Je-sus hath died.

245 *Jesus hath died.*

2 Lord, I confess to Thee,
   Sadly, my sin;
   All I am tell I Thee,
   All I have been.
   Purge Thou my sin away,
   Wash Thou my soul this day;
   Lord, make me clean.

3 Faithful and just art Thou,
   Forgiving all;
   Loving and kind art Thou
   When poor ones call.
   Lord, let the cleansing blood—
   Blood of the Lamb of God—
   Pass o'er my soul

Rev. Horatius Bonar (1808—),

SALVATION SOUGHT AND FOUND.

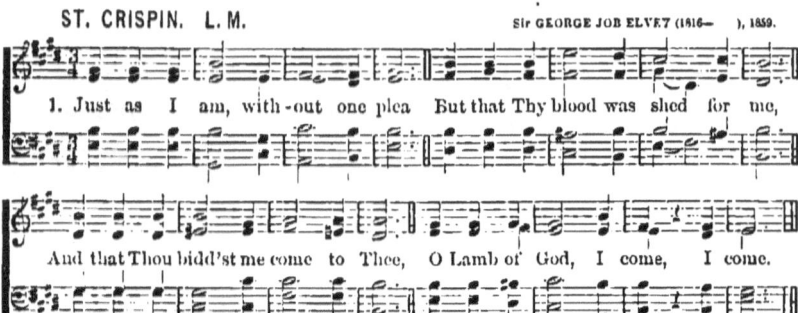

ST. CRISPIN. L. M.   Sir GEORGE JOB ELVEY (1816–), 1859.

1. Just as I am, with-out one plea But that Thy blood was shed for me, And that Thou bidd'st me come to Thee, O Lamb of God, I come, I come.

246   *"Just as I am."*
John vi. 37.

2 Just as I am, and waiting not
To rid my soul of one dark blot, [spot,
To Thee, whose blood can cleanse each
O Lamb of God, I come.

3 Just as I am, though tossed about
With many a conflict, many a doubt,
With fears within, and foes without,
O Lamb of God, I come.

4 Just as I am, poor, wretched, blind;
Sight, riches, healing of the mind,
Yea, all I need, in Thee to find,
O Lamb of God, I come.

5 Just as I am, Thou wilt receive,
Wilt welcome, pardon, cleanse, relieve:
Because Thy promise I believe,
O Lamb of God, I come.

6 Just as I am, Thy love unknown
Has broken every barrier down:
Now, to be Thine, yea, Thine alone,
O Lamb of God, I come.
    Miss Charlotte Elliot (1789–1871), 1836.

247   *"Thou hast died."*
1 Jesus, the sinner's Friend, to Thee,
Lost and undone, for aid I flee;
Weary of earth, myself, and sin,
Open Thine arms and take me in.

2 At last I own it cannot be
That I should fit myself for Thee:
Here, then, to Thee I all resign;
Thine is the work, and only Thine.

3 What can I say Thy grace to move?
Lord, I am sin,—but Thou art love:
I give up every plea beside,
Lord, I am lost,—but Thou hast died!
    Rev. Charles Wesley (1708–1788).

248   *"Come to Me!"*
1 With tearful eyes I look around;
Life seems a dark and stormy sea;
Yet 'midst the gloom I hear a sound,
A heavenly whisper, "Come to Me!"

2 It tells me of a place of rest,
It tells me where my soul may flee:
O, to the weary, faint, opprest,
How sweet the bidding, "Come to Me!"

3 "Come, for all else must fail and die;
Earth is no resting-place for thee;
Heavenward direct thy weeping eye;
I am thy portion; Come to Me!"

4 O voice of mercy, voice of love,
In conflict, grief, and agony,
Support me, cheer me from above,
And gently whisper, "Come to Me!"
    Miss Charlotte Elliot. 1841.

WOODWORTH. L. M.   WILLIAM BATCHELDER BRADBURY (1816–1868), 1849.

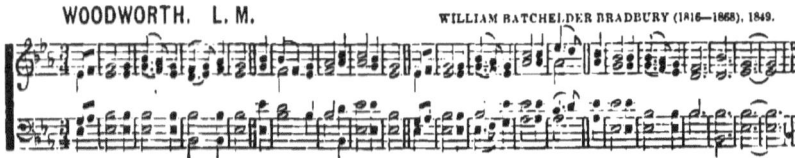

OUR REFUGE AND REST.

ATHENS. C. M. D. FELICE GIARDINI (1716–1796), 1769.

1. I heard the voice of Jesus say, "Come unto Me and rest; Lay down, thou weary one, lay down Thy head upon My breast." I came to Jesus as I was, Weary, and worn, and sad;

D.S.—I found in Him a resting-place, And He has made me glad.

249 *The Voice from Galilee.*
John i. 16.

2 I heard the voice of Jesus say,
"Behold, I freely give
The living water; thirsty one,
Stoop down, and drink, and live."

I came to Jesus, and I drank
Of that life-giving stream;
My thirst was quenched, my soul revived,
And now I live in Him.

3 I heard the voice of Jesus say,
"I am this dark world's Light;
Look unto Me, thy morn shall rise,
And all thy day be bright."
I looked to Jesus, and I found
In Him my Star, my Sun;
And in that Light of Life I'll walk
Till all my journey's done.

Rev. Horatius Bonar (1808—), 1850. Sl. alt.

SUBJECTION. S. M. GIOVANNI PAISIELLO (1741–1816), 1788.

1. Dear Lord and Master mine, Thy happy servant see: My Conqu'ror, with what joy divine Thy captive clings to Thee.

250 *Sweet Subjection.*

2 I would not walk alone,
But still with Thee, my God;
At every step my blindness own,
And ask of Thee the road.

3 The weakness I enjoy
That casts me on Thy breast;

The conflicts that Thy strength employ
Make me divinely blest.

4 Dear Lord and Master mine,
Still keep Thy servant true;
My Guardian and my Guide divine,
Bring, bring Thy pilgrim through.

Thomas Hornblower Gill (1819—), 1867. Ab.

WILTSHIRE. C. M.
Sir GEORGE SMART (1784—1869).

1. All that I was, my sin, my guilt, My death was all my own,
All that I am I owe to Thee, My gra - cious God, a - lone.

251 *Jesus all in all.*
1 Cor. xv. 10.

2 The evil of my former state
Was mine, and only mine;
The good in which I now rejoice
Is Thine, and only Thine.

3 The darkness of my former state,
The bondage, all was mine,
The light of life in which I walk,
The liberty, is Thine.

4 Thy grace first made me feel my sin,
It taught me to believe;
Then in believing, peace I found,
And now I live, I live.

5 All that I am, even here on earth,
All that I hope to be,
When Jesus comes, and glory dawns,
I owe it, Lord, to Thee.
Rev. Horatius Bonar (1808—).

GRAPE. P. M.
JOHN THOMAS GRAPE (1833—), 1865.

1. { I hear the Saviour say, Thy strength indeed is small;
Child of weakness, watch and pray, (Omit) . . . . Find in Me thine all in all.

CHORUS.

Je-sus paid it all, All to Him I owe; Sin had left a crimson stain: He wash'd it white as snow.

252 *Jesus paid it all.*

2 Lord, now indeed I find
Thy power, and Thine alone,
Can change the leper's spots,
And melt the heart of stone.—CHO.

3 For nothing good have I
Whereby Thy grace to claim—
I'll wash my garment white
In the blood of Calvary's Lamb.—CHO.

4 When from my dying bed
My ransomed soul shall rise,
Then "Jesus paid it all"
Shall rend the vaulted skies.—CHO.

5 And when before the throne
I stand in Him complete;
I'll lay my trophies down,
All down at Jesus' feet.—CHO.
Mrs. Elvina Mabel Myers (1818—), 1865.

ST. ULRICH. 7, 6, D. C. H. PURDAY (—),

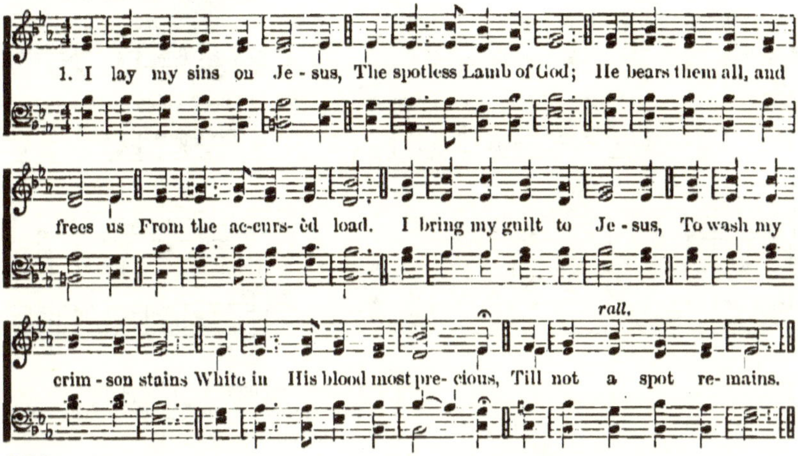

1. I lay my sins on Jesus, The spotless Lamb of God; He bears them all, and frees us From the accursed load. I bring my guilt to Jesus, To wash my crimson stains White in His blood most precious, Till not a spot remains.

253
The Substitute.

2 I lay my wants on Jesus;
  All fulness dwells in Him;
 He heals all my diseases,
  He doth my soul redeem.
 I lay my griefs on Jesus,
  My burdens and my cares;
 He from them all releases,
  He all my sorrows shares.

3 I rest my soul on Jesus,
  This weary soul of mine;
 His right hand me embraces,
  I on His breast recline.
 I love the name of Jesus,
  Immanuel, Christ, the Lord;
 Like fragrance on the breezes,
  His name abroad is poured.

Rev. Horatius Bonar, 1843. Ab.

GORDON. 11. A. J. GORDON (—),

1. { My Jesus, I love Thee, I know Thou art mine,
    { For Thee all the follies of sin I resign; } My gracious Re-
D.C.—If ever I lov'd Thee, my (Omit) . . . . . Jesus 'tis now.

-deemer, my Saviour art Thou,

D.C. If ever I loved Thee, my Jesus, 'tis now.

3 I'll love Thee in life, I will love Thee in
    death, [me breath;
 And praise Thee as long as Thou lendest
 And say when the death-dew lies cold on
    my brow,
 If ever I loved Thee, my Jesus, 'tis now.

4 In mansions of glory and endless delight,
 I'll ever adore Thee in Heaven so bright;
 I'll sing with the glittering crown on my
    brow,
 If ever I loved Thee, my Jesus, 'tis now.

London Hymn Book, 1864.

254
"Altogether lovely."

2 I love Thee, because Thou hast first loved
    me, [tree;
 And purchased my pardon on Calvary's
 I love Thee for wearing the thorns on
    Thy brow;

SALVATION SOUGHT AND FOUND.

NEWCASTLE. 8, 6, 8, 8, 6.   HENRY L. MORLEY (—).

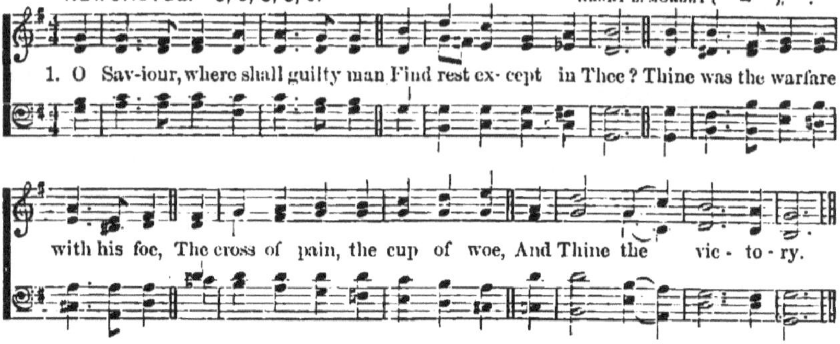

1. O Sav-iour, where shall guilty man Find rest ex-cept in Thee? Thine was the warfare with his foe, The cross of pain, the cup of woe, And Thine the vic-to-ry.

255   *"Behold, what manner of love!"*

2 How came the everlasting Son,
   The Lord of life, to die?
Why didst Thou meet the tempter's [power,
Why, Jesus, in Thy dying hour,
   Endure such agony?

2 To save us by Thy precious blood,
   To make us one in Thee,

That ours might be Thy perfect life,
Thy thorny crown, Thy cross, Thy strife,
   And ours the victory.

4 O make us worthy, gracious Lord,
   Of all Thy love to be;
To Thy blest will our wills incline,
That unto death we may be Thine,
   And ever live in Thee.

                               C. E. May (—), 1861.

HERMAS. 6. 5. D.   Miss FRANCES RIDLEY HAVERGAL (1836—1879), 1872.

1. Je-sus, I will trust Thee, Trust Thee with my soul; Guilt-y, lost, and help-less, Thou canst make me whole; There is none in heav-en Or on earth like Thee: Thou hast died for sin-ners; Therefore, Lord, for me.

256   *Trusting Jesus.*
      Ps. ix. 10.

2 Jesus, I may trust Thee,
   Name of matchless worth,
Spoken by the angel
   At Thy wondrous birth!

Written, and forever,
   On Thy cross of shame;
Sinners read and worship,
   Trusting in that Name.

3 Jesus, I must trust Thee,
  Pondering Thy ways,
  Full of love and mercy
  All Thine earthly days;
  Sinners gathered round Thee,
  Lepers sought Thy face,
  None too vile or loathsome
  For a Saviour's grace.
4 Jesus, I can trust Thee,
  Trust Thy written word,
  Though Thy voice of pity
  I have never heard:

When Thy Spirit teacheth,
  To my taste how sweet!
  Only may I hearken,
  Sitting at Thy feet.
5 Jesus, I do trust Thee,
  Trust without a doubt!
  Whosoever cometh,
  Thou wilt not cast out;
  Faithful is Thy promise,
  Precious is Thy blood;
  These my soul's salvation,
  Thou my Saviour God!
    Mrs. Mary Jane Walker (—   ), 1864.

ALL HALLOWS. C. M. 6 l. ARTHUR HENRY BROWN (1830—   ).

1. O Christ, what burdens bowed Thy head! Our load was laid on Thee;
Thou stood-est in the sin-ner's stead, Didst bear all ill for me:
A vic-tim led, Thy blood was shed; Now there's no load for me.

257 *In the Sinner's stead.*
  Is. liii. 5.

2 Death and the curse were in our cup;
    O Christ, 'twas full for Thee!
  But Thou hast drained the last dark drop;
    'Tis empty now for me!
  That bitter cup—Love drank it up;
    Now blessing's draught for me.
3 The tempest's awful voice was heard;
    O Christ, it broke on Thee!
  Thy open bosom was my ward;
    It braved the storm for me:
  Thy form was scarred, Thy visage marred;
    Now cloudless peace for me.

4 The Holy One did hide His face;
    O Christ, 'twas hid from Thee!
  Dumb darkness wrapt Thy soul a space;
    The darkness due to me:
  But now that face of radiant grace
    Shines forth in light on me.
5 For me, Lord Jesus, Thou hast died,
    And I have died in Thee!
  Thou'rt risen; my bands are all untied;
    And now Thou liv'st in me:
  When purified, made white, and tried,
    Thy glory then for me!
        Mrs. Anne Ross Cousin (—   ).

BRADEN. S. M. WILLIAM BATCHELDER BRADBURY (1816–1868), 1844.

1. I bless the Christ of God;
   I rest on love divine;
   And with unfalt'ring lip and heart,
   I call this Saviour mine.

258 "*I bless the Christ of God.*"

2 His cross dispels each doubt;
   I bury in His tomb
   Each thought of unbelief and fear,
   Each lingering shade of gloom.

3 I praise the God of grace;
   I trust His truth and might;
   He calls me His, I call Him mine,
   My God, my Joy, my Light.

4 'Tis He who saveth me,
   And freely pardon gives;
   I love because He loveth me,
   I live because He lives.

5 My life with Him is hid,
   My death has passed away,
   My clouds have melted into light,
   My midnight into day.

   Rev. Horatius Bonar (1808–   ), 1863. Ab.

SILVER STREET. S. M. ISAAC SMITH (1735–1800). 1770.

1. Grace, 'tis a charming sound,
   Harmonious to mine ear;
   Heav'n with the echo shall resound,
   And all the earth shall hear.

259 "*Saving Grace.*" Eph. ii. 5.

2 Grace first contrived a way
   To save rebellious man,
   And all the steps that grace display,
   Which drew the wondrous plan.

3 Grace taught my wandering feet
   To tread the heavenly road;
   And new supplies each hour I meet,
   While pressing on to God.

4 Grace all the work shall crown,
   Through everlasting days;
   It lays in Heaven the topmost stone,
   And well deserves the praise.

   Rev. Philip Doddridge (1702–1751), 1755.

260 "*The Song of Moses and the Lamb.*" Rev. xv. 3.

1 Awake, and sing the song
   Of Moses and the Lamb;
   Wake every heart and every tongue,
   To praise the Saviour's Name.

2 Sing of His dying love;
   Sing of His rising power;
   Sing how He intercedes above
   For those whose sins He bore.

3 Sing on your heavenly way,
   Ye ransomed sinners sing;
   Sing on, rejoicing every day
   In Christ th' eternal King.

4 Soon shall ye hear Him say,
   "Ye blessed children, come;"
   Soon will He call you hence away,
   And take His wanderers home.

5 There shall our raptured tongue
   His endless praise proclaim,
   And sweeter voices swell the song
   Of Moses and the Lamb.

   Rev. William Hammond (–1783), 1745. Ab. and alt.
   Rev. Martin Madan (1726–1790), 1760. First 4 vs.

LOVE TO CHRIST.

FERGUSON. S. M.
George Kingsley (1811–1884). 1843.

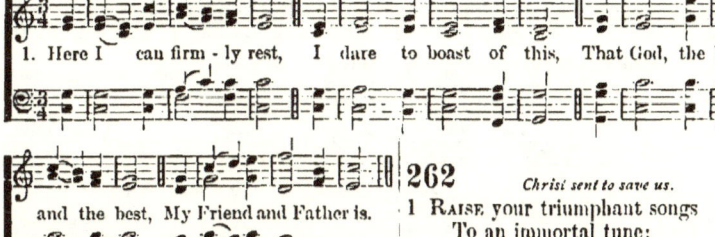

1. Here I can firm-ly rest, I dare to boast of this, That God, the high-est and the best, My Friend and Father is.

261 *"Ist Gott für mich so trete."*

2 He whispers in my breast
  Sweet words of holy cheer,
How he who seeks in God his rest
  Shall ever find Him near;

3 How God hath built above
  A city fair and new,
Where eye and heart shall see and prove
  What faith has counted true.

4 My heart for gladness springs,
  It cannot more be sad,
For very joy it laughs and sings,
  Sees naught but sunshine glad.

5 The Sun that glads my eyes
  Is Christ the Lord of love:
I sing for joy of that which lies
  Stored up for us above.

Rev. Paul Gerhardt (1606–1676), 1650.
Tr. by Miss Catherine Winkworth (1827–1878), 1855. Ab.

262 *Christ sent to save us.*

1 Raise your triumphant songs
  To an immortal tune;
Let the wide world resound the deeds
  Celestial grace has done.

2 Sing how Eternal Love
  Its chief belovèd chose,
And bade Him raise our wretched race
  From their abyss of woes.

3 'Twas mercy filled the throne,
  And wrath stood silent by,
When Christ was sent with pardons
  To rebels doomed to die.   [down

4 Now, sinners, dry your tears,
  Let hopeless sorrow cease;
Bow to the sceptre of His love,
  And take the offered peace.

5 Lord, we obey Thy call;
  We lay a humble claim
To the salvation Thou hast brought
  And love and praise Thy name.

Rev. Isaac Watts (1674–1748), 1709. Ab.

DAWN. S. M.
Rev. Edwin Pond Parker (1836–   ), 1871.

1. Je-sus, I live to Thee, The love-li-est and best; My life in Thee, Thy life in me, In Thy blest love I rest.

263 *"We are the Lord's."* Rom. xiv. 8.

2 Jesus, I die to Thee,
  Whenever death shall come;
To die in Thee is life to me,
  In my eternal home.

3 Whether to live or die,
  I know not which is best;
To live in Thee is bliss to me,
  To die is endless rest.

4 Living or dying, Lord,
  I ask but to be Thine;
My life in Thee, Thy life in me,
  Makes Heaven forever mine.

Rev. Henry Harbaugh (1818–1867), 1850.

GRACE MAGNIFIED.

NETTLETON. 8. 7. D. Rev. JOHN WYETH (1792—1858), 1812.

1. Come, Thou Fount of ev'ry blessing, Tune my heart to sing Thy grace; Teach me some melodious sonnet, Sung by flaming tongues above; Streams of mercy nev-er ceas-ing, Call for songs of loudest praise:
D. C.—Praise the mount I'm fix'd upon it; Mount of God's unchanging love.

264 *Grateful Recollection.*

2 Here I raise my Ebenezer,
　Hither by Thy help I'm come;
　And I hope, by Thy good pleasure,
　Safely to arrive at home:
　Jesus sought me, when a stranger,
　Wandering from the fold of God;
　He, to rescue me from danger,
　Interposed His precious blood.

3 O to grace how great a debtor,
　Daily I'm constrained to be;
　Let that grace now, like a fetter,
　Bind my wandering heart to Thee:
　Prone to wander, Lord, I feel it,
　Prone to leave the God I love;
　Here's my heart, O take and seal it,
　Seal it from Thy courts above.
　　　　Rev. Robert Robinson (1735—1790), 1757.

FABEN. 8. 7. D. JOHN HENRY WILLCOX (1827—1875), 1849.

1. Hail, my ev-er bless-ed Je-sus! On-ly Thee I wish to sing; To my soul Thy Name is precious, Thou my Prophet, Priest, and King: O, what mercy flows from Heaven, O what joy and hap-pi-ness! Love I much, I've much forgiven; I'm a mir-a-cle of grace.

265 *"I'm a Miracle of Grace."*

2 Once with Adam's race in ruin,
　Unconcerned in sin I lay,
　Swift destruction still pursuing,
　Till my Saviour passed that way.
　Witness, all ye host of Heaven,
　My Redeemer's tenderness.
　Love I much, I've much forgiven;
　I'm a miracle of grace!

3 Shout, ye bright, angelic choir,
　Praise the Lamb enthroned above,
　While, astonished, I admire
　God's free grace and boundless love.
　That blest moment I received Him
　Filled my soul with joy and peace.
　Love I much, I've much forgiven;
　I'm a miracle of grace.
　　　　John Wingrove (1720—1793), 1785.

THE JOY OF FAITH.

266 *Praise for pardoning Grace.* 8. 7. D.

1 Lord, with glowing heart I'd praise Thee
   For the bliss Thy love bestows,
For the pardoning grace that saves me,
   And the peace that from it flows.
Help, O God, my weak endeavor,
   This dull soul to rapture raise;
Thou must light the flame, or never
   Can my love be warmed to praise.

2 Praise, my soul, the God that sought thee,
   Wretched wanderer, far astray;
Found thee lost, and kindly brought thee
   From the paths of death away.
Praise, with love's devoutest feeling,
   Him who saw thy guilt-born fear,
And, the light of hope revealing,
   Bade the blood-stained cross appear.

3 Lord, this bosom's ardent feeling
   Vainly would my lips express;
Low before Thy footstool kneeling,
   Deign Thy suppliant's prayer to bless.
Let Thy grace, my soul's chief treasure,
   Love's pure flame within me raise;
And since words can never measure,
   Let my life show forth Thy praise.

   Francis Scott Key (1779—1843), 1857.

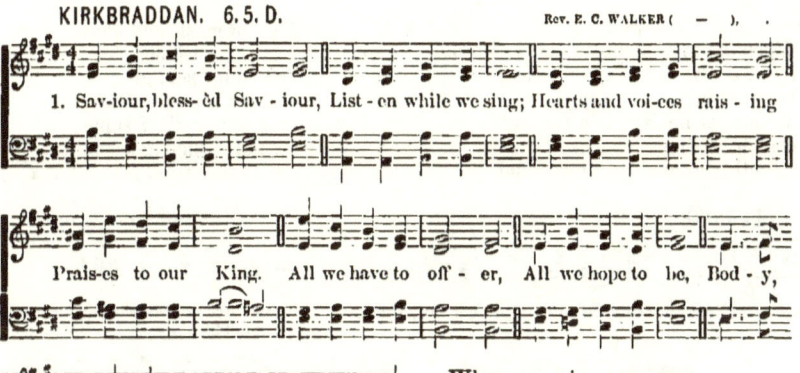

KIRKBRADDAN. 6. 5. D.   Rev. E. C. WALKER (—),

1. Sav-iour, bless-èd Sav-iour, List-en while we sing; Hearts and voi-ces rais-ing
Prais-es to our King. All we have to off-er, All we hope to be, Bod-y,
soul, and spir-it, All we yield to Thee.

267 *"Praises to our King."*

2 Nearer, ever nearer,
   Christ, we draw to Thee,
Deep in adoration
   Bending low the knee.
Thou, for our redemption,
   Cam'st on earth to die;
Thou, that we might follow,
   Hast gone up on high.

3 Great, and ever greater,
   Are Thy mercies here;
True and everlasting
   Are the glories there;
Where no pain nor sorrow,
   Toil nor care is known
Where the angel-legions
   Circle round Thy throne.

4 Onward, ever onward,
   Journeying o'er the road
Worn by saints before us,
   Journeying on to God;
Leaving all behind us,
   May we hasten on,
Backward never looking,
   Till the prize is won.

5 Higher then, and higher,
   Bear the ransomed soul,
Earthly toils forgotten,
   Saviour, to its goal;
Where, in joys unthought of,
   Saints with angels sing,
Never weary, raising
   Praises to their King.

   Rev. Godfrey Thring (1823—), 1862. Ab.

STELLA. L. M. 6 l.   From "Crown of Jesus."

1. { My hope is built on nothing less Than Jesus' blood and righteousness;
   { I dare not trust the sweetest frame, But wholly omit . . . . } lean on
Jesus' name. On Christ, the solid rock, I stand; All other ground is sinking sand.

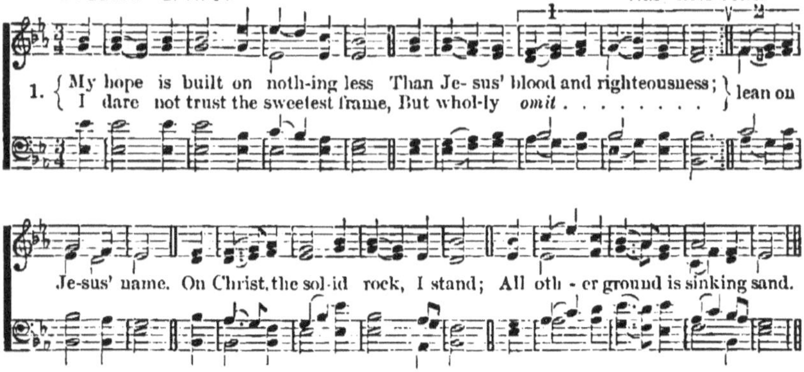

268 *The solid Rock.*

2 When darkness seems to vail His face,
I rest on His unchanging grace;
In every high and stormy gale,
My anchor holds within the vail:
On Christ, the solid rock, I stand;
All other ground is sinking sand.

3 His oath, His covenant, and blood,
Support me in the whelming flood:
When all around my soul gives way,
He then is all my hope and stay:
On Christ, the solid rock, I stand;
All other ground is sinking sand.

Rev. Edward Mote (—), 1865.

LEBANON. S. M. D.   JOHN ZUNDEL (1815—1882), 1855.

1. I was a wandering sheep, I did not love the fold; I did not love my Shepherd's voice,
D.S. I did not love my Father's voice,
I would not be controlled: I was a wayward child, I did not love my home,
I loved afar to roam.

269 *Lost but found.*

2 The Shepherd sought His sheep,
   The Father sought His child,
They followed me o'er vale and hill,
   O'er deserts waste and wild:
They found me nigh to death,
   Famished, and faint, and lone;
They bound me with the bands of love;
   They saved the wandering one.

3 Jesus my Shepherd is,
   'Twas He that loved my soul,
'Twas He that washed me in His blood,
   'Twas He that made me whole;
'Twas He that sought the lost,
   That found the wandering sheep,
'Twas He that brought me to the fold,
   'Tis He that still doth keep.

Rev. Horatius Bonar (1808—), 1844. Ab

FAITH IN CHRIST.

OLIVET. 6. 6. 4. 6. 6. 6. 4. LOWELL MASON (1792—1872), 1830.

1. My faith looks up to Thee, Thou Lamb of Cal-va-ry, Sav-iour di-vine:
{ Now hear me while I pray, } { Take all my guilt a-way, } O let me from this day Be whol-ly Thine.

270 *"My Faith looks up to Thee."*

2 May Thy rich grace impart
  Strength to my fainting heart,
    My zeal inspire;
  As Thou hast died for me,
  O may my love to Thee,
  Pure, warm, and changeless be,
    A living fire.

3 While life's dark maze I tread,
  And griefs around me spread,
    Be Thou my Guide;
  Bid darkness turn to day,
  Wipe sorrow's tears away,
  Nor let me ever stray,
    From Thee aside.

4 When ends life's transient dream,
  When death's cold, sullen stream
    Shall o'er me roll;
  Blest Saviour, then, in love,
  Fear and distrust remove;
  O bear me safe above;
    A ransomed soul.

Rev. Ray Palmer (1808—1887), 1830.

LYTE. 6. 6. 4. 6. 6. 6. 4. JOSEPH PERRY HOLBROOK (1822—   ).

1. Je-sus, Thy Name I love, All oth-er names a-bove, Je-sus, my Lord!
{ O Thou art all to me; } { Nothing to please I see, } Noth-ing a-part from Thee, Je-sus, my Lord!

271 *"Jesus, my Lord."*

2 When unto Thee I flee,
  Thou wilt my Refuge be,
    Jesus, my Lord!
  What need I now to fear?
  What earthly grief or care,
  Since Thou art ever near,
    Jesus, my Lord!

3 Soon Thou wilt come again:
  I shall be happy then,
    Jesus, my Lord!
  Then Thine own face I'll see,
  Then I shall like Thee be,
  Then evermore with Thee,
    Jesus, my Lord!

James George Deck (1802—   ), 1837. Ab.

GRACE MAGNIFIED.

MESSIAH. 7. D.

LOUIS JOSEPH FERDINAND HEROLD (1791—1833), 1830.
Arr. by GEORGE KINGSLEY (1811—1884), 1838.

1. Christ, of all my hopes the Ground, Christ, the Spring of all my joy, Still in Thee may I be found, (*Omit*) .... Still for Thee my pow'rs employ. Fountain of o'er-flow-ing grace, Free-ly from Thy ful-ness give; Till I close my earth-ly race, May I prove it, "Christ to live."

272 *"To live is Christ, and to die is Gain."*
Phil. i. 21.

2 When I touch the blessèd shore,
Back the closing waves shall roll:
Death's dark stream shall never more
Part from Thee my ravished soul.
Thus, O thus, an entrance give
To the land of cloudless sky;
Having known it, "Christ to live,"
Let me know it, "Gain to die."

3 Gain, to part from all my grief;
Gain, to bid my sins farewell;
Gain, of all my gains the chief,
Ever with the Lord to dwell:
This Thy people's portion, Lord,
Peace on earth, and bliss on high;
This their ever-sure reward,
"Christ to live, and gain to die."

Rev. Ralph Wardlaw (1779—1853), 1817.

SPANISH HYMN. 7. 6l.

Spanish Melody.

1. Blessèd Saviour, Thee I love, All my oth-er joys a-bove; All my hopes in Thee abide,
D.C.—Ev-er let my glo-ry be, On-ly, on-ly, on-ly Thee. Thou my hope, and naught beside;

273 *"Only Thee."*

2 Once again beside the cross,
All my gain I count but loss;
Earthly pleasures fade away;
Clouds they are that hide my day:
Hence, vain shadows, let me see
Jesus, crucified for me.

3 From beneath that thorny crown
Trickle drops of cleansing down;
Pardon from Thy piercèd hand
Now I take, while here I stand;
Only then I live to Thee,
When Thy wounded side I see.

4 Blessèd Saviour, Thine am I,
Thine to live, and Thine to die;
Height or depth, or earthly power,
Ne'er shall hide my Saviour more:
Ever shall my glory be,
Only, only, only Thee.

Rev. George Duffield (1818—1888), 1859.

TRUSTING IN CHRIST.

274 *Happy Trust.* 7. 6 l.

1 SAVIOUR, happy would I be,
 If I could but trust in Thee;
 Trust Thy wisdom me to guide;
 Trust Thy goodness to provide;
 Trust Thy saving love and power;
 Trust Thee every day and hour:

2 Trust Thee as the only light
 In the darkest hour of night;
 Trust in sickness, trust in health;
 Trust in poverty and wealth;
 Trust in joy, and trust in grief;
 Trust Thy promise for relief:

3 Trust Thy blood to cleanse my soul;
 Trust Thy grace to make me whole;
 Trust Thee living, dying, too;
 Trust Thee all my journey through;
 Trust Thee till my feet shall be
 Planted on the crystal sea.

 Rev. Edwin Henry Nevin (1814–), 1857.

275 *Numbered with God's Sons.* 7. 6 l.

1 BLESSED are the sons of God,
 They are bought with Jesus' blood;
 They are ransomed from the grave,
 Life eternal they shall have:
 With them numbered may we be,
 Here, and in eternity.

2 God did love them in His Son,
 Long before the world begun;
 All their sins are washed away;
 They shall stand in God's great day:
 With them numbered may we be,
 Here, and in eternity.

3 They are lights upon the earth,
 Children of a heavenly birth,
 One with God, with Jesus one;
 Glory is in them begun:
 With them numbered may we be,
 Here, and in eternity.

 Rev. Joseph Humphreys (1720–), 1743. Ab.

HENDON. 7. 5 l. Rev. CÆSAR HENRI ABRAHAM MALAN (1787–1861), 1828.

1. Ask ye what great thing I know That delights and stirs me so? What the high reward I win? Whose the name I glory in? Jesus Christ, the Crucified.

276 *"The Crucified."*

2 What is faith's foundation strong?
 What awakes my lips to song
 He who bore my sinful load,
 Purchased for me peace with God,
  Jesus Christ, the Crucified.

3 Who defeats my fiercest foes?
 Who consoles my saddest woes?
 Who revives my fainting heart,
 Healing all its hidden smart?
  Jesus Christ, the Crucified.

4 Who is Life in life to me?
 Who the Death of death will be?
 Who will place me on His right
 With the countless hosts of light?
  Jesus Christ, the Crucified.

5 This is that great thing I know;
 This delights and stirs me so:
 Faith in Him who died to save,
 Him who triumphed o'er the grave,
  Jesus Christ, the Crucified.

 Rev. Benjamin Hall Kennedy (1804–), 1863.

GRACE MAGNIFIED.

ARIEL. C. P. M.
Arr. from MOZART by LOWELL MASON (1792–1872), 1836.

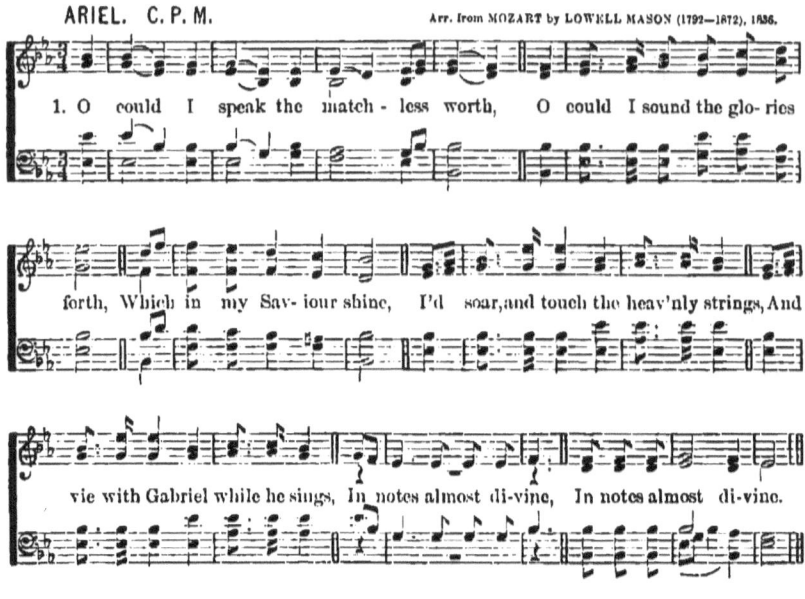

1. O could I speak the matchless worth, O could I sound the glories forth, Which in my Saviour shine, I'd soar, and touch the heav'nly strings, And vie with Gabriel while he sings, In notes almost divine, In notes almost divine.

277   *"The Matchless Worth."*
Ps. lxvi. 2.

2 I'd sing the precious blood He spilt,
My ransom from the dreadful guilt
Of sin, and wrath divine;
I'd sing His glorious righteousness,
In which all-perfect, heavenly dress
My soul shall ever shine.

3 I'd sing the characters He bears,
And all the forms of love He wears,
Exalted on His throne;
In loftiest songs of sweetest praise,
I would to everlasting days
Make all His glories known.

4 Well, the delightful days will come
When my dear Lord will bring me home,
And I shall see His face;
Then with my Saviour, Brother, Friend,
A blest eternity I'll spend,
Triumphant in His grace.

Rev. Samuel Medley (1738–1799), 1789. Ab.

BREMEN. C. P. M.
THOMAS HASTINGS (1784–1872), 1836.

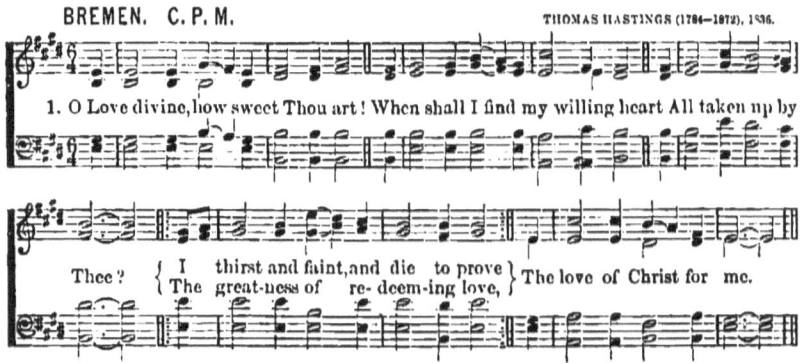

1. O Love divine, how sweet Thou art! When shall I find my willing heart All taken up by Thee? { I thirst and faint, and die to prove } The love of Christ for me. { The greatness of redeeming love, }

THE OLD, OLD STORY.

278   *"Love Divine."*

2 God only knows the love of God;
   O that it now were shed abroad
   In this poor, stony heart!
   For love I sigh, for love I pine:
   This only portion, Lord, be mine,
     Be mine this better part.

3 O that I could forever sit
   With Mary at the Master's feet!
   Be this my happy choice,
   My only care, delight and bliss,
   My joy, my heaven on earth, be this,
     To hear the Bridegroom's voice.
        Rev. Charles Wesley (1708—1788), 1749. Ab.

TELL THE STORY. 7, 6, D.   WILLIAM GUSTAVUS FISCHER (1835—), 1869.

1. I love to tell the story, Of unseen things above, Of Jesus and His glory, Of Jesus and His love. I love to tell the story, Because I know 'tis true; It satisfies my longings, As nothing else can do.

CHORUS.
I love to tell the story, 'Twill be my theme in glory, To tell the old, old story Of Jesus and His love.

279   *"I love to tell the Story."*

2 I love to tell the story;
   More wonderful it seems,
   Than all the golden fancies
     Of all our golden dreams.
   I love to tell the story,
     It did so much for me!
   And that is just the reason
     I tell it now to thee.

3 I love to tell the story;
   'Tis pleasant to repeat,
   What seems, each time I tell it,
     More wonderfully sweet.
   I love to tell the story,
     For some have never heard
   The message of salvation,
     From God's own holy word.

4 I love to tell the story;
   For those who know it best,
   Seem hungering and thirsting
     To hear it like the rest.
   And when, in scenes of glory,
     I sing the New, New song,
   'Twill be the Old, Old story
     That I have loved so long.
        Miss Kate Hankey (—), 1865.

VALENTIA. C. M. TRAUGOTT MAXIMILIAN EBERWEIN (1775—1831), Arr. by GEORGE KINGSLEY (1811—1884), 1853.

1. O gift of gifts! O grace of faith! My God, how can it be
That Thou, who hast dis-cern-ing love, Shouldst give that gift to me?

280 *Converting Grace.*

2 How many hearts Thou mightst have had
More innocent than mine,
How many souls more worthy far
Of that sweet touch of Thine!

3 Ah, grace, into unlikeliest hearts
It is thy boast to come,
The glory of thy light to find
In darkest spots a home.

4 O happy, happy that I am!
If thou canst be, O faith,
The treasure that thou art in life,
What wilt thou be in death?
Rev. Frederick William Faber (1814—1863), 1848. Ab.

281 *"Jesu, Rex admirabilis."*

1 O JESUS, King most wonderful,
Thou Conqueror renowned,
Thou Sweetness most ineffable,
In whom all joys are found:

2 When once Thou visitest the heart,
Then truth begins to shine,
Then earthly vanities depart,
Then kindles love divine.

3 O Jesus, Light of all below,
Thou Fount of life and fire,
Surpassing all the joys we know,
And all we can desire:

4 May every heart confess Thy Name,
And ever Thee adore;
And, seeking Thee, itself inflame
To seek Thee more and more.

5 Thee may our tongues forever bless;
Thee may we love alone;
And ever in our lives express
The image of Thine own.
Bernard of Clairvaux (1091—1153), 1140.
Tr. by Rev. Edward Caswall (1814—1878), 1849. Sl. alt.

282 *Converting Grace commemorated.*

1 O FOR a thousand tongues to sing
My dear Redeemer's praise;
The glories of my God and King,
The triumphs of His grace.

2 My gracious Master and my God,
Assist me to proclaim,
To spread, through all the earth abroad,
The honors of Thy Name.

3 Jesus, the Name that charms our fears,
That bids our sorrows cease;
'Tis music in the sinner's ears,
'Tis life, and health, and peace.

4 He breaks the power of cancelled sin,
He sets the prisoners free;
His blood can make the foulest clean,
His blood availed for me.
Rev. Charles Wesley (1708—1788), 1740. Ab.

DEDHAM. C. M. WILLIAM GARDINER (1770—1853), 1822.

CHRIST PRAISED.

GEER. C. M. — HENRY WELLINGTON GREATOREX (1811–1858), 1849.

1. Jesus, these eyes have nev-er seen That ra-diant form of Thine;
The veil of sense hangs dark be-tween Thy bless-ed face and mine.

283 *Unseen, but loved.*
1 Pet. i. 8.

2 I see Thee not, I hear Thee not,
   Yet art Thou oft with me;
And earth had ne'er so dear a spot,
   As where I meet with Thee.

3 Yet though I have not seen, and still
   Must rest in faith alone,
I love Thee, dearest Lord,—and will,
   Unseen, but not unknown.

4 When death these mortal eyes shall seal,
   And still this throbbing heart,
The rending veil shall Thee reveal,
   All-glorious as Thou art.
      Rev. Ray Palmer (1808—1887), 1858. Ab.

284 *"Amazing Grace."*

1 Amazing grace, how sweet the sound
   That saved a wretch like me!
I once was lost, but now am found,
   Was blind, but now I see.

2 'Twas grace that taught my heart to fear,
   And grace my fears relieved;
How precious did that grace appear
   The hour I first believed!

3 Through many dangers, toils, and snares,
   I have already come;
'Tis grace has brought me safe thus far,
   And grace will lead me home.

4 The Lord has promised good to me,
   His word my hope secures;
He will my Shield and Portion be,
   As long as life endures.
      Rev. John Newton (1725—1807), 1779. Ab.

285 *Christ our Strength and Righteousness.*
Ps. lxxi.

1 My Saviour, my Almighty Friend,
   When I begin Thy praise,
Where will the growing numbers end,
   The numbers of Thy grace?

2 Thou art my everlasting trust,
   Thy goodness I adore;
And since I knew Thy graces first,
   I speak Thy glories more.

3 My feet shall travel all the length
   Of the celestial road,
And march with courage in Thy strength
   To see my Father, God.
      Rev. Isaac Watts (1674—1748), 1719. Ab.

286 *Fear disarmed.*

1 The Saviour! O what endless charms
   Dwell in the blissful sound!
Its influence every fear disarms,
   And spreads sweet comfort round.

2 The almighty Former of the skies
   Stooped to our vile abode;
While angels viewed with wondering eyes,
   And hailed the incarnate God.

3 O the rich depths of love divine,
   Of bliss a boundless store!
Dear Saviour, let me call Thee mine;
   I cannot wish for more.

4 On Thee alone my hope relies,
   Beneath Thy cross I fall,
My Lord, my Life, my Sacrifice,
   My Saviour, and my All.
      Miss Anne Steele (1717—1778), 1760. Ab.

GRACE MAGNIFIED.

HOLY TRINITY. C. M. — JOSEPH BARNBY (1838—).

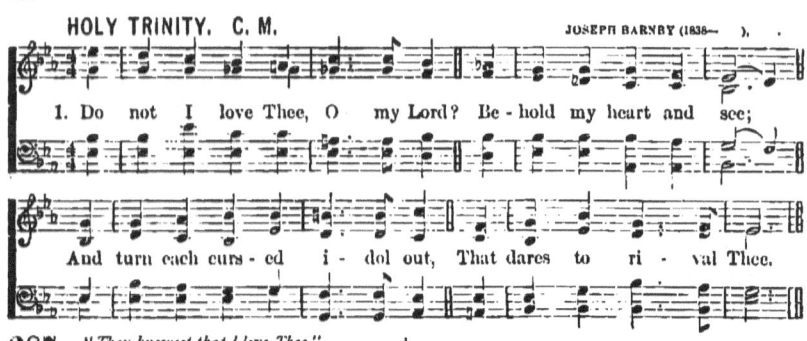

1. Do not I love Thee, O my Lord? Behold my heart and see;
And turn each cursed idol out, That dares to rival Thee.

287 *"Thou knowest that I love Thee."*
John xxi. 15.

2 Do not I love Thee from my soul?
Then let me nothing love;
Dead be my heart to every joy,
When Jesus cannot move.

3 Is not Thy Name melodious still
To mine attentive ear?
Doth not each pulse with pleasure bound
My Saviour's voice to hear?

4 Thou know'st I love Thee, dearest Lord,
But O, I long to soar
Far from the sphere of mortal joys,
And learn to love Thee more.
   Rev. Philip Doddridge (1702—1751), 1755. Ab.

288 *Christ precious.*
1 Pet. ii. 7.

1 Jesus, I love Thy charming Name,
'Tis music to mine ear;
Fain would I sound it out so loud
That earth and Heaven should hear.

2 All my capacious powers can wish
In Thee doth richly meet;
Not to mine eyes is light so dear,
Nor friendship half so sweet.

3 Thy grace still dwells upon my heart,
And sheds its fragrance there;
The noblest balm of all its wounds,
The cordial of its care.

4 I'll speak the honors of Thy Name
With my last laboring breath;
Then, speechless, clasp Thee in mine arms,
The Conqueror of death.
   Rev. Philip Doddridge, 1755. Ab.

ST. AGNES. C. M. — Rev. JOHN BACCHUS DYKES (1823—1876), 1858.

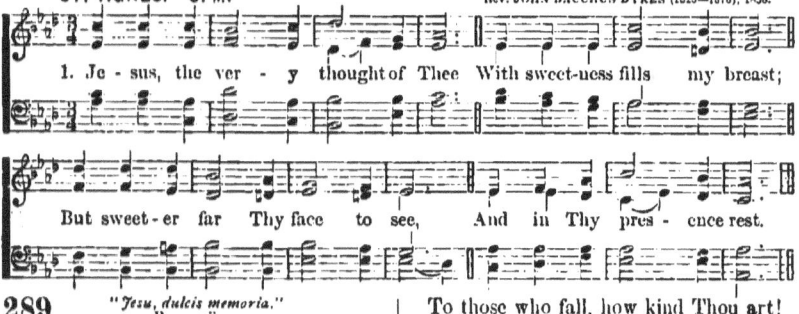

1. Jesus, the very thought of Thee With sweetness fills my breast;
But sweeter far Thy face to see, And in Thy presence rest.

289 *"Jesu, dulcis memoria."*
Rev. xxii. 4.

2 Nor voice can sing, nor heart can frame,
Nor can the memory find
A sweeter sound than Thy blest Name,
O Saviour of mankind!

3 O Hope of every contrite heart,
O Joy of all the meek,
To those who fall, how kind Thou art!
How good to those who seek!

4 Jesus, our only Joy be Thou,
As Thou our Prize wilt be;
Jesus, be Thou our Glory now,
And through eternity.
   Bernard of Clairvaux (1091—1153), 1140.
   Tr. by Rev. Edward Caswall (1814—1878), 1849.

LOVE AND PRAISE.

LOVING-KINDNESS. L. M.   American Melody. 1830.

1. A-wake, my soul, in joy-ful lays, And sing thy great Re-deem-er's praise;
He just-ly claims a song from me, His lov-ing-kind-ness is so free,
Lov-ing-kindness, lov-ing-kindness, His lov-ing-kind-ness is so free.

290 *"The Loving-kindness of the Lord."*
Is. lxiii. 7.

2 He saw me ruined in the fall,
Yet loved me notwithstanding all,
And saved me from my lost estate,
His loving-kindness is so great.

3 Through mighty hosts of cruel foes,
Where earth and hell my way oppose,
He safely leads my soul along,
His loving-kindness is so strong.

Rev. Samuel Medley (1738—1799), 1787. **Ab.**

SONG. 8. 8. 8. 5.   German Melody; Adams' Church Pastorals. 1904.

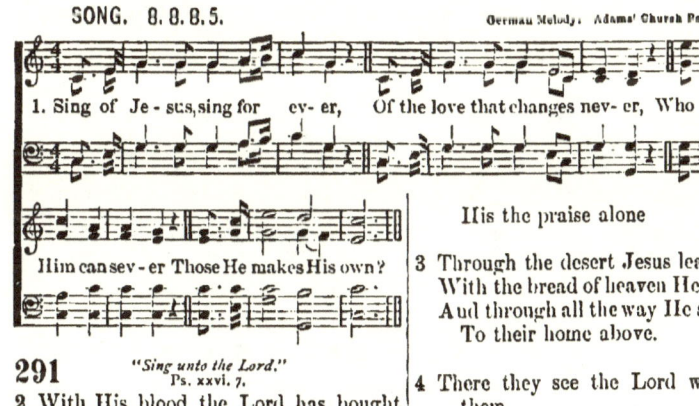

1. Sing of Je-sus, sing for ev-er, Of the love that changes nev-er, Who or what from Him can sev-er Those He makes His own?

His the praise alone

291 *"Sing unto the Lord."*
Ps. xxvi. 7.

2 With His blood the Lord has bought them;   [them,
When they knew Him not, He sought
And from all their wanderings brought them;

3 Through the desert Jesus leads them,
With the bread of heaven He feeds them,
And through all the way He speeds them
To their home above.

4 There they see the Lord who bought them,   [them,
Him who came from Heaven, and sought
Him who by His Spirit taught them,
Him they serve and love.

Rev. Thomas Kelly (1769—1855), 1815. **Ab.**

SELF-SURRENDER. P. M.
Anonymous

1. I left it all with Jesus long ago, All my sins I brought Him, and my woe; When by faith I saw Him on the tree, Heard His small, still whisper, "Tis for thee," From my heart the burden rolled away! Happy day! From my heart the burden rolled away! Happy day!

292 *Leaving all with Jesus.*
1 Pet. v. 7.

2 I leave it all with Jesus, for He knows
How to steal the bitter from life's woes;
How to gild the tear-drop with His smile,
Make the desert garden bloom awhile:
When my weakness leaneth on His might
    All seems light.

3 I leave it all with Jesus, day by day;
Faith can firmly trust Him, come what
    may: [her rest
Hope has dropped her anchor, found
In the calm, sure haven of His breast:
Love esteems it Heaven to abide
    At His side.

4 O leave it all with Jesus, drooping soul!
Tell not half thy story, but the whole.
Worlds on worlds are hanging on His
    hand,   [mand;
Life and death are waiting His com-
Yet His tender bosom makes thee room—
    O come home.
        Miss Ellen H. Willis (—),

MANCHESTER. C. M.
ROBERT WAINWRIGHT (1747–1782), c. 1774.

1. How sweet the Name of Jesus sounds In a believer's ear; It soothes his sorrows, heals his wounds, And drives away his fear.

293
The sweet Name.

2 It makes the wounded spirit whole,
    And calms the troubled breast;
  'Tis manna to the hungry soul,
    And to the weary rest.

3 By Thee my prayers acceptance gain,
    Although with sin defiled;
  Satan accuses me in vain,
    And I am owned a child.

4 Weak is the effort of my heart,
    And cold my warmest thought;
  But when I see Thee as Thou art,
    I'll praise Thee as I ought.
Rev. John Newton (1725—1807), 1779.

294
Singing for Joy.   **C. M.**

1 I've found the pearl of greatest price,
  My heart doth sing for joy;
And sing I must; for Christ is mine,
  Christ shall my song employ.

2 Christ is my Prophet, Priest, and King;
  A Prophet full of light,
My great High-Priest before the throne,
  My King of heavenly might.

3 For He indeed is Lord of lords,
  And He the King of kings;
He is the Sun of righteousness,
  With healing in His wings.

4 Christ is my peace; He died for me,
  For me He gave His blood;
And as my wondrous Sacrifice,
  Offered Himself to God.

5 Christ Jesus is my All in all,
  My Comfort and my Love,
My Life below, and He shall be
  My Joy and Crown above.
Rev. John Mason (1634—1694), 1683. Ab. and alt.

AMOR CHRISTI. 10, 10, 10, 10, 4.   A. CROIL FALCONER (1850—), 1886.

1. It passeth knowledge, that dear love of Thine, My Saviour, Jesus! yet this soul of mine Would of Thy love, in all its breadth and length, Its height and depth, its everlasting strength, Know more and more.

295
Love, passing Knowledge.
    Eph. iii. 19.

2 It passeth telling, that dear love of Thine,
My Saviour, Jesus! yet these lips of mine
  Would fain proclaim to sinners, far and
    near,
  A love which can remove all guilty fear,
    And love beget.

3 But though I cannot sing or tell or know
The fulness of Thy love, while here
  below,
My empty vessel I may freely bring;
O Thou who art of love the living spring,
  My vessel fill.

4 O, fill me, Jesus, Saviour, with Thy love!
Lead, lead me to the living fount above!
  Thither may I, in simple faith, draw
    nigh,
  And never to another fountain fly,
    But unto Thee.
Miss Mary Shekleton (—). . Ab.

AUTUMN. 8.7. D. — Spanish Melody.

1. Gen-tly, Lord, O gen-tly lead us, Pil-grims in this vale of tears,
Through the tri-als yet de-creed us, Till our last great change ap-pears.
D.S.—Let Thy good-ness nev-er fail us, Lead us in Thy per-fect way.
When temp-ta-tion's darts as-sail us, When in de-vious paths we stray.

296   *"Gently, Lord."*

2 In the hour of pain and anguish,
In the hour when death draws near,
Suffer not our hearts to languish,
Suffer not our souls to fear;
And, when mortal life is ended,
Bid us in Thine arms to rest,
Till, by angel bands attended,
We awake among the blest.

Thomas Hastings (1784—1872), 1830, 1850, 1859.

SEGUR. 8.7.4. — JOSEPH PERRY HOLBROOK (1822—), 1862.

1. Guide me, O Thou great Je-ho-vah, Pilgrim through this bar-ren land;
I am weak, But Thou art mighty; (*Omit*). . . . .
Hold me with Thy pow'r-ful hand; Bread of Heav-en, Bread of Heav-en,
Feed me till I want no more.

297   *Prayer for Guidance.*

2 Open now the crystal fountain,
Whence the healing stream doth flow;
Let the fire and cloudy pillar
Lead me all my journey through:
Strong Deliverer,
Be Thou still my strength and shield.

3 When I tread the verge of Jordan,
  Bid my anxious fears subside;
  Death of deaths, and hell's destruction,
  Land me safe on Canaan's side:

Songs of praises,
I will ever give to Thee.
  Rev. Peter Williams (1719—1796), 1771. v. 1.
  Rev. William Williams (1717—1791), 1773. Ab.

STRACATHRO. C. M.
Rev. CHARLES HUTCHISON (1792—1856), c. 1815.

1. O God of Beth-el, by whose hand Thy peo-ple still are fed;
Who through this wea-ry pil-grim-age Hast all our fa-ther's led;

298 *Jacob's Vow.*
Gen. xxviii. 20—22.

2 Our vows, our prayers, we now present
  Before Thy throne of grace:
  God of our fathers, be the God
  Of their succeeding race.

3 Through each perplexing path of life
  Our wandering footsteps guide;

Give us each day our daily bread,
  And raiment fit provide.

4 O spread Thy covering wings around,
  Till all our wanderings cease,
  And, at our Father's loved abode,
  Our souls arrive in peace.
  Rev. Philip Doddridge (1702—1751), 1737.
  Michael Bruce (1746—1767), 1781. Alt.

ASAPH. L. M.
FELIX MENDELSSOHN-BARTHOLDY (1805—1847).

1. O Thou, to whose all-search-ing sight The dark-ness shin-eth as the light,
Search, prove my heart, it pants for Thee; O burst these bonds and set it free.

299 *"Seelenbräutigam, o Du Gottes-Lamm."*

2 Wash out its stains, refine its dross;
  Nail my affections to the cross;
  Hallow each thought; let all within
  Be clean, as Thou, my Lord, art clean.

3 If in this darksome wild I stray,
  Be Thou my Light, be Thou my Way;
  No foes, no violence I fear,
  No fraud, while Thou, my God, art near.

4 When rising floods my soul o'erflow,
  When sinks my heart in waves of woe,
  Jesus, Thy timely aid impart,
  And raise my head, and cheer my heart.

5 Saviour, where'er Thy steps I see,
  Dauntless, untired, I follow Thee;
  O let Thy hand support me still,
  And lead me to Thy holy hill.
  Gerhard Tersteegen (1697—1769).
  Tr. by Rev. John Wesley (1703—1791), 1738. Ab.

PILGRIMAGE.

NUREMBURG. 7. JOHANN RUDOLPH AHLE (1625—1673), 1664.

1. Chil-dren of the heav'n-ly King, As ye jour-ney, sweet-ly sing; Sing your Sav-iour's worth-y praise, Glo-rious in His works and ways.

300 *"Travelling Home."*

2 We are travelling home to God,
  In the way the fathers trod:
  They are happy now, and we
  Soon their happiness shall see.

3 Shout, ye little flock, and blest,
  You on Jesus' throne shall rest;
  There your seat is now prepared,
  There your kingdom and reward.

4 Fear not, brethren, joyful stand
  On the borders of your land;
  Jesus Christ, your Father's Son,
  Bids you undismayed go on.

5 Lord, obediently we go,
  Gladly leaving all below;
  Only Thou our Leader be,
  And we still will follow Thee.

  Rev. John Cennick (1717—1755), 1742. Ab.

301 *"Redeeming Love."*

1 Now begin the heavenly theme,
  Sing aloud in Jesus' name;
  Ye who Jesus' kindness prove,
  Triumph in redeeming love.

2 Ye who see the Father's grace
  Beaming in the Saviour's face,
  As to Canaan on ye move,
  Praise and bless redeeming love.

3 Mourning souls, dry up your tears;
  Banish all your guilty fears;
  See your guilt and curse remove,
  Cancelled by redeeming love.

5 Hither, then, your music bring,
  Strike aloud each joyful string;
  Mortals, join the host above,
  Join to praise redeeming love.

  John Langford (— —), 1767. Ab.

BADEA. S. M. German Melody.

1. Your harps, ye trembling saints, Down from the willows take; Loud to the praise of love di-vine Bid ev-'ry string a-wake.

302 *Weak Believers encouraged.*

2 Though in a foreign land,
    We are not far from home;
  And nearer to our house above
    We every moment come.

3 His grace will to the end
    Stronger and brighter shine;
  Nor present things, nor things to come,
    Shall quench the spark divine.

4 Blest is the man, O God,
    That stays himself on Thee;
  Who wait for Thy salvation, Lord,
    Shall Thy salvation see.

Rev. Augustus Montague Toplady (1740—1778), 1772. Ab.

303
"Sweet is Thy Mercy."
Ps. cix. 20.   S. M.

1 Sweet is Thy mercy, Lord;
    Before Thy mercy-seat
   My soul, adoring, pleads Thy word,
    And owns Thy mercy sweet.

2 My need, and Thy desires,
    Are all in Christ complete;
   Thou hast the justice truth requires,
    And I Thy mercy sweet.

3 Light Thou my weary way,
    Place Thou my weary feet,
   That while I stray on earth I may
    Still find Thy mercy sweet.

4 Thus shall the heavenly host
    Hear all my songs repeat
   To Father, Son, and Holy Ghost,
    My joy, Thy mercy sweet.

Rev. John Samuel Bewley Monsell (1811—1875), 1862.

AMSTERDAM. 7. 6. D.

German Choral. Author unknown.
Attributed to JAMES NARES (1715—1783), 1778.

1. { Rise, my soul, and stretch thy wings, Thy better portion trace; }
   { Rise from transitory things Towards Heav'n, thy native place: }
   Sun and moon and stars decay; Time shall soon this earth remove;
   Rise, my soul, and haste away To seats prepar'd above.

304
"Rise, my Soul."

2 Rivers to the ocean run,
    Nor stay in all their course;
   Fire, ascending, seeks the sun;
    Both speed them to their source:
   So a soul, that's born of God,
    Pants to view His glorious face,
   Upward tends to His abode,
    To rest in His embrace

3 Cease, ye pilgrims, cease to mourn,
    Press onward to the prize;
   Soon our Saviour will return
    Triumphant in the skies:
   Yet a season, and you know
    Happy entrance will be given,
   All our sorrows left below,
    And earth exchanged for Heaven.

Rev. Robert Seagrave (1693—   ), 1742. Ab.

305
"Time is winging us away."

1 Time is winging us away
    To our eternal home;
   Life is but a winter's day,
    A journey to the tomb;
   Youth and vigor soon will flee,
    Blooming beauty lose its charms;
   All that's mortal soon shall be
    Enclosed in death's cold arms.

2 Time is winging us away
    To our eternal home;
   Life is but a winter's day,
    A journey to the tomb;
   But the Christian shall enjoy
    Health and beauty soon, above,
   Far beyond the world's annoy,
    Secure in Jesus' love.

John Burton (1773—1822), 1815.

PILGRIMAGE.

LUX BENIGNA. 10, 4, 10, 10.   Rev. JOHN BACCHUS DYKES (1823–1876), 1861.

1. Lead, kindly Light, amid th' encircling gloom, Lead Thou me on; The night is dark, and I am far from home, Lead Thou me on; Keep Thou my feet; I do not ask to see The dis-tant scene, one step e-nough for me.

306   *"Lead Thou me on."*

2 I was not ever thus, nor prayed that Thou
    Shouldst lead me on;
  I loved to choose and see my path; but now
    Lead Thou me on!
  I loved the garish day, and, spite of fears,
  Pride ruled my will. Remember not past
    years!

3 So long Thy Power has blest me, sure it still
    Will lead me on
  O'er moor and fen, o'er crag and torrent, till
    The night is gone,
  And with the morn those angel faces smile
  Which I have loved long since, and lost
    awhile!
        Rev. John Henry Newman (1801–   ), 1833.

PRINCETON. P. M.   Arr. from FELIX MENDELSSOHN-BARTHOLDY (1809–1847).

1. He leadeth me, O blessèd thought, O words with heav'nly comfort fraught, What e'er I do, where e'er I be, Still 'tis God's hand that leadeth me, He leadeth me, He leadeth me, He leadeth me.

307   *"He leadeth Me."*

2 Sometimes 'mid scenes of deepest gloom,
  Sometimes where Eden's bowers bloom,
  By waters still, o'er troubled sea,
  Still 'tis His hand that leadeth me.—REF.

3 Lord, I would clasp Thy hand in mine,
  Nor ever murmur nor repine;
  Content, whatever lot I see,
  Since 'tis my God that leadeth me.—REF.

4 And when my task on earth is done,
  When, by Thy grace, the victory's won,
  E'en death's cold wave I will not flee,
  Since God thro' Jordan leadeth me.—REF.
        Rev. Joseph H. Gilmore (–   ), 1859.

PILGRIMAGE.

CLINTON. C. M. — JOSEPH PERRY HOLBROOK (1822—).

1. When I can read my ti-tle clear To mansions in the skies, I bid farewell to ev'ry fear, And wipe my weeping eyes.

308 *Heavenly Hope.*

2 Should earth against my soul engage,
And hellish darts be hurled,
Then I can smile at Satan's rage,
And face a frowning world.

3 Let cares like a wild deluge come,
And storms of sorrow fall;
May I but safely reach my home,
My God, my Heaven, my All.

4 There shall I bathe my weary soul
In seas of heavenly rest,
And not a wave of trouble roll
Across my peaceful breast.
   —Rev. Isaac Watts (1674—1748), 1709.

LANGRAN. 10. — JAMES LANGRAN (1835—). 1863.

1. My feet are worn and weary with the march O'er the rough road and up the steep hill-side,
O Cit-y of our God, I fain would see Thy pastures green, where peaceful waters glide.

309 *"Worn and Weary."*

2 My garments, travel-worn and stained with dust,
Oft rent by briers and thorns that crowd my way,
Would fain be made, O Lord, my Righteousness,
Spotless and white in Heaven's unclouded ray.

3 My heart is weary of its own deep sin:
Sinning, repenting, sinning still again;
When shall my soul Thy glorious presence feel,
And find, dear Saviour, it is free from stain;

4 Patience, poor soul! the Saviour's feet were worn,
The Saviour's heart and hands were weary, too;
His garments stained and travel-worn, and old,
His vision blinded with a pitying dew.

5 Love thou the path of sorrow that He trod;
Toil on, and wait in patience for thy rest;
O City of our God, we soon shall see
Thy jasper walls, home of the loved and blest.
   —Mrs. Sarah Roberts Boyle (1812—1869), 1853.

PILGRIMAGE AND WARFARE.

ST. EDMUND. 6, 4, 6, 4, 6, 6, 6, 4.   ARTHUR SULLIVAN (1842–), 1872.

1. I'm but a stranger here, Heav'n is my home; Earth is a desert drear, Heav'n is my home; Danger and sorrow stand Round me on ev'ry hand; Heav'n is my fatherland, Heav'n is my home.

310   *"Heaven is my home."* Heb. xi. 16.

2 What though the tempest rage,
   Heaven is my home;
Short is my pilgrimage,
   Heaven is my home;
Time's wild and wintry blast
Soon will be overpast;
I shall reach home at last,
   Heaven is my home.

3 There at my Saviour's side—
   Heaven is my home—
I shall be glorified,
   Heaven is my home;
There are the good and blest,
Those I loved most and best,
And there I too shall rest;
   Heaven is my home.

Thomas Rawson Taylor (1807–1836), 1835. Ab.

LABAN. S. M.   LOWELL MASON (1792–1872), 1830.

1. My soul, be on thy guard; Ten thousand foes arise, And hosts of sin are

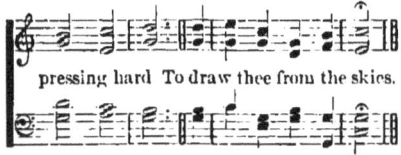

pressing hard To draw thee from the skies.

4 Fight on, my soul, till death
   Shall bring thee to thy God;
He'll take thee, at thy parting breath,
   To His divine abode.

George Heath (—), 1781.

311   *"Be on thy Guard."*

2 O watch, and fight, and pray,
   The battle ne'er give o'er;
Renew it boldly every day,
   And help divine implore.

3 Ne'er think the victory won,
   Nor once at ease sit down;
Thine arduous work will not be done
   Till thou receive thy crown.

312   *"Keep the Charge of the Lord."* Lev. viii. 35.

1 A CHARGE to keep I have
   A God to glorify,
A never-dying soul to save,
   And fit it for the sky;

2 To serve the present age,
   My calling to fulfil:
O may it all my powers engage
   To do my Master's will.

3 Arm me with jealous care,
   As in Thy sight to live,
   And O Thy servant, Lord, prepare
   A strict account to give.

4 Help me to watch and pray,
   And on Thyself rely,
   Assured, if I my trust betray,
   I shall for ever die.
            Rev. Charles Wesley (1708—1788), 1762.

313 *"Weigh not thy Life."*

1 My soul, weigh not thy life
   Against thy heavenly crown,
   Nor suffer Satan's deadliest strife
   To beat thy courage down.

2 With prayer and crying strong,
   Maintain the fearful fight,
   And let the breaking day prolong
   The wrestling of the night.

3 The battle soon will yield,
   If thou thy part fulfil;
   For strong as is the hostile shield,
   Thy sword is stronger still.

4 Thine armor is divine,
   Thy feet with victory shod;
   And on thy head shall quickly shine
   The diadem of God.
            Rev. Leonard Swain (1821—1869), 1858. Sl. alt.

314 *Marching on.*

1 Rejoice, ye pure in heart,
   Rejoice, give thanks and sing;
   Your festal banner wave on high,
   The cross of Christ your King.

2 Still lift your standard high,
   Still march in firm array,
   As warriors through the darkness toil,
   Till dawns the golden day.

3 At last the march shall end,
   The wearied ones shall rest,
   The pilgrims find the Father's house,
   Jerusalem the blest.

4 Then on, ye pure in heart;
   Rejoice, give thanks, and sing;
   Your festal banner wave on high,
   The cross of Christ your King.
            Rev. Edward Hayes Plumptre (1821—   ),   Ab.

315 *Cross and Crown.*

1 O what, if we are Christ's,
   Is earthly shame or loss?
   Bright shall the crown of glory be,
   When we have borne the cross.

2 Keen was the trial once,
   Bitter the cup of woe,
   When martyred saints, baptized in blood,
   Christ's sufferings shared below.

3 Bright is their glory now,
   Boundless their joy above,
   Where, on the bosom of their God,
   They rest in perfect love.

4 Lord, may that grace be ours,
   Like them in faith to bear
   All that of sorrow, grief, or pain
   May be our portion here.
            Rev. Sir Henry Williams Baker (1821—1877), 1852. Ab.

316 *Phil. ii. 12. 13.*

1 Heirs of unending life,
   While yet we sojourn here,
   O let us our salvation work
   With trembling and with fear.

2 God will support our hearts
   With might before unknown;
   The work to performed is ours,
   The strength is all His own.

3 Assisted by His grace,
   We still pursue our way;
   And hope at last to reach the prize,
   Secure in endless day.

4 'Tis He that works to will,
   'Tis He that works to do;
   His is the power by which we act,
   His be the glory too.
            Rev. Benjamin Beddome (1717—1795),   Ab. and alt.

GLORY. S. M.   Rev. RALPH HARRISON (1748—1810), 1786.

WEBB. 7. 6. D. GEORGE JAMES WEBB (1803–1887), 1830.

1. Go forward, Christian soldier, Beneath His banner true: The Lord himself, thy Leader,
D.S.—He can, with bread of Heaven.

Shall all thy foes subdue. His love foretells thy tri-als, He knows thine hourly need;
Thy fainting spir-it feed.

317 *"Go forward, Christian Soldier"*

2 Go forward, Christian soldier,
 Fear not the secret foe;
 Far more are o'er thee watching
 Than human eyes can know.
 Trust only Christ, thy Captain,
 Cease not to watch and pray;
 Heed not the treach'rous voices,
 That lure thy soul astray.

3 Go forward, Christian soldier,
 Nor dream of peaceful rest,
 Till Satan's host is vanquished,
 And Heaven is all possest;
 Till Christ Himself shall call thee
 To lay thine armor by,
 And wear, in endless glory,
 The crown of victory.

4 Go forward, Christian soldier,
 Fear not the gathering night;
 The Lord has been thy shelter,
 The Lord will be thy light;
 When morn His face revealeth,
 Thy dangers all are past;
 O pray that faith and virtue
 May keep thee to the last.
   Rev. Lawrence Tuttiett (1825—), 1866.

UNSELD. 7. 6. D. BENJAMIN CARL UNSELD (1843–), 1883.

1. Stand up, stand up for Je-sus, Ye soldiers of the cross; Lift high His royal ban-ner, It must not suf-fer loss: From vic-t'ry un-to vic-t'ry His ar-my shall He lead, Till ev-'ry foe is vanquish'd, And Christ is Lord in-deed.

318 *"Stand up, stand up for Jesus."*

2 Stand up, stand up for Jesus,
 The trumpet call obey;
Forth to the mighty conflict,
 In this His glorious day:
"Ye that are men, now serve Him"
 Against unnumbered foes;
Let courage rise with danger,
 And strength to strength oppose.

3 Stand up, stand up for Jesus,
 Stand in His strength alone;
The arm of flesh will fail you,
 Ye dare not trust your own:
Put on the gospel armor,
 Each piece put on with prayer;
Where duty calls or danger,
 Be never wanting there.

4 Stand up, stand up for Jesus,
 The strife will not be long;
This day, the noise of battle,
 The next, the victor's song:
To him that overcometh,
 A crown of life shall be;
He with the King of Glory
 Shall reign eternally.
 Rev. George Duffield (1818—1888), 1856. Ab.

CHRISTMAS. C. M.   GEORGE FREDERICK HANDEL (1685—1759). 1728.

1. Am I a soldier of the cross, A foll'wer of the Lamb? And shall I fear to own His cause, Or blush to speak His Name? Or blush to speak His Name?

319 *"Quit you like Men."*
 1 Cor. xvi. 13.

2 Must I be carried to the skies
 On flowery beds of ease,
While others fought to win the prize,
 And sailed through bloody seas?

3 Are there no foes for me to face?
 Must I not stem the flood?
Is this vile world a friend to grace,
 To help me on to God?

4 Sure I must fight, if I would reign;
 Increase my courage, Lord;
I'll bear the toil, endure the pain,
 Supported by Thy word.
 Rev. Isaac Watts (1674—1748), 1720. Ab.

320 *Pressing on.*
 Phil. iii. 12—14.

1 AWAKE, my soul, stretch every nerve,
 And press with vigor on:
A heavenly race demands thy zeal,
 And an immortal crown.

2 A cloud of witnesses around
 Hold thee in full survey;
Forget the steps already trod,
 And onward urge thy way.

3 'Tis God's all-animating voice
 That calls thee from on high;
'Tis His own hand presents the prize
 To thine aspiring eye:—

4 That prize with peerless glories bright,
 Which shall new lustre boast,
When victor's wreaths and monarch's gems
 Shall blend in common dust.

5 Blest Saviour, introduced by Thee,
 Have I my race begun;
And crowned with victory, at Thy feet
 I'll lay my honors down.
 Rev. Philip Doddridge (1702—1751), 1755.

PARK STREET. L. M.
FREDERICK MARC ANTOINE VENUA (1788–), 1810.

1. Fight the good fight with all thy might, Christ is thy strength, and Christ thy right; Lay hold on life, and it shall be Thy joy and crown eter-nal-ly, Thy joy and crown eter-nal-ly.

321   *"The good Fight."*   1 Tim. vi. 12.

2 Run the straight race through God's good grace,
  Lift up thine eyes, and seek His face;
  Life with its way before us lies,
  Christ is the path, and Christ the prize.

3 Cast care aside, upon thy guide
  Lean, and His mercy will provide;
  Lean, and the trusting soul shall prove
  Christ is its life, and Christ its love.

4 Faint not nor fear, His arms are near,
  He changeth not, and thou art dear:
  Only believe, and thou shalt see
  That Christ is all in all to thee.
  Rev. John Samuel Bewley Monsell (1811–1875), 1862.

MENDON. L. M.
German. Arr. by LOWELL MASON (1792–1872), 1830.

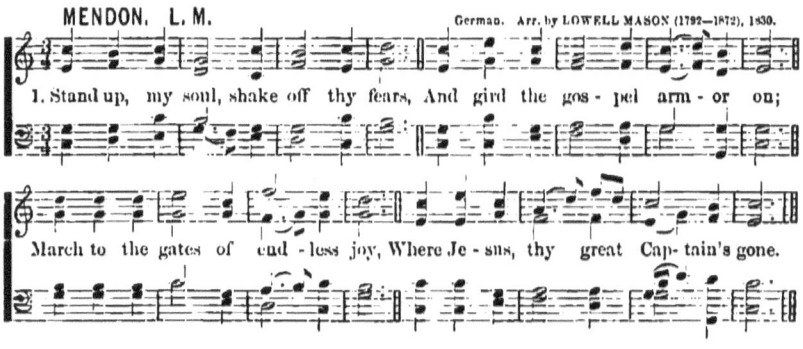

1. Stand up, my soul, shake off thy fears, And gird the gos-pel arm-or on; March to the gates of end-less joy, Where Je-sus, thy great Cap-tain's gone.

322   *"March boldly on."*

2 Hell and thy sins resist thy course,
  But hell and sin are vanquished foes;
  Thy Jesus nailed them to the cross,
  And sung the triumph when He rose.

3 Then let my soul march boldly on,
  Press forward to the heavenly gate:
  There peace and joy eternal reign,
  And glittering robes for conquerors wait.

4 There shall I wear a starry crown,
  And triumph in almighty grace;
  While all the armies of the skies
  Join in my glorious Leader's praise.
  Rev. Isaac Watts (1674–1748), 1709. Ab. and alt.

323   *Walking by Faith.*

1 'Tis by the faith of joys to come,
  We walk through deserts dark as night;
  Till we arrive at Heaven, our home,
  Faith is our guide, and faith our light.

2 The want of sight she well supplies;
  She makes the pearly gates appear;
  Far into distant worlds she pries,
  And brings eternal glories near.

CONFLICT AND CROWN. 135

3. Cheerful we tread the desert through,
   While faith inspires a heavenly ray;
   Though lions roar and tempest blow,
   And rocks and dangers fill the way.

4 So Abr'am, by divine command,
  Left his own house to walk with God;
  His faith beheld the promised land,
  And fired his zeal along the road.
  Rev. Isaac Watts, 1709.

2 True, 'tis a straight and thorny road,
  And mortal spirits tire and faint;
  But they forget the mighty God,
  Who feeds the strength of every saint.

3 The mighty God, whose matchless power,
  Is ever new, and ever young,
  And firm endures, while endless years
  Their everlasting circles run.

324   *The Christian Race.*   **L. M.**
Is. xl. 28–31.

1 Awake, our souls, away our fears,
  Let every trembling thought be gone;
  Awake, and run the heavenly race,
  And put a cheerful courage on.

4 From Thee, the overflowing spring,
  Our souls shall drink a full supply;
  While such as trust their native strength,
  Shall melt away, and droop, and die.
  Rev. Isaac Watts, 1709. Ab.

VIGILATE. 7. 7. 7. 3.   WILLIAM HENRY MONK (1823—), 1874.

1. Chris-tian, seek not yet re - pose, Cast thy dreams of ease a - way; Thou art

in the midst of foes: Watch and pray.

Ambushed lies the evil one:
    Watch and pray.

3 Hear the victors who o'ercame;
  Still they mark each warrior's way;
  All with warning voice exclaim:
      Watch and pray.

4 Watch, as if on that alone
  Hung the issue of the day;
  Pray that help may be sent down:
      Watch and pray.
  Miss Charlotte Elliott (1789–1871), 1859. Ab. and alt.

325   *"Watch and pray."*
Mark xiv. 38. Col. iv. 2.

2 Gird thy heavenly armor on,
  Wear it ever, night and day;

Ascribed to THEOBALD, King of Navarre (1201–1253).

INNOCENTS. 7.

1. Soldiers, who are Christ's below, Strong in faith resist the foe: Boundless is the pledg'd re -

- ward   Un-to them who serve the Lord.

Joys are his, serene and pure,
Light, that ever shall endure.

3 For the souls that overcome,
  Waits the beauteous heavenly home,
  Where the blessèd evermore
  Tread, on high, the starry floor.

4 Father, who the crown dost give,
  Saviour, by whose death we live,
  Spirit, who our hearts dost raise,
  Three in One, Thy Name we praise.
  Paris Breviary, 1716.
Tr. by Rev. J. H. Clark (—). Ab.

326   *"He that overcometh."*
Rev. iii. 21.

2 'Tis no palm of fading leaves
  That the conqueror's hand receives;

WARFARE AND VICTORY.

FRANCONIA. S. M. German Melody, circa 1720.

1. Sol-diers of Christ, a-rise, And put your ar-mor on, Strong

in the strength which God sup-plies Through His e-ter-nal Son.

327 *"The whole Armor."*
Eph. vi. 11—18.

2 Strong in the Lord of hosts,
  And in His mighty power,
  Who in the strength of Jesus trusts,
  Is more than conqueror.

3 Stand, then, in His great might,
  With all His strength endued,
  And take, to arm you for the fight,
  The panoply of God.

4 Leave no unguarded place,
  No weakness of the soul;
  Take every virtue, every grace,
  And fortify the whole.

5 To keep your armor bright,
  Attend with constant care,
  Still walking in your Captain's sight,
  And watching unto prayer.

Rev. Charles Wesley (1708—1788), 1749. Ab.

RATHBURN. 8, 7. ITHAMAR CONKEY (1815—1867), 1847.

1. In the cross of Christ I glo-ry, Tow-'ring o'er the wrecks of time;

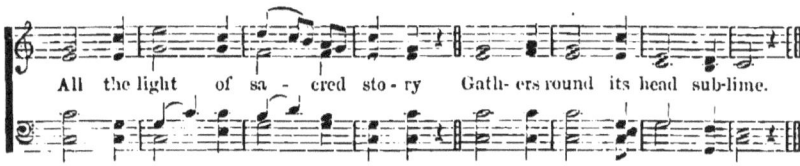

All the light of sa-cred sto-ry Gath-ers round its head sub-lime.

328 *"In the Cross of Christ I glory."*
Gal. vi. 14.

2 When the woes of life o'ertake me,
  Hopes deceive, and fears annoy,
  Never shall the cross forsake me;
  Lo, it glows with peace and joy.

3 When the sun of bliss is beaming
  Light and love upon my way,
  From the cross the radiance streaming
  Adds more lustre to the day.

4 Bane and blessing, pain and pleasure,
  By the cross are sanctified;
  Peace is there, that knows no measure,
  Joys that through all time abide.

5 In the cross of Christ I glory,
  Towering o'er the wrecks of time;
  All the light of sacred story
  Gathers round its head sublime.

Sir John Bowring (1792—1872), 1825.

THE CHRISTIAN LIFE.

329 *Hasting on.* 8. 7.

1 Take, my soul, thy full salvation,
  Rise o'er sin, and fear, and care;
  Joy to find in every station
  Something still to do or bear.

2 Think what Spirit dwells within thee;
  What a Father's smile is thine;
  What a Saviour died to win thee:
  Child of Heaven, shouldst thou repine?

3 Haste thee on from grace to glory,
  Armed by faith, and winged by prayer;
  Heaven's eternal day's before thee,
  God's own hand shall guide thee there.

4 Soon shall close thy earthly mission,
  Swift shall pass thy pilgrim days,
  Hope soon change to glad fruition,
  Faith to sight, and prayer to praise.
  Rev. Henry Francis Lyte (1793—1847), 1824. Ab.

330 *"Follow Me."* 8. 7.

1 Jesus calls us: o'er the tumult
  Of our life's wild, restless sea,
  Day by day His sweet voice soundeth,
  Softly, clearly—"Follow Me."

2 Jesus calls us, from the evil
  In a world we cannot flee,
  From each idol that would keep us,
  Softly, clearly—"Follow Me."

3 Still in joy and still in sadness
  We discern our own decree;
  Still He calls, in cares and pleasures,
  Softly, clearly—"Follow Me."

4 Thou dost call us! may we ever
  To Thy call attentive be;
  Give our hearts to Thine obedience,
  Rise, leave all, and follow Thee.
  Mrs. Cecil Francis Alexander (1823—), 1858. Ab. and alt.

FEDERAL STREET. L. M.   HENRY KEMBLE OLIVER (1800—1885), 1832.

1. Jesus, and shall it ever be, A mortal man asham'd of Thee? Asham'd of Thee whom angels praise, Whose glories shine through endless days?

331 *Not ashamed of Jesus.*
       Rom. i. 16. Heb. ii. 11.

2 Ashamed of Jesus, that dear Friend,
  On whom my hopes of Heaven depend!
  No, when I blush, be this my shame,
  That I no more revere His name.

3 Ashamed of Jesus! yes I may,
  When I've no guilt to wash away,
  No tear to wipe, no good to crave,
  No fear to quell, no soul to save.

4 Till then, nor is my boasting vain,
  Till then I boast a Saviour slain;
  And O, may this my glory be,
  That Christ is not ashamed of me.
  Rev. Joseph Grigg (—1763), 1765. Ab. and alt.
  Rev. Benjamin Francis (1734—1799), 1787.

332 *"Take up thy Cross"*
       Matt. xvi. 24.

1 Take up thy cross, the Saviour said,
  If thou wouldst my disciple be;
  Deny thyself, the world forsake,
  And humbly follow after Me.

2 Take up thy cross; let not its weight
  Fill thy weak spirit with alarm;
  His strength shall bear thy spirit up,
  And brace thy heart, and nerve thine arm.

3 Take up thy cross, nor heed the shame,
  Nor let thy foolish pride rebel:
  Thy Lord for thee the cross endured,
  To save thy soul from death and hell.

4 Take up thy cross, and follow Christ,
  Nor think till death to lay it down;
  For only he who bears the cross
  May hope to wear the starry crown.
  Rev. Charles William Everest (1814—1877), 1833. Ab. and alt.

BAYLEY. 8.7. D.   Arr. by JOSEPH PERRY HOLBROOK (1822–).

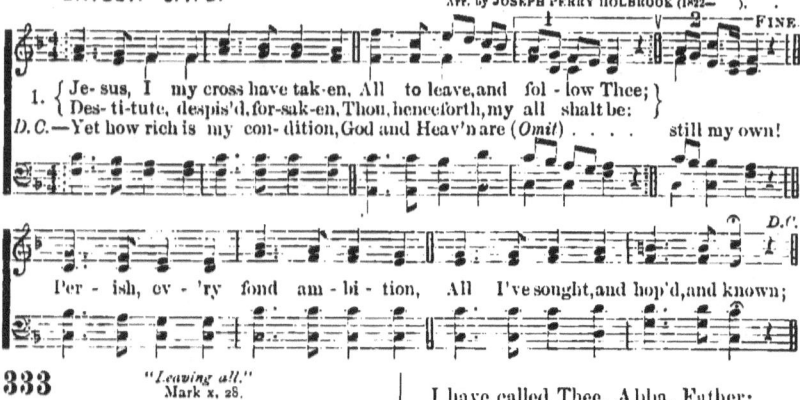

1. Je-sus, I my cross have tak-en, All to leave, and fol-low Thee;
   Des-ti-tute, despis'd, for-sak-en, Thou, henceforth, my all shalt be:
   D.C.—Yet how rich is my con-dition, God and Heav'n are (*Omit*) . . . still my own!
   Per-ish, ev-'ry fond am-bi-tion, All I've sought, and hop'd, and known;

333 "*Leaving all.*"
Mark x. 28.

2 Let the world despise and leave me,
    They have left my Saviour, too;
  Human hearts and looks deceive me;
    Thou art not, like man, untrue;
  And while Thou shalt smile upon me,
    God of wisdom, love, and might,
  Foes may hate, and friends may shun me,
    Show Thy face, and all is bright.

3 Go, then, earthly fame and treasure;
    Come, disaster, scorn, and pain!
  In Thy service, pain is pleasure;
    With Thy favor, loss is gain.

    I have called Thee, Abba, Father;
      I have stayed my heart on Thee:
    Storms may howl, and clouds may gather,
      All must work for good to me.

4 Man may trouble and distress me,
    'Twill but drive me to Thy breast;
  Life with trials hard may press me,
    Heaven will bring me sweeter rest.
  O 'tis not in grief to harm me,
    While Thy love is left to me;
  O 'twere not in joy to charm me,
    Were that joy unmixed with Thee.

Rev. Henry Francis Lyte (1793–1847), 1824.

BREMEN. C. P. M.   THOMAS HASTINGS (1784–1872), 1836.

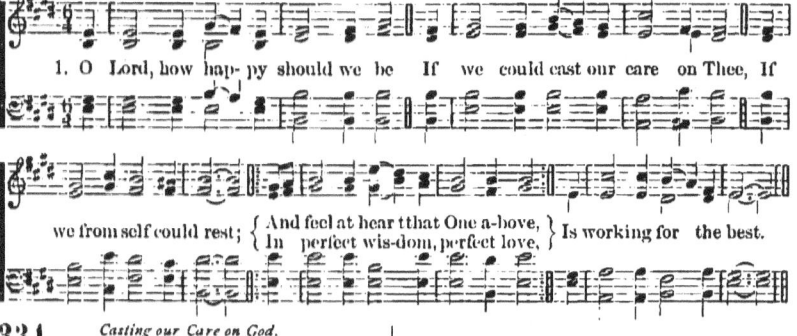

1. O Lord, how hap-py should we be If we could cast our care on Thee, If
   we from self could rest; And feel at heart that One a-bove, Is working for the best.
   In perfect wis-dom, perfect love,

334 *Casting our Care on God.*
1 Pet. v. 7.

2 Could we but kneel and cast our load,
    E'en while we pray, upon our God,
      Then rise with lightened cheer;
    Sure that the Father, who is nigh
    To still the famished raven's cry,
      Will hear in that we fear.

3 We cannot trust Him as we should;
    So chafes weak nature's restless mood
      To cast its peace away;
    But birds and flowerets round us preach,
    All, all the present evil teach
      Sufficient for the day.

TRUSTING IN CHRIST.

4 Lord, make these faithless hearts of ours
Such lessons learn from birds and flowers;
Make them from self to cease,
Leave all things to a Father's will,
And taste, before Him lying still,
E'en in affliction, peace.
    Prof. Joseph Anstice (1808–1836), 1836. Ab.

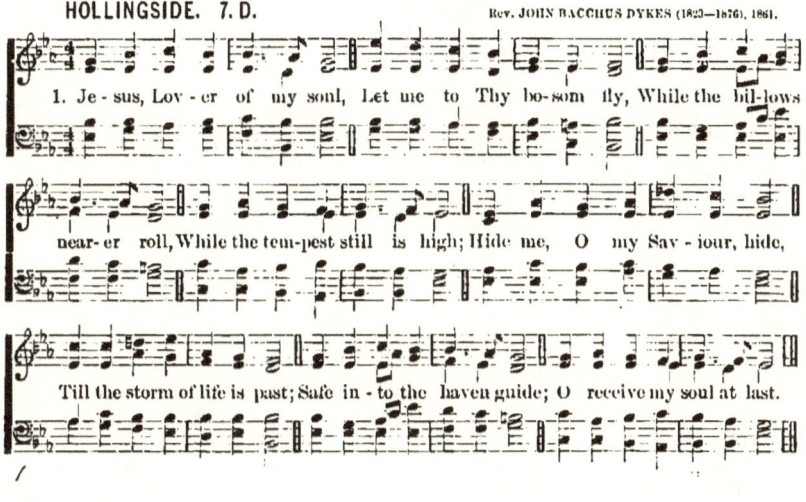

HOLLINGSIDE. 7. D. Rev. JOHN BACCHUS DYKES (1823–1876), 1861.

1. Jesus, Lover of my soul, Let me to Thy bosom fly, While the billows nearer roll, While the tempest still is high; Hide me, O my Saviour, hide, Till the storm of life is past; Safe into the haven guide; O receive my soul at last.

335 *"Jesus, Lover of my Soul."*

2 Other refuge have I none;
Hangs my helpless soul on Thee;
Leave, ah! leave me not alone,
Still support and comfort me
All my trust on Thee is stayed,
All my help from Thee I bring;
Cover my defenceless head
With the shadow of Thy wing.

3 Wilt Thou not regard my call?
Wilt Thou not accept my prayer?
Lo, I sink, I faint, I fall!
Lo, on Thee I cast my care.
Reach me out Thy gracious hand,
While I of Thy strength receive,
Hoping against hope I stand,
Dying, and behold I live.

4 Thou, O Christ, art all I want;
More than all in Thee I find:
Raise the fallen, cheer the faint,
Heal the sick, and lead the blind.
Just and holy is Thy Name;
I am all unrighteousness;
False and full of sin I am,
Thou art full of truth and grace.

5 Plenteous grace with Thee is found,
Grace to cover all my sin:
Let the healing streams abound,
Make and keep me pure within
Thou of life the Fountain art;
Freely let me take of Thee;
Spring Thou up within my heart,
Rise to all eternity.
    Rev. Charles Wesley (1708–1788), 1740. Sl. alt.

MARTYN. 7. D. SIMEON BUTLER MARSH (1798–1875), 1834.

THE CHRISTIAN LIFE.

MAITLAND. C. M. — AMZI CHAPIN (1768–), c. 1820.

1. Must Jesus bear the cross alone, And all the world go free?

No, there's a cross for ev'ry one, And there's a cross for me.

336 *No Cross, no Crown.*

2 How happy are the saints above,
    Who once went sorrowing here!
But now they taste unmingled love,
    And joy without a tear.

3 The consecrated cross I'll bear,
    Till death shall set me free;
And then go home my crown to wear
    For there's a crown for me.

4 O precious cross! O glorious crown!
    O resurrection day!
Ye angels, from the stars come down,
    And bear my soul away.

*Thomas Shepherd (1665–1739), 1692. Vs. 1. Alt.
Prof. George Nelson Allen (1812–1877), 1849. Vs. 2, 3.
Plymouth Collection, 1855. Vs. 4.*

337 *Christ our Example. John xv. 13.*

1 Lord, as to Thy dear cross we flee,
    And plead to be forgiven,
So let Thy life our pattern be,
    And form our souls for Heaven.

2 Help us, through good report and ill,
    Our daily cross to bear;
Like Thee, to do our Father's will,
    Our brethren's griefs to share.

3 If joy shall at Thy bidding fly,
    And grief's dark day come on,
We in our turn would meekly cry,
    Father, Thy will be done.

4 Kept peaceful in the midst of strife,
    Forgiving and forgiven,
O may we lead the pilgrim's life,
    And follow Thee to Heaven.

Rev. John Hampden Gurney (1802–1862), 1838. Ab.

338 *"I am not ashamed." 2 Tim. i. 12.*

1 I'm not ashamed to own my Lord,
    Or to defend His cause,
Maintain the honor of His word,
    The glory of His cross.

2 Jesus, my God! I know His name,
    His name is all my trust;
Nor will He put my soul to shame,
    Nor let my hope be lost.

3 Firm as His throne His promise stands,
    And He can well secure
What I've committed to His hands,
    Till the decisive hour.

4 Then will He own my worthless name
    Before His Father's face,
And in the New Jerusalem
    Appoint my soul a place.

Rev. Isaac Watts (1674–1748), 1709.

339 *Humble Reliance.*

1 My God, my Father, blissful Name,
    O may I call Thee mine?
May I with sweet assurance claim
    A portion so divine?

2 This only can my fears control,
    And bid my sorrows fly;
What harm can ever reach my soul
    Beneath my Father's eye?

3 What'er Thy providence denies,
    I calmly would resign,
For Thou art good and just and wise:
    O bend my will to Thine.

Miss Anne Steele, (1717–1778), 1760. Ab.

BEATITUDE. C. M.   Rev. JOHN BACCHUS DYKES (1823—1876).

1. O for a heart to praise my God, A heart from sin set free; A heart that al-ways feels Thy blood So free-ly shed for me.

340   *"Make me a clean Heart."* Ps. li. 10.

2 A heart resigned, submissive, meek,
   My dear Redeemer's throne;
Where only Christ is heard to speak,
   Where Jesus reigns alone.

3 A humble, lowly, contrite heart,
   Believing, true and clean;
Which neither life nor death can part
   From Him that dwells within.

4 A heart in every thought renewed,
   And full of love divine;
Perfect, and right, and pure, and good,
   A copy, Lord, of Thine.

5 Thy nature, dearest Lord, impart;
   Come quickly from above;
Write Thy new Name upon my heart,
   Thy new, best Name of Love.

          Rev. Charles Wesley (1708—1788), 1742. Ab. and sl. alt.

BYEFIELD. C. M.   THOMAS HASTINGS (1784—1872), 1840.

1. God moves in a mys-te-rious way His won-ders to per-form; He plants His foot-steps in the sea, And rides up-on the storm.

341   *The Mysteries of Providence.*

2 Deep in unfathomable mines
   Of never-failing skill,
He treasures up His bright designs,
   And works His sovereign will.

3 Judge not the Lord by feeble sense,
   But trust Him for His grace;
Behind a frowning providence
   He hides a smiling face.

4 His purposes will ripen fast,
   Unfolding every hour;
The bud may have a bitter taste,
   But sweet will be the flower.

5 Blind unbelief is sure to err,
   And scan His work in vain:
God is His own interpreter,
   And He will make it plain.

          William Cowper (1731—1800), 1774. Ab.

DUNDEE. C. M.

From Hart's Psalter. 1615.

1. God, my Sup-port-er and my Hope, My Help for-ev-er near,
Thine arm of mer-cy held me up When sink-ing in de-spair.

342 *God our Portion here and hereafter.*
Ps. lxxiii. 23–28.

2 Thy counsels, Lord, shall guide my feet
 Through this dark wilderness;
 Thy hand conduct me near Thy seat,
 To dwell before Thy face.

3 Were I in heaven without my God,
 'Twould be no joy to me;
 And while this earth is my abode,
 I long for none but Thee.

4 What if the springs of life were broke,
 And flesh and heart should faint?
 God is my soul's eternal Rock,
 The Strength of every saint.

5 But to draw near to Thee, my God,
 Shall be my sweet employ:
 My tongue shall sound Thy works abroad,
 And tell the world my joy.

Rev. Isaac Watts (1674–1748), 1719. Ab.

NAOMI. C. M.

HANS GEORG NAEGELI (1773–1836), 1832.
Arr. by LOWELL MASON (1792–1872), 1836.

1. Fa-ther, what-e'er of earth-ly bliss Thy sov-'reign will de-nies,
Ac-cept-ed at Thy throne of grace, Let this pe-ti-tion rise:—

343 *"A calm, a thankful Heart."*

2 Give me a calm, a thankful heart,
 From every murmur free;
 The blessings of Thy grace impart,
 And make me live to Thee.

3 Let the sweet hope that Thou art mine
 My life and death attend;
 Thy presence through my journey shine,
 And crown my journey's end.

Miss Anne Steele (1717–1778), 1760. Ab.

344 *"Sweet Will of God."*

1 I worship Thee, sweet Will of God,
 And all Thy ways adore;
 And every day I live, I seem
 To love Thee more and more.

2 I have no cares, O blessed Will,
 For all my cares are Thine;
 I live in triumph, Lord, for Thou
 Hast made Thy triumphs mine.

CONFIDENCE IN GOD.

3 He always wins who sides with God,
  To him no chance is lost;
  God's will is sweetest to him when
  It triumphs at his cost,

4 Ill that He blesses is our good,
  And unblest good is ill;
  And all is right that seems most wrong
  If it be His sweet will.
  Rev. Frederick William Faber (1814—1863), 1849. Ab.

STEPHENS. C. M. — *Rev. WILLIAM JONES (1726—1800), 1784.*

1. Through all the chang-ing scenes of life, In troub-le and in joy, The prais-es of my God shall still My heart and tongue em-ploy.

345 *Safety in God.*
Ps. xxxiv.

2 Of His deliverance I will boast,
  Till all that are distressed,
  From my example comfort take,
  And charm their griefs to rest.

3 The hosts of God encamp around
  The dwellings of the just;
  Deliverance He affords to all
  Who on His succor trust.

4 Fear Him, ye saints, and you will then
  Have nothing else to fear;
  Make you His service your delight,
  Your wants shall be His care.
  Tate and Brady, 1696. Ab.

OAKSVILLE. C. M. — *HEINRICH CHRISTOPHER ZEUNER (1795—1857), 1839.*

1. My God, the Spring of all my joys, The Life of my de-lights, The Glo-ry of my bright-est days, And Com-fort of my nights!

346 *Light in Darkness.*

2 In darkest shades if He appear,
  My dawning is begun;
  He is my soul's sweet Morning Star,
  And He my Rising Sun.

3 The opening heavens around me shine
  With beams of sacred bliss,
  While Jesus shows His heart is mine,
  And whispers, I am His.

4 My soul would leave this heavy clay
  At that transporting word;
  Run up with joy the shining way,
  T'embrace my dearest Lord.
  Rev. Isaac Watts, 1709. Ab.

MEAR. C. M. — Anon. c. 1740.

1. O for a closer walk with God, A calm and heav'nly frame, A light to shine upon the road That leads me to the Lamb.

347   *"A closer Walk."*   Gen. v. 24. 1 John ii. 6.

2 Return, O holy Dove, return,
   Sweet messenger of rest:
I hate the sins that made Thee mourn,
   And drove Thee from my breast.

3 The dearest idol I have known,
   Whate'er that idol be;
Help me to tear it from Thy throne,
   And worship only Thee.

4 So shall my walk be close with God,
   Calm and serene my frame;
So purer light shall mark the road
   That leads me to the Lamb.
      William Cowper (1731–1800), 1774. Ab.

348   *"Let us return."*   Hos. vi. 1-3.

1 Long hath the night of sorrow reigned;
   The dawn shall bring us light;
God shall appear, and we shall rise
   With gladness in His sight.

2 Our hearts, if God we seek to know,
   Shall know Him and rejoice;
His coming like the morn shall be,
   Like morning songs His voice.

3 As dew upon the tender herb,
   Diffusing fragrance round;
As showers that usher in the spring,
   And cheer the thirsty ground;

4 So shall His presence bless our souls,
   And shed a joyful light;
That hallowed morn shall chase away
   The sorrows of the night.
      Rev. John Morrison (1749–1798), 1781. Ab.

HEATH. C. M. — LOWELL MASON (1792–1872), 1835.

1. As pants the hart for cooling streams, When heated in the chase, So pants my soul, O Lord, for Thee, And Thy refreshing grace.

349   *Panting for God.*   Ps. xliii.

2 For Thee, the Lord, the living Lord,
   My thirsty soul doth pine:
O when shall I behold Thy face,
   Thou majesty Divine?

3 I sigh to think of happier days,
   When Thou, O Lord, wast nigh;
When every heart was tuned to praise,
   And none so blest as I.

4 Why restless, why cast down, my soul?
   Trust God, and thou shalt sing
His praise again, and find Him still
   Thy health's eternal Spring.
      Tate and Brady, 1696. Alt.
      Rev. Henry Francis Lyte (1793–1847), 1834.

CONFIDENCE IN GOD.

DOMINUS REGIT ME. 8. 7.   Rev. JOHN BACCHUS DYKES (1823—1876), 1868.

1. The King of love my Shepherd is, Whose goodness faileth never; I nothing lack if I am His, And He is mine for-ev-er.

350 *Never-failing Goodness.*

2 Where streams of living water flow
  My ransomed soul He leadeth,
And, where the verdant pastures grow,
  With food celestial feedeth.

3 Perverse and foolish oft I strayed,
  But yet in love He sought me,
And on His shoulder gently laid,
  And home, rejoicing, brought me.

4 In death's dark vale I fear no ill
  With Thee, dear Lord, beside me;
Thy rod and staff my comfort still,
  Thy cross before to guide me.

5 And so through all the length of days
  Thy goodness faileth never;
Good Shepherd, may I sing Thy praise
  Within Thy house for ever.

Rev. Sir Henry Williams Baker (1821—1877), 1868. Ab.

ST. BEDE. C. M. 6 l.   Rev. JOHN BACCHUS DYKES, 1868.

1. Father, I know that all my life Is portion'd out for me; The changes that are sure to come I do not fear to see: I ask Thee for a present mind, Intent on pleasing Thee.

351 *"My Times are in Thy Hand."*
Ps. xxxi. 15.

2 I would not have the restless will
  That hurries to and fro,
Seeking for some great thing to do,
  Or secret thing to know:
I would be treated as a child,
  And guided where I go.

3 In service which Thy will appoints
  There are no bonds for me;
My inmost heart is taught the truth
  That makes Thy children free:
A life of self-renouncing love
  Is one of liberty.

Miss Anne Lætitia Waring (1820—), 1850. Ab. and alt.

ASWARBY. S. M.
SAMUEL WESLEY (1766—1837), 1798.

1. How gen- tle God's commands! How kind His pre-cepts are! "Come, cast your burdens on the Lord, And trust His constant care."

352 *God's Care a Remedy for ours.*
1 Pet. v. 7.

2 While Providence supports,
Let saints securely dwell;
That hand, which bears all nature up,
Shall guide His children well.

3 Why should this anxious load
Press down your weary mind?
Haste to your heavenly Father's throne,
And sweet refreshment find.

4 His goodness stands approved
Down to the present day;
I'll drop my burden at His feet,
And bear a song away.
Rev. Philip Doddridge (1702—1751), 1755.

353 *"All in all."*
Ps. lxxiii. 25.

1 My God, my Life, my Love,
To Thee, to Thee I call;
I cannot live if Thou remove,
For Thou art All in all.

2 Not all the harps above
Can make a heavenly place,
If God His residence remove,
Or but conceal His face.

3 Nor earth, nor all the sky,
Can one delight afford;
No, not a drop of real joy,
Without Thy presence, Lord.
Rev. Isaac Watts (1674—1748), 1709. Ab.

354 *"Befiehl du deine Wege."*

1 Give to the winds thy fears;
Hope, and be undismayed;
God hears thy sighs, and counts thy tears;
God shall lift up thy head.

2 Through waves and clouds and storms,
He gently clears thy way:
Wait thou His time, so shall this night
Soon end in joyous day.

3 Far, far above thy thought
His counsel shall appear,
When fully He the work hath wrought
That caused thy needless fear.
Rev. Paul Gerhardt (1606—1676), 1659.
Tr. by Rev. John Wesley (1703—1791), 1739. Ab.

355 *"Blessed are the pure in heart."*

1 Blest are the pure in heart,
For they shall see their God:
The secret of the Lord is theirs;
Their soul is Christ's abode.

2 The Lord, who left the sky
Our life and peace to bring,
And dwelt in lowliness with men,
Their pattern and their King,—

3 Still to the lowly soul
He doth Himself impart;
And for His dwelling and His throne
Chooseth the pure in heart.

4 Lord, we Thy presence seek;
May ours this blessing be;
Give us a pure and lowly heart,
A temple meet for Thee!
Rev. John Keble (1792—1866),
William John Hall (—), 1836.

FRANKLIN SQUARE. S. M.
SYLVANUS BILLINGS POND (1792—1871), before 1850.

ST. BEES. 7.   Rev. JOHN BACCHUS DYKES (1823—1876), 1871.

1. Hark, my soul, it is the Lord; 'Tis thy Saviour, hear His word; Jesus speaks, and

speaks to thee: "Say, poor sinner, lovest thou Me?"

356   *"Lovest thou Me?"*

2 "I delivered thee, when bound,
And, when wounded, healed thy wound;
Sought thee wandering, set thee right,
Turned thy darkness into light.

3 "Mine is an unchanging love,
Higher than the heights above,
Deeper than the depths beneath,
Free and faithful, strong as death.

4 "Thou shalt see My glory soon,
When the work of grace is done;
Partner of My throne shalt be;
Say, poor sinner, lovest thou Me?"

5 Lord, it is my chief complaint,
That my love is weak and faint;
Yet I love Thee, and adore;
O for grace to love Thee more!
      William Cowper (1731—1800), 1768. Ab.

357   *"Loving Him who first loved me."*

1 Saviour, teach me, day by day,
Love's sweet lesson to obey:
Sweeter lesson cannot be,
Loving Him who first loved me.

2 Teach me all Thy steps to trace,
Strong to follow in Thy grace:
Learning how to love from Thee,
Loving Him who first loved me.

3 Thus may I rejoice to show
That I feel the love I owe:
Singing, till Thy face I see,
Of His love who first loved me.
      Miss Jane Elizabeth Leeson (—), 1842. Ab.

358   *The Heavenly Shepherd.*
      Ps. xxiii.

1 To Thy pastures fair and large,
Heavenly Shepherd, lead Thy charge,
And my couch, with tenderest care,
Mid the springing grass prepare.

2 When I faint with summer's heat
Thou shalt guide my weary feet
To the streams that, still and slow,
Through the verdant meadows flow.

3 Constant to my latest end,
Thou my footsteps shalt attend;
And shalt bid Thy hallowed dome
Yield me an eternal home.
      Rev. James Merrick (1720—1769), 1765. Ab. and alt.

359   *"Cast thy burden upon the Lord."*
      Ps. lv. 22.

1 Cast thy burden on the Lord,
Only lean upon His word;
Thou shalt soon have cause to bless
His eternal faithfulness.

2 Ever in the raging storm
Thou shalt see His cheering form,
Hear His pledge of coming aid:
"It is I, be not afraid."

3 He will gird thee by His power,
In thy weary, fainting hour;
Lean, then, loving, on His word;
Cast thy burden on the Lord.
      Rev. Rowland Hill (1744—1833), 1783. V. 1.
George Rawson (1807—1885), 1857. Ab. and much alt.

ESHTEMOA. 7.   THOMAS B. MASON (—).

HANFORD. 8.8.8.4. Sir ARTHUR SULLIVAN (1842–), 1872.

360 *"Thy Will be done."*

1. My God and Father, while I stray
Far from my home, on life's rough way,
O teach me from my heart to say,
"Thy will be done."

2 Though dark my path, and sad my lot,
Let me be still and murmur not,
Or breathe the prayer divinely taught,
"Thy will be done."

3 Renew my will from day to day;
Blend it with Thine, and take away
All that now makes it hard to say,
"Thy will be done."

4 Then when on earth I breathe no more,
The prayer oft mixed with tears before
I'll sing upon a happier shore:
"Thy will be done."

Miss Charlotte Elliott (1789–1871), 1834. Ab.

PORTUGUESE HYMN. 11. MARC ANTOINE PORTOGALLO (1763–1830).

1. How firm a foundation, ye saints of the Lord,
Is laid for your faith in His excellent Word!
What more can He say than to you He hath said,
You who unto Jesus for refuge have fled?
You who unto Jesus for refuge have fled?

361 *"Exceeding great and precious Promises."*
2 Pet. i. 4.

2 "Fear not, I am with thee, O be not dismayed,
For I am thy God, and will still give thee aid;
I'll strengthen thee, help thee, and cause thee to stand,
Upheld by My righteous, omnipotent hand.

3 "When through the deep waters I call thee to go,
The rivers of woe shall not thee overflow;
For I will be with thee thy troubles to bless,
And sanctify to thee thy deepest distress.

OUR SHEPHERD AND LEADER.

4 "E'en down to old age, all My people shall prove
My sovereign, eternal, unchangeable love;
And when hoary hairs shall their temples adorn,
Like lambs they shall still in My bosom be borne.

5 "The soul that on Jesus hath leaned for repose
I will not, I will not desert to his foes;
That soul, though all hell should endeavor to shake,
I'll never, no never, no never forsake."

R. Kirke—George Keith, 1787. Ab.

GOSHEN. 11.   Greek Melody.

1. The Lord is my Shep-herd, no want shall I know; I feed in green pastures, safe fold-ed I rest; He leadeth my soul where the still wa-ters flow,
D.S.—Re-stores me when wand'ring, re-deems when oppress'd.

362   *"I will fear no Evil."*
Ps. xxiii. 4.

2 Through the valley and shadow of death though I stray,
Since Thou art my Guardian, no evil I fear;
Thy rod shall defend me, Thy staff be my stay;
No harm can befall, with my Comforter near.

3 In the midst of affliction my table is spread;
With blessings unmeasured my cup runneth o'er;
With perfume and oil Thou anointest my head;
O what shall I ask of Thy providence more?

4 Let goodness and mercy, my bountiful God,
Still follow my steps till I meet Thee above;
I seek, by the path which my forefathers trod,
Through the land of their sojourn, Thy kingdom of love.

James Montgomery (1771—1854), 1822.

363   *"Faint, yet pursuing."*

1 Though faint, yet pursuing, we go on our way;
The Lord is our Leader, His Word is our stay;
Though suffering, and sorrow, and trial be near,
The Lord is our Refuge, and whom can we fear?

2 Though clouds may surround us, our God is our Light;
Though storms rage around us, our God is our Might;
So faint, yet pursuing, still onward we come;
The Lord is our Leader, and Heaven is our home.

Rev. John Nelson Darby (1800—1882), 1858. Ab.

NEWLAND. S.M.   HENRY JOHN GAUNTLETT (1806—1876), 1857.

1. The Lord my Shepherd is, I shall be well supplied; Since He is mine, and

I am His, What can I want be-side?

364   *The Lord our Shepherd.*
              Ps. xxiii.

2 He leads me to the place
    Where heavenly pasture grows;
    Where living waters gently pass,
    And full salvation flows.

3 If e're I go astray,
    He doth my soul reclaim;
    And guides me, in His own right way,
    For His most holy Name.

4 While He affords His aid,
    I cannot yield to fear; [dark shade,
    Though I should walk through death's
    My Shepherd's with me there.
          Rev. Isaac Watts (1674—1748), 1719. Ab.

365   *Safety in God.*
       Ps. xxxvi.

1 My spirit, on Thy care,
    Blest Saviour, I recline:
    Thou wilt not leave me to despair,
    For Thou art Love divine.

2 In Thee I place my trust,
    On Thee I calmly rest;
    I know Thee good, I know Thee just,
    And count Thy choice the best.

3 Whate'er events betide,
    Thy will they all perform;
    Safe in Thy breast my head I hide,
    Nor fear the coming storm.

4 Let good or ill befall,
    It must be good for me;
    Secure of having Thee in all,
    Of having all in Thee.
      Rev. Henry Francis Lyte (1793—1847), 1834.

WARD. L.M.   Old Scotch Melody. Arr. by LOWELL MASON (1792—1872), 1839.

1. God is the Ref-uge of His saints, When storms of sharp distress in-vade;
Ere we can of-fer our complaints, Be-hold Him pres-ent with His aid.

366   *God our Refuge.*

2 There is a stream whose gentle flow
    Supplies the city of our God;
    Life, love, and joy still gliding through,
    And watering our divine abode.

3 That sacred stream, Thy holy Word,
    Our grief allays, our fear controls;
    Sweet peace Thy promises afford,
    And give new strength to fainting souls.

4 Zion enjoys her Monarch's love,
    Secure against a threat'ning hour;
    Nor can her firm foundations move,
    Built on His truth, and armed with
    power.
               Rev. Isaac Watts, 1719. Ab. and alt.

TRUST.

367 *Watching and Praying.* **L. M.**

1 They pray the best who pray and watch,
  They watch the best who watch and pray,
  They hear Christ's fingers on the latch,
  Whether He comes by night or day.

2 Whether they guard the gates and watch,
  Or, patient, toil for Him, and wait,
  They hear His fingers on the latch,
  If early He doth come, or late.

3 With trembling joy they hail their Lord,
  And haste His welcome feet to kiss,
  While He, well pleased, doth speak the word
  That thrills them with unending bliss:

4 "Well done, My servants, now receive,
  For faithful work, reward and rest,
  And wreaths which busy angels weave,
  To crown the men who serve Me best."

Rev. Edward Hopper (1818—   ), 1873.

368 *"Ye shall live also."* John xiv. 19. **L. M.**

1 When sins and fears prevailing rise,
  And fainting hope almost expires,
  Jesus, to Thee I lift mine eyes;
  To Thee I breathe my soul's desires.

2 Art Thou not mine, my living Lord?
  And can my hope, my comfort die?
  Fixed on Thine everlasting word,
  That word which built the earth and sky?

3 If my Immortal Saviour lives,
  Then my immortal life is sure;
  His word a firm foundation gives;
  Here let me build, and rest secure.

4 Here, O my soul, thy trust repose;
  If Jesus is forever mine,
  Not death itself, that last of foes,
  Shall break a union so divine.

Miss Anne Steele (1717—1778), 1760. Ab.

BRATTLE STREET. C. M. D.

IGNAZ JOSEPH PLEYEL (1757—1831), 1791.
Arr. by NAHUM MITCHELL (1770—1853), 1812.

1. While Thee I seek, pro-tect-ing Pow'r, Be my vain wish-es still'd;
   And may this con-se-cra-ted hour (Omit). . . . . With
   bet-ter hopes be fill'd. Thy love the pow'rs of thought bestow'd, To Thee my thoughts would soar; Thy mer-cy o'er my life has flow'd, That mer-cy I a-dore.

369 *Habitual Devotion.*

2 In each event of life, how clear
    Thy ruling hand I see:
  Each blessing to my soul more dear,
    Because conferred by Thee.
  In every joy that crowns my days,
    In every pain I bear,
  My heart shall find delight in praise,
    Or seek relief in prayer.

3 When gladness wings my favored hour,
    Thy love my thoughts shall fill;
  Resigned, when storms of sorrow lower,
    My soul shall meet Thy will.
  My lifted eye, without a tear,
    The lowering storm shall see;
  My steadfast heart shall know no fear,
    That heart shall rest on Thee.

Miss Helen Maria Williams (1762—1827), 1786.

AURELIA. 7, 6. D.   SAMUEL SEBASTIAN WESLEY (1810—1876), c. 1868.

1. I need Thee, precious Jesus, For I am full of sin; My soul is dark and guilty, My heart is dead within; I need the cleansing fountain Where I can always flee, The blood of Christ most precious, The sinner's perfect plea.

370 *"He is precious."* 1 Pet. ii. 7.

2 I need Thee, precious Jesus,
   For I am very poor;
A stranger and a pilgrim,
   I have no earthly store;
I need the love of Jesus
   To cheer me on my way,
To guide my doubting footsteps,
   To be my strength and stay.

3 I need Thee, precious Jesus,
   And hope to see Thee soon,
Encircled with the rainbow,
   And seated on Thy throne:
There, with Thy blood-bought children,
   My joy shall ever be,
To sing Thy praises, Jesus,
   To gaze, my Lord, on Thee.

Rev. Frederick Whitfield (1829—), 1859. Ab. and sl. alt.

371 *"Still keep me."*

1 O Lamb of God, still keep me
   Near to Thy wounded side;
'Tis only there in safety
   And peace I can abide.
What foes and snares surround me,
   What doubts and fears within!
The grace that sought and found me
   Alone can keep me clean.

2 Soon shall my eyes behold Thee
   With rapture face to face;
One half hath not been told me
   Of all Thy power and grace;
Thy beauty, Lord, and glory,
   The wonders of Thy love,
Shall be the endless story,
   Of all Thy saints above.

James George Deck (1802—), 1857. Ab.

372 *"I will fear no evil."* Ps. xxiii. 4.

1 In heavenly love abiding,
   No change my heart shall fear;
And safe is such confiding,
   For nothing changes here.
The storm may roar without me,
   My heart may low be laid,
But God is round about me,
   And can I be dismay'd?

2 Wherever He may guide me,
   No want shall turn me back;
My Shepherd is beside me,
   And nothing can I lack.
His wisdom ever waketh,
   His sight is never dim,
He knows the way He taketh,
   And I will walk with Him.

3 Green pastures are before me,
   Which yet I have not seen;
   Bright skies will soon be o'er me,
   Where darkest clouds have been.

My hope I cannot measure,
   My path to life is free,
   My Saviour has my treasure,
   And He will walk with me.

Miss Anna Lætitia Waring (1820—), 1850. Sl. alt.

DOANE. 6. 4. 6. 4. 6. 6. 4.
WILLIAM HOWARD DOANE (1832—), 1869.

1. More love to Thee, O Christ, More love to Thee, Hear Thou the pray'r I make On bended knee; This is my earnest plea, More love, O Christ, to Thee, More love to Thee! More love to Thee!

373 *"More Love to Thee."*
John xxi. 17

2 Once earthly joy I craved,
   Sought peace and rest;
   Now Thee alone I seek,
   Give what is best:
   This all my prayer shall be,
   More love, O Christ, to Thee,
   More love to Thee!

3 Let sorrow do its work,
   Send grief and pain;
   Sweet are Thy messengers,
   Sweet their refrain,
   When they can sing with me,
   More love, O Christ, to Thee,
   More love to Thee.

4 Then shall my latest breath
   Whisper Thy praise;
   This be the parting cry
   My heart shall raise,
   This still its prayer shall be,
   More love, O Christ, to Thee,
   More love to Thee.

Mrs. Elizabeth Payson Prentiss (1819—1878), 1869.

374 *"Nearer, my God, to Thee."*
Gen. xxviii. 10—12.

1 NEARER, my God, to Thee,
   Nearer to Thee:
   E'en though it be a cross
   That raiseth me;
   Still all my song shall be,
   Nearer, my God, to Thee,
   Nearer to Thee.

2 Though like the wanderer,
   The sun gone down,
   Darkness be over me,
   My rest a stone;
   Yet in my dreams I'd be
   Nearer, my God, to Thee,
   Nearer to Thee.

3 There let the way appear
   Steps unto Heaven;
   All that Thou sendest me,
   In mercy given;
   Angels to beckon me
   Nearer, my God, to Thee,
   Nearer to Thee.

4 Then, with my waking thoughts
   Bright with Thy praise,
   Out of my stony griefs
   Bethel I'll raise;
   So by my woes to be
   Nearer, my God, to Thee,
   Nearer to Thee.

Mrs. Sarah Flower Adams (1805—1848), 1840. Ab.

BETHANY. 6. 4. 6. 4. 6. 6. 4.
Arr. by LOWELL MASON (1792—1872), 1859.

1. { Nearer, my God, to Thee, Nearer to Thee:
    E'en though it be a cross (*Omit*) . . . } That raiseth me; Still all my song shall be, Nearer, my God, to Thee,
   Nearer, my God, to Thee, (*Omit*) . . . Near-er to Thee.

ST. THOMAS. S. M. — GEORGE FREDERICK HANDEL (1685—1759). Coll. of AARON WILLIAMS (1731—1776), 1762.

1. We give Thee but Thine own, What-e'er the gift may be: All that we have is Thine a-lone, A trust, O Lord, from Thee.

375 *"Thine alone."*

2 To comfort and to bless,
   To find a balm for woe,
   To tend the lone and fatherless,
   Is angels' work below.

3 The captive to release,
   To God the lost to bring,
   To teach the way of life and peace,
   It is a Christ-like thing.

4 And we believe Thy word,
   Though dim our faith may be;
   Whate'er for Thine we do, O Lord,
   We do it unto Thee.

Bp. William Walsham How (1823—), 1854. Ab.

376 *Waiting Orders from Heaven.*

1 HAPPY the man, who knows
   His Master to obey;
   Whose life of care and labor flows,
   Where God points out the way.

2 He riseth to his task,
   Soon as the word is given;
   Nor waits, nor doth a question ask,
   When orders come from Heaven.

3 Nothing he calls his own;
   Nothing he hath to say;
   His feet are shod for God alone,
   And God alone obey.

4 Give us, O God, this mind,
   Which waits for Thy command,
   And doth its highest pleasure find
   In Thy great work to stand.

Rev. Thomas Cogswell Upham (1799—1872), 1872.

377 *Bearing One Another's Burdens.*
Gal. vi. 2.

1 O PRAISE our God to-day,
   His constant mercy bless,
   Whose love hath helped us on our way,
   And granted us success.

2 His arm the strength imparts
   Our daily toil to bear;
   His grace alone inspires our hearts,
   Each other's load to share.

3 O happiest work below,
   Earnest of joy above,
   To sweeten many a cup of woe,
   By deeds of holy love!

4 Lord, may it be our choice
   This blessed rule to keep,
   "Rejoice with them that do rejoice,
   And weep with them that weep."

Rev. Sir Henry Williams Baker (1821—1877), 1861. Ab.

378 *Revive Thy work.*

1 REVIVE Thy work, O Lord!
   Exalt Thy precious name;
   And by the Holy Ghost our love
   For Thee and Thine inflame.

2 Revive Thy work, O Lord!
   Give power unto Thy word;
   Grant that Thy blessed Gospel may
   In living faith be heard.

3 Revive Thy work, O Lord!
   And give refreshing showers;
   The glory shall be all Thine own,
   The blessing, Lord, be ours!

Albert Midlane (1825—), 1860. Ab.

WINN. S. M. — WILLIAM WINN (1828—), 1872.

CHRISTIAN ACTIVITY.

ST. MICHAEL. S. M. — From the Psalter (.563) of JOHN DAYE (1522—1584).

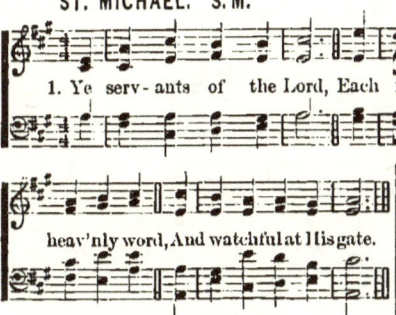

1. Ye serv-ants of the Lord, Each in his of-fice wait, Ob-serv-ant of His heav'nly word, And watchful at His gate.

379   *"The watchful Servant."* Luke xii. 35-38.

2 Let all your lamps be bright,
   And trim the golden flame;
Gird up your loins as in His sight,
   For awful is His Name.

3 Watch! 'tis your Lord's command;
   And while we speak He's near:
Mark the first signal of His hand,
   And ready all appear.

4 O happy servant he,
   In such a posture found!
He shall his Lord with rapture see,
   And be with honor crowned.

Rev. Philip Doddridge (1702—1751), 1755. Ab. and sl. alt.

380   *Sowing beside all Waters.* Is. xxxii. 20.

1 Sow in the morn thy seed,
   At eve hold not thy hand;
To doubt and fear give thou no heed,
   Broadcast it o'er the land.

2 Thou canst not toil in vain;
   Cold, heat, the moist and dry,
Shall foster and mature the grain
   For garners in the sky.

3 Then, when the glorious end,
   The day of God shall come,
The angel-reapers shall descend,
   And heaven sing, "Harvest home!"

James Montgomery (1771—1854), 1825. Ab.

381   *A word in Season.*

1 A FITLY spoken word,
   It hath mysterious powers;
Its far-off echoes shall be heard
   Ringing through future hours.

2 An honest, truthful word,
   It has a tongue of flame;
On wings of wind it flies abroad,
   And wins a heavenly fame.

3 A gentle, gracious word,
   'Tis music in the heart;
Thrilling its very inmost chord,
   Till tears unbidden start.

4 Speak thou, then, lovingly,
   Out of a Christ-like soul;
Thy words a blessèd balm shall be,
   To make the sin-sick whole.

5 Speak, for the love of God,—
   Speak, for the love of man;
The words of truth love sends abroad,
   Shall never be in vain.

George B. Bubier (—1869).

382   *Work for Christ.*

1 LAB'RERS of Christ, arise,
   And gird you for the toil;
The dew of promise from the skies
   Already cheers the soil.

2 Go where the sick recline,
   Where mourning hearts deplore;
And where the sons of sorrow pine,
   Dispense your hallow'd lore.

3 So shall you share the wealth
   That earth may ne'er despoil,
And the blest Gospel's saving health
   Repay your arduous toil.

Mrs. Lydia Howard Huntley Sigourney (1791—1865). Ab.

LEIGHTON. S. M. — HENRY WELLINGTON GREATOREX (1811—1858), 1849.

BISHOP. L. M. JOSEPH PERRY HOLBROOK (1822–), 1862.

1. My gracious Lord, I own Thy right To ev-'ry ser-vice I can pay,
And call it my supreme de-light To hear Thy dic-tates and o-bey.

383 *Serving Christ.*
Phil. i. 22.

2 I would not breathe for worldly joy,
Or to increase my worldly good;
Nor future days nor powers employ
To spread a sounding name abroad.

3 'Tis to my Saviour I would live,
To Him who for my ransom died;
Nor could the bowers of Eden give
Such bliss as blossoms at His side.

4 His work my hoary age shall bless,
When youthful vigor is no more;
And my last hour of life confess
His dying love, His saving power.
   Rev. Philip Doddridge (1702–1751), 1755. Ab. and alt.

384 *"Go, labor on."*

1 Go, labor on; spend and be spent,
Thy joy to do the Father's will:
It is the way the Master went;
Should not the servant tread it still?

2 Go, labor on; 'tis not for naught;
Thine earthly loss is heavenly gain:
Men heed thee, love thee, praise thee not;
The Master praises,—what are men?

3 Go, labor on; enough, while here,
If He shall praise thee, if He deign
Thy willing heart to mark and cheer:
No toil for Him shall be in vain.

4 Toil on, and in thy toil rejoice;
For toil comes rest, for exile, home;
Soon shalt thou hear the Bridegroom's voice,
The midnight peal: "Behold, I come!"
   Rev. Horatius Bonar (1808–), 1857. Ab.

385 *Adorning the Doctrine.*
Titus. ii. 10–13.

1 So let our lips and lives express
The holy gospel we profess;
So let our works and virtues shine,
To prove the doctrine all divine.

2 Thus shall we best proclaim abroad
The honors of our Saviour God;
When His salvation reigns within,
And grace subdues the power of sin.

3 Our flesh and sense must be denied,
Passion and envy, lust and pride;
While justice, temperance, truth and love,
Our inward piety approve.

4 Religion bears our spirits up,
While we expect that blessed hope,
The bright appearance of the Lord,
And faith stands leaning on His word.
   Rev. Isaac Watts (1674–1748), 1709. Sl. alt.

386 *For Grace to surrender all.*

1 Jesus, our best beloved Friend,
Draw out our souls in pure desire;
Jesus, in love to us descend,
Baptize us with Thy Spirit's fire.

2 Our souls and bodies we resign,
To fear and follow Thy commands;
O take our hearts, our hearts are Thine,
Accept the service of our hands.

3 Firm, faithful, watching unto prayer,
May we Thy blessed will obey;
Toil in Thy vineyard here, and bear
The heat and burden of the day.
   James Montgomery (1771–1854), 1825. Ab.

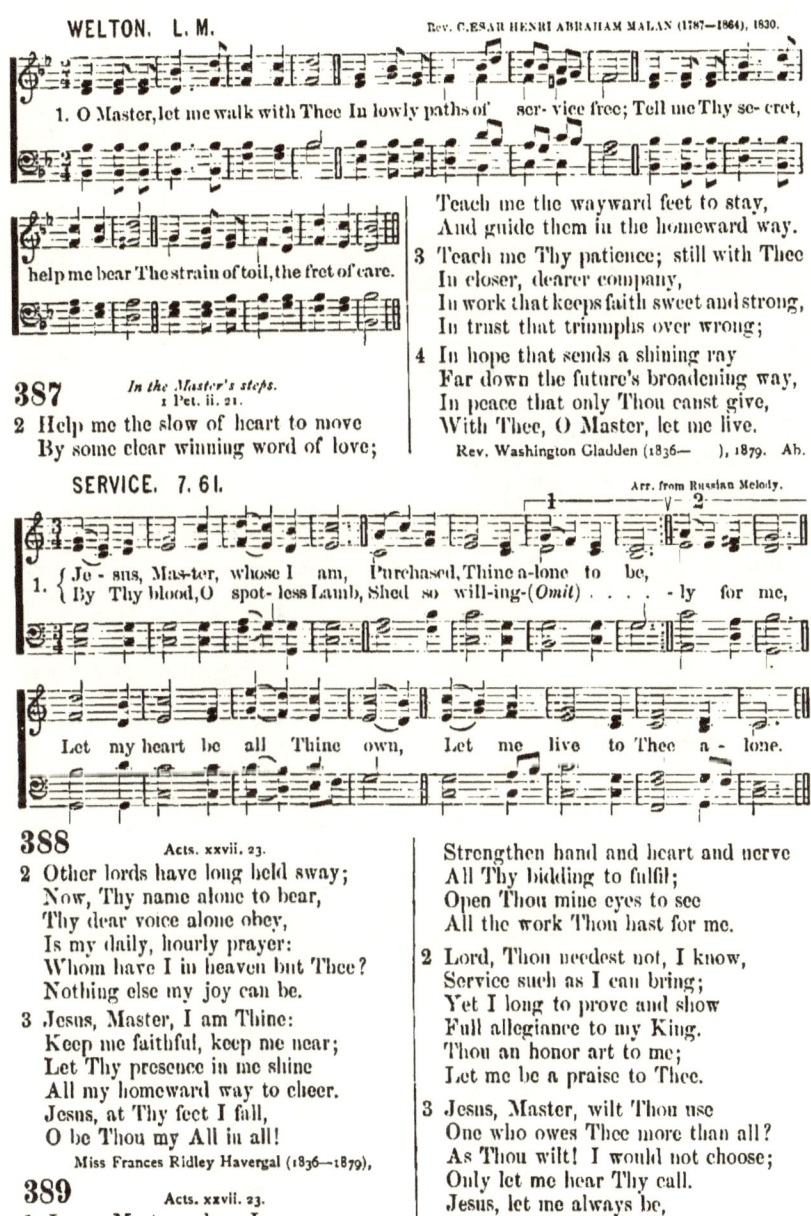

WELTON. L. M. — Rev. CÆSAR HENRI ABRAHAM MALAN (1787—1864), 1830.

1. O Master, let me walk with Thee
In lowly paths of service free;
Tell me Thy secret, help me bear
The strain of toil, the fret of care.

387 *In the Master's steps.* 1 Pet. ii. 21.

2 Help me the slow of heart to move
By some clear winning word of love;
Teach me the wayward feet to stay,
And guide them in the homeward way.

3 Teach me Thy patience; still with Thee
In closer, dearer company,
In work that keeps faith sweet and strong,
In trust that triumphs over wrong;

4 In hope that sends a shining ray
Far down the future's broadening way,
In peace that only Thou canst give,
With Thee, O Master, let me live.
Rev. Washington Gladden (1836—   ), 1879. Ab.

SERVICE. 7. 6 l. — Arr. from Russian Melody.

1. Jesus, Master, whose I am,
Purchased, Thine alone to be,
By Thy blood, O spotless Lamb,
Shed so willing-(Omit) . . . ly for me,
Let my heart be all Thine own,
Let me live to Thee alone.

388 Acts. xxvii. 23.

2 Other lords have long held sway;
Now, Thy name alone to bear,
Thy dear voice alone obey,
Is my daily, hourly prayer:
Whom have I in heaven but Thee?
Nothing else my joy can be.

3 Jesus, Master, I am Thine:
Keep me faithful, keep me near;
Let Thy presence in me shine
All my homeward way to cheer.
Jesus, at Thy feet I fall,
O be Thou my All in all!
Miss Frances Ridley Havergal (1836—1879).

389 Acts. xxvii. 23.

1 Jesus, Master, whom I serve,
Though so feebly and so ill,
Strengthen hand and heart and nerve
All Thy bidding to fulfil;
Open Thou mine eyes to see
All the work Thou hast for me.

2 Lord, Thou needest not, I know,
Service such as I can bring;
Yet I long to prove and show
Full allegiance to my King.
Thou an honor art to me;
Let me be a praise to Thee.

3 Jesus, Master, wilt Thou use
One who owes Thee more than all?
As Thou wilt! I would not choose;
Only let me hear Thy call.
Jesus, let me always be,
In Thy service, glad and free!
Miss Frances Ridley Havergal,

THE CHRISTIAN LIFE.

SOUTHPORT. C. M. — GEORGE KINGSLEY (1811–1884), 1853.

1. Work-man of God, O lose not heart, But learn what God is like;

And in the dark-est bat-tle-field Thou shalt know where to strike.

390 *The winning Side.*

2 Thrice blest is he to whom is given
  The instinct that can tell
That God is on the field, when He
  Is most invisible.

3 Blest too is he who can divine,
  Where real right doth lie,
And dares to take the side that seems
  Wrong to man's blindfold eye.

4 For right is right, since God is God,
  And right the day must win;
To doubt would be disloyalty,
  To falter would be sin.
  Rev. Frederick William Faber (1814—1863), 1849. Ab.

391 *Waiting for Light.*

1 O VERY God of very God,
  And very Light of Light,
Whose feet this earth's dark valley trod,
  That so it might be bright.

2 Our hopes are weak, our fears are strong,
  Thick darkness blinds our eyes;
Cold is the night, and O we long
  That Thou, our Sun, wouldst rise.

3 O guide us till our path is done,
  And we have reached the shore
Where Thou, our everlasting Sun,
  Art shining evermore.

4 We wait in faith, and turn our face
  To where the daylight springs,
Till Thou shalt come our gloom to chase,
  With healing on Thy wings.
  Rev. John Mason Neale (1818—1866), 1846. Ab.

392 *"The Poor always with you."* Matt. xxvi. 11.

1 LORD, lead the way the Saviour went,
  By lane and cell obscure,
And let our treasures still be spent,
  Like His, upon the poor.

2 Like Him, through scenes of deep distress,
  Who bore the world's sad weight,
We, in their crowded loneliness,
  Would seek the desolate.

3 For Thou hast placed us side by side
  In this wide world of ill;
And that Thy followers may be tried,
  The poor are with us still.

4 Mean are all offerings we can make;
  But Thou hast taught us, Lord,
If given for the Saviour's sake,
  They lose not their reward.
  Rev. William Croswell (1804—1851), 1831.

393 *Charitableness.*

1 THINK gently of the erring one;
  And let us not forget,
However darkly stained by sin,
  He is our brother yet.

2 Heir of the same inheritance,
  Child of the self-same God;
He hath but stumbled in the path
  We have in weakness trod.

3 Forget not thou hast often sinned,
  And sinful yet must be:
Deal gently with the erring one,
  As God has dealt with thee.
  Miss Fletcher, 1846.

ST. MATTHEW. C. M. D.
WILLIAM CROFT (1677—1727).

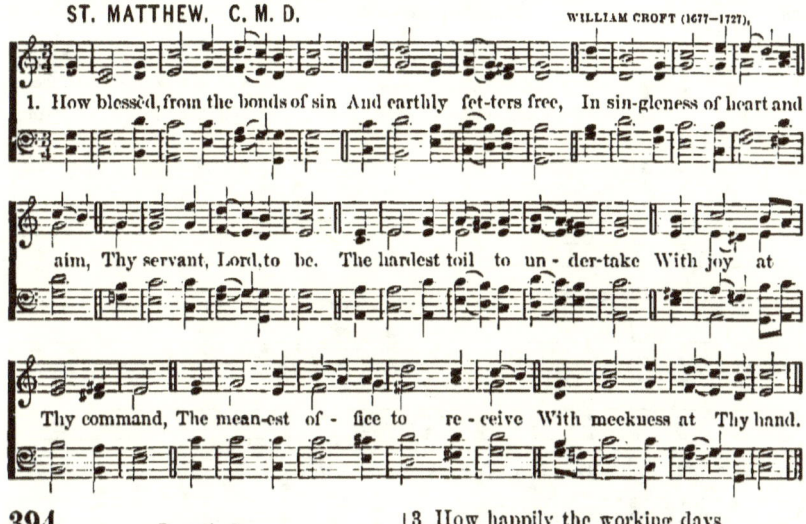

1. How blesséd, from the bonds of sin And earthly fet-ters free, In sin-gleness of heart and aim, Thy servant, Lord, to be. The hardest toil to un-der-take With joy at Thy command, The mean-est of - fice to re-ceive With meekness at Thy hand.

394 Ps. cxvi. 13.

2 Thus may I serve Thee, gracious Lord;
　Thus ever Thine alone,
My soul and body given to Thee,
　The purchase Thou hast won;
Through evil or through good report
　Still keeping by Thy side;
And by my life, or by my death,
　Let Christ be magnified.

3 How happily the working days
　In this dear service fly!
How rapidly the closing hour,
　The time of rest draws nigh!
When all the faithful gather home,
　A joyful company,
And ever where the Master is
　Shall His blest servants be.

Rev. Carl Johann Philipp Spitta (1801—1859), 1843.
Tr. by Miss Jane Borthwick (1813—), 1854. Ab.

ALMSGIVING. 8. 8. 8. 4.
Rev. JOHN BACCHUS DYKES (1823—1876).

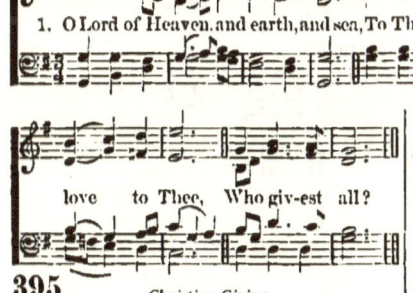

1. O Lord of Heaven, and earth, and sea, To Thee all praise and glo-ry be; How shall we show our love to Thee, Who giv-est all?

395 Christian Giving.

2 Thou didst not spare Thine only Son,
But gavest Him for a world undone,
And freely with that blessèd One
　Thou givest all.

3 Thou givest the Spirit's blessèd dower,
Spirit of life, and love, and power,
And dost His sevenfold graces shower
　Upon us all.

4 For souls redeemed, for sins forgiven,
For means of grace, and hopes of Heaven,
What can to Thee, O Lord, be given,
　Who givest all?

Bp. Christopher Wordsworth (1807—1885), 1863. Ab.
and alt.

160 THE CHRISTIAN LIFE.

RESCUE. P. M. WILLIAM HOWARD DOANE (1832–). 1870.

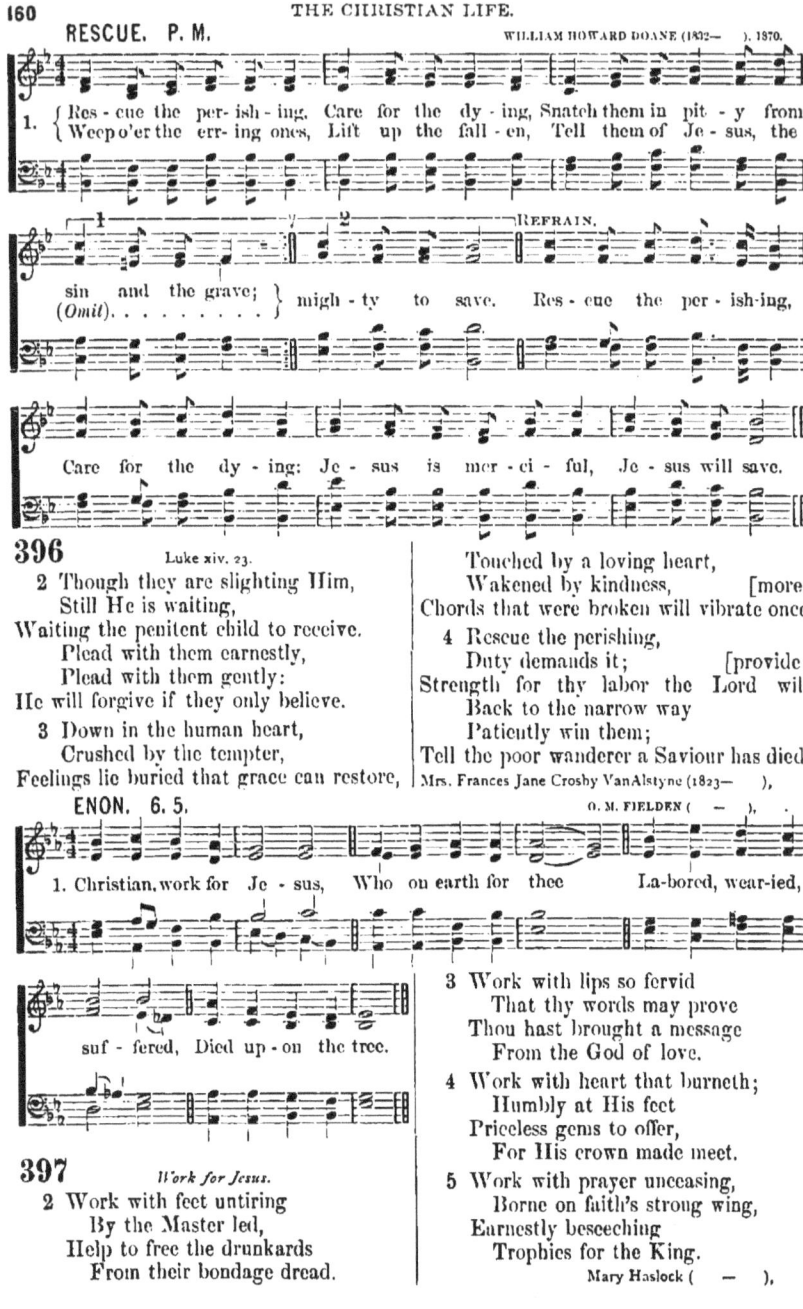

1. Rescue the perishing, Care for the dying, Snatch them in pity from sin and the grave; Weep o'er the erring ones, Lift up the fallen, Tell them of Jesus, the (Omit)......... mighty to save. Rescue the perishing, Care for the dying: Jesus is merciful, Jesus will save.

396   Luke xiv. 23.

2 Though they are slighting Him,
   Still He is waiting,
Waiting the penitent child to receive.
   Plead with them earnestly,
   Plead with them gently:
He will forgive if they only believe.

3 Down in the human heart,
   Crushed by the tempter,
Feelings lie buried that grace can restore,
   Touched by a loving heart,
   Wakened by kindness, [more.
Chords that were broken will vibrate once

4 Rescue the perishing,
   Duty demands it; [provide:
Strength for thy labor the Lord will
   Back to the narrow way
   Patiently win them;
Tell the poor wanderer a Saviour has died.

Mrs. Frances Jane Crosby VanAlstyne (1823–),

ENON. 6. 5. O. M. FIELDEN (–),

1. Christian, work for Jesus, Who on earth for thee Labored, wearied, suffered, Died upon the tree.

397   *Work for Jesus.*

2 Work with feet untiring
   By the Master led,
   Help to free the drunkards
   From their bondage dread.

3 Work with lips so fervid
   That thy words may prove
   Thou hast brought a message
   From the God of love.

4 Work with heart that burneth;
   Humbly at His feet
   Priceless gems to offer,
   For His crown made meet.

5 Work with prayer unceasing,
   Borne on faith's strong wing,
   Earnestly beseeching
   Trophies for the King.

Mary Haslock (–),

TEMPTATION. P. M. HENRY R. PALMER (—), 1868.

1. Yield not to tempta-tion, For yielding is sin,
Each vict'ry will help you
Fight man-ful-ly on-ward, Dark passions sub-due,
Look ev-er to Je-sus,
Some oth-er to win;
(Omit) . . . . . . He'll car-ry you through.

REFRAIN.
Ask the Saviour to help you, Comfort strengthen, and keep you He is will-ing to aid you, He will car-ry you through.

398 1 Cor. x. 13.

2 Shun evil companions,
  Bad language disdain,
God's name hold in rev'rence,
  Nor take it in vain;
Be thoughtful and earnest,
  Kind-hearted and true,
Look ever to Jesus,
  He will carry you through.—REF.

3 To him that o'ercometh
  God giveth a crown,
Thro' faith we shall conquer,
  Though often cast down;
He, who is our Saviour,
  Our strength will renew,
Look ever to Jesus,
  He will carry you through.—REF.

Henry R. Palmer.

SWABIA. S. M. Arr. from German.

1. Mourn for the thousands slain, The youthful and the strong; Mourn for the winecup's fear-ful reign, And the de-lu-ded throng.

399 *Intemperance.*

2 Mourn for the ruined soul,
  Eternal life and light
Lost by the fiery, maddening bowl,
  And turned to hopeless night.

3 Mourn for the lost, but call,
  Call to the strong, the free;
Rouse them to shun the dreadful fall,
  And to the refuge flee.

4 Mourn for the lost, but pray,
  Pray to our God above,
To break the fell destroyer's sway,
  And show His saving love.

Rev. Seth Collins Brace (1811—), 1843.

WORK. 7, 6, 7, 5, D. LOWELL MASON (1792–1872).

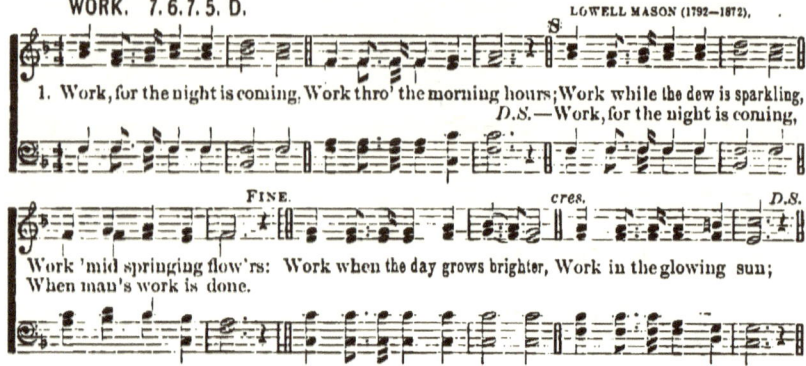

1. Work, for the night is coming, Work thro' the morning hours; Work while the dew is sparkling,
D.S.—Work, for the night is coming,
Work 'mid springing flow'rs: Work when the day grows brighter, Work in the glowing sun;
When man's work is done.

400 *Work.*

2 Work, for the night is coming,
　Work through the sunny noon;
　Fill brightest hours with labor,
　Rest comes sure and soon.
　Give every flying minute
　Something to keep in store:
　Work, for the night is coming,
　When man works no more.

3 Work, for the night is coming,
　Under the sunset skies;
　While their bright tints are glowing,
　Work, for daylight flies.
　Work till the last beam fadeth,
　Fadeth to shine no more;
　Work while the night is dark'ning,
　When man's work is o'er.

　　　　　Anna L. Walker (—), 1868.

PAX TECUM. 10, 10. G. T. CALDBECK (—).

1. Peace, perfect peace, in this dark world of sin? The blood of Jesus whispers peace with-in.

401　Is. xxvi. 3.

2 Peace, perfect peace, by thronging duties pressed?
　To do the will of Jesus, this is rest.

3 Peace, perfect peace, with sorrows surging round?
　On Jesus' bosom nought but calm is found.

4 Peace, perfect peace, with loved ones far away?
　In Jesus' keeping we are safe, and they.

5 Peace, perfect peace, our future all unknown?
　Jesus we know, and He is on the throne.

6 Peace, perfect peace, death shadowing us and ours?
　Jesus has vanquished death and all its powers.

7 It is enough: earth's struggle soon shall cease
　And Jesus call us to heaven's perfect peace.

　　　　　Bp. Edward Henry Bickersteth (1825–), 1883.

CONSECRATION. 6.4.6.4.6.6.6.4.

Rev. ROBERT LOWRY (1826—), 1871.

1. Saviour, Thy dying love Thou gavest me,
Nor should I aught withhold, Dear Lord from Thee;
In love my soul would bow,
My heart fulfill its vow,
Some offering bring Thee now,
Something for Thee.

402   Acts. ix 6.

2 At the blest mercy-seat,
   Pleading for me,
My feeble faith looks up,
   Jesus, to Thee:
Help me the cross to bear,
Thy wondrous love declare,
Some song to raise, or prayer,
   Something for Thee.

3 Give me a faithful heart—
   Likeness to Thee—
That each departing day
   Henceforth may see

Some work of love begun,
Some deed of kindness done,
Some wand'rer sought and won,
   Something for Thee.

4 All that I am and have—
   Thy gifts so free—
In joy, in grief, through life,
   Dear Lord, for Thee!
And when Thy face I see,
My ransomed soul shall be,
Through all eternity,
   Something for Thee.

Rev. Sylvanus Dryden Phelps (1816—),

PLEYEL'S HYMN. 7.

IGNAZ JOSEPH PLEYEL (1757—1831), 1800.

1. Take my life, and let it be Consecrated, Lord, to Thee: Take my moments and my days, Let them flow in ceaseless praise.

403   *Consecration Hymn.*

2 Take my hands, and let them move
At the impulse of Thy love:
Take my feet, and let them be
Swift and beautiful for Thee.

3 Take my silver and my gold;
Not a mite would I withhold:

Take my intellect, and use
Every power as Thou dost choose.

4 Take my will, and make it Thine;
It shall be no longer mine:
Take my heart: it is Thine own;
It shall be Thy royal throne.

5 Take my love: my Lord, I pour
At Thy feet its treasure-store:
Take myself, and I will be
Ever, only, all for Thee!

Miss Frances Ridley Havergal (1836—1879), 1873. Ab.

THE LORD'S SUPPER.

LUDWIG. 7, 6. D. LUDWIG von BEETHOVEN (1770—1827). 1824.

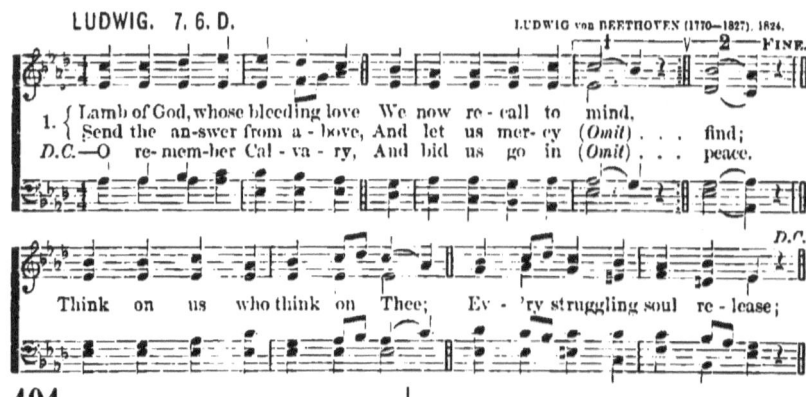

1. Lamb of God, whose bleeding love We now re-call to mind,
Send the an-swer from a-bove, And let us mer-cy (*Omit*) . . . find;
D.C.—O re-mem-ber Cal-va-ry, And bid us go in (*Omit*) . . . peace.
Think on us who think on Thee; Ev-'ry struggling soul re-lease;

404 "*Bid us go in Peace.*"

2 By Thine agonizing pain
And bloody sweat, we pray,
By Thy dying love to man,
Take all our sins away;
Burst our bonds and set us free,
From iniquity release;
O remember Calvary,
And bid us go in peace.

3 Let Thy blood, by faith applied,
The sinner's pardon seal;
Speak us freely justified,
And all our sickness heal;
By Thy passion on the tree,
Let our griefs and troubles cease;
O remember Calvary,
And bid us go in peace.

Rev. Charles Wesley (1708—1788), 1745. Ab. and alt. sl.

DAY OF REST. 7, 6. D. J. W. ELLIOTT (1816—).

1. O Je-sus, I have promised To serve Thee to the end; Be Thou for-ev-er
near me, My Mas-ter and my Friend! I shall not fear the bat-tle If Thou art
by my side, Nor wan-der from the path-way If Thou wilt be my guide.

405 "*Lord, I will follow Thee.*"

2 O let me hear Thee speaking
In accents clear and still,
Above the storms of passion,
The murmurs of self-will.

O speak to re-assure me,
To hasten or control:
O speak, and make me listen,
Thou Guardian of my soul!

CONSECRATION AND CONFESSION.

3 O Jesus Thou hast promised
 To all who follow Thee,
That, where Thou art in glory,
 There shall Thy servant be;
And, Jesus, I have promised
 To serve Thee to the end;
O give me grace to follow
 My Master and my Friend.
John Ernest Bode (1816—1874). . Ab.

BENEDICTION. L. M. 6 l.   JOSEPH BARNBY (1838—), 1872.

406
Adoring Love.

2 Jesus, too late I Thee have sought,
 How can I love Thee as I ought;
 And how extol Thy matchless fame,
 The glorious beauty of Thy Name?
 Jesus, my Lord, I Thee adore,
 O make me love Thee more and more.

3 Jesus, what didst Thou find in me,
 That Thou hast dealt so lovingly?
 How great the joy that Thou hast brought,
 So far exceeding hope or thought!
 Jesus, my Lord, I Thee adore,
 O make me love Thee more and more.

4 Jesus, of Thee shall be my song,
 To Thee my heart and soul belong;
 All that I have or am is Thine,
 And Thou, blest Saviour, Thou art mine;
 Jesus, my Lord, I Thee adore,
 O make me love Thee more and more.
Rev. Henry Collins (—), 1852.

ZURICH. S. M.   HANS GEORG NAGELI (1773—1836).

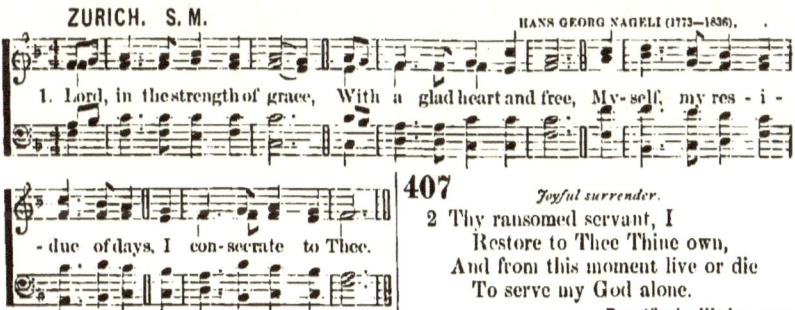

407
Joyful surrender.

2 Thy ransomed servant, I
 Restore to Thee Thine own,
And from this moment live or die
 To serve my God alone.
Rev. Charles Wesley, 1745.

THE LORD'S SUPPER.

CULFORD. 7. D. — EDWARD JOHN HOPKINS (1818—).

1. People of the living God, I have sought the world around, Paths of sin and sorrow trod, Peace and comfort no-where found, Now to you my spirit turns, Turns, a fugitive unbless'd; Brethren where your altar burns, O receive me into rest.

408 *Choosing the Portion of God's Heritage.*
Ruth i. 16, 17.

2 Lonely I no longer roam,
  Like the cloud, the wind, the wave;
Where you dwell shall be my home,
  Where you die shall be my grave;

Mine the God whom you adore,
  Your Redeemer shall be mine;
Earth can fill my heart no more,
  Every idol I resign.

James Montgomery (1771—1854), 1819, 1853. Ab.

ELLESDIE. 8. 7. D. — Arr. from JOHANN C. W. A. MOZART (1756—1791).

1. Sweet the moments, rich in blessing, Which before the cross I spend; Life and health and peace possessing, From the sinner's dying Friend.
D.S.—Precious drops, my soul bedewing, Plead and claim my peace with God.

Here I'll sit, forever viewing Mercy's streams in streams of blood.

CONSECRATION. 167

409 *Before the Cross.*

2 Truly blessèd is this station,
　Low before His cross to lie,
While I see divine compassion
　Floating in His languid eye.
Here it is I find my Heaven,
　While upon the Lamb I gaze;
Love I much? I've much forgiven;
　I'm a miracle of grace.

3 Love and grief my heart dividing,
　With my tears His feet I'll bathe,
Constant still, in faith abiding,
　Life deriving from His death.
May I still enjoy this feeling,
　In all need to Jesus go;
Prove His blood each day more healing,
　And Himself most deeply know.
　　　Rev. James Allen (1734—1804), 1757. Alt.
　　Hon. and Rev. Walter Shirley (1725—1786), 1771.

BUDLEIGH. 6, 4, 6, 4, 10, 10.　　THOMAS MOLLISON MUDIE (1809—1876).

1. I lift my heart to Thee, Sav-iour Di-vine! For Thou art all to me, And I am Thine. Is there on earth a clos-er bond than this, That "my Be-lov-ed's mine, and I am His?"

410 *Devotion to Christ.*

2 Thine am I by all ties;
　But chiefly Thine,
That through Thy sacrifice
　Thou, Lord, art mine.
By Thine own chords of love, so sweetly wound
Around me, I to Thee am closely bound.

3 To Thee, Thou bleeding Lamb,
　I all things owe;
All that I have and am,
　And all I know.
All that I have is now no longer mine,
And I am not mine own; Lord, I am Thine.

4 How can I, Lord, withhold
　Life's brightest hour
From Thee; or gathered gold,
　Or any power?
Why should I keep one precious thing from Thee,
When Thou hast given Thine own dear Self for me?

5 I pray Thee, Saviour, keep
　Me in Thy love,
Until death's holy sleep
　Shall me remove
To that far realm where, sin and sorrow [o'er,
Thou and Thine own are one for evermore.
　　　Charles Edward Mudie (1818—　).

THE LORD'S SUPPER.

NEEDHAM. C. M.
SAMUEL SEBASTIAN WESLEY (1810–1876), 1872.

1. What shall I render to my God For all His kindness shown? My feet shall visit Thine abode, My songs address Thy throne.

411   Ps. cxvi.

2 How happy all Thy servants are!
    How great Thy grace to me!
My life, which Thou hast made Thy care,
    Lord, I devote to Thee.

3 Now I am Thine—for ever Thine;
    Nor shall my purpose move;
Thy hand hath loosed my bonds of pain,
    And bound me with Thy love.

4 Here, in Thy courts, I leave my vow,
    And Thy rich grace record;
Witness, ye saints, who hear me now,
    If I forsake the Lord.

Rev. Isaac Watts (1674–1748), 1719. Ab.

412   *Self Consecration.*

1 My God accept my heart this day,
    And make it always Thine,
That I from Thee no more may stray,
    No more from Thee decline.

2 Before the cross of Him who died,
    Behold, I prostrate fall;
Let every sin be crucified,
    Let Christ be all in all.

3 May the dear blood once shed for me
    My blest atonement prove,
That I from first to last may be
    The purchase of Thy love.

4 Let every thought, and work, and word
    To Thee be ever given;
Then life shall be Thy service, Lord!
    And death the gate of Heaven.

Matthew Bridges (1800–   ), 1848.

413   *Yielding to Christ.*

1 Witness, ye men and angels, now,
    Before the Lord we speak;
To Him we make our solemn vow,
    A vow we dare not break—

2 That long as life itself shall last
    Ourselves to Christ we yield;
Nor from His cause will we depart,
    Nor ever quit the field.

3 We trust not in our native strength,
    But on His grace rely;
That, with returning wants the Lord,
    Will all our need supply.

4 O guide our doubtful feet aright,
    And keep us in Thy ways;
And while we turn our vows to prayers,
    Turn Thou our prayers to praise.

Rev. Benjamin Beddome (1717–1795), 1787.

ARMENIA. C. M.
SYLVANUS BILLINGS POND (1792–1871).

SELF DEDICATION.

DORRNANCE. 8. 7. ISAAC BAKER WOODBURY (1819—1858), 1850.

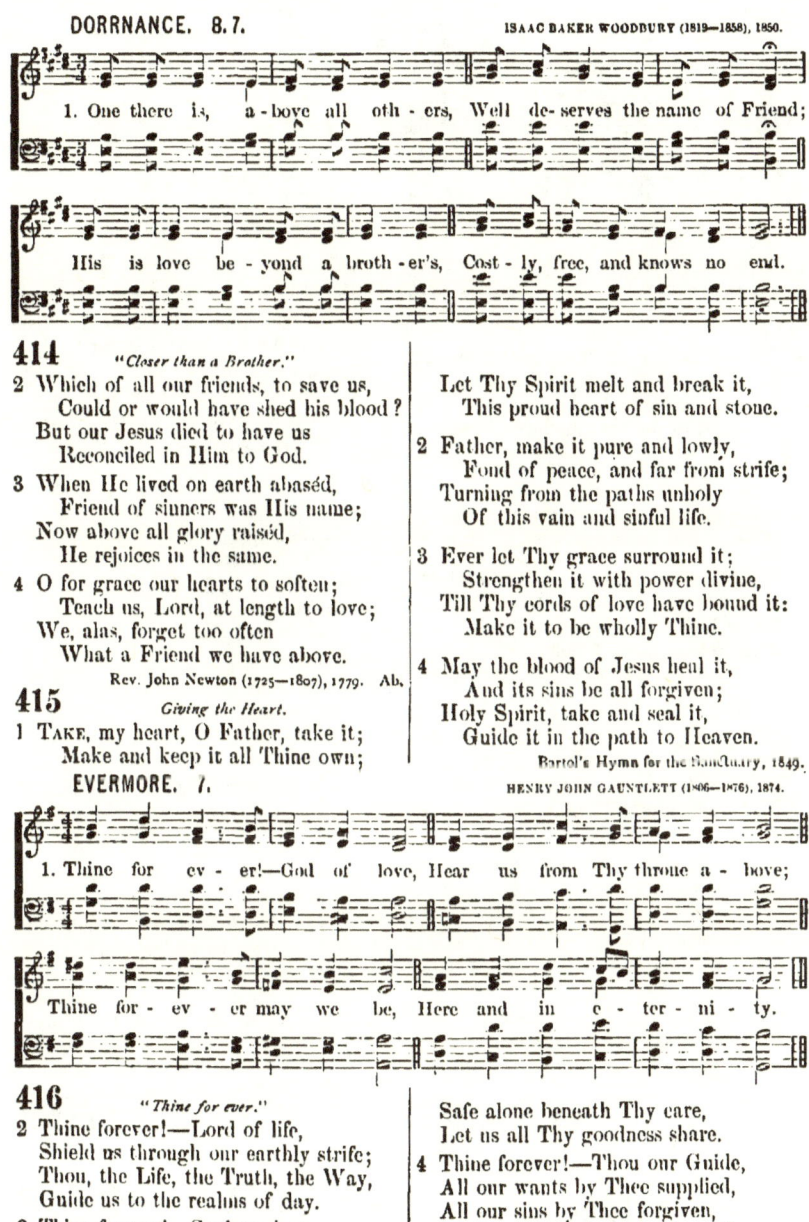

1. One there is, above all others, Well deserves the name of Friend;
His is love beyond a brother's, Costly, free, and knows no end.

414 *"Closer than a Brother."*

2 Which of all our friends, to save us,
   Could or would have shed his blood?
But our Jesus died to have us
   Reconciled in Him to God.

3 When He lived on earth abased,
   Friend of sinners was His name;
Now above all glory raised,
   He rejoices in the same.

4 O for grace our hearts to soften;
   Teach us, Lord, at length to love;
We, alas, forget too often
   What a Friend we have above.
     Rev. John Newton (1725—1807), 1779. Ab.

415 *Giving the Heart.*

1 Take, my heart, O Father, take it;
   Make and keep it all Thine own;
Let Thy Spirit melt and break it,
   This proud heart of sin and stone.

2 Father, make it pure and lowly,
   Fond of peace, and far from strife;
Turning from the paths unholy
   Of this vain and sinful life.

3 Ever let Thy grace surround it;
   Strengthen it with power divine,
Till Thy cords of love have bound it:
   Make it to be wholly Thine.

4 May the blood of Jesus heal it,
   And its sins be all forgiven;
Holy Spirit, take and seal it,
   Guide it in the path to Heaven.
     Bartol's Hymn for the Sanctuary, 1849.

EVERMORE. 7. HENRY JOHN GAUNTLETT (1806—1876), 1874.

1. Thine forever!—God of love, Hear us from Thy throne above;
Thine forever may we be, Here and in eternity.

416 *"Thine for ever."*

2 Thine forever!—Lord of life,
   Shield us through our earthly strife;
Thou, the Life, the Truth, the Way,
   Guide us to the realms of day.

3 Thine forever!—Saviour, keep
   These Thy frail and trembling sheep;
Safe alone beneath Thy care,
   Let us all Thy goodness share.

4 Thine forever!—Thou our Guide,
   All our wants by Thee supplied,
All our sins by Thee forgiven,
   Lead us, Lord, from earth to Heaven.
     Mrs. Mary Fawler Maude (—), 1848. Ab.

CRASSELIUS. L. M.
Hamburger Musikalisches Handbuch (1690—), c. 1690.

1. O hap-py day, that fix'd my choice On Thee, my Sav-iour and my God;
Well may this glow-ing heart re-joice, And tell its rap-tures all a-broad.

417 *Rejoicing in our Covenant-Engagements.*
2 Chron. xv. 15.

2 'Tis done, the great transaction's done;
  I am my Lord's, and He is mine:
  He drew me, and I followed on,
  Charmed to confess the voice divine.

3 Now rest, my long divided heart,
  Fixed on this blissful centre, rest;
  With ashes who would grudge to part,
  When called on angels' bread to feast?

4 High Heaven, that heard the solemn vow,
  That vow renewed shall daily hear,
  Till in life's latest hour I bow,
  And bless in death a bond so dear.
      Rev. Philip Doddridge (1702—1751), 1755. Ab.

418 *"Entirely Thine."*

1 LORD, I am Thine, entirely Thine,
  Purchased and saved by blood divine;
  With full consent Thine I would be,
  And own Thy sovereign right in me.

2 Grant one poor sinner more a place
  Among the children of Thy grace;
  A wretched sinner, lost to God,
  But ransomed by Immanuel's blood.

3 Thine would I live, Thine would I die,
  Be Thine through all eternity;
  The vow is passed beyond repeal;
  And now I set the solemn seal.

4 Here at that cross where flows the blood
  That bought my guilty soul for God,
  Thee, my new Master now I call,
  And consecrate to Thee my all.
      Rev. Samuel Davies (1724—1761), 1769. Ab.

419 *Trusting the Merits of Christ.*
Phil. iii. 7-9.

1 No more, my God, I boast no more
  Of all the duties I have done;
  I quit the hopes I held before,
  To trust the mercies of Thy Son.

2 Now for the love I bear His name,
  What was my gain I count my loss;
  My former pride I call my shame,
  And nail my glory to His cross.

3 Yes, and I must and will esteem
  All things but loss for Jesus' sake;
  O may my soul be found in Him,
  And of His righteousness partake.
      Rev. Isaac Watts (1674—1748), 1709. Ab.

420 *The sweet Wonders of the Cross.*

1 O the sweet wonders of that cross
  Where my Redeemer loved and died;
  Her noblest life my spirit draws
  From His dear wounds, and bleeding side.

2 I would forever speak His name
  In sounds to mortal ears unknown;
  With angels join to praise the Lamb,
  And worship at His Father's throne.
      Rev. Isaac Watts 1709. Ab.

HEBRON. L. M.
LOWELL MASON (1792—1872), 1830.

CONSECRATION.

ST. JUDE. 8, 7, 8, 7. CHARLES VINCENT (1852–).

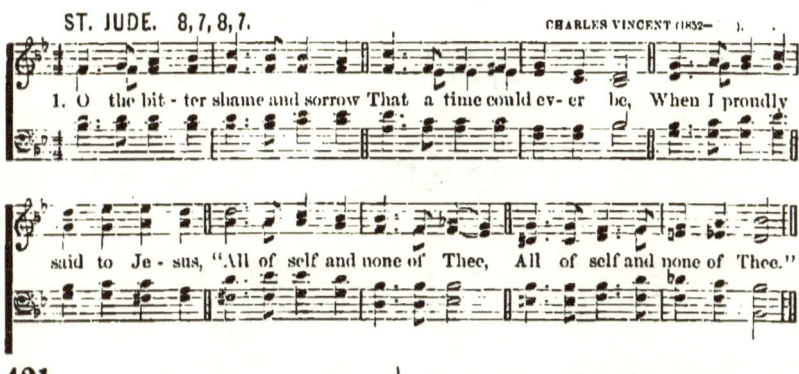

1. O the bitter shame and sorrow That a time could ever be, When I proudly said to Jesus, "All of self and none of Thee, All of self and none of Thee."

421   *"None of Self."*

2 Yet He found me, I beheld Him
Bleeding on th' accursèd tree,
And my wistful heart said faintly,
"Some of self, and some of Thee."

3 Day by day His tender mercy
Healing, helping, full and free,
Brought me lower, while I whispered,
"Less of self, and more of Thee."

4 Higher than the highest heavens,
Deeper than the deepest sea,
Lord, Thy love at last has conquered;
"None of self, and all of Thee."
           Rev. Theodore Monod (—).

BLISS. 6. 6. 6. 6. 8. 6. PHILIP P. BLISS (1838–1876).

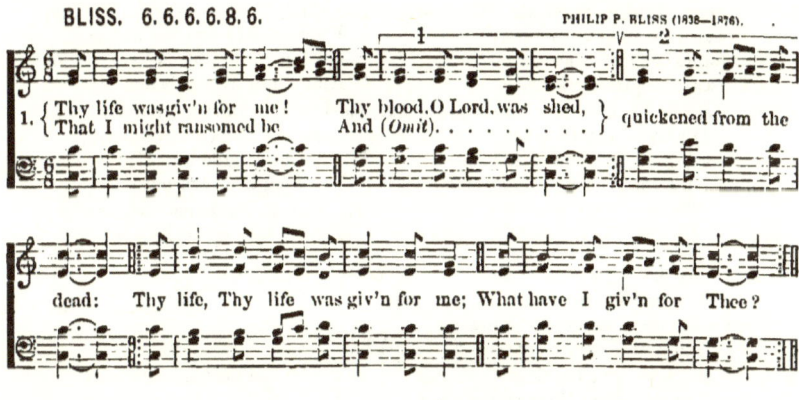

1. Thy life was giv'n for me! That I might ransomed be, Thy blood, O Lord, was shed, And (*Omit*). . . . . quickened from the dead: Thy life, Thy life was giv'n for me; What have I giv'n for Thee?

422   2 Cor. viii. 5.

2 Thy Father's home of light,
Thy rainbow-circled throne,
Were left for earthly night,
For wanderings sad and lone;
Yea, all, yea, all was left for me:
Have I left aught for Thee?

3 And Thou hast brought to me,
Down from Thy home above,
Salvation full and free,
Thy pardon and Thy love;
Great gifts, great gifts Thou broughtest me:
What have I brought to Thee?

4 O let my life be given,
My years for Thee be spent;
World-fetters all be riven,
And joy with suffering blent:
Thou gav'st, Thou gav'st Thyself for me,
I give myself to Thee!
   Miss Frances Ridley Havergal (1836–1879).   . Ab. and alt.

THE COMMUNION OF SAINTS.

CHRISTMAS. C. M.   GEORGE FREDERICK HANDEL (1685–1759).

1, Give me the wings of faith, to rise With-in the veil, and see The saints above, how great their joys, How bright their glo-ries be, How bright their glo-ries be.

423   *"The Saints above."*

2 I ask them, whence their victory came?
    They, with united breath,
Ascribe their conquest to the Lamb
    Their triumph to His death.

3 They marked the footsteps that He trod;
    His zeal inspired their breast;
And following their incarnate God,
    Possess the promised rest.

4 Our glorious Leader claims our praise,
    For His own pattern given,
While the long cloud of witnesses
    Show the same path to Heaven.
            Rev. Isaac Watts (1674–1748), 1709. Ab.

424   *One Church, one Army.*

1 LET saints below in concert sing
    With those to glory gone;
For all the servants of our King
    In earth and Heaven are one.

2 One family, we dwell in Him,
    One Church above, beneath;
Though now divided by the stream,
    The narrow stream of death.

3 One army of the living God,
    To His command we bow;
Part of the host have crossed the flood,
    And part are crossing now.

4 Dear Saviour, be our constant Guide;
    Then, when the word is given,
Bid Jordan's narrow stream divide,
    And land us safe in Heaven.
      Rev. Charles Wesley (1708–1788), 1759. Ab. and alt.

425   *One Song.*

1 HAPPY the souls to Jesus joined,
    And saved by grace alone;
Walking in all Thy ways, we find
    Our Heaven on earth begun.

2 The Church triumphant in Thy love
    Their mighty joys we know;
They sing the Lamb in hymns above,
    And we in hymns below.

3 Thee in Thy glorious realm, they praise,
    And bow before Thy throne;
We, in the kingdom of Thy grace:
    The kingdoms are but one.

4 The holy to the holiest leads;
    From hence our spirits rise;
And he that in Thy statutes treads
    Shall meet Thee in the skies.
                Rev. Charles Wesley, 1745.

426   *At Parting.*

1 BLEST be the dear, uniting love,
    That will not let us part;
Our bodies may far off remove,
    We still are joined in heart.

2 Joined in one spirit to our Head,
    Where He appoints we go,
And still in Jesus' footsteps tread,
    And do His work below.

3 Partakers of the Saviour's grace,
    The same in mind and heart,
Nor joy, nor grief, nor time, nor place,
    Nor life, nor death, can part.
                Rev. Charles Wesley, 1742. Ab.

MONSELL. S. M.   JOSEPH BARNBY (1338—), 1868.

1. Blest be the tie that binds Our hearts in christian love: The fel-low-ship of

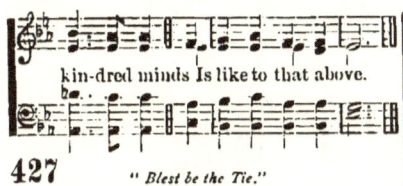

kin-dred minds Is like to that above.

427
"Blest be the Tie."

2 Before our Father's throne
  We pour our ardent prayers;
Our fears, our hopes, our aims are one,
  Our comforts and our cares.

3 We share our mutual woes;
  Our mutual burdens bear;
And often for each other flows
  The sympathizing tear.

4 When we asunder part
  It gives us inward pain;
But we shall still be joined in heart,
  And hope to meet again.
        Rev. John Fawcett (1739—1817), 1772. Ab.

428
Love to the Church.
Ps. cxxxvii.

1 I LOVE Thy kingdom, Lord,
  The house of Thine abode,
The Church our blest Redeemer saved
  With His own precious blood.

2 I love Thy Church, O God:
  Her walls before Thee stand,
Dear as the apple of Thine eye,
  And graven on Thy hand.

3 For her my tears shall fall,
  For her my prayers ascend;
To her my cares and toils be given,
  Till toils and cares shall end.

4 Beyond my highest joy
  I prize her heavenly ways,

Her sweet communion, solemn vows,
  Her hymns of love and praise.

5 Sure as Thy truth shall last,
  To Zion shall be given
The brightest glories earth can yield,
  And brighter bliss of Heaven.
        Rev. Timothy Dwight (1752—1817), 1800. Ab.

429
Adoption.
1 John iii. 1.   Gal. iv. 6.

1 BEHOLD what wondrous grace
  The Father has bestowed
On sinners of a mortal race,
  To call them sons of God.

2 Nor doth it yet appear
  How great we must be made;
But when we see our Saviour here,
  We shall be like our Head.

3 A hope so much divine
  May trials well endure,
May purge our souls from sense and sin,
  As Christ the Lord is pure.
        Rev. Isaac Watts, 1709. Ab.

430
Christian Union.

1 LET party names no more
  The christian world o'erspread;
Gentile and Jew, and bond and free,
  Are one in Christ their Head.

2 Among the saints on earth,
  Let mutual love be found;
Heirs of the same inheritance,
  With mutual blessings crowned.

3 Thus will the Church below
  Resemble that above;
Where streams of pleasure ever flow,
  And every heart is love.
        Rev. Benjamin Beddome (1717—1795), 1759.

BOYLSTON. S. M.   LOWELL MASON (1792—1872), 1832.

FOR CHILDREN.

ROSE HILL. L. M.
JOSEPH EMERSON SWEETZER (1825—1873), 1849.

1. A little child the Saviour came, The mighty God was still His Name, And angels worshipped, as He lay, The seeming infant of a day.

431 *"Let little Children come to Me."*

2 He who, a little child, began
The life divine to show to man,
Proclaims from heaven the message free,
"Let little children come to Me."

3 O give Thine angels charge, good Lord,
Them safely in Thy way to guard;
Thy blessings on their lives command,
And write their names upon Thy hand.
Rev. William Robertson (—1743), 1751. Ab.

432 *Prayer for the Children of the Church.*

1 Dear Saviour, if these lambs should stray
From Thy secure enclosure's bound,
And, lured by worldly joys away,
Among the thoughtless crowd be found;

2 Remember still that they are Thine,
That Thy dear sacred name they bear;
Think that the seal of love divine,
The sign of covenant grace, they wear.

3 In all their erring, sinful years,
O let them ne'er forgotten be;
Remember all the prayers and tears
Which made them consecrate to Thee.

4 And when these lips no more can pray,
These eyes can weep for them no more,
Turn Thou their feet from folly's way,
The wanderers to Thy fold restore.
Mrs. Ann Bradley Hyde (—1872), 1824.

SILOAM. C. M.
ISAAC BAKER WOODBURY (1819—1858), 1850.

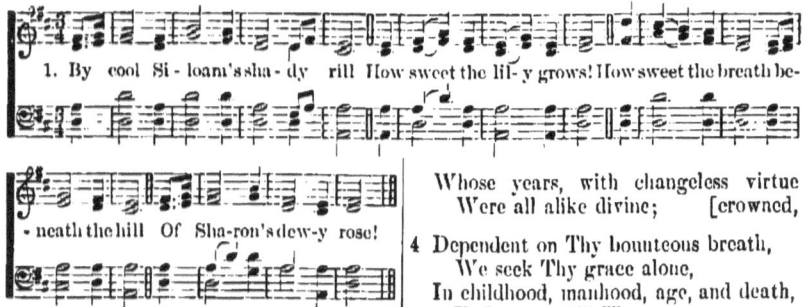

1. By cool Siloam's shady rill How sweet the lily grows! How sweet the breath beneath the hill Of Sharon's dewy rose!

433 *Christ a Pattern for Children.*
Luke ii. 40.

2 Lo, such the child whose early feet
The paths of peace have trod;
Whose secret heart, with influence sweet,
Is upward drawn to God.

3 O Thou, whose infant feet were found
Within Thy Father's shrine,
Whose years, with changeless virtue crowned,
Were all alike divine;

4 Dependent on Thy bounteous breath,
We seek Thy grace alone,
In childhood, manhood, age, and death,
To keep us still Thine own.
Bp. Reginald Heber (1783—1826), 1812. Ab.

434 *Christ's Regard for Children.*
Mark x. 13-16.

1 See, Israel's gentle Shepherd stands,
With all-engaging charms;
Hark, how He calls the tender lambs,
And folds them in His arms!

FOR CHILDREN.

2 "Permit them to approach," He cries,
 "Nor scorn their humble name;
For 'twas to bless such souls as these,
 The Lord of angels came."

3 We bring them, Lord, in thankful hands,
 And yield them up to Thee;
Joyful that we ourselves are Thine,
 Thine let our offspring be.
   Rev. Philip Doddridge (1702–1751), 1755. Ab.

ST. SYLVESTER. 8.7.
Rev. JOHN BACCHUS DYKES (1823–1876), 1862.

1. Saviour, who Thy flock art feeding, With the shepherd's kindest care, All the feeble gently leading, While the lambs Thy bosom share;

435 *Committed to the Shepherd's care.*

2 Now, these little ones receiving,
 Fold them in Thy gracious arm;
There, we know, Thy word believing,
 Only there, secure from harm.

3 Never, from Thy pasture roving,
 Let them be the lion's prey;
Let Thy tenderness, so loving,
 Keep them all life's dangerous way.

4 Then, within Thy fold eternal,
 Let them find a resting-place;
Feed in pastures ever vernal,
 Drink the rivers of Thy grace.
   Rev. William Augustus Muhlenberg (1796–1877), 1826.

ITALIAN HYMN. 6.6.4.6.6.6.4.
FELICE GIARDINI (1716–1796), 1765.

1. Shepherd of tender youth, Guiding in love and truth Thro' devious ways; Christ, our triumphant King, We come Thy Name to sing; Hither our children bring, To shout Thy praise.

436 Στόμιον πώλων ἀδαῶν.

2 Thou art our Holy Lord,
 The all-subduing Word,
  Healer of strife;
 That didst Thyself abase,
 That from sin's deep disgrace
 Thou mightest save our race,
  And give us life.

3 Ever be Thou our Guide,
 Our Shepherd and our Pride,
  Our Staff and Song;
 Jesus, Thou Christ of God,

By Thy perennial Word
 Lead us where Thou hast trod,
  Make our faith strong.

4 So now, and till we die,
 Sound we Thy praises high,
  And joyful sing:
 Infants, and the glad throng
 Who to Thy Church belong,
 Unite to swell the song
  To Christ our King.
   From Clement of Alexandria (—217),
   Tr. by Rev. Henry Martyn Dexter (1821–   ), 1846,
 1849. Ab.

THE CHURCH OF GOD.

AUSTRIAN HYMN. 8, 7. D.   FRANCIS JOSEPH HAYDN (1732—1809), 1797.

1. Glorious things of thee are spoken, Zion, city of our God!
   He whose word cannot be broken, Formed thee for His own abode:
   On the Rock of ages founded, What can shake thy sure repose?
   With salvation's walls surrounded, Thou may'st smile at all thy foes.

437   *The City of God.*
Is. xxxiii. 20, 21.

2 See the streams of living waters,
   Springing from eternal love,
Well supply thy sons and daughters,
   And all fear of want remove:
Who can faint, while such a river
   Ever flows their thirst t'assuage?
Grace, which, like the Lord, the Giver,
   Never fails from age to age.

3 Round each habitation hovering,
   See the cloud of fire appear,
For a glory and a covering,
   Showing that the Lord is near:
Thus deriving from their banner
   Light by night, and shade by day,
Safe they feed upon the manna
   Which He gives them when they pray.
         Rev. John Newton (1725—1807), 1779.

438   *Prayer for Revival.*

1 Saviour, visit Thy plantation,
   Grant us, Lord, a gracious rain:
All will come to desolation,
   Unless Thou return again.
Keep no longer at a distance,
   Shine upon us from on high,
Lest, for want of Thine assistance,
   Every plant should droop and die.

2 Once, O Lord, Thy garden flourished;
   Every part looked gay and green;
Then Thy word our spirits nourished;
   Happy seasons we have seen.
But a drought has since succeeded,
   And a sad decline we see:
Lord, Thy help is greatly needed,
   Help can only come from Thee.

3 Let our mutual love be fervent;
   Make us prevalent in prayer;
Let each one esteemed Thy servant
   Shun the world's bewitching snare.
Break the tempter's fatal power,
   Turn the stony heart to flesh,
And begin from this good hour
   To revive Thy work afresh.
         Rev. John Newton, 1779. Ab. and alt.

MIDDLETON. 8. 7. D.   English Melody.

REGENT SQUARE. 8. 7. 4.   HENRY SMART (1812—1879), 1867.

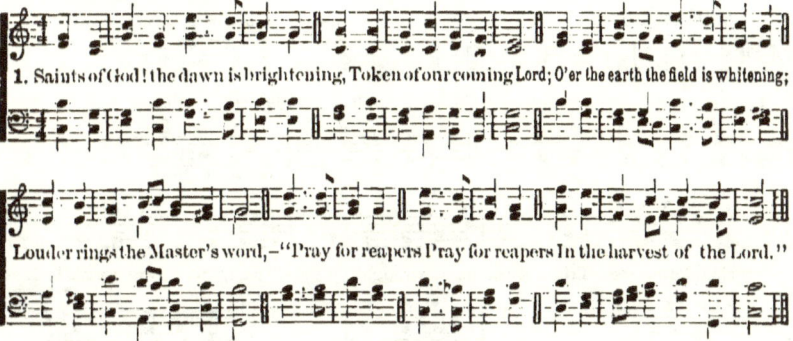

1. Saints of God! the dawn is brightening, Token of our coming Lord; O'er the earth the field is whitening;
Louder rings the Master's word,—"Pray for reapers Pray for reapers In the harvest of the Lord."

439   *Home Missions.*

2 Now, O Lord! fulfil Thy pleasure,
   Breathe upon Thy chosen band,
And, with pentecostal measure,
   Send forth reapers o'er our land,—
     Faithful reapers,
   Gathering sheaves for Thy right hand.

3 Broad the shadow of our nation,
   Eager millions hither roam;
Lo! they wait for Thy salvation;
   Come, Lord Jesus! quickly come!
     By Thy Spirit,
   Bring Thy ransomed people home.

4 Soon shall end the time of weeping,
   Soon the reaping time will come,—
Heaven and earth together keeping
   God's eternal Harvest Home.
     Saints and angels!
   Shout the world's great Harvest Home.
      Mrs. Mary Robertson Maxwell (—   ), 1875.

440   *Light in the Darkness.*
      Matt. iv. 16.

1 O'er the gloomy hills of darkness,
   Look, my soul, be still and gaze;
Sun of Righteousness, arising,
   Bring the bright, the glorious day:
     Send the Gospel
   To the earth's remotest bound.

2 Kingdoms wide that sit in darkness,
   Grant them, Lord, Thy glorious light,
And from eastern coast to western
   May the morning chase the night;
     And redemption,
   Freely purchased, win the day.

3 Fly abroad, thou mighty Gospel,
   Win and conquer, never cease!
May thy lasting, wide dominions
   Multiply, and still increase;
     Sway Thy sceptre,
   Saviour, all the world around.
      Rev. William Williams (1717—1791), 1772. Ab. and alt.

ZION. 8. 7. 4.   THOMAS HASTINGS (1784—1872). 1830.

MISSIONS.

ANVERN. L.M.
German. Arr. by LOWELL MASON (1792—1872), 1840.

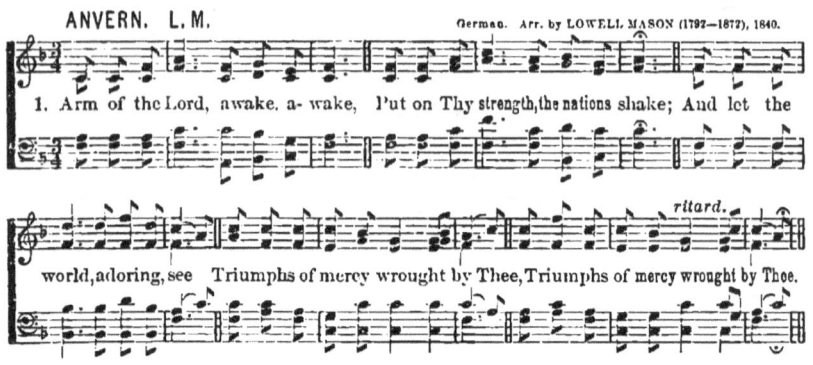

1. Arm of the Lord, awake, awake, Put on Thy strength, the nations shake; And let the world, adoring, see Triumphs of mercy wrought by Thee, Triumphs of mercy wrought by Thee.

441   *"Awake, awake."* Is. li. 9.

2 Say to the heathen from Thy throne,
"I am Jehovah, God alone!"
Thy voice their idols shall confound,
And cast their altars to the ground.

3 No more let human blood be spilt,
Vain sacrifice for human guilt;
But to each conscience be applied
The blood that flowed from Jesus' side.

4 Almighty God, Thy grace proclaim,
In every clime, of every name,
Till adverse powers before Thee fall,
And crown the Saviour, Lord of all.

William Shrubsole, Jr. (1759—1829), 1795. Ab.

442   *Prayer for speedy Triumph.*

1 Soon may the last glad song arise
Through all the millions of the skies,
That song of triumph, which records
That all the earth is now the Lord's.

2 Let thrones, and powers, and kingdoms be
Obedient, mighty God, to Thee;
And over land, and stream, and main,
Wave Thou the sceptre of Thy reign.

3 O that the anthem now might swell,
And host to host the triumph tell,
That not one rebel heart remains,
But over all the Saviour reigns.

Baptist Magazine, 1816.

HARMONY GROVE. L.M.
HENRY KEMBLE OLIVER (1800—1885), 1839.

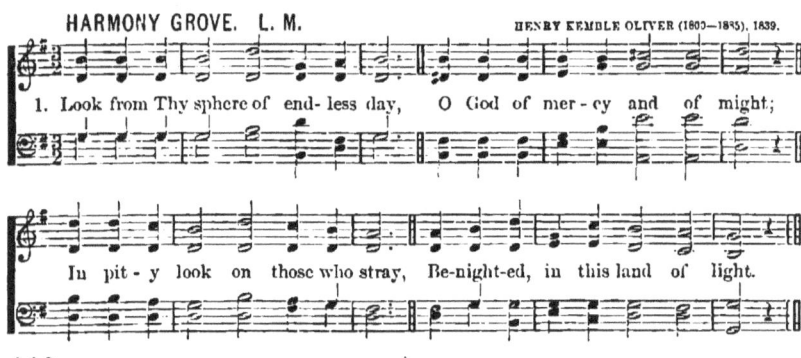

1. Look from Thy sphere of endless day, O God of mercy and of might; In pity look on those who stray, Benighted, in this land of light.

443   *Prayer for Home Missions.*

2 In peopled vale, in lonely glen,
In crowded mart, by stream or sea,
How many of the sons of men
Hear not the message sent from Thee.

3 Send forth Thy heralds, Lord, to call
The thoughtless young, the hardened old,
A scattered, homeless flock, till all
Be gathered to Thy peaceful fold.

CHRIST'S MINISTERS.

4 Send them Thy mighty word to speak,
Till faith shall dawn, and doubt depart,
To awe the bold, to stay the weak,
And bind and heal the broken heart.

5 Then all these wastes, a dreary scene,
That make us sadden as we gaze,
Shall grow with living waters green,
And lift to Heaven the voice of praise.

William Cullen Bryant (1794—1878), 1840.

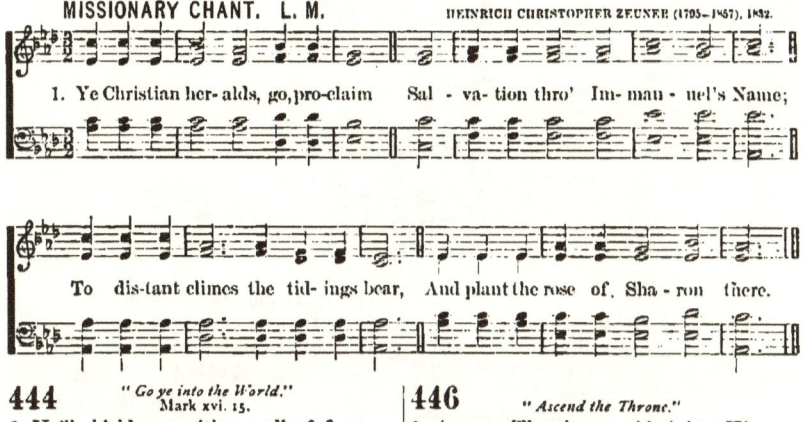

MISSIONARY CHANT. L. M. HEINRICH CHRISTOPHER ZEUNER (1795—1857), 1832.

1. Ye Christian heralds, go, proclaim
Salvation thro' Immanuel's Name;
To distant climes the tidings bear,
And plant the rose of Sharon there.

444 *"Go ye into the World."* Mark xvi. 15.

2 He'll shield you with a wall of fire,
With flaming zeal your breast inspire,
Bid raging winds their fury cease,
And hush the tempest into peace.

3 And when our labors all are o'er,
Then we shall meet to part no more,
Meet, with the blood-bought throng to fall,
And crown our Jesus Lord of all.

Rev. Bourne Hall Draper (1778—1843), 1803. Ab. and sl. alt.

445 *The Spirit accompanying the Word.*

1 O Spirit of the living God,
In all Thy plenitude of grace,
Where'er the foot of man hath trod,
Descend on our apostate race.

2 Give tongues of fire, and hearts of love,
To preach the reconciling word;
Give power and unction from above,
Whene'er the joyful sound is heard.

3 Be darkness, at Thy coming, light,
Confusion, order in Thy path;
Souls without strength inspire with
Bid mercy triumph over wrath. [might;

4 Baptize the nations; far and nigh
The triumphs of the cross record;
The name of Jesus glorify,
Till every kindred call Him Lord.

James Montgomery (1771—1854), 1825. Ab.

446 *"Ascend the Throne."*

1 Ascend Thy throne, Almighty King,
And spread Thy glories all abroad;
Let Thine own arm salvation bring,
And be Thou known the gracious God.

2 Let millions bow before Thy seat,
Let humble mourners seek Thy face,
Bring daring rebels to Thy feet,
Subdued by Thy victorious grace.

3 O let the kingdoms of the world
Become the kingdom of the Lord!
Let saints and angels praise Thy Name,
Be Thou through heaven and earth adored.

Rev. Benjamin Beddome (1717—1795), 1787.

447 *Light in Darkness.* Is. ix. 2.

1 Though now the nations sit beneath
The darkness of o'erspreading death;
God will arise with light divine,
On Zion's holy towers to shine.

2 That light shall shine on distant lands,
And wandering tribes in joyful bands,
Shall come Thy glory, Lord, to see,
And in Thy courts to worship Thee.

3 O light of Zion, now arise,
Let the glad morning bless our eyes:
Ye nations catch the kindling ray,
And hail the splendors of the day.

Rev. Leonard Bacon (1802—1881), 1845.

MISSIONS.

DUKE STREET. L. M.
JOHN HATTON (—1793), c. 1790.

1. Je - sus shall reign where'er the sun Does his suc - ces - sive journeys run; His king-dom stretch from shore to shore, Till moons shall wax and wane no more.

448 *Christ's Dominion.*
Ps. lxxii.

2 To Him shall endless prayer be made,
And praises throng to crown His head;
His Name, like sweet perfume, shall rise
With every morning sacrifice.

3 Blessings abound where'er He reigns;
The prisoner leaps to lose his chains;
The weary find eternal rest,
And all the sons of want are blest.

4 Let every creature rise and bring
Peculiar honors to our King;
Angels descend with songs again,
And earth repeat the loud Amen.
Rev. Isaac Watts (1674—1748), 1719. Ab. and sl. alt.

449 *"Fling out the Banner."*

1 FLING out the banner: let it float
Skyward and seaward, high and wide;
The sun, that lights its shining folds,
The cross, on which the Saviour died.

2 Fling out the banner: heathen lands
Shall see from far the glorious sight;
And nations, crowding to be born,
Baptize their spirits in its light.

3 Fling out the banner: let it float
Skyward and seaward, high and wide:

Our glory only in the cross,
Our only hope, the Crucified.

4 Fling out the banner: wide and high,
Seaward and skyward let it shine;
Nor skill, nor might, nor merit ours;
We conquer only in that sign.
Bp. George Washington Doane (1799—1859), 1848. Ab.

450 *Christ's coming.*

1 JESUS Thy church, with longing eyes,
For Thine expected coming waits;
When will the promised light arise,
And glory beam from Zion's gates?

2 Ev'n now, when tempests round us fall,
And wintry clouds o'ercast the sky,
Thy words with pleasure we recall,
And deem that our redemption's nigh.

3 O come and reign o'er every land;
Let Satan from his throne be hurled;
All nations bow to Thy command,
And grace revive a dying world.

4 Teach us, in watchfulness and prayer,
To wait for the appointed hour;
And fit us, by Thy grace, to share
The triumphs of Thy conquering power.
Rev. William Hiley Bragge-Bathurst (1796—1877), 1830.

ENSIGN. L. M.
JOHN BAPTISTE CALKINS (1827—   ). 1872.

DOWNS. C. M. LOWELL MASON (1792—1872), 1832.

1. On Zi-on and on Leb-an-on, On Car-mel's bloom-ing height,
On Sha-ron's fer-tile plains, once shone The glo-ry, pure and bright.

451 *Home Missions.*

2 From thence its mild and cheering ray
 Streamed forth from land to land;
 And empires now behold its day;
 And still its beams expand.

3 But ah, our deserts deep and wild
 See not this heavenly light;
 No sacred beams, no radiance mild,
 Dispel their dreary night.

4 Thou, who didst lighten Zion's hill,
 On Carmel who didst shine,
 Our deserts let Thy glory fill,
 Thy excellence divine.

Bp. Henry Ustick Onderdonk (1789—1858), 1826. Ab.

452 *National.*

1 LORD, while for all mankind we pray,
 Of every clime and coast,
 O hear us for our native land,
 The land we love the most.

2 O guard our shores from every foe,
 With peace our borders bless,
 With prosperous times our cities crown,
 Our fields with plenteousness.

3 Unite us in the sacred love
 Of knowledge, truth, and Thee,

And let our hills and valleys shout
 The songs of liberty.

4 Lord of the nations, thus to Thee
 Our country we commend;
 Be Thou her refuge and her trust,
 Her everlasting friend.

Rev. John Reynell Wreford (1800—1881), 1830.

453 *The Gospel for all Nations.*
Mark xiii. 10.

1 GREAT God, the nations of the earth
 Are by creation Thine;
 And in Thy works, by all beheld,
 Thy radiant glories shine.

2 But, Lord, Thy greater love has sent
 Thy gospel to mankind,
 Unveiling what rich stores of grace
 Are treasured in Thy mind.

3 Lord, when shall these glad tidings spread
 The spacious earth around,
 Till every tribe, and every soul,
 Shall hear the joyful sound?

4 Smile, Lord, on each divine attempt
 To spread the gospel's rays,
 And build on sin's demolished throne
 The temples of Thy praise.

Rev. Thomas Gibbons (1720—1785), 1769. Ab. and alt.

ARLINGTON. C. M. THOMAS AUGUSTINE ARNE (1710—1778), 1762.

MISSIONS.

MISSIONARY HYMN. 7. 6. D. LOWELL MASON (1792–1872). 1823.

1. From Greenland's icy mountains, From India's coral strand, Where Afric's sunny fountains Roll down their golden sand; From many an ancient river, From many a palmy plain, They call us to deliver Their land from error's chain.

454 *"From Greenland's icy Mountains."*

2 What though the spicy breezes
   Blow soft o'er Ceylon's isle,
   Though every prospect pleases,
   And only man is vile:
In vain with lavish kindness
   The gifts of God are strown,
The heathen in his blindness
   Bows down to wood and stone.

3 Can we, whose souls are lighted
   With wisdom from on high,
Can we to men benighted
   The lamp of life deny?
Salvation, O salvation!
   The joyful sound proclaim,
Till each remotest nation
   Has learned Messiah's Name.

4 Waft, waft, ye winds, His story,
   And you, ye waters, roll,
Till, like a sea of glory,
   It spreads from pole to pole;
Till o'er our ransomed nature,
   The Lamb for sinners slain,
Redeemer, King, Creator,
   In bliss returns to reign.
                    Bp. Reginald Heber (1783—1826), 1819.

455 *"Hail to the Lord's Anointed."*

1 HAIL to the Lord's Anointed,
   Great David's greater Son;
Hail, in the time appointed,
   His reign on earth begun!

He comes to break oppression,
   To set the captive free,
To take away transgression,
   And rule in equity.

2 He comes with succor speedy
   To those who suffer wrong;
To help the poor and needy,
   And bid the weak be strong;
To give them songs for sighing,
   Their darkness turn to light,
Whose souls, condemned and dying,
   Were precious in His sight.

3 For Him shall prayer unceasing,
   And daily vows ascend;
His kingdom still increasing,
   A kingdom without end.
O'er every foe victorious,
   He on His throne shall rest,
From age to age more glorious,
   All-blessing and all-blest.
              James Montgomery (1771—1854), 1822.   Ab.

456   *Home Missions.*

1 OUR country's voice is pleading,
   Ye men of God, arise!
His providence is leading,
   The land before you lies;
Day-gleams are o'er it brightening,
   And promise clothes the soil;
Wide fields for harvest whitening,
   Invite the reaper's toil.

THE TRIUMPH.

2 Go, where the waves are breaking
  On California's shore,
Christ's precious Gospel taking,
  More rich than golden ore;
On Alleghany's mountains,
  Through all the western vale,
Beside Missouri's fountains,
  Rehearse the wondrous tale.

3 The love of Christ unfolding,
  Speed on from east to west,
Till all, His cross beholding,
  In Him are fully blest.
Great Author of salvation,
  Haste, haste the glorious day,
When we, a ransomed nation,
  Thy sceptre shall obey.
    Mrs. Maria Frances Anderson (1819—   ), 1848. A b.

WEBB. 7. 6. D.
GEORGE JAMES WEBB (1803—1887), 1830.

1. The morning light is breaking, The darkness disappears; The sons of earth are waking
   To peni-i-tential tears: Each breeze that sweeps the o-cean Brings tidings from a-far
   D.S.— Of nations in commo-tion.
   Prepar'd for Zion's war.

457 *"The Morning Light is breaking."*

2 See heathen nations bending
    Before the God we love,
  And thousand hearts ascending,
    In gratitude above;
  While sinners, now confessing,
    The gospel call obey,
  And seek the Saviour's blessing,
    A nation in a day.

3 Blest river of salvation,
    Pursue thine onward way;
  Flow thou to every nation,
    Nor in thy riches stay;
  Stay not, till all the lowly
    Triumphant reach their home;
  Stay not, till all the holy
    Proclaim, "The Lord is come."
      Rev. Samuel Francis Smith (1808—   ), 1831. Ab.

458 *The final Triumph.*

1 When shall the voice of singing
    Flow joyfully along,
  When hill and valley ringing,
    With one triumphant song,
  Proclaim the contest ended,
    And Him, who once was slain,
  Again to earth descended,
    In righteousness to reign?

2 Then from the craggy mountains
    The sacred shout shall fly;
  And shady vales and fountains
    Shall echo the reply:
  High tower and lowly dwelling
    Shall send the chorus round,
  And hallelujah swelling
    In one eternal sound.
      James Edmeston (1791—1867), 1822. Alt.

459 *The good Tidings.*

1 How beauteous on the mountains,
    The feet of him that brings,
  Like streams from living fountains,
    Good tidings of good things;
  That publisheth salvation,
    And jubilee release,
  To every tribe and nation,
    God's reign of joy and peace.

2 Lift up thy voice, O watchman,
    And shout, from Zion's towers,
  Thy hallelujah chorus,
    "The victory is ours!"
  The Lord shall build up Zion
    In glory and renown,
  And Jesus, Judah's Lion,
    Shall wear His rightful crown.
      Benjamin Gough (1805—   ), 1865. Ab. and sl. alt.

MISSIONS.

ONIDO. 7. D.
IGNAZ JOSEPH PLEYEL (1757—1831),
Arr. by LOWELL MASON (1792—1872), 1840.

1. Has-ten, Lord, the glorious time, When, beneath Messiah's sway, Ev-'ry nation, ev-'ry clime Shall the gospel call obey. Mightiest kings His pow'r shall own, Heathen tribes His Name a-dore; Satan and his host o'erthrown, Bound in chains, shall hurt no more.

460 *The Victory anticipated.*
Ps. lxxii.

2 Then shall wars and tumults cease,
Then be banished grief and pain;
Righteousness, and joy, and peace,
Undisturbed shall ever reign.

3 Time shall sun and moon obscure,
Seas be dried, and rocks be riven,
But His reign shall still endure,
Endless as the days of Heaven.

Miss Harriet Auber (1773—1862), 1829. Ab.

LANCASHIRE. 7. 6. D.
HENRY SMART (1812—1879), 1836?

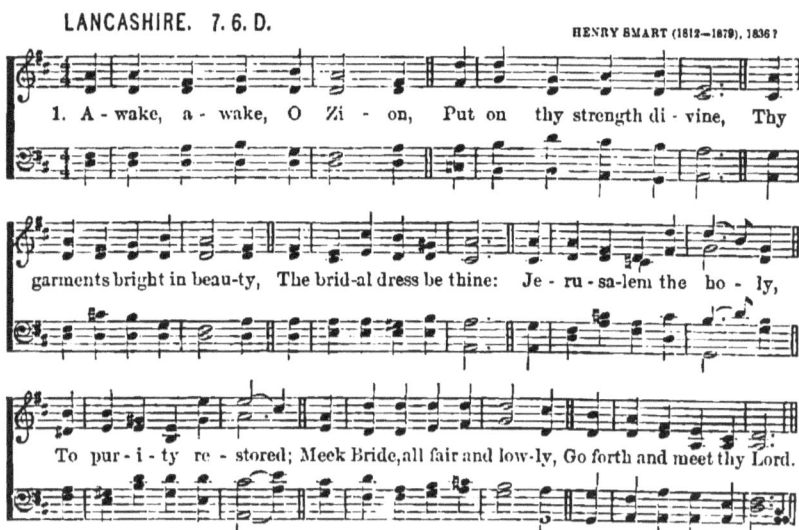

1. A-wake, a-wake, O Zi-on, Put on thy strength di-vine, Thy garments bright in beauty, The bridal dress be thine: Je-ru-sa-lem the ho-ly, To pu-ri-ty re-stored; Meek Bride, all fair and low-ly, Go forth and meet thy Lord.

THY KINGDOM COME.

461 *Meeting the Bridegroom.*

2 The Lamb who bore our sorrows
   Comes down to earth again;
No sufferer now, but Victor,
   For evermore to reign;
To reign in every nation,
   To rule in every zone:
O world-wide coronation,
   In every heart a throne.

3 Awake, awake, O Zion,
   The bridal day draws nigh,
The day of signs and wonders,
   And marvels from on high:
Thy sun uprises slowly,
   But keep thou watch and ward;
Fair Bride, all pure and lowly,
   Go forth to meet thy Lord.
Benjamin Gough (1805—), 1865. Ab.

MIRIAM. 7.6. D.   JOSEPH PERRY HOLBROOK (1822—), 1865.

1. Now be the Gospel banner In ev-'ry land unfurled, And be the shout, "Hosan-na!"
D.S.—Re-ceive the great sal-va-tion,
Re-echoed thro' the world: Till ev-'ry isle and na-tion, Till ev-'ry tribe and tongue,
And join the happy throng.

462 *"The Gospel Banner."*

2 Yes, Thou shalt reign for ever,
   O Jesus, King of kings:
Thy light, Thy love, Thy favor,
   Each ransomed captive sings.
The isles for Thee are waiting,
   The deserts learn Thy praise,
The hills and valleys greeting,
   The song responsive raise.
Thomas Hastings (1784–1872), 1830. Ab.

463 *"The blood-red Banner."*

1 UPLIFT the blood-red banner,
   And shout, with trumpet's sound,
Deliverance to the captive,
   And freedom to the bound;
Earth's jubilee of glory,
   The year of full release:
O tell the wondrous story,
   Go forth and publish peace.

2 Go forth, Confessors, Martyrs,
   With zeal and love unpriced,
And preach the blood of sprinkling,
   And live, or die, for Christ;
For Christ claim every nation,
   Your banner wide unfurled;
Go forth and preach salvation,
   Salvation for the world.
Benjamin Gough, 1865. Ab.

464 *The Salvation of Israel.* Ps. xiv.

1 O THAT the Lord's salvation
   Were out of Zion come,
To heal His ancient nation,
   To lead His outcasts home.
How long the holy city
   Shall heathen feet profane?
Return, O Lord, in pity;
   Rebuild her walls again.

2 Let fall Thy rod of terror,
   Thy saving grace impart;
Roll back the veil of error,
   Release the fettered heart.
Let Israel, home returning,
   Her lost Messiah see;
Give oil of joy for mourning,
   And bind Thy Church to Thee
Rev. Henry Francis Lyte (1793–1847), 1834.

MISSIONS.

BAVARIA. 8. 7. D. — German Melody.

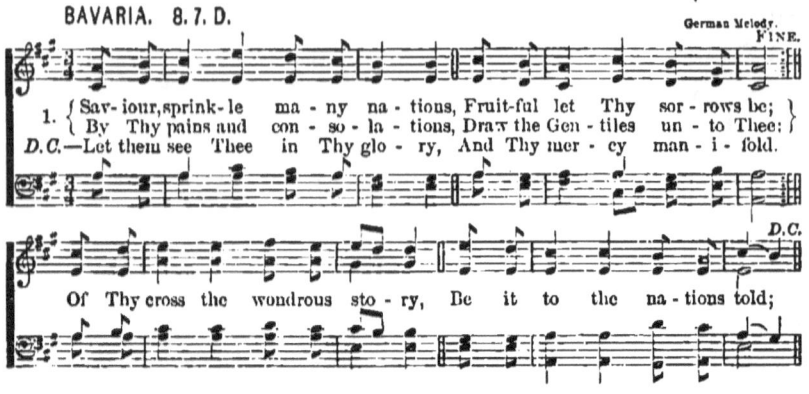

1. Saviour, sprinkle many nations, Fruitful let Thy sorrows be;
By Thy pains and consolations, Draw the Gentiles unto Thee:
D.C.—Let them see Thee in Thy glory, And Thy mercy manifold.

Of Thy cross the wondrous story, Be it to the nations told;

465 *"So shall He sprinkle many Nations."*
Is. lii. 15.

2 Far and wide, though all unknowing,
Pants for Thee each mortal breast;
Human tears for Thee are flowing,
Human hearts in Thee would rest,
Thirsting, as for dews of even,
As the new-mown grass for rain;
Thee, they seek, as God of Heaven,
Thee, as Man, for sinners slain.

3 Saviour, lo, the isles are waiting,
Stretched the hand, and strained the sight,
For Thy Spirit, new creating
Love's pure flame and wisdom's light;
Give the word, and of the preacher
Speed the foot, and touch the tongue,
Till on earth by every creature
Glory to the Lamb be sung.

Bp. Arthur Cleveland Coxe (1818—), 1851.

466 *"Come over and help us."*
Acts xvi. 9.

1 Hark, what mean those lamentations,
Rolling sadly through the sky?
'Tis the cry of heathen nations,
"Come and help us, or we die."
Lost and helpless and desponding,
Wrapt in error's night they lie;
To their cries your hearts responding,
Haste to help them ere they die.

2 Hark, again those lamentations
Rolling sadly through the sky;
Louder cry the heathen nations,
"Come and help us, or we die."
Hear the heathen's sad complaining;
Christians, hear their dying cry;
And the love of Christ constraining,
Join to help them ere they die.

Rev. John Cawood (1775—1852), 1819.

OLIVET. 6. 6. 4. 6. 6. 6. 4. — LOWELL MASON (1792—1872), 1830.

1. Christ for the world we sing; The world to Christ we bring, With loving zeal;
The poor, and them that mourn, The faint and overborne,
Sin-sick and sorrow-worn, Whom Christ doth heal.

467 *"Christ for the World."*

2 Christ for the world we sing;
The world to Christ we bring,
With fervent prayer:
The wayward and the lost,
By reckless passion tossed,
Redeemed, at countless cost,
From dark despair.

3 Christ for the world we sing;
　The world to Christ we bring,
　　With one accord;
　With us the work to share,
　With us reproach to dare,
　With us the cross to bear,
　　For Christ our Lord.

4 Christ for the world we sing;
　The world to Christ we bring,
　　With joyful song;
　The new-born souls, whose days,
　Reclaimed from error's ways,
　Inspired with hope and praise,
　　To Christ belong.
　　　　Rev. Samuel Wolcott (1813—), 1869.

WESTON. 6.6.4.6.6.6.4.　　　ARTHUR E. DYER (—).

1. Lord of all pow'r and might, Father of love and light, Speed on Thy Word;
O let the gospel sound All the wide world around, Wherever man is found: God speed His Word.

468 *"Speed on Thy Word."*

2 Hail, blesséd Jubilee:
　Thine, Lord, the glory be;
　　Hallelujah!
　Thine was the mighty plan,
　From Thee the work began;
　Away with praise of man,
　　Glory to God!

3 Onward shall be our course,
　Despite of fraud or force;
　　God is before:
　His Word ere long shall run
　Free as the noon-day sun;
　His purpose must be done:
　　God bless His Word.
　　　Rev. Hugh Stowell (1799—1865), 1854. Ab. and sl. alt.

469 *"Let there be Light."*
　　　Gen. i. 3.　2 Cor. iv. 6.

1 THOU, whose almighty word
　Chaos and darkness heard,
　　And took their flight;
　Hear us, we humbly pray,
　And where the gospel's day
　Sheds not its glorious ray,
　　"Let there be light!"

2 Thou, who didst come to bring
　On Thy redeeming wing
　　Healing and sight,
　Health to the sick in mind,
　Sight to the inly blind,
　O now to all mankind
　　"Let there be light!"

3 Spirit of truth and love,
　Life-giving, holy Dove,
　　Speed forth Thy flight:
　Move o'er the water's face,
　Bearing the lamp of grace,
　And in earth's darkest place
　　"Let there be light!"

4 Blesséd and Holy Three,
　Glorious Trinity,
　　Wisdom, Love, Might;
　Boundless as ocean's tide,
　Rolling in fullest pride,
　Through the world, far and wide,
　　"Let there be light!"
　　　Rev. John Marriott (1780—1825), 1816.

DAWN. S. M. Rev. EDWIN POND PARKER (1836–   ), 1871.

1. One sweet-ly sol-emn thought Comes to me o'er and o'er, Near-er my part-ing hour am I Than e'er I was be-fore.

470 *Nearing Home.*

2 Nearer my Father's house,
  Where many mansions be;
 Nearer the throne where Jesus reigns,
  Nearer the crystal sea;

3 Nearer my going home,
  Laying my burden down,
 Leaving my cross of heavy grief,
  Wearing my starry crown.

4 Jesus, to Thee I cling:
  Strengthen my arm of faith;
 Stay near me while my way-worn feet
  Press through the stream of death.
 Miss Phœbe Cary (1825–1871), 1852. Ab. and alt.

471 *"The Death of the Righteous."*

1 O for the death of those
  Who slumber in the Lord:
 O be like theirs my last repose,
  Like theirs my last reward.

2 Their bodies in the ground,
  In silent hope may lie,
 Till the last trumpet's joyful sound
  Shall call them to the sky.

3 Their ransomed spirits soar,
  On wings of faith and love,
 To meet the Saviour they adore,
  And reign with Him above.

4 With us their names shall live
  Through long-succeeding years,
 Embalmed with all our hearts can give,
  Our praises and our tears.
 James Montgomery (1771–1854), 1804. Ab. and much alt.

472 *Far from Home.*
  Ps. cxxxvii.

1 Far from my heavenly home,
  Far from my Father's breast,
 Fainting I cry, "Blest Spirit, come,
  And speed me to my rest."

2 My spirit homeward turns,
  And fain would thither flee;
 My heart, O Zion, droops and yearns,
  When I remember thee.

3 God of my life, be near:
  On Thee my hopes I cast;
 O guide me through the desert here,
  And bring me home at last.
 Rev. Henry Francis Lyte (1793–1847). 1834. Ab.

473 *"Forever with the Lord."*

1 Forever with the Lord:
  Amen, so let it be;
 Life from the dead is in that word,
  'Tis immortality.

2 Here in the body pent,
  Absent from Him I roam,
 Yet nightly pitch my moving tent
  A day's march nearer home.

3 My Father's house on high,
  Home of my soul, how near,
 At times, to faith's foreseeing eye,
  Thy golden gates appear.

4 "Forever with the Lord;"
  Father, if 'tis Thy will,
 The promise of that faithful word
  E'en here to me fulfil.
   James Montgomery, 1835.

GREENWOOD. S. M. JOSEPH EMERSON SWEETSER (1825–1873), 1849.

FUNERAL HYMNS.

REST. L. M.   WILLIAM BATCHELDER BRADBURY (1816—1868), 1843.

1. A-sleep in Je - sus: bless-ed sleep, From which none ev - er wakes to weep,
A calm and un - dis-turb'd re-pose, Un- bro-ken by the last of foes.

474 *"Asleep in Jesus."*

2 Asleep in Jesus: O how sweet
To be for such a slumber meet;
With holy confidence to sing,
That death hath lost his venomed sting.

3 Asleep in Jesus: peaceful rest,
Whose waking is supremely blest;
No fear, no woe, shall dim that hour
That manifests the Saviour's power.

4 Asleep in Jesus: O for me
May such a blissful refuge be;
Securely shall my ashes lie,
Waiting the summons from on high.
  Mrs. Margaret Mackay (1801—), 1832. Ab.

475 *The Death of the Righteous.*
  Num. xxiii. 10.

1 How blest the righteous, when he dies,
When sinks a weary soul to rest:

How mildly beam the closing eyes,
How gently heaves th' expiring breast.

2 So fades a summer cloud away;
So sinks the gale, when storms are o'er;
So gently shuts the eye of day;
So dies a wave along the shore.

3 A holy quiet reigns around,
A calm which life nor death destroys;
And naught disturbs that peace profound,
Which his unfettered soul enjoys.

4 Life's labor done, as sinks the clay,
Light from its load the spirit flies;
While Heaven and earth combine to say,
"How blest the righteous when he dies!"
  Mrs. Anna Lætitia Barbauld (1743—1825), 1809. Ab. and alt.

VESPER. 8. 7.   Arr. from FRIEDRICH FREIHERR von FLOTOW (1812—1883), 1847.

1. This is not my place of resting; Mine's a cit-y yet to come; Onward to it I am hast-ing, On to my e-ter-nal home.

476 *"This is not your Rest."*
  Micah. ii. 10.

2 In it all is light and glory;
O'er it shines a nightless day:
Every trace of sin's sad story,
All the curse, hath passed away.

3 There the Lamb, our Shepherd, leads us,
By the streams of life along,
On the freshest pastures feeds us,
Turns our sighing into song.

4 Soon we pass the desert dreary,
Soon we bid farewell to pain;
Never more are sad or weary,
Never, never sin again.
  Rev. Horatius Bonar (1808—), 1845.

THE JUDGMENT.

MERIBAH. C. P. M.   LOWELL MASON (1792—1872), 1839.

1. O God, mine in-most soul con-vert, And deep-ly on my thoughtful heart E-ternal things impress; { Give me to feel their solemn weight, And tremble on the brink of fate, } And wake to righteousness.

477   *Death and Judgment anticipated.*

2 Before me place, in dread array,
   The pomp of that tremendous day,
     When Thou with clouds shalt come
   To judge the nations at Thy bar;
   And tell me, Lord, shall I be there
     To meet a joyful doom.

3 Be this my one great business here,
   With holy trembling, holy fear,
     To make my calling sure,
   Thine utmost counsel to fulfil,
   And suffer all Thy righteous will,
     And to the end endure.

4 Then, Saviour, then my soul receive,
   Transported from this vale to live
     And reign with Thee above,
   Where faith is sweetly lost in sight,
   And hope in full, supreme delight,
     And everlasting love.
      Rev. Charles Wesley (1708—1788), 1749. Ab. and alt. v. 3.

TAPPAN. C. M. 5 l.   GEORGE KINGSLEY (1811—1884), 1838.

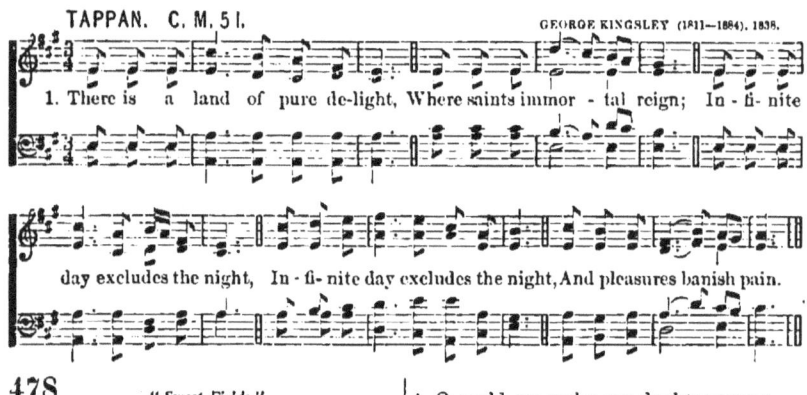

1. There is a land of pure de-light, Where saints immor-tal reign; In-fi-nite day excludes the night, In-fi-nite day excludes the night, And pleasures banish pain.

478   *"Sweet Fields."*

2 There, everlasting spring abides,
     And never-withering flowers:
   Death, like a narrow sea, divides
     This heavenly land from ours.

3 Sweet fields, beyond the swelling flood,
     Stand dressed in living green:
   So to the Jews old Canaan stood,
     While Jordan rolled between.

4 O could we make our doubts remove,
     Those gloomy doubts that rise,
   And see the Canaan that we love,
     With unbeclouded eyes;

5 Could we but climb where Moses stood,
     And view the landscape o'er, [flood,
   Not Jordan's stream, nor death's cold
     Should fright us from the shore.
      Rev. Isaac Watts (1674—1748), 1709. Ab.

HEAVEN.

RHINE. C. M. 51. Air. from FRIEDRICH BURGMULLER (1804—   ). c. 1810.

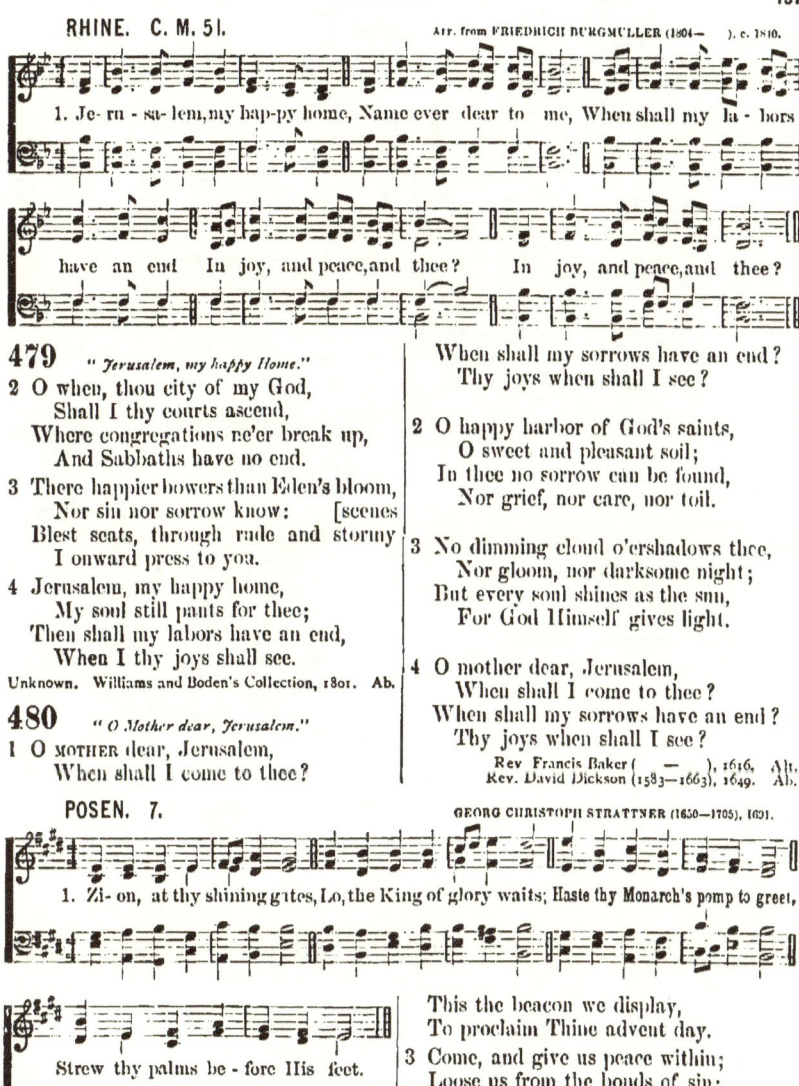

1. Je-ru-sa-lem, my hap-py home, Name ever dear to me, When shall my la-bors have an end In joy, and peace, and thee? In joy, and peace, and thee?

479 *"Jerusalem, my happy Home."*

2 O when, thou city of my God,
   Shall I thy courts ascend,
Where congregations ne'er break up,
   And Sabbaths have no end.

3 There happier bowers than Eden's bloom,
   Nor sin nor sorrow know: [scenes
Blest seats, through rude and stormy
   I onward press to you.

4 Jerusalem, my happy home,
   My soul still pants for thee;
Then shall my labors have an end,
   When I thy joys shall see.

Unknown. Williams and Boden's Collection, 1801. Ab.

480 *"O Mother dear, Jerusalem."*

1 O MOTHER dear, Jerusalem,
   When shall I come to thee?
When shall my sorrows have an end?
   Thy joys when shall I see?

2 O happy harbor of God's saints,
   O sweet and pleasant soil;
In thee no sorrow can be found,
   Nor grief, nor care, nor toil.

3 No dimming cloud o'ershadows thee,
   Nor gloom, nor darksome night;
But every soul shines as the sun,
   For God Himself gives light.

4 O mother dear, Jerusalem,
   When shall I come to thee?
When shall my sorrows have an end?
   Thy joys when shall I see?

Rev. Francis Baker (—   ), 1616. Alt.
Rev. David Dickson (1583—1663), 1649. Ab.

POSEN. 7. GEORG CHRISTOPH STRATTNER (1650—1705), 1691.

1. Zi-on, at thy shining gates, Lo, the King of glory waits; Haste thy Monarch's pomp to greet, Strew thy palms be-fore His feet.

481 *"Peace within."*

2 Christ, for Thee their triple light,
   Faith, and hope, and love unite;
This the beacon we display,
To proclaim Thine advent day.

3 Come, and give us peace within;
   Loose us from the bonds of sin;
Give us grace Thy yoke to wear;
Give us strength Thy cross to bear.

4 So, when Thou shalt come again,
   Judge of angels and of men,
We, with all Thy saints, shall sing
Hallelujahs to our King.

Rev. Benjamin Hall Kennedy (1804—   ), 1863. Ab

EWING. 7. 6. D.   ALEXANDER EWING (1830—), 1853.

1. Je-ru-sa-lem, the gold-en, With milk and hon-ey blest Be-neath thy con-tem-pla-tion Sink heart and voice op-prest: I know not, O I know not, What so-cial joys are there; What ra-dian-cy of glo-ry, What light be-yond compare.

482   *"Urbs Syon aurea."*

2 They stand, those halls of Zion,
   All jubilant with song,
And bright with many an angel,
   And all the martyr throng:
The Prince is ever in them,
   The daylight is serene;
The pastures of the blessèd
   Are decked in glorious sheen.

3 There is the throne of David;
   And there, from care released,
The shout of them that triumph,
   The song of them that feast;
And they who, with their Leader,
   Have conquered in the fight,
Forever, and forever,
   Are clad in robes of white.

Bernard of Cluny, c. 1145.
Tr. by Rev. John Mason Neale (1818—1866), 1851. Alt.

483   *"Hic breve vivitur."*

1 Brief life is here our portion;
   Brief sorrow, short-lived care;
The life that knows no ending,
   The tearless life, is there.
O happy retribution:
   Short toil, eternal rest;
For mortals and for sinners
   A mansion with the blest.

2 And now we fight the battle,
   But then shall wear the crown
Of full, and everlasting,
   And passionless renown.
But He whom now we trust in
   Shall then be seen and known;
And they that know and see Him
   Shall have Him for their own.

3 The morning shall awaken,
   The shadows shall decay,
And each true-hearted servant
   Shall shine as doth the day.
There God our King and Portion,
   In fulness of His grace,
Shall we behold forever,
   And worship face to face.

Bernard of Cluny, c. 1145.
Tr. by Rev. John Mason Neale, 1851. Alt.

484   *"O bona Patria."*

1 For thee, O dear, dear country,
   Mine eyes their vigils keep;
For very love, beholding
   Thy happy name, they weep.
The mention of thy glory
   Is unction to the breast,
And medicine in sickness,
   And love, and life, and rest.

2 O one, O only mansion,
   O paradise of joy,
Where tears are ever banished,
   And smiles have no alloy;
The Lamb is all thy splendor,
   The Crucified thy praise;
His laud and benediction
   Thy ransomed people raise.

Bernard of Cluny, c. 1145.
Tr. by Rev. John Mason Neale, 1851. Alt.

RUTHERFORD. P.M.   CHARLES D'URHAN (—), 1815.

1. The sands of time are sink-ing, The dawn of Heav-en breaks; The summer morn I've sigh'd for, The fair, sweet morn a-wakes: Dark, dark hath been the mid-night, But day-spring is at hand, And glo-ry, glo-ry dwell-eth In Im-man-uel's land.

485   *"Immanuel's Land."*

2 O Christ, He is the fountain,
   The deep, sweet well of love;
The streams on earth I've tasted,
   More deep I'll drink above.
There to an ocean fulness
   His mercy doth expand,
And glory, glory dwelleth
   In Immanuel's land.

3 The bride eyes not her garment,
   But her dear bridegroom's face;
I will not gaze at glory,
   But on my King of grace;
Not at the crown He giveth,
   But on His pierced hand:
The Lamb is all the glory
   Of Immanuel's land.

          Mrs. Anne Ross Cousin (—), 1857. Ab.

NEANDER. 8.7.7.7.   JOACHIM NEANDER (1610—1680), 1679.

1. { Hark, ten thousand harps and voices Sound the note of praise a-bove! } See, He sits on yonder throne; Je-sus rules the world alone.
   { Je - sus reigns, and heaven rejoic-es; Je - sus reigns, the God of love; }

Those whom Thou hast made Thine
Happy objects of Thy grace,   [own;
Destined to behold Thy face.

486   *Worshipped of Angels.*
        Heb. i. 6.

2 King of glory, reign forever!
   Thine an everlasting crown;
Nothing from Thy love shall sever

3 Saviour, hasten Thine appearing;
   Bring, O bring the glorious day,
When, the awful summons hearing,
   Heaven and earth shall pass away:
Then, with golden harps, we'll sing,
   "Glory, glory to our King!"

       Rev. Thomas Kelly (1769—1855), 1804. Ab.

HEAVEN.

PARADISE. P. M. — JOSEPH BARNBY (1838–), 1866.

1. O Par-a-dise! O Par-a-dise! Who doth not crave for rest? Who would not seek the happy land Where they that lov'd are blest? Where loy-al hearts and true

CHORUS.
Where loy-al hearts and true Stand ev-er in the light, All rapt-ure thro' and through, In God's most holy sight?

487 *Paradise.*

2 O Paradise! O Paradise!
　The world is growing old;
Who would not be at rest and free
　Where love is never cold.—Cho.

3 O Paradise! O Paradise!
　I greatly long to see
The special place my dearest Lord
　In love prepares for me;—Cho.

4 Lord Jesus, King of Paradise,
　O keep me in Thy love,
And guide me to that happy land
　Of perfect rest above;—Cho.

Rev. Frederick William Faber (1814–1863), 1854. Ab. and alt.

WOODLAND. C. M. 5 l. — NATHANIEL D. GOULD (1781–1864). 1832.

1. There is an hour of peaceful rest, To mourning wand'rers giv'n; There is a joy for souls dis-trest, A balm for ev-'ry wounded breast,'Tis found a-bove, in Heaven.

488 *The Heavenly Rest.*

2 There is a home for weary souls
　By sin and sorrow driven;
When tossed on life's tempestuous shoals,
Where storms arise, and ocean rolls,
　And all is drear but Heaven.

3 There, fragrant flowers, immortal, bloom,
　And joys supreme are given;
There, rays divine disperse the gloom:
Beyond the confines of the tomb
　Appears the dawn of Heaven.

Rev. William Bingham Tappan (1794–1849). 1818. Ab

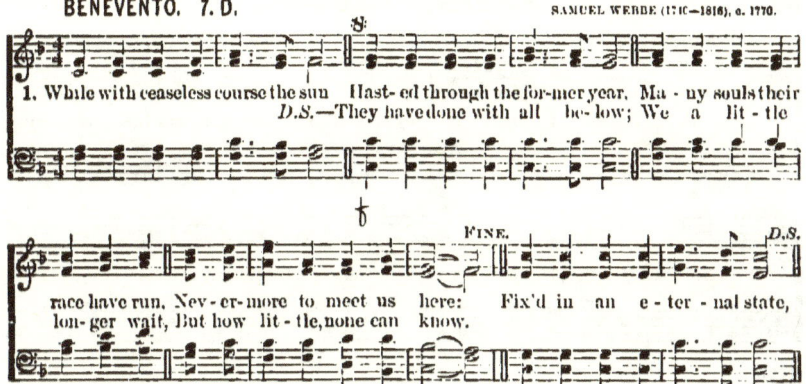

BENEVENTO. 7. D. — SAMUEL WEBBE (1740—1816), c. 1770.

1. While with ceaseless course the sun Hast-ed through the for-mer year, Ma-ny souls their race have run, Nev-er-more to meet us here: Fix'd in an e-ter-nal state,
D.S.—They have done with all be-low; We a lit-tle lon-ger wait, But how lit-tle, none can know.

489 *The New Year.*

2 As the wingèd arrow flies
Speedily the mark to find;
As the lightning from the skies
Darts and leaves no trace behind;
Swiftly thus our fleeting days
Bear us down life's rapid stream:
Upward, Lord, our spirits raise,
All below is but a dream.

3 Thanks for mercies past receive;
Pardon of our sins renew;
Teach us henceforth how to live
With eternity in view:
Bless Thy word to young and old;
Fill us with a Saviour's love;
And when life's short tale is told,
May we dwell with Thee above.
Rev. John Newton (1725—1807), 1779.

490 *For New Year's Eve.*

1 FOR Thy mercy and Thy grace,
Faithful through another year,
Hear our songs of thankfulness,
Father and Redeemer, hear.
In our weakness and distress,
Rock of strength, be Thou our stay;
In the pathless wilderness
Be our true and living way.

2 Who of us death's awful road
In the coming year shall tread?
With Thy rod and staff, O God,
Comfort Thou his dying bed.

Keep us faithful, keep us pure,
Keep us evermore Thine own;
Help Thy servants to endure,
Fit us for the promised crown.
Rev. Henry Downton (1818—), 1839. Ab.

491 *The Old Year.*

1 THOU who roll'st the year around,
Crowned with mercies large and free,
Rich Thy gifts to us abound,
Warm our thanks shall rise to Thee:
Kindly to our worship bow,
While our grateful praises swell,
That, sustained by Thee, we now
Bid the parting year farewell.

2 All its numbered days are sped,
All its busy scenes are o'er,
All its joys for ever fled,
All its sorrows felt no more:
Mingled with th' eternal past,
Its remembrance shall decay;
Yet to be revived at last
At the solemn judgment-day.

3 All our follies, Lord, forgive;
Cleanse each heart and make us Thine;
Let Thy grace within us live,
As our future suns decline;
Then, when life's last eve shall come,
Happy spirits, let us fly
To our everlasting home,
To our Father's house on high.
Rev. Ray Palmer (1808—1887), 1850.

TIMES AND SEASONS.

GERMANY. L. M.
LUDWIG von BEETHOVEN (1770—1827).

1. E-ter-nal Source of ev-'ry joy, Well may Thy praise our lips em-ploy, While in Thy tem-ple we ap-pear, Whose goodness crowns the cir-cling year.

492   *For New Year's Day.*
Ps. lxv. ii.

2 The flowery spring, at Thy command,
Perfumes the air and paints the land;
The summer rays with vigor shine,
To raise the corn and cheer the vine.

3 Thy hand in autumn richly pours
Through all our coasts redundant stores;
And winters, softened by Thy care,
No more a face of horror wear.

4 Seasons, and months, and weeks, and days,
Demand successive songs of praise;
And be the grateful homage paid,
With morning light and evening shade.
     Rev. Philip Doddridge (1702—1751), 1755. Ab. and alt.

493   *Help obtained of God.*
Acts xxvi. 22.

1 Great God, we sing that mighty hand,
By which supported still we stand:
The opening year Thy mercy shows;
Let mercy crown it till it close.

2 By day, by night, at home, abroad,
Still we are guided by our God;
By His incessant bounty fed,
By His unerring counsel led.

3 With grateful hearts the past we own;
The future, all to us unknown,
We to Thy guardian care commit,
And peaceful leave before Thy feet.

4 In scenes exalted or deprest,
Be Thou our joy, be Thou our rest;
Thy goodness all our hopes shall raise,
Adored through all our changing days.
     Rev. Philip Doddridge, 1755. Ab. and alt.

494   *Forefathers' Day.*

1 O God, beneath Thy guiding hand,
Our exiled fathers crossed the sea;
And when they trod the wintry strand,
With prayer and psalm they worshipped Thee.

2 Thou heard'st, well pleased, the song, the prayer;
Thy blessing came, and still its power
Shall onward through all ages bear
The memory of that holy hour.

3 Laws, freedom, truth, and faith in God
Came with those exiles o'er the waves;
And where their pilgrim feet have trod,
The God they trusted guards their graves.

4 And here Thy Name, O God of love,
Their children's children shall adore,
Till these eternal hills remove,
And spring adorns the earth no more.
     Rev. Leonard Bacon (1802—1881), 1845. Ab.

OLD HUNDREDTH. L. M.
LOUIS BOURGEOIS, 1551.

THANKSGIVING.

ST. GEORGE'S CHAPEL. 7. D.   Sir. GEORGE JOB ELVEY (1816—). 1-59.

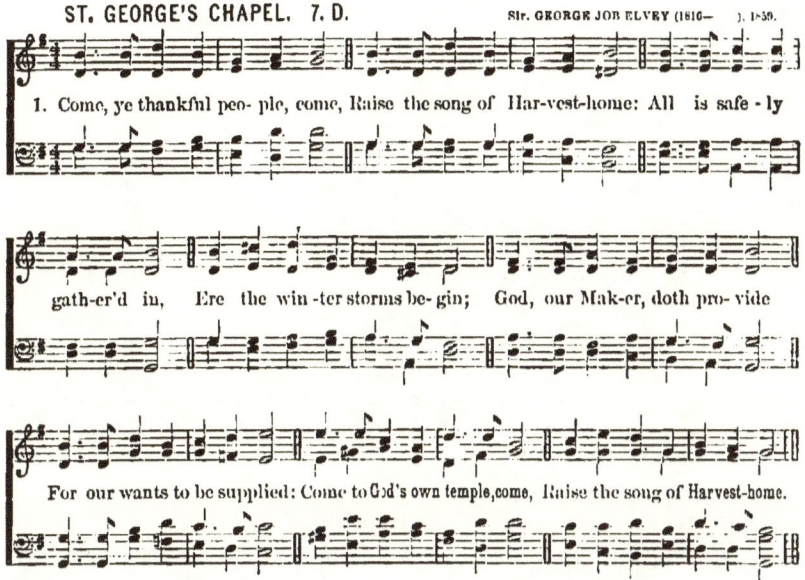

1. Come, ye thankful peo-ple, come, Raise the song of Har-vest-home: All is safe-ly gath-er'd in, Ere the win-ter storms be-gin; God, our Mak-er, doth pro-vide For our wants to be supplied: Come to God's own temple, come, Raise the song of Harvest-home.

495   *Harvest Hymn.*

2 All the world is God's own field,
Fruit unto His praise to yield;
Wheat and tares together sown,
Unto joy or sorrow grown;
First the blade, and then the ear,
Then the full corn shall appear:
Lord of Harvest, grant that we
Wholesome grain and pure may be.

3 For the Lord our God shall come,
And shall take His harvest home;
From His field shall in that day
All offences purge away;
Give His angels charge at last
In the fire the tares to cast;
But the fruitful ears to store
In His garner evermore.

4 Even so, Lord, quickly come
To Thy final Harvest-home;
Gather Thou Thy people in,
Free from sorrow, free from sin;
There, forever purified,
In Thy presence to abide:
Come, with all Thine angels, come,
Raise the glorious Harvest-home.

         Rev. Henry Alford (1810—1871), 1844.

496   *Thanksgiving or Fast.*

1 Christ, by heavenly hosts adored,
Gracious, mighty, sovereign Lord,
God of nations, King of kings,
Head of all created things,
By the Church with joy confest,
God o'er all forever blest;
Pleading at Thy throne we stand,
Save Thy people, bless our land.

2 On our fields of grass and grain
Drop, O Lord, the kindly rain;
O'er our wide and goodly land
Crown the labors of each hand;
Let Thy kind protection be
O'er our commerce on the sea;
Open, Lord, Thy bounteous hand,
Bless Thy people, bless our land.

3 Let our rulers ever be
Men that love and honor Thee;
Let the powers by Thee ordained,
Be in righteousness maintained;
In the people's hearts increase
Love of piety and peace;
Thus, united we shall stand
One wide, free, and happy land.

     Rev. Henry Harbaugh (1818—1867), 1860. Ab. and alt.

RUTH. 6.5. D. SAMUEL SMITH (1804—1873).

1. Summer suns are glowing Over land and sea; Happy light is flowing, Bountiful and free. Ev'rything rejoices In the mellow rays; All earth's thousand voices Swell the psalm of praise.

497 *A Summer Song.*

2 God's free mercy streameth
  Over all the world,
  And His banner gleameth,
  Everywhere unfurled.
  Broad, and deep, and glorious,
  As the Heaven above,
  Shines in might victorious
  His eternal love.

3 Lord, upon our blindness,
  Thy pure radiance pour;
  For Thy loving-kindness
  Makes us love Thee more.

And when clouds are drifting
  Dark across our sky,
  Then, the vail uplifting,
  Father, be Thou nigh.

4 We will never doubt Thee,
  Though Thou vail Thy light;
  Life is dark without Thee,
  Death with Thee is bright.
  Light of light, shine o'er us
  On our pilgrim way,
  Go Thou still before us
  To the endless day.
        Bp. William Walsham How (1823—).

ST. MARTIN'S. C. M. WILLIAM TANSUR (1700—1783), 1735.

1. Let children hear the mighty deeds, Which God performed of old; Which in our younger years we saw, And which our fathers told.

498 *The Story handed down.*
Ps. lxxviii.

2 He bids us make His glories known,
  His works of power and grace;
  And we'll convey His wonders down
  Through every rising race.

3 Our lips shall tell them to our sons,
  And they again to theirs,

That generations yet unborn
  May teach them to their heirs,
4 Thus shall they learn, in God alone
  Their hope securely stands;
  That they may ne'er forget His works,
  But practise His commands.

Rev. Isaac Watts (1674—1748), 1719.

ST. HUGH. C. M. EDWARD JOHN HOPKINS (1818—).

1. Lord, in Thy name Thy ser-vants plead, And Thou hast sworn to hear;
Thine is the har-vest, Thine the seed, The fresh and fad-ing year.

499 *Spring Time.*

2 Our hope when autumn winds blew wild,
  We trusted, Lord, in Thee:
  And still, now spring has on us smiled,
  We wait on Thy decree.

3 The former and the latter rain,
  The summer sun and air,

The green ear, and the golden grain,
  All Thine, are ours by prayer.
4 So grant the precious things brought forth
  By sun and moon below,
  That Thee in Thy new heaven and earth
  We never may forego.

Rev. John Keeble (1792—1866), 1857. Ab.

COLUMBA. 7. JOHN BAPTISTE CALKIN (1827—), 1872.

1. Praise to God, im-mor-tal praise, For the love that crowns our days! Bounteous Source of

ev-'ry joy, Let Thy praise our tongues employ.

500 *Thanksgiving.*
Ps. lxv.

2 For the blessings of the field,
  For the stores the gardens yield;
  For the fruits in full supply,
  Ripened 'neath the summer sky;

3 Flocks that whiten all the plain;
  Yellow sheaves of ripened grain;
  Clouds that drop their fattening dews;
  Suns that temperate warmth diffuse;
4 All that spring with bounteous hand
  Scatters o'er the smiling land;
  All that liberal autumn pours
  From her rich o'erflowing stores;
5 These to Thee, my God, we owe,
  Source whence all our blessings flow;
  And for these my soul shall raise
  Grateful vows and solemn praise.

Mrs. Anna Lætitia Barbauld (1743—1825), 1772. Ab. and alt.

TIMES AND SEASONS.

AMERICA. 6.6.4.6.6.6.4.   HENRY CAREY (1663–1743). 1740. Har. 1745.

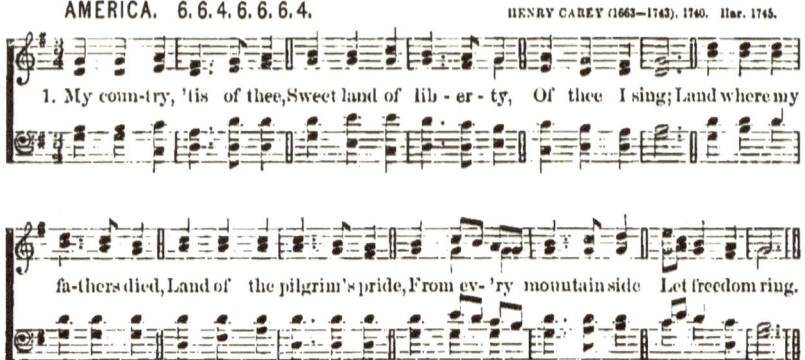

1. My coun-try, 'tis of thee, Sweet land of lib-er-ty, Of thee I sing; Land where my fa-thers died, Land of the pilgrim's pride, From ev-'ry mountain side Let freedom ring.

501   *"My Country."*

2 My native country, thee,
  Land of the noble, free,
    Thy name I love;
  I love thy rocks and rills,
  Thy woods and templed hills;
  My heart with rapture thrills
    Like that above.

3 Let music swell the breeze,
  And ring from all the trees
    Sweet freedom's song:
  Let mortal tongues awake,
  Let all that breathe partake,
  Let rocks their silence break,
    The sound prolong.

4 Our fathers' God, to Thee,
  Author of liberty,
    To Thee we sing;
  Long may our land be bright
  With freedom's holy light;
  Protect us by Thy might,
    Great God, our King.
      Rev. Samuel Francis Smith (1808–), 1832.

502   *"God save the State."*

1 GOD bless our native land:
  Firm may she ever stand,
    Through storm and night;
  When the wild tempests rave,
  Ruler of wind and wave,
  Do Thou our country save
    By Thy great might.

2 For her our prayer shall rise
  To God, above the skies;
    On Him we wait;
  Thou who art ever nigh,
  Guarding with watchful eye,
  To Thee aloud we cry,
    God save the State.
      Rev. Charles Timothy Brooks (1813–1883), 1835.
      Alt. by Rev. John Sullivan Dwight (1813–), 1844.

503   *Thanksgiving for Harvest.*

1 THE God of harvest praise,
  In loud thanksgivings raise
    Hand, heart, and voice;
  The valleys laugh and sing,
  Forests and mountains ring,
  The plains their tribute bring,
    The streams rejoice.

2 Yea, bless His holy Name,
  And joyous thanks proclaim
    Through all the earth;
  To glory in your lot
  Is comely; but be not
  God's benefits forgot
    Amidst your mirth.

3 The God of harvest praise;
  Hands, hearts, and voices raise
    With one accord;
  From field to garner throng,
  Bearing your sheaves along,
  And in your harvest-song
    Bless ye the Lord.
      James Montgomery (1771–1854), 1822. Ab. and alt.

DOXOLOGIES.

1   C. M.
To Father, Son, and Holy Ghost,
  The God whom we adore,
Be glory, as it was, is now,
  And shall be evermore.
Tate and Brady, 1696.

2   S. M.
To God, the Father, Son,
  And Spirit, One and Three,
Be glory, as it was, is now,
  And shall forever be.
Rev. John Wesley (1703—1791), 1741.

3   L. M.
Praise God, from whom all blessings flow;
Praise Him, all creatures here below:
Praise Him above, ye heavenly host;
Praise Father, Son, and Holy Ghost.
Bp. Thomas Ken (1637—1711), 1697.

4   L. M.
To God the Father, God the Son,
And God the Spirit, Three in One,
Be honor, praise, and glory given,
By all on earth, and all in Heaven.
Rev. Isaac Watts (1674—1748), 1709.

5   L. M. 6 l.
To God the Father, God the Son,
And God the Spirit, Three in One,
Be honor, praise, and glory given,
By all on earth, and all in Heaven;
As was through ages heretofore,
Is now, and shall be evermore.
Rev. Isaac Watts, 1709. First 4 lines.

6   C. P. M.
To Father, Son, and Holy Ghost,
The God whom Heaven's triumphant host
  And saints on earth adore;
Be glory as in ages past,
As now it is, and so shall last,
  When time shall be no more.
Tate and Brady, 1696. Alt.

7   L. P. M.
Now to the great and sacred Three,
The Father, Son, and Spirit, be
  Eternal praise and glory given,
Through all the worlds where God is
    known,
By all the angels near the throne,
And all the saints in earth and Heaven.
Rev. Isaac Watts, 1719.

8   H. M.
O God, for ever blest,
  To Thee all praise be given;
Thy Name Triune confessed
  By all in earth and Heaven;
As heretofore it was, is now,
And shall be so for evermore.
Rev. Edward Henry Bickersteth (1825—   ), 1870.

9   8, 7.
Praise the Father, earth and Heaven,
  Praise the Son, the Spirit praise,
As it was, and is, be given
  Glory through eternal days.
Unknown Author, 1327.

10   8, 7. D.
Worship, honor, glory, blessing,
  Lord, we offer to Thy Name:
Young and old their praise expressing,
  Join Thy goodness to proclaim,
As the saints in Heaven adore Thee,
  We would bow before Thy throne;
As the angels serve before Thee,
  So on earth Thy will be done.
Edward Osler (1798—1863), 1836.

11   8, 7. 4.
Glory be to God the Father,
  Glory be to God the Son,
Glory be to God the Spirit,
  Great Jehovah, Three in One:
    Glory, glory,
  While eternal ages run.
Rev. Horatius Bonar (1808—   ), 1866.

12   7, 6. D.
FATHER, Son, and Holy Ghost,
  One God whom we adore,
Join we with the heavenly host,
  To praise Thee evermore:
Live, by Heaven and earth adored,
  Three in One, and One in Three,
Holy, holy, holy Lord,
  All glory be to Thee.
Rev. Charles Wesley (1708—1788), 1746. Alt.

13   7.
SING we to our God above
Praise eternal as His love:
Praise Him, all ye heavenly host,
Father, Son, and Holy Ghost.
Rev. Charles Wesley, 1740.

14   7. 6 l.
PRAISE the Name, of God most high,
Praise Him, all below the sky,
Praise Him, all ye heavenly host,
Father, Son, and Holy Ghost;
As through countless ages past,
Evermore His praise shall last.
Unknown Author, 1827.

15   7. 6 l.
GOD the Father, God of grace,
Saviour, born of mortal race,
Comforter, our Life and Light,
One in essence, love and might;
Thee, whom all in Heaven adore,
We would worship evermore.
Rev. Ray Palmer (1808—), 1873.

16   7. D.
PRAISE our glorious King and Lord,
Angels waiting on His word,
Saints that walk with Him in white,
Pilgrims walking in His light:
Glory to the Eternal One,
Glory to His Only Son,
Glory to the Spirit be
Now, and through eternity.
Rev. Alexander Ramsay Thompson (1822—), 1869.

17   6, 4.
To the great One in Three
The highest praises be,
  Hence evermore;
His sovereign majesty
May we in glory see,
And to eternity
  Love and adore.
Rev. Charles Wesley, 1755.

18   6, 4.
To God, the Father, Son,
And Spirit, Three in One,
  All praise be given:
Crown Him in every song;
To Him your hearts belong,
Let all His praise prolong
  On earth, in Heaven.
Rev. Edwin Francis Hatfield (1807—1883), 1843.

19   10.
ALL praise and glory to the Father be
And Son and Spirit, undivided Three,
As hath been alway, shall be, and is now,
To Thee, O God, the everlasting Thou.
Bp. Edward Henry Bickersteth (1825—), 1870.

20   10, 11.
ALL glory to God, the Father and Son,
And Spirit of grace, the great Three in One;
Let highest ascriptions forever be given
By all the creation on earth and in Heaven.
Rippon's Collection, 1773.

21   11..
O FATHER Almighty, to Thee be addressed
With Christ and the Spirit, One God ever blest,
All glory and worship, from earth and from Heaven,
As was, and is now, and shall ever be given.
Unknown Author.

ALPHABETICAL INDEX OF TUNES.

A.	PAGE		PAGE	D.	PAGE
Abridge	73	Bethany	153	Dallas	71
Aldersgate	50	Bethel	101	Dawn	109, 188
Aletta	97	Bishop	156	Day of Rest	164
All Hallows	107	Blendon	29	Dedham	118
Alleluia	63	Bliss	171	Dennis	36
Almsgiving	14, 159	Blumenthal	83	Diademata	55
America	200	Boardman	65	Dijon	97
Amor Christi	123	Bonar	75	Dix	13, 42
Amsterdam	127	Boylston	173	Doane	153
Angel Tower	74	Braden	108	Dominus Regit Me	145
Angelus	23	Bradford	38	Doncaster	49
Antioch	43	Brattle Street	151	Dorrnance	96, 169
Anvern	178	Bremen	116, 138	Dort	56
Ariel	116	Brest	49	Downs	181
Arlington	181	Brown	52	Duke Street	180
Armagh	30	Budleigh	167	Dundee	142
Armenia	168	Burnham	93		
Asaph	125	Byefield	141	E.	
Ashwell	48			Edina	56
Aswarby	146	C.		Elizabethtown	44
Athens	103	Capetown	24	Ellers	26
Aurelia	152	Ceylon	41	Ellesdie	166
Austrian Hymn	35, 176	Chesterfield	70	Elvet	64
Autumn	54, 124	Chimes	52	Enon	160
Avon	48	Christmas	133, 172	Ensign	180
Azmon	64	Church	39	Eric	76
		Clinton	129	Ernan	68
B.		Cluff	85	Eshtemoa	147
Baden	126	Columba	199	Even Me	88
Barnby	70	Come unto Me	74	Evening Hymn	16
Bartimeus	96	Come, ye Disconsolate	78	Eventide	27
Batty	19	Consecration	163	Evermore	169
Bavaria	186	Cooling	95	Ewing	192
Bayley	138	Coronation	59	Expostulation	88
Beatitude	141	Cowper	95		
Belmont	15	Crasselius	170	F.	
Benediction	165	Culbach	5	Faben	110
Benevento	195	Culford	166	Federal Street	137
Bera	80	Cyprus	82	Ferguson	109

203

ALPHABETICAL INDEX OF TUNES.

	PAGE
Ferrier	10
Flemming	22
Franconia	136
Franklin Square	146
Fulton	37

G.

Geer	119
Geneva	39
Germany	196
Gethsemane	47, 99
Gilead	7
Glastonbury	99
Globe Field	10
Glory	131
Gordon	105
Gorton	79
Goshen	119
Grape	104
Greenville	9
Greenwood	100, 188
Grostete	60

H.

Halle	25
Hamburg	46
Hanford	148
Harmony Grove	178
Haydn	67
Hazelwood	23
Heath	144
Heber	58
Hebron	170
Hendon	115
Hermas	106
Holley	11
Hollingside	139
Holy Trinity	120
Horton	82
Houghton	40
Howard	53
Humility	17
Hummel	73
Hursley	17

I.

Innocents	22, 135
Invitation	87
Italian Hymn	8, 175

K.

Kirkbradden	111

L.

	PAGE
Laban	130
Lancashire	184
Langran	129
Laus Matutina	20
Lebanon	112
Leighton	155
Lenox	92
Lisbon	28
Louvan	91
Loving-kindness	121
Ludwig	164
Lux Benigna	128
Lyons	40
Lyte	113

M.

Maitland	140
Majesty	34
Manchester	122
Manoah	44
Marcellus	51
Marlow	71
Martyn	83, 139
Mear	144
Melcombe	6
Mendebras	29
Mendon	134
Mercy	66
Meribah	89, 190
Merrial	21
Messiah	114
Middleton	176
Migdol	51
Miles' Lane	59
Miriam	185
Missionary Chant	35, 179
Missionary Hymn	182
Monkland	36
Monsell	173
Mornington	13

N.

Naomi	142
Nativity	53
Neander	193
Needham	168
Nettleton	110
New Haven	62
New Castle	106
Newland	150
Nuremburg	126

O.

	PAGE
Oak	101
Oaksville	143
Old Hundredth	32, 196
Oliphant	77
Olive's Brow	46
Olivet	113, 186
Olmutz	67
Olney	79
Onido	184

P.

Paradise	104
Park Street	134
Pax Dei	26
Pax Tecum	162
Penitentia	90
Pentecost	66
Pleyel's Hymn	163
Portuguese Hymn	148
Posen	191
Princeton	128

R.

Rathbun	31, 136
Regent Square	12, 177
Renovation	20
Rescue	160
Rest	189
Retreat	14
Rhine	191
Rivaulx	8
Rock of Ages	98
Rockingham	6
Rose Hill	174
Rosefield	78
Russian Hymn	33
Ruth	198
Rutherford	193

S.

Sabbath	24
Salisbury	61
Samson	60
Segur	124
Self-surrender	122
Seraph	84
Service	157
Seymour	11
Shawmut	50
Shirland	12
Siloam	174
Silver Street	108
Solitude	37

	PAGE
Song	121
Southport	158
Spanish Hymn	114
St. Agnes	120
St. Alkmund	7
St. Ann	38
St. Bede	145
St. Bees	147
St. Crispin	102
St. Edmund	130
St. George's Chapel	197
St. Helen's	89
St. Hugh	199
St. John	94
St. Jude	171
St. Leonard	94
St. Martin's	198
St. Matthew	159
St. Maura	92
St. Michael	155
St. Raphael	9
St. Regulus	86
St. Sylvester	175
St. Thomas	154
St. Ulrich	105
State Street	100
Stella	112
Stephanos	76
Stephens	143
Stockton	84

	PAGE
Stockwell	18
Stracathro	125
Stuttgard	18
Subjection	103
Swabia	161

T.

	PAGE
Tappan	190
Tarring	86
Tell the Story	117
Temptation	161
Thatcher	12
To-day	82
Toplady	98
Treves	31
Tribute	35
Troyland	81
Truro	32
Trusting	72

U.

	PAGE
Unseld	132
Uxbridge	72

V.

	PAGE
Valentia	118
Varina	45
Vesper	189
Victory	57
Vigilate	135

W.

	PAGE
Ward	150
Ware	34
Wareham	68
Warner	90
Warwick	30
Watchman	28
Webb	132, 183
Wells	81
Welton	157
Wesley	62
Westminster	19
Weston	187
Wilmot	43
Wiltshire	104
Winn	154
Woodland	194
Woodstock	15
Woodworth	102
Work	162

Y.

	PAGE
Yoakley	21

Z.

	PAGE
Zebulon	69
Zephyr	80
Zion	177
Zurich	105

METRICAL INDEX OF TUNES.

C. M.	PAGE		PAGE		PAGE
Abridge	73	Miles' Lane	59	Ashwell	48
Antioch	43	Naomi	142	Bera	80
Arlington	181	Nativity	53	Bishop	156
Armagh	30	Needham	108	Blendon	29
Armenia	168	Oaksville	143	Crasselius	170
Avon	48	Siloam	174	Doncaster	49
Azmon	64	Southport	158	Duke Street	180
Barnby	70	St. Agnes	120	Ensign	180
Beatitude	141	St. Ann	38	Ernan	68
Belmont	15	St. Hugh	199	Evening Hymn	16
Boardman	65	St. John	94	Federal Street	137
Bradford	38	St. Leonard	94	Germany	196
Brown	52	St. Martin's	198	Gilead	7
Byefield	141	Stephens	143	Grostete	60
Chesterfield	70	Stracathro	125	Hamburg	46
Chimes	52	Valentia	118	Harmony Grove	178
Christmas	133, 172	Warwick	30	Hebron	170
Church	39	Wiltshire	104	Humility	17
Clinton	129	Woodstock	15	Hursley	17
Cooling	95			Louvan	91
Coronation	59	**C. M. 5 Lines.**		Loving-kindness	121
Cowper	95	Rhine	191	Majesty	34
Dedham	118	Tappan	190	Melcombe	6
Downs	181	Woodland	194	Mendon	134
Dundee	142			Migdol	51
Elizabethtown	44	**C. M. 6 Lines.**		Missionary Chant	33, 170
Elvet	64	All Hallows	107	Old Hundredth	32, 196
Geer	119	St. Bede	145	Olive's Brow	46
Geneva	39			Park Street	134
Heath	144	**C. M. D.**		Rest	189
Heber	58	Athens	103	Retreat	14
Holy Trinity	120	Brattle Street	151	Rivaulx	8
Howard	53	St. Matthew	159	Rockingham	6
Hummel	73	Varina	45	Rose Hill	174
Maitland	140			Russian Hymn	33
Manchester	122	**L. M.**		Samson	60
Manoah	44	Angelus	23	St. Alkmund	7
Marlow	71	Anvern	178	St. Crispin	102
Mear	144	Asaph	125	Troyland	81

206

	PAGE		S. M. D.	PAGE		PAGE
Truro	32	Diademata		55	Italian Hymn	8, 175
Uxbridge	72	Lebanon		112	Lyte	113
Ward	150				New Haven	62
Ware	34	**C. P. M.**			Olivet	113, 186
Wareham	68	Ariel		116	Weston	187
Warner	90	Bremen		116, 138		
Wells	81	Meribah		89, 190	**6. 5.**	
Welton	157				Enon	160
Woodworth	102	**H. M.**			Merrial	21
Zephyr	80	Burnham		93		
		Lenox		92	**6. 5. D.**	
		Stockton		84	Edina	56
L. M. 6 Lines.		St. Maura		92	Hermas	166
Benediction	165	Zebulon		69	Kirkbradden	111
Stella	112				Ruth	198
Yoakley	21	**P. M.**				
		Cluff		85	**6. 6. 6. 6. 8. 6.**	
S. M.		Grape		104	Bliss	171
Aldersgate	50	Invitation		87		
Aswarby	146	Paradise		194	**7.**	
Badea	126	Princeton		128	Aletta	97
Boylston	173	Rescue		160	Columba	199
Braden	108	Rutherford		193	Culbach	5
Dawn	109, 188	Salisbury		61	Cyprus	82
Dennis	36	Seraph		84	Dallas	71
Ferguson	109	Self-surrender		122	Dijon	97
Franconia	136	Tarring		86	Eshtemoa	147
Franklin Square	146	Temptation		161	Evermore	169
Glory	131				Ferrier	10
Gorton	79	**5. 5. 5. 6. D.**			Fulton	37
Greenwood	100, 188	Houghton		40	Globe Field	10
Haydn	67	Lyons		40	Holley	11
Laban	130				Horton	82
Leighton	155	**6. 4.**			Innocents	22, 135
Lisbon	28	To-day		82	Mercy	66
Monsell	173				Monkland	36
Mornington	13	**6. 4. 6. 4. 6. 6. 4.**			Nuremburg	120
Newland	150	Bethany		153	Pleyel's Hymn	163
Olmutz	67	Bethel		101	Posen	191
Olney	79	Doane		153	Seymour	11
Renovation	20				Solitude	37
Shawmut	50	**6. 4. 6. 4. 6. 6. 6. 4.**			St. Bees	147
Shirland	12	Consecration		163	Trusting	72
Silver Street	108	Oak		101		
St. Michael	155	St. Edmund		130	**7. 5 Lines.**	
St. Thomas	154				Hendon	115
State Street	100	**6. 4. 6. 4. 10. 10.**				
Subjection	103	Budleigh		107	**7. 6 Lines.**	
Swabia	161				Dix	13, 42
Thatcher	12	**6. 6. 4. 6. 6. 6. 4.**			Gethsemane	47, 99
Watchman	28	America		200	Glastonbury	99
Winn	154	Dort		56	Halle	25
Zurich	165	Hazelwood		23	Rock of Ages	98
					Rosefield	78

	PAGE
Sabbath	24
Service	157
– Spanish Hymn	114
– Toplady	98

7. D.

– Benevento	195
– Blumenthal	83
Culford	166
Hollingside	139
– Martyn	83, 139
– Messiah	114
– Onido	184
– St. George's Chapel	197

7. 6. D.

– Amsterdam	127
Angel Tower	74
– Aurelia	152
Bonar	75
Ceylon	41
Come unto Me	74
Day of Rest	164
– Ewing	192
Lancashire	184
Ludwig	164
Mendebras	29
– Miriam	185
– Missionary Hymn	182
St. Ulrich	105
– Tell the Story	117
Unfeld	132
– Webb	132, 183

7. 6. 7. 5. D.

– Work	162

7. 7. 7. 3.

Vigilate	135

7. 7. 7. 5.

Capetown	24
Pentecost	66
Treves	31

8. 5. 8. 3.

St. Helen's	89

	PAGE
Stephanos	76

8. 6. 8. 8. 6.

Newcastle	106

8. 7.

Bartimeus	96
Batty	19
Dominus Regit Me	145
Dorrnance	96, 169
Rathbun	31, 136
Stockwell	18
St. Sylvester	175
Stuttgard	18
Vesper	189
Westminster	19
Wilmot	43

8. 7. D.

Austrian Hymn	176
Autumn	54, 124
Bavaria	186
Bayley	138
Ellesdie	166
Erie	76
Faben	110
Middleton	176
Nettleton	110
Wesley	62

8. 7. 3. 3. 7.

Even Me	88

8. 7. 4.

Austrian Hymn	35
Brest	49
Greenville	9
Oliphant	77
Regent Square	42, 177
Segur	124
St. Raphael	9
Tribute	35
Victory	57
Zion	177

8. 7. 7. 7.

Neander	193

	PAGE
8. 7. 8. 7. 7.	
St. Jude	171
8. 8. 8. 4.	
Almsgiving	14, 159
Hanford	148
Marcellus	51
8. 8. 8. 5.	
Song	121
8. 8. 6. 8. 8. 6.	
Alleluia	63
10. 2 Lines.	
Pax Tecum	162
10.	
Ellers	26
Eventide	27
Langran	129
Pax Dei	26
Penitentia	90
10. 4, 10. 10.	
Lux Benigna	128
10. 10. 4. 6.	
St. Regulus	86
10. 10. 10. 10. 4.	
Amor Christi	123
11.	
Expostulation	88
Gordon	105
Goshen	149
Portuguese Hymn	148
11. 10.	
Come, ye Disconsolate	78
Laus Matutina	20
11. 11. 11. 5.	
Flemming	22

INDEX OF AUTHORS.

The figures refer to the numbers of the hymns.

ADAMS, Mrs. Sarah Flower (1805-1848). 18, 374.
Addison, Joseph (1672-1719). 92.
Alexander, Mrs. Cecil Frances (1823—). 330.
Alford, Rev. Henry (1810-1871). 495.
Alfred, King of England (849-901). 50.
Allen, Prof. George Nelson (1812-1877). 336.
Allen, Rev. James (1734-1804). 132, 409.
Ambrose of Milan (340-397). 35.
Anderson, Mrs. Maria Frances (1819—). 456.
Anstice, Prof. Joseph (1808-1836). 55, 334.
Auber, Miss Harriet (1773-1862). 43, 460.

BACON, Rev. Leonard (1802-1881). 447, 494.
Baker, Rev. Francis. 480.
Baker, Rev. Sir Henry Williams (1821-1877). 80, 110, 117, 241, 315, 350, 377.
Bakewell, Rev. John (1721-1819). 126, 127.
Bancroft, Mrs. Charitie Lees (1841—). 184.
Barbauld, Mrs. Anna Lætitia (1743-1825). 202, 475, 500.
Bathurst, William Hiley Bragge (1796-1877). 450.
Beddome, Rev. Benjamin (1717-1795). 166, 176, 242, 316, 413, 430, 446.
Bernard of Clairvaux (1091-1153). 281, 289.
Bernard of Cluny. 482, 483, 484.
Bethune, Rev. George Washington (1805-1862). 103.
Bevan, Emma Frances (1827—). 238.
Bickersteth, Bp. Edward Henry (1825—). 60, 96, 401.
Bode, John Ernest (1816-1874). 405.
Boden, Rev. James (1757-1841). 12, 205.
Bonar, Rev. Horatius (1808—). 74, 81, 209, 223, 235, 245, 249, 251, 253, 258, 269, 384, 476.
Bonar, Mrs. Jane Catherine Lundie. 244.

Borthwick, Miss Jane (1813—). 218, 394.
Bowring, Sir John (1792-1872). 70, 328.
Boyle, Mrs. Sarah Roberts (1812-1869). 309.
Brace, Rev. Seth Collins (1811—). 399.
Bridges, Matthew (1800—). 131, 412.
Brooks, Rev. Charles Timothy (1813-1883). 502.
Brown, Mrs. Phœbe Hinsdale (1783-1861). 32, 162.
Browne, Rev. Simon (1680-1732). 167.
Bruce, Michael (1746-1767). 141, 298.
Bryant, William Cullen (1794-1878). 443.
Bubier, George B. (—1869). 381.
Burder, Rev. George (1752-1832). 88.
Burnham, Rev. Richard (1749-1810). 228.
Burns, Rev. James Drummond (1823-1864). 234.
Burton, John (1773-1822). 175, 305.
Burton, John, Jr. (1803—). 170.

CARY, Miss Phœbe (1825-1871). 470.
Caswall, Rev. Edward (1814-1878). 164, 281, 289.
Cawood, Rev. John (1775-1852). 99, 466.
Cennick, Rev. John (1717-1755). 300.
Chandler, Rev. John (1806-1876). 35.
Clark, Rev. J. H. 326.
Clement of Alexandria (—217). 436.
Cluff, S. O'Maley. 207.
Codner, Mrs. Elizabeth. 212.
Coffin, Prof. Charles (1676-1749). 151.
Collins, Rev. Henry. 406.
Collyer, Rev. William Bengo (1782-1854). 195, 199.
Conder, Josiah (1789-1855). 44.
Contractus, Hermannus (1013-1054). 146.
Cooper, Edward (1770-1833). 75.
Cotterill, Rev. Thomas (1779-1823). 8, 155, 176.
Cousin, Mrs. Anne Ross. 257, 485.

INDEX OF AUTHORS.

Cowper, William (1731–1800). 172, 226, 341, 347, 356.
Coxe, Bp. Arthur Cleveland (1818—). 107, 465.
Crabbe, Rev. George (1754–1832). 203.
Crosswell, Rev. William (1804–1851). 392.

DARBY, Rev. John Nelson (1800–1882). 363.
Davies, Rev. Samuel (1724–1761). 418.
Deck, James George (1802—). 105, 271, 371.
Denny, Sir Edward (1796–). 102.
Dexter, Rev. Henry Martyn (1821—). 436.
Dickson, Rev. David (1583–1663). 480.
Dix, William Chatterton (1837—). 98, 183.
Doane, Bp. George Washington (1799–1859). 21, 135, 449.
Dobell, John (1757–1840). 194.
Doddridge, Rev. Philip (1702–1751). 25, 154, 165, 193, 259, 287, 288, 298, 320, 352, 379, 383, 417, 434, 492, 493.
Downton, Rev. Henry (1818—). 490.
Draper, Rev. Bourne Hall (1778–1843). 444.
Duffield, Rev. George (1818–1888). 273, 318.
Dwight, John Sullivan (1813—). 502.
Dwight, Rev. Timothy (1752–1817). 196, 428.
Dyer, Rev. Sidney (1814—). 201.

EDMESTON, James (1791–1867). 39, 458.
Ellerton, Rev. John (1826—). 59.
Elliott, Miss Charlotte (1789–1871). 30, 246, 248, 325, 360.
Elven, Rev. Cornelius (1797—). 216.
Enfield, Prof. William (1741–1797). 101.
Evans, Rev. Jonathan (1749–1809). 115.
Everest, Rev. Charles William (1814–1877). 332.

FABER, Rev. Frederick William (1814–1863). 47, 186, 280, 344, 390, 487.
Fawcett, Rev. John (1739–1817). 14, 173, 427.
Fletcher, Miss. 393.
Follen, Mrs. Eliza Lee (1787–1860). 20.
Francis, Rev. Benjamin (1734–1799). 331.

GANSE, Rev. Hervey Doddridge (1822—). 230.
Gerhardt, Rev. Paul (1606–1676). 261, 354.
Gibbons, Rev. Thomas (1720–1785). 453.
Gill, Thomas Hornblower (1819—). 136, 250.

Gilmore, Rev. Joseph H. 307.
Gladden, Rev. Washington (1836—). 387.
Gough, Benjamin (1805—). 459, 461, 463.
Gould, Rev. Sabine Baring (1834—). 48.
Grant, Sir Robert (1788–1838). 94.
Gregory the Great (540–604). 140.
Grigg, Rev. Joseph (—1768). 197, 331.
Gurney, Rev. John Hampden (1802–1862). 337.

HALL, William John. 355.
Hammond, Rev. William (—1783). 15, 260.
Hankey, Miss Kate. 279.
Harbaugh, Rev. Henry (1818–1867). 263, 496.
Hart, Rev. Joseph (1712–1768). 10, 160, 188.
Haslock, Mary. 397.
Hastings, Thomas (1784–1872). 56, 57, 189, 200, 208, 211, 296, 462.
Havergal, Miss Frances Ridley (1836–1879). 148, 214, 220, 388, 389, 403, 422.
Haweis, Rev. Thomas (1732–1820). 190.
Hawker, Rev. Robert (1753–1827). 130.
Heath, George. 311.
Heber, Bp. Reginald (1783–1826). 433, 454.
Hervey, Rev. James (1714–1758). 91.
Hill, Rev. Rowland (1744–1833). 359.
Holden, Oliver (1765–1844). 16.
Hope, Henry Joy McCracken (1809–1872). 243.
Hopper, Rev. Edward (1818—). 367.
How, Bp. William Walsham (1823—). 113, 182, 375, 497.
Humphreys, Rev. Joseph (1720—). 275.
Hunter, Rev. William. 206.
Hyde, Mrs. Ann Bradley (—1872). 432.

KEBLE, Rev. John (1792–1866). 37, 355, 499.
Keith, George. 361.
Kelly, Rev. Thomas (1769–1855). 7, 13, 121, 134, 291, 486.
Ken, Bp. Thomas (1637–1711). 33, 34.
Kennedy, Rev. Benjamin Hall (1804—). 276, 481.
Key, Francis Scott (1779–1843). 266.

LANGFORD, John. 301.
Leeson, Miss Jane Elizabeth. 151, 357.
Lynch, Rev. Thomas Toke (1818–1871). 104.
Lyte, Rev. Henry Francis (1793–1847). 28,

60, 80, 242, 329, 333, 319, 365, 464, 472.

MacDonald, Rev. William (1820—). 178.
MacKay, Mrs. Margaret (1801—). 474.
MacKellar, Thomas (1812—). 231.
Madan, Rev. Martin (1726-1790). 260.
Marriott, Rev. John (1780-1825). 469.
Mason, Rev. John (1634-1694). 66, 152, 294.
Mason, Rev. William (1725-1797). 58.
Maude, Mrs. Mary Fawler. 416.
Maurus, Rabanus (776-856). 164.
Maxwell, Mrs. Mary Robertson. 439.
May, C. E. 255.
Medley, Rev. Samuel (1738-1799). 119, 277, 290.
Merrick, Rev. James (1720-1769). 358.
Midlane, Albert (1825—). 378.
Millard, Rev. James Elwin (1821—). 86.
Milton, John (1608-1674). 85.
Monod, Rev. Theodore. 421.
Monsell, Rev. John Samuel Bewley (1811-1875). 303, 321.
Montgomery, James (1771-1854). 1, 31, 87, 97, 109, 142, 161, 210, 362, 380, 386, 408, 445, 455, 471, 478, 503.
Moore, Thomas (1779-1852). 189.
Morris, Mrs. Eliza Fanny (1821—). 68.
Morrison, Rev. John (1749-1798). 348.
Mote, Rev. Edward, 268. *1797-1874*.
Mudie, Charles Edward (1818—). 410.
Muhlenberg, Rev. William Augustus (1796-1877). 192, 435.
Myers, Mrs. Elvina Mabel (1818—). 252.

Neale, Rev. John Mason (1818-1866). 46, 185, 391, 482, 483, 484.
Nelson, Earl Horatio (1823—). 50.
Neumeister, Rev. Erdmann (1671-1756). 238.
Nevin, Rev. Edwin Henry (1814—). 129, 274.
Newman, Rev. John Henry (1801—). 306.
Newton, Rev. John (1725-1807). 17, 19, 22, 24, 26, 41, 54, 225, 284, 293, 414, 437, 438, 489.
Noel, Miss Caroline M. 133.

Onderdonk, Bp. Henry Ustick (1789-1858). 191, 451.

Palmer, Henry R. 398.

Palmer, Rev. Ray (1808-1887). 112, 140, 146, 220, 270, 283, 491.
Parr, Miss Harriet. 42.
Perronet, Rev. Edward (—1792). 139.
Phelps, Rev. Sylvanus Dryden (1816—). 402.
Pirie, Rev. Alexander (—1804). 123.
Plumptre, Rev. Edward Hayes (1821—). 314.
Pott, Rev. Francis (1832—). 118.
Prentiss, Mrs. Elizabeth Payson (1819-1878). 373.

Rawson, George (1807-1885). 52, 159, 359.
Reed, Rev. Andrew (1787-1862). 153, 157.
Robertson, Rev. William (—1743). 431.
Robinson, Rev. George Wade (1838-1877). 239.
Robinson, Rev. Richard Hayes (1842—). 69.
Robinson, Rev. Robert (1735-1790). 264.
Rorison, Rev. Gilbert (1821-1869). 53.
Russell, Arthur Tozer (1851—). 147.

Scriven, Joseph (1829-1886). 187.
Seagrave, Rev. Robert (1693—). 304.
Shekleton, Miss Mary. 295.
Shepherd, Thomas (1665-1739). 336.
Shirley, Hon. and Rev. Walter (1725-1786). 409.
Shrubsole, William, Jr. (1759-1829). 441.
Sigourney, Mrs. Lydia Howard Huntley (1791-1865). 163, 582.
Smith, Mrs. Caroline Sprague (1827—). 40.
Smith, Rev. Samuel Francis (1808—). 200, 457, 501.
Spitta, Rev. Carl Johann Philipp (1801-1859). 394.
Steele, Miss Anne (1717-1778). 36, 120, 171, 179, 286, 339, 343, 368.
Stennett, Rev. Samuel (1727-1795). 5, 62, 137, 224.
Stephen of St. Sabas (725-794). 185.
Stewart, John. 168.
Stocker, John. 156.
Stone, Rev. Samuel John (1839—). 215.
Stowell, Rev. Hugh (1799-1865). 29, 468.
Swain, Rev. Leonard (1821-1869). 313.

Tappan, Rev. William Bingham (1794-1849), 108, 488.
Taylor, Thomas Rawson (1807-1836). 310.
Tersteegen, Gerhard (1697-1769). 218, 299.

Thomson, Rev. John (1782-1818). 93.
Thring, Rev. Godfrey (1823—). 267.
Toplady, Rev. Augustus Montague (1740-1778). 126, 127, 213, 236, 237, 302.
Tuttiett, Rev. Lawrence (1825—). 317.
Twells, Rev. Henry (1823—). 51.

UPHAM, Rev. Thomas Cogswell (1799-1872). 376.

VAN ALSTYNE, Mrs. Frances Jane Crosby (1823—). 396.

WALKER, Anna L. 400.
Walker, Mrs. Mary Jane. 256.
Wardlaw, Rev. Ralph (1779-1853). 272.
Waring, Miss Anna Lætitia (1820—). 351, 372.
Watts, Rev. Isaac (1674-1748). 2, 3, 4, 6, 9, 23, 61, 63, 67, 71, 72, 73, 76, 77, 78, 79, 82, 83, 89, 90, 100, 106, 111, 114, 116, 122, 124, 125, 138, 143, 144, 149, 150, 169, 174, 177, 180, 181, 198, 217, 219, 222, 227, 262, 285, 308, 319, 322, 323, 324, 338, 342, 346, 353, 364, 366, 385, 411, 419, 420, 423, 429, 448, 478, 498.
Wesley, Rev. Charles (1708-1788). 11, 27, 38, 95, 145, 158, 204, 221, 232, 233, 247, 278, 282, 312, 327, 335, 340, 404, 407, 424, 425, 426, 477.
Wesley, Rev. John (1703-1791). 233, 290, 354.
Whitfield, Rev. Frederick (1829—). 370.
Wigner, John M. 210. urch (1644—).
Williams, Rev. Benjamin. 84.
Williams, Miss Helen Maria (1762-1827). 369.
Williams, Rev. Peter (1719-1796). 297.
Williams, Rev. William (1717-1791). 297, 440.
Willis, Miss Ellen H. 292.
Wingrove, John (1720-1793). 265.
Winkworth, Miss Catherine (1827-1878). 49, 261.
Wolcott, Rev. Samuel (1813—). 467.
Woodford, Bp. James Russell (1820—). 128.
Wordsworth, Bp. Christopher (1807-1885). 64, 395.
Wreford, Rev. John Reynell (1800-1881). 452.

INDEX OF COMPOSERS.

The figures refer to the number of the page.

ABBEY, Alonzo Judson (1825-1887). 95.
Ahle, Johann Rudolph (1625-1673). 126.
Arne, Thomas Augustine (1710-1778). 181.

BAILLOT, Pierre-Marie-Francois de Sales (1771-1842). 77.
Baker, Rev. Sir Henry Williams (1821-1877). 76.
Barnby, Joseph (1838—). 21, 70, 75, 120, 165, 173, 194.
Beadle, Harry Hobart (1828—). 57.
Beethoven, Ludwig von (1770-1827). 79, 164, 196.
Bliss, Philip P. (1838-1876). 171.
Blumenthal, Jacques (1829—). 83.
Bourgeois, Louis. 32, 196.
Bradbury, William Batchelder (1816-1868). 36, 37, 46, 52, 80, 88, 97, 102, 108, 189.
Brown, Arthur Henry (1830—). 107.
Burgmüller, Friedrich (1804—). 191.
Burney, Charles (1726-1814). 32.

CALDBECK, G. T. 162.
Calkin, John Baptiste (1827—). 180, 199.
Carey, Henry (1663-1743). 200.
Chapin, Amzi (1768—). 140.
Cherubini, Maria Luigi (1760-1842). 71.
Cole, John (1774-1853). 39.
Conkey, Ithamar (1815-1867). 31, 136.
Converse, Charles Crozart (1834—). 76.
Croft, William (1677-1727). 38, 93, 159.

DAYE, John (1522-1584). 155.
Dearle, Edward (1806—). 90.
Devereux, Lewis. 65.
Doane, William Howard (1832—). 153, 160.
Downes, Lewis Thomas (1827—). 37.
D'Urban, Charles. 193.

Dutton, Deodatus, Jr. 15.
Dyer, Arthur E. 187.
Dykes, Rev. John Bacchus (1823-1876). 8, 10, 14, 26, 59, 64, 74, 98, 99, 120, 128, 139, 141, 145, 147, 159, 175.

EDERWEIN, Traugott Maximilian (1775-1831). 118.
Edson, Lewis (1748-1820). 92.
Elliott, J. W. (1816—). 164.
Elvey, Sir George Job (1816—). 55, 102, 197.
Ewing, Alexander (1830—). 192.

FALCONER, A. Croil (1850—). 86, 123.
Fielden, O. M. 160.
Filitz, Friedrich (1804-1860). 24.
Fischer, William Gustavus (1835—). 72, 117.
Flemming, Friedrich Ferdinand (1778-1813). 22.
Flotow, Friedrich Freiherr von (1812-1883). 189.

GARDINER, William (1770-1853). 118.
Gauntlett, Henry John (1806-1876). 31, 40, 150, 169.
Giardini, Felice (1716-1796). 8, 29, 103, 175.
Gläser, Carl Gotthilf (1784-1829). 64.
Goldschmidt, Otto (1829—). 63.
Gordon, A. J. 105.
Goss, Sir John (1800-1880). 35.
Gottschalk, Louis Moreau (1829-1869). 66.
Gould, John Edgar (1822-1875). 80.
Gould, Nathaniel D. (1781-1864). 194.
Grape, John Thomas (1833—). 104.
Greatorex, Henry Wellington (1811-1858). 11, 44, 60, 119, 155.

HANDEL, George Frederick (1685-1759). 12, 38, 43, 60, 133, 154, 172.

INDEX OF COMPOSERS.

Harrison, Rev. Ralph (1748-1810). 131.
Hastings, Thomas (1784-1872). 14, 62, 98, 116, 138, 141, 177.
Hatton, John (—1793). 180.
Havergal, Miss Frances Ridley (1836-1879). 106.
Havergal, Rev. William Henry (1793-1870). 5.
Haweis, Rev. Thomas (1732-1820). 70.
Haydn, Francis Joseph (1732-1809). 34, 35, 40, 44, 67, 176.
Herold, Louis Joseph Ferdinand (1791-1833). 114.
Hews, George (1806-1873). 11.
Holbrook, Joseph Perry (1822—). 19, 39, 113, 124, 129, 138, 156, 185.
Holden, Oliver (1765-1844). 59.
Holdroyd, Israel. 81.
Hopkins, Edward John (1818—). 9, 23, 26, 86, 166, 199.
Hopkins, Rev. Josiah (1786-1862). 88.
Howard, Samuel (1710-1782). 53.
Hummel, Johann Nepomuk (1778-1837). 20.
Hutchinson, Rev. Charles (1792-1856). 125.

JENKS, Stephen (1772-1856). 96.
Jones, Rev. Darius Eliot (1815-1881). 18.
Jones, Rev. William (1726-1800). 143.
Josephi, Georg. 23.

KINGSLEY, George (1811-1884). 34, 44, 58, 65, 90, 109, 114, 118, 158, 190.
Knapp, William (1698 1768). 68.
Kocher, Conrad (1786-1872). 13.

LAHEE, Henry (1826—). 53.
Langran, James (1835—). 129.
Leach, James (1762-1797). 28.
Longhurst, William Henry (1819—). 74.
Lowry, Rev. Robert (1826—). 163.
Lvoff, Alexis Feodorovitch (1799-1870). 33.

MAKER, F. C. (1844—). 87.
Malan, Rev. Cæsar Henri Abraham (1787-1864). 78, 115, 157.
Marsh, Simeon Butler (1798-1875). 83, 139.
Mason, Lowell (1792-1872). 6, 13, 24, 29, 43, 46, 48, 49, 50, 51, 52, 56, 64, 67, 68, 69, 71, 72, 77, 79, 82, 89, 95, 101, 113, 116, 130, 134, 142, 144, 150, 153, 162, 170, 173, 178, 181, 182, 184, 186, 190.
Mason, Thomas B. 147.
Mehul, Etienne Henri (1763-1817). 7.
Mendelssohn, Felix Bartholdy (1809-1847). 82, 125, 128.
Merrick, Rev. Sir G. P. 50.
Miller, Edward (1731-1807). 49.
Mitchell, Nahum (1770-1853). 151.
Monk, William Henry (1823—). 13, 17, 27, 42, 76, 135.
Morley, Henry L. 106.
Mozart, Johann C. W. A. (1756-1791). 166.
Mudie, Thomas Mollison (1809-1876). 167.

NAEGELI, Hans Georg (1773-1836). 36, 142, 165.
Nares, James (1715-1783). 127.
Neander, Joachim (1610-1680). 193.

OAKELEY, Sir Herbert Stanley (1830—). 56.
Oliver, Henry Kemble (1800-1885). 137, 178.

PAISIELLO, Giovanni (1741-1816). 103.
Palestrina, Giovanni Pierluigi da (1524?-1594). 51.
Palmer, Henry R. 161.
Parker, Edwin Pond (1836—). 109, 188.
Pleyel, Ignaz Joseph (1757-1831). 151, 163, 184.
Pond, Sylvanus Billings (1792-1871). 146, 168.
Portogallo, Marc Antoine (1763-1830). 148.
Purday, C. H. 105.

REAY, Samuel (1828—). 41.
Redhead, Richard (1820—). 47, 99.
Reed, Daniel (1757-1836). 28.
Ritter, Peter (1760-1846). 17, 25.
Root, George Frederick (1820—). 45.
Rossini, Gioacchimo (1792-1868). 90.
Rousseau, Jean Jacques (1712-1778). 9.

SANKEY, Ira D. (1840—). 85.
Shrubsole, William (1758-1806). 59.
Smart, Sir George (1784-1869). 104.
Smart, Henry (1812-1879). 42, 94, 177, 184.
Smith, Isaac (1735-1800). 73, 108.
Smith, Samuel (1804-1873). 198.
Spratt, A. B. 101.

INDEX OF COMPOSERS.   215

Stainer, John (1840—). 20.
Stanley, Samuel (1767-1822). 12, 30.
Statham, Francis R. 81.
Stewart, Sir Robert Prescott (1825—). 89.
Stockton, Rev. J. H. 84.
Störl, Johann Georg Christian (1676-1743). 18.
Strattner, Georg Christoph (1650-1705). 191.
Sullivan, Sir Arthur (1842—). 66, 92, 130, 148.
Sweetser, Joseph Emerson (1825-1873). 100, 174, 188.

TALLIS, Thomas (1529-1585). 16.
Tansur, William (1700-1783). 198.
Taylor, Virgil Corydon (1817—). 91.
Theobald, King of Navarre (1201-1253). 22, 135.
Tuckerman, Samuel Parkman (1819—). 17.
Turle, James (1802-1882). 30, 94.

UNSELD, Benjamin Carl (1843—). 132.

VENUA, Frederick Marc Antoine (1788—). 134.
Vincent, Charles (1852—). 171.

WAINWRIGHT, Robert (1747-1782). 122.
Walker, Rev. E. C. 111.
Wartensee, Xavier Schnyder von (1786-1868). 82.
Webb, George James (1803-1887). 132, 183.
Webbe, Samuel (1740-1816). 6, 15, 78, 195.
Weber, Carl Maria von (1786-1826). 11, 43.
Wellesley, Garret Colley (1735-1781). 13.
Wesley, Samuel (1766-1837). 146.
Wesley, Samuel Sebastian (1810-1876). 152, 168.
Wilkes, John P. 36.
Willcox, John Henry (1827-1875). 110.
Williams, Aaron (1731-1776). 154.
Wilson, Hugh (1764-1824). 48.
Winn, William (1828—). 154.
Woodbury, Isaac Baker (1819-1858). 96, 169, 174.
Woodman, Jonathan Call (1813—). 100.
Wyeth, Rev. John (1792-1858). 110.

YOAKLEY, William. 21.

ZEUNER, Heinrich Christopher (1795-1857). 33, 73, 143, 179.
Zundel, John (1815-1882). 62, 112.

INDEX OF SCRIPTURE TEXTS.

GENESIS.
	HYMN
1 : 3	469
3 : 24	125
5 : 24	347
7 : 1	192
7 : 8, 9	192, 240
12 : 1–4	323
19 : 17	199, 223
24 : 63	30, 32
26 : 24	361
27 : 34	212
28 : 10–12	480
28 : 17	7
28 : 20–22	298
32 : 21–32	313
32 : 26	15
49 : 10	462

EXODUS.
3 : 8	482
10 : 11	318
13 : 21, 22	297
14 : 15	317
20 : 8–11	58
23 : 16	195, 503
25 : 17–22	29
33 : 15	490
34 : 23	503

LEVITICUS.
8 : 35	312
16 : 2	29
16 : 21, 22	116

NUMBERS.
7 : 89	29
14 : 24	330
23 : 10	471, 475

DEUTERONOMY.
10 : 12, 13	389
11 : 27	376
12 : 9	476
15 : 11	392
28 : 1–14	376
31 : 6–8	361
33 : 27	335, 361, 366
34 : 1–4	478

JOSHUA.
1 : 2	478

	HYMN
1 : 9, 16	300
4 : 6, 7	498
24 : 15	417

JUDGES.
8 : 4	363

RUTH.
1 : 16, 17	408

1st SAMUEL.
2 : 10	455
3 : 10	13
7 : 12	264
15 : 22	376

2d SAMUEL.
22 : 3	214, 366
23 : 4	457

1st KINGS.
2 : 3	312
3 : 5	19, 26
19 : 12	162

2d KINGS.
6 : 15–17	390
6 : 17	345

1st CHRONICLES.
29 : 11, 12	77
29 : 14	375
29 : 15	310

2d CHRONICLES.
15 : 15	417
16 : 9	16
32 : 7, 8	390

NEHEMIAH.
8 : 9–12	495
9 : 19	297

ESTHER.
4 : 16	225, 239

JOB.
5 : 9	6
13 : 15	369
19 : 25	119, 120

	HYMN
29 : 23	438
33 : 13	341
38 : 7	1

PSALMS.
2	454
3	390
3 : 5	33
4 : 8	34
5	67
5 : 3	33
9 : 9, 10	335, 366
9 : 10	256
16 : 5–9	342
16 : 8	38
18 : 2	214
20 : 5	314, 449
23	350, 358, 362, 364, 372
24 : 3, 4	355
24 : 7–10	139
26 : 7	291
27 : 1	47
27 : 1–3	339, 342
30 : 5	354, 457
31 : 15	351
34	345
34 : 18	189, 219
35 : 28	36
36	365
36 : 5–9	71
36 : 7	290
37 : 3–7	334, 339
37 : 23, 24	339
37 : 37	471, 475
38 : 4	233
39 : 4, 5	305
40 : 2	268
40 : 8	344
40 : 12	220
42 : 5	354
42 : 8	9
43	349
43 : 3	45, 307, 301
45 : 2	102, 137
45 : 3–6	77
46	366
46 : 9	460
48	437
51	217, 219
51 : 6, 7	299

216

HYMN		HYMN		HYMN
51 : 10....................340	118 : 24..................64	25 : 8....................118
51 : 15....................219	119.......................171	25 : 9....................100
51 : 17....................189	119 : 97..................175	26 : 3....................401
51 : 18....................464	119 : 105.................173	26 : 4........236, 261, 274
52 : 8................214, 256	119 : 130.................172	32 : 2....................335
55 : 6....................240	119 : 136.................242	32 : 20...................380
55 : 22......233, 334, 352, 359	119 : 148..................32	33 : 20, 21...............437
56........................365	119 : 176.................269	35 : 1, 2..................154
57 : 7, 8............260, 415	121........................39	35 : 10...................302
61 : 4....................267	126 : 2...................291	40 : 11..............296, 435
62 : 8....................274	126 : 5, 6...........380, 382	40 : 28–31................324
63 : 1...............309, 349	127.........................43	41 : 10, 13, 14...........361
63 : 6.....................32	130.................216, 241	42 : 4....................465
65...................492, 500	130 : 7...................186	42 : 7..............440, 447
66 : 2...............219, 277	136..................76, 85	43 : 2....................361
66 : 16...................207	137............302, 428, 472	44 : 5....................417
67.........................28	139..................93, 299	45 : 7......................9
68 : 9....................438	139 : 7–10............16, 20	45 : 19....................15
71...................285, 365	139 : 17....................4	48 : 17...................307
71 : 16...................300	141 : 8...................214	48 : 22...................240
71 : 23, 24................36	143 : 1, 2................217	49 : 15...................356
72..............448, 455, 460, 462	143 : 9...................223	50 : 4....................381
72 : 6....................154	143 : 10.............343, 360	50 : 10...................214
73 : 23–28................342	145........................6	51 : 9....................441
73 : 24....................42	145 : 1, 2................281	51 : 11..............458, 483
73 : 25........271, 353, 388	145 : 15, 16.........493, 500	52........................437
73 : 26...................339	147.......................497	52 : 1, 2.................461
74 : 17...................497	147 : 7...................260	52 : 7–9..................459
77 : 12....................32	147 : 15..................468	52 : 15...................465
78....................79, 498	148.......................495	53 : 4, 5, 12........237, 253
84 : 10....................61	149 : 2....................23	53 : 4–6..................117
85...................496, 502		53 : 5...........111, 223, 257
85 : 6.........160, 162, 378, 438	**PROVERBS.**	53 : 6....................269
87 : 3....................437	1 : 10–20.................398	53 : 6, 9, 12.............213
89 : 6....................277	1 : 20–23.................218	55 : 1..............179, 249
90................89, 90, 96	2 : 3–5...................171	55 : 1, 2.................180
90 : 9....................189	3 : 24.....................48	55 : 4....................317
91.........................39	4 : 11, 15................398	55 : 7....................195
91 : 1.....................34	8 : 4.....................179	55 : 12.............296, 458
92 : 1, 2...................9	8 : 17...............235, 433	57 : 21...................240
93 : 1.....................77	14 : 32..............471, 475	58 : 8....................457
94 : 19....................32	15 : 3.....................16	60 : 3, 4.................162
95 : 1–6...............65, 83	15 : 23...................381	60 : 20...................483
95 : 2....................211	16 : 3....................334	61 : 1....................189
95 : 7...............200, 201	18 : 24........187, 243, 414	61 : 12...................455
97 : 2....................341	25 : 11...................381	62 : 6..............414, 459
103...................72, 80	29 : 25...................214	63 : 7..............290, 369
103 : 1–7.........82, 92, 491		
103 : 3, 4................253	**ECCLESIASTES.**	**JEREMIAH.**
103 : 8...................186	9 : 10..........198, 397, 400	3 : 22....................195
104........................94	11 : 16...................380	8 : 22....................206
104 : 1, 2.................77		9 : 1.....................242
104 : 20–24.............9, 49	**CANTICLES.**	23 : 24....................16
104 : 27, 28..............492	1 : 3.....................282	24 : 7....................195
105.......................291	2 : 16..............244, 410	29 : 13....................15
106.......................291	5 : 2..............182, 197	31 : 18–20................195
107........................87	5 : 10......................7	35 : 15...................195
107 : 1, 2................267	5 : 16..........254, 271, 414	36 : 3–7..................195
107 : 7...................296	6 : 3..............244, 258, 410	50 : 4, 5.................203
109 : 21..................305		
112 : 7...................256	**ISAIAH.**	**LAMENTATIONS.**
116.......................411	1 : 18....................252	3 : 23..................9, 92
116 : 7–9...........261, 401	2 : 4.....................460	
116 : 12, 13....264, 267, 395, 402	2 : 5......................45	**EZEKIEL.**
116 : 16, 17..............265	4 : 6.....................335	11 : 19..............340, 415
116 : 18..................394	7 : 14....................136	18 : 31, 32......204, 205, 208
117...................73, 87	9 : 2.....................447	34 : 26...................378
118.......................100	12 : 2..........214, 261, 365	36 : 25...................465

INDEX OF SCRIPTURE TEXTS.

	HYMN
36 : 26	340, 415
36 : 37	165

DANIEL.
4 : 35	341
7 : 9-14	94
7 : 10	486
7 : 14	132, 442
7 : 27	442
12 : 3	396
14 : 27	446

HOSEA.
6 : 1	195
6 : 1-3	348, 438
10 : 12	438
11 : 8	232
14 : 1-4	195

JOEL.
2 : 11	477
2 : 17	242
2 : 28, 29	154, 161

JONAH.
2 : 2	241

MICAH.
2 : 10	476
4 : 3	160
6 : 6, 7	236
7 : 8	47

NAHUM.
1 : 2-7	94
1 : 15	159

HABAKKUK.
3 : 2	378, 438
3 : 18	369

HAGGAI.
2 : 7	441

ZECHARIAH.
9 : 10	148
10 : 1	438
12 : 10	154, 224
13 : 1	220, 226
14 : 7	69

MALACHI.
3 : 7	195
3 : 10	378
4 : 2	391
4 : 5	477

MATTHEW.
1 : 23	136
2 : 10	98
4 : 16	440, 447
4 : 19	330
4 : 24	206
5 : 8	340, 355
5 : 16	385
6 : 25-34	334, 352
7 : 7	19
7 : 24, 25	268

	HYMN
8 : 2	245
8 : 22	330
9 : 9	330
9 : 10-13	238
9 : 12	206
9 : 13	188
9 : 37, 38	439
10 : 10, 24, 25	384
10 : 38	332, 336
10 : 42	392
11 : 19	247
11 : 28	183, 185
11 : 28-30	188, 202, 240, 248, 249, 337
13 : 3-8	380
13 : 44	171
13 : 44-46	174, 294
14 : 15-27	104
14 : 27	359
16 : 24	332, 333, 336
18 : 12-14	432
18 : 20	5
19 : 13-16	431, 434
19 : 21	330
19 : 27-29	333
20 : 1-16	386
21 : 15, 16	436
22 : 4	190
22 : 9	443
23 : 6-10	250
23 : 37	232
24 : 14	453
24 : 35	185
24 : 42-46	367, 379
25 : 13-30	367
25 : 40	375, 392
26 : 11	392
26 : 36-45	108, 109, 110
26 : 41	311, 325
26 : 42	360
27 : 32	336
27 : 45	111
27 : 50	117
28 : 19, 20	129, 444
28 : 58	128

MARK.
1 : 32	51
1 : 40	245
2 : 14	330
2 : 17	188, 206
2 : 27	64
4 : 3-8	380
6 : 35-50	104
6 : 50	359
6 : 56	206
8 : 34	330, 332, 333, 336
8 : 38	331
10 : 13-16	431, 434
10 : 21	331, 333
10 : 28	333
10 : 38	332
10 : 46-48	212
10 : 51, 52	230
13 : 10	453
13 : 30	185
13 : 33-37	367
14 : 32-42	108, 109, 110

	HYMN
14 : 38	311, 325
15 : 21	336
15 : 33	111
15 : 37	117
16 : 15	444

LUKE.
1 : 68	301
1 : 74, 75	394
2 : 9-11	99
2 : 10	97
2 : 32	440, 447
2 : 40	433
4 : 13	189
4 : 18	455
5 : 12	245
5 : 22	188
5 : 27	330
5 : 31	206
6 : 40	384
7 : 34	247
7 : 47	254, 265, 410
8 : 5-15	380
9 : 10-17	104
9 : 23	330, 332, 333, 336
9 : 58	46
9 : 59	330
10 : 2	439
10 : 7	384
10 : 42	278
11 : 1	31
11 : 2	360
11 : 13	170
12 : 22-31	334
12 : 32	300
12 : 35-38	379
12 : 37, 38	367
13 : 34	232
14 : 16, 17	190
14 : 16-24	205, 209
14 : 23	396, 443
14 : 27	336
15 : 3-7	238, 269
15 : 20-24	195
18 : 1-7	24, 27
18 : 13	216, 232, 241
18 : 15, 16	431, 434
18 : 28	333
18 : 35-39	212
19 : 41, 42	232, 242
21 : 33	185
21 : 36	367
22 : 39-46	108, 109, 110
23 : 24	221
23 : 26	336
23 : 42, 43	226, 228, 234, 487
23 : 44	111
23 : 46	117
24 : 29	37, 40, 60

JOHN.
1 : 9	391
1 : 12	275
1 : 13	181
1 : 14	136, 286
1 : 16	249
1 : 29	110, 246, 253, 270
1 : 43	330

INDEX OF SCRIPTURE TEXTS.

	HYMN
3 : 5, 6	160, 181
3 : 8	153
3 : 14	249
3 : 15	225, 231
3 : 36	231
4 : 35–38	380
6 : 1–21	104
6 : 20	359
6 : 35	249
6 : 37	246, 256
6 : 44, 65	280
6 : 63	150, 155, 177
6 : 68	220, 223
7 : 37	179, 180, 190, 249
8 : 12	249
9 : 4	400
9 : 5	249
10 : 3	307
11 : 3–5	187
11 : 11	474
12 : 26	330
12 : 32	113
13 : 1	243
13 : 7	341, 376
14 : 1–3	470
14 : 2	487
14 : 3	473
14 : 6	135, 199
14 : 16	148, 170
14 : 19	256, 368
14 : 26	148, 154
14 : 27	18, 59, 401
15 : 13	337, 414
16 : 13, 14	155, 164
16 : 24	19
16 : 33	401
17 : 4	115
17 : 9–11	416
18 : 1, 2	108, 109, 110
19 : 30	115, 117
19 : 34	296
20 : 19	5
21 : 15	287
21 : 15–17	356, 373
21 : 19–22	330

ACTS.

2 : 1–4	153, 155, 158, 161, 445
2 : 17, 18	154, 161
2 : 37–39	217
2 : 46, 47	394
3 : 1	30
3 : 8, 9	276
7 : 60	474
9 : 6	402
9 : 11	31
10 : 28	392
10 : 36	125, 139
10 : 38	101
10 : 44	154
11 : 23	413
14 : 22	332
16 : 9	406
16 : 22	493
20 : 35	377
21 : 14	360
27 : 23	388

ROMANS.

	HYMN
1 : 16	331
2 : 16	477
3 : 20–24	217
3 : 24	218
5 : 5	151, 154, 163, 168, 278
5 : 6–10	215
5 : 7, 8	414
5 : 17–21	227
5 : 19	213
5 : 21	284
6 : 6	412
6 : 13	403
6 : 16–22	394
8 : 1	255
8 : 1–3	138
8 : 14–16	149, 152
8 : 15	159, 160
8 : 17	121, 430
8 : 18	315
8 : 26	31, 159
8 : 31	300
8 : 37	327
8 : 38, 39	243, 273, 368
10 : 4	115
10 : 12	139
10 : 15	459
10 : 18	153
11 : 33	6
12 : 1	267, 383, 402, 403, 418, 422
12 : 5	424, 427
12 : 11	38
12 : 15	377
14 : 8	263, 273
14 : 17	157
15 : 1	377
15 : 13	168

1st CORINTHIANS.

1 : 9, 10	214
1 : 22–30	138
2 : 9	261
2 : 10–14	166
2 : 13, 14	169
3 : 8, 9	382
3 : 16	145, 155, 164
4 : 2	383
6 : 9–11	215
6 : 19, 20	267, 383, 388, 402, 403, 418
7 : 22, 23	394
10 : 13	398
12 : 12	424
12 : 13	430
12 : 26	427
13 : 1–8	393
13 : 13	151, 393
15 : 10	251
15 : 27	139
15 : 47, 49	136
15 : 58	380, 384
16 : 13	313, 318, 319

2d CORINTHIANS.

1 : 22	156
3 : 18	145, 157, 158
4 : 4	172
4 : 6	469

	HYMN
4 : 17	315
5 : 1, 2	310
5 : 5	156
5 : 7	323
5 : 14, 15	111, 112, 114, 255, 395, 402, 422
5 : 19	125, 237, 418
5 : 21	213, 221, 257
6 : 2	194, 200, 201, 212
6 : 20	114
8 : 5	403, 413, 422
12 : 9	324
12 : 10	252
13 : 14	41

GALATIANS.

2 : 20	178, 257, 263
3 : 13	116, 213, 237, 257
3 : 28	430
4 : 26	480
5 : 24	412
6 : 1	393, 396
6 : 2	377
6 : 14	328

EPHESIANS.

1 : 4	275
1 : 6	259
1 : 7	252
1 : 9	246
1 : 13, 14	149, 152
1 : 20–22	133, 139
2 : 1–9	215
2 : 5	259
2 : 8	259, 280, 284
3 : 6	430
3 : 16–19	2
3 : 19	295
4 : 4–6	424
5 : 13	469
5 : 19	260
5 : 20	369
6 : 6	344
6 : 11–13	311, 318, 322
6 : 14	379
6 : 18	311, 325, 327

PHILIPPIANS.

1 : 9	373
1 : 21	103, 272
1 : 22	383
2 : 5	105, 106, 337
2 : 9	222
2 : 10	133, 134
2 : 12, 13	316
3 : 3	276
3 : 7, 8	114, 178, 273, 276, 328, 419
3 : 13, 14	304, 320
3 : 18	242
4 : 6, 7	30, 59, 187, 354, 352, 401
4 : 19	370

COLOSSIANS.

1 : 12	308
2 : 15	118
3 : 3	308
3 : 5	332

INDEX OF SCRIPTURE TEXTS.

	HYMN
3 : 11	294, 430
3 : 16	88
4 : 2	325

1st THESSALONIANS.
2 : 13	177
4 : 14	474
4 : 17	473
5 : 9, 10	258
5 : 17	24, 27

2d THESSALONIANS.
3 : 1	468
3 : 16	59

1st TIMOTHY.
1 : 15	188, 234
1 : 17	81
3 : 16	138
6 : 12	319, 321
6 : 20	214

2d TIMOTHY.
1 : 8	338
1 : 12	256, 338
2 : 11, 12	121
2 : 21	250
3 : 16	173
4 : 1	477
4 : 7, 8	317, 320, 321

TITUS.
2 : 10-13	385
2 : 11	259
2 : 12	4
2 : 14	397, 402
3 : 5, 6	151, 157, 158, 227

HEBREWS.
1 : 1, 2	176
1 : 6	486
2 : 1	201
2 : 3	232
2 : 9	131
2 : 10	121
2 : 11	331
2 : 14	138
3 : 2	162
3 : 7-16	200, 201, 211
4 : 9	483, 488
4 : 14-16	123, 141, 187
4 : 16	26
6 : 17-19	366
6 : 18	361
6 : 20	25
7 : 22	221
7 : 25	188

	HYMN
9 : 13, 14	116, 226, 257
9 : 24	123
10 : 1-14	115
10 : 19-22	141, 187, 221
10 : 23	405
10 : 29	232
10 : 30	477
10 : 36	344, 360
11 : 6	19
11 : 7	192
11 : 8	323
11 : 10	309
11 : 13	297
11 : 13-16	304, 476
11 : 16	310
12 : 1, 2	304, 320, 324
12 : 22, 23	424, 479, 482
13 : 5	361
13 : 15	293
13 : 20, 24	22, 59
13 : 21	316

JAMES.
1 : 12	321, 322
1 : 17	375, 395
1 : 18	181
1 : 21	176
1 : 25	376
4 : 7	398
4 : 13-15	193
5 : 20	393, 396

1st PETER.
1 : 4	308
1 : 8	271, 283
1 : 13	379
1 : 19	270, 388
1 : 23	181
2 : 6	261
2 : 7	288, 370
2 : 9	266
2 : 12	385
2 : 21	101, 106, 107, 387
2 : 22, 24	213, 237
2 : 24	111, 116, 257
2 : 25	269
3 : 18	112, 150, 237, 257
3 : 22	128, 139
4 : 5	477
5 : 7	292, 334, 352
5 : 8, 9	311, 317, 325, 327

2d PETER.
1 : 4	361
3 : 9	188, 224, 225
3 : 11-13	305, 367

1st JOHN.
	HYMN
1 : 7	116, 236, 245, 246, 252
1 : 9	220
2 : 1	25
2 : 6	337, 347
2 : 20	164
2 : 27	164, 165
3 : 1, 2	275
3 : 5	213
4 : 8	70
4 : 9, 10	262
4 : 10	357
4 : 17	477
4 : 19	357
4 : 29	254
5 : 6	236

REVELATION.
1 : 5, 6	132, 143, 147, 262
1 : 18	119, 120
2 : 7	487
2 : 7, 11, 17	326
2 : 10	405
3 : 2, 3	367
3 : 5, 12	326
3 : 12	479
3 : 17, 18	236, 246
3 : 20	179, 180, 182, 197, 218
3 : 21	318, 319, 322, 326, 398
4 : 11	12
5 : 6-12	124
5 : 8-14	95, 126, 127, 131, 132, 142, 147
5 : 11	480
5 : 11-13	122
5 : 12	12
7 : 9-12	126, 127
7 : 9-17	423
7 : 10-13	95
11 : 15	442, 446, 460
12 : 11	423
13 : 15	439
15 : 3	260, 425
17 : 14	134
17 : 17-20	191
19 : 12	131
19 : 16	134
21 : 1-4	479
21 : 8	240
21 : 10-27	480
21 : 27	215
22	484
22 : 1-5	487
22 : 4	289
22 : 17	179, 249

INDEX OF SUBJECTS.

The figures refer to the numbers of the hymns.

ABBA FATHER.
  429 Behold what wondrous
  159 Holy Ghost, the Infinite
  333 Jesus, I my cross
ACCEPTED TIME.
  188 Come, ye sinners, poor
  218 God calling yet! shall I
  194 Now is the accepted
  200 To-day the Saviour calls
  191 The Spirit in our hearts
ACCESS TO GOD.
  221 Arise, my soul, arise
  26 Behold the throne of
  125 Come let us lift our
  25 Our heavenly Father
ACTIVITY—See *Christian Activity*.
ADOPTION.
  429 Behold what wondrous
  275 Blessed are the sons of
  261 Here I can firmly rest
ADORATION—See *Christ, God, Holy Spirit,* and *Trinity*.
ADVENT—See *Christ, Advent of*.
ADVOCATE—See *Christ*.
AFFLICTIONS:
  BLESSINGS OF.
    341 God moves in a
    374 Nearer, my God, to Thee
    91 Since all the varying
  COMFORT UNDER.
    189 Come, ye disconsolate
    361 How firm a foundation
    352 How gentle God's
    488 There is an hour of
  COURAGE IN.
    319 Am I a soldier of the
    359 Cast thy burden on the
    329 Take, my soul, thy full
    362 The Lord is my
  DELIVERANCE FROM.
    354 Give to the winds thy
    361 How firm a foundation
    348 Long hath the night of
    345 Through all the
  PRAYER IN.
    270 My faith looks up to
    374 Nearer, my God, to Thee
    299 O Thou, to whose
    187 What a Friend we have
  REFUGE IN.
    359 Cast thy burden on the
    29 From every stormy wind

AFFLICTIONS:
  366 God is the Refuge of
  361 How firm a foundation
  352 How gentle God's
  335 Jesus, Lover of my soul
  365 My spirit on Thy care
  141 Where high the heavenly
REJOICING IN.
  354 Give to the winds thy
  249 I heard the voice of
  346 My God, the Spring of
  315 O what, if we are Christ's
  369 While Thee I seek,
SUBMISSION UNDER.
  351 Father, I know that all
  313 Father, whate'er of
  344 I worship Thee, sweet
  360 My God and Father,
  334 O Lord, how happy
ALARM.
  477 O God, mine inmost
  240 O where shall rest be
  224 Prostrate, dear Jesus, at
ANGELS:
  ADORATION OF.
    1 Songs of praise the
    8 Thee we adore, Eternal
    95 Ye servants of God
  AT THE ADVENT OF CHRIST.
    97 Angels from the realms
    99 Hark, what mean those
  CORONATION OF CHRIST.
    130 All hail the power of
    122 Come, let us join our
    1 Songs of praise the
  MINISTRY OF.
    46 Almighty God, to-night
    49 Now God be with us, for
    39 Saviour, breathe an
ASHAMED OF JESUS.
  338 I'm not ashamed to own
  331 Jesus, and shall it soon
  332 Take up thy cross, the
ASPIRATIONS:
  FOR CHRIST.
    297 Guide me, O Thou great
    7 How sweet to leave the
    370 I need Thee, precious
    335 Jesus, Lover of my soul
    271 Jesus, Thy Name I love
    373 More love to Thee, O
    254 My Jesus, I love Thee
    280 O gift of gifts! O grace

ASPIRATIONS:
  371 O Lamb of God, still
  278 O Love Divine, how
  FOR DIVINE GRACE.
    2 Come, dearest Lord.
    3 Far from my thoughts,
    406 Jesus, my Lord, my God
    340 O for a heart to praise
  FOR GOD.
    349 As pants the hart for
    4 My God, permit me not
    346 My God, the Spring of
    374 Nearer, my God, to Thee
    229 Take me, O my Father
  FOR HEAVEN.
    472 Far from my heavenly
    473 Forever with the Lord
    484 For thee, O dear, dear
    479 Jerusalem, my happy
    480 O mother dear,
    487 O Paradise, O Paradise
    304 Rise, my soul, and
    485 The sands of time are
    476 This is not my place of
  FOR HOLINESS.
    270 My faith looks up to
    347 O for a closer walk with
    340 O for a heart to praise
    299 O Thou, to whose
    215 Weary of earth and
  FOR THE HOLY SPIRIT.
    146 Come, Holy Ghost, in
    157 Holy Ghost, with light
    145 Love Divine, all love
  FOR PEACE AND REST.
    233 Jesus, full of truth and
    309 My feet are worn and
    298 O God of Bethel, by
    240 O where shall rest be
    215 Weary of earth and
  OF FAITH—See *Faith*.
  OF HOPE—See *Hope*.
ASSURANCE:
  DECLARED.
    300 Children of the heavenly
    258 I bless the Christ of God
    249 I heard the voice of
    292 I left it all with Jesus
    119 I know that my
    294 I've found the pearl of
    372 In heavenly love abiding
  DESIRED.
    221 Arise, my soul, arise

INDEX OF SUBJECTS.

ASSURANCE:
  213 O Thou that hearest the
  149 Why should the children
  302 Your harps, ye trembling
ATONEMENT:
 COMPLETED.
  125 Come, let us lift our
  190 From the cross uplifted
  116 Not all the blood of
  237 Surely Christ thy griefs
 NEEDED.
  138 Dearest of all the names
  116 Not all the blood of
  236 Rock of ages, cleft for
 SUFFICIENT.
  188 Come, ye sinners, poor
  190 From the cross uplifted
  126 Hail, Thou once despised
  186 There's a wideness in
  135 Thou art the Way, to
BACKSLIDING—See *Declension.*
BAPTISM:
 ADULT—See *Confession.*
 INFANT.
  431 A little child the Saviour
  432 Dear Saviour, if these
  435 Saviour, who Thy flock
  434 See Israel's gentle
  436 Shepherd of tender
 OF HOLY SPIRIT.
  154 Great Father of each
  161 Lord God, the Holy
BELIEVERS—See *Christians and Saints.*
BENEVOLENCE—See *Charity.*
BEREAVEMENT—See *Afflictions, Death.*
BIBLE—See *Word of God.*
CALVARY.
  109 Go to dark Gethsemane
  115 Hark, the voice of love
  113 Lord Jesus, when we
  234 Thou, who didst on
 Also see *Christ, Crucified.*
CHARITY.
  392 Lord, lead the way then
  393 Think gently of the
  375 We give Thee but Thine
 Also see *Communion of Saints.*
CHILDREN.
  431 A little child the Saviour
  433 By cool Siloam's shady
  432 Dear Saviour, if these
  48 Now the day is over
  435 Saviour, who Thy flock
  434 See Israel's gentle
  436 Shepherd of tender
CHRIST:
 ABIDING WITH BELIEVERS.
  60 Abide with me; fast falls
  37 Sun of my soul, Thou
 ADORATION OF.
  124 Behold the glories of the
  122 Come, let us join our
  125 Come, let us lift our
  132 Glory to God on high
  126 Hail, Thou once despised
  406 Jesus, my Lord, my God

CHRIST:
  289 Jesus, the very thought
  271 Jesus, thy Name I love
  262 Raise your triumphant
 ADVENT, FIRST.
  97 Angels from the realms
  99 Hark, what mean those
  100 Joy to the world, the
 ADVENT, SECOND—See *Second Coming of.*
 ADVOCATE—See *Priest.*
 ALL IN ALL.
  252 I hear the Saviour say
  294 I've found the pearl
  365 My spirit on Thy care
 ALPHA AND OMEGA.
  145 Love Divine, all love
 ATONEMENT OF.
  111 Alas! and did my
  221 Arise, my soul, arise
  126 Hail, Thou once despised
  116 Not all the blood of
  257 O Christ, what burdens
  112 O Jesus, sweet the tears
  117 O perfect life of love
  213 O Thou, that hearest the
  237 Surely Christ thy griefs
 BEAUTY OF.
  137 Majestic sweetness sits
 BIRTH OF—See *Advent.*
 BLOOD OF—See *Passion.*
 CAPTAIN.
  317 Go forward, Christian
  327 Soldiers of Christ, arise
  322 Stand up, my soul, shake
  318 Stand up, stand up for
 CHARACTER OF.
  101 Behold, where in a
  107 How beauteous were the
  106 My dear Redeemer and
  94 O worship the King
 COMPASSION OF—See *Love of.*
 CONDESCENSION OF—See *Humanity of.*
 CONQUEROR.
  133 At the Name of Jesus
  134 Look, ye saints, the
 CORONATION OF.
  139 All hail the power of
  131 Crown Him with many
  134 Look, ye saints, the
  121 The head that once was
 CROSS OF—See *Cross.*
 CRUCIFIXION OF—See *Sacrifice* and *Passion.*
 DIVINITY OF.
  139 All hail the power of
  138 Dearest of all the names
  140 O Christ, our King.
  104 O where is He that trod
 EXALTED.
  139 All hail the power of
  124 Behold the glories of the
  128 Christ, above all glory
  134 Look, ye saints, the
  131 Crown Him with many
  121 The head that once was
 EXAMPLE.
  101 Behold, where, in a

CHRIST:
  109 Go to dark Gethsemane
  337 Lord, as to Thy dear
  106 My dear Redeemer and
  387 O Master, let me walk
  102 What grace, O Lord and
 EXCELLENCY OF.
  145 Love Divine, all love
  137 Majestic sweetness sits
  277 O could I speak
 FOUNTAIN.
  220 I bring my sins to Thee
  249 I heard the voice of
  485 The sands of time are
  226 There is a fountain
 FRIEND.
  370 I need Thee, precious
  285 My Saviour, my
  243 Now I have found a
  414 One there is, above all
  187 What a Friend we have
 FRIEND OF SINNERS.
  196 Behold, a Stranger at
  247 Jesus, the sinner's
  238 Sinners Jesus will
 FULLNESS OF.
  249 I heard the voice of
  119 I know that my
  253 I lay my sins on Jesus
  294 I've found the pearl
  335 Jesus, Lover of my soul
 GLORYING IN.
  338 I'm not ashamed to own
  328 In the cross of Christ I
  331 Jesus, and shall it ever
  332 Take up thy cross the
 GLORY OF—See *Exalted.*
 GRACE OF.
  284 Amazing grace! how
  259 Grace, 'tis a charming
  137 Majestic sweetness sits
  286 O gift of gifts! O grace
  117 O perfect life of love
  291 Sing of Jesus, sing for
 HIDING-PLACE.
  335 Jesus, Lover of my soul
  236 Rock of ages, cleft for
 HIGH PRIEST.
  221 Arise, my soul, arise
  123 Come, let us join in
  119 I know that my
  143 Now to the Lord, who
  141 Where high the heavenly
 HUMANITY OF.
  51 At even, ere the sun was
  101 Behold, where in a
  123 Come, let us join in
  138 Dearest of all the names
  107 How beauteous were the
  106 My dear Redeemer, and
  136 O mean may seem this
  141 Where high the heavenly
 HUMILITY OF.
  101 Behold, where in a
  107 How beauteous were the
 IMMANUEL.
  138 Dearest of all the names
  136 O mean may seem this
 INCARNATE—See *Humanity of.*

INDEX OF SUBJECTS.

CHRIST:
IN GETHSEMANE.
  109 Go to dark Gethsemane
  108 'Tis midnight; and on
  110 Zion's daughter, weep
INTERCESSION OF.
  221 Arise, my soul, arise
  126 Hail, thou once despised
  120 He lives, the great
  141 Where high the heavenly
INVITATION OF.
  185 Art thou weary, art thou
  202 Come, said Jesus' sacred
  249 I heard the voice of
  248 With tearful eyes I look
JUDGE.
  477 O God, mine inmost
  196 While life prolongs its
KING OF GLORY.
  128 Christ above all glory
  486 Hark, ten thousand
  100 Joy to the world, the
KING OF SAINTS.
  113 Now to the Lord, who
  94 O worship the King
  267 Saviour, blessed Saviour
  95 Ye servants of God
KING, SOVEREIGN.
  446 Ascend Thy throne
  131 Crown Him with many
  222 Join all the glorious
  100 Joy to the world, the
  281 O Jesus, King most
KNOCKING.
  197 Behold, a Stranger at
  182 O Jesus, Thou art
LAMB OF GOD.
  124 Behold the glories of the
  122 Come, let us join our
  112 Come, let us sing the
  132 Glory to God on high
  126 Hail, Thou once despised
  253 I lay my sins on Jesus
  246 Just as I am, without
  404 Lamb of God, whose
  116 Not all the blood of
LEADER.
  317 Go forward, Christian
  297 Guide me, O Thou
  307 He leadeth me, O blessed
  306 Lead, kindly Light.
  322 Stand up, my soul, shake
LIFE.
  272 Christ, of all my hopes
  249 I heard the voice of
LIFE OF—See *Ministry of*.
LIGHT.
  249 I heard the voice of
  346 My God, the Spring of
LONG-SUFFERING OF.
  197 Behold, a Stranger at
  232 Depth of mercy, can
  182 O Jesus, Thou art
  184 The King of glory
LORD.
  139 All hail the power of
  122 Come, let us join our
  271 Jesus, Thy Name I love
  121 The head that once was

CHRIST:
LOVE OF.
  232 Depth of mercy, can
  123 Come, let us join in
  356 Hark, my soul, it is the
  279 I love to tell the story
  295 It passeth knowledge
  145 Love Divine, all love
  278 O Love divine, how
  117 O perfect life of love
  414 One there is above all
  357 Saviour, teach me day
  102 What grace, O Lord
LOVELINESS OF.
  283 Jesus, these eyes have
  289 Jesus, the very thought
  137 Majestic sweetness sits
  281 O Jesus, King most
LOVING-KINDNESS OF .
  290 Awake, my soul, in
MAN OF SORROWS.
  237 Surely Christ thy griefs
  141 Where high the heavenly
MASTER.
  250 Dear Lord and Master
  389 Jesus, Master, whom I
  388 Jesus, Master, whose I
  418 Lord, I am Thine
MEDIATOR—See *Intercession of*.
  221 Arise, my soul, arise
  123 Come, let us join in
MEEKNESS OF.
  101 Behold, where in a
  107 How beauteous were
  106 My dear Redeemer, and
  105 O Lord, when we the
  102 What grace, O Lord, and
MERCY OF.
  232 Depth of mercy, can
  303 Sweet is Thy mercy
MINISTRY OF.
  51 At even, ere the sun was
  101 Behold, where in a
  106 My dear Redeemer, and
  105 O Lord, when we the
  104 O where is He that trod
MIRACLES OF—See *Ministry of*.
NAME OF.
  139 All hail the power of
  133 At the Name of Jesus
  138 Dearest of all the names
  293 How sweet the Name of
  288 Jesus, I love Thy
  271 Jesus, Thy Name I love
  282 O for a thousand tongues
NAMES OF.
  294 I've found the pearl of
  222 Join all the glorious
NATIVITY—See *Advent*.
OFFICES OF.
  265 Hail, my ever-blessed
  126 Hail, Thou once despised
  119 I know that my
  222 Join all the glorious
  143 Now to the Lord, who
OUR PASSOVER.
  126 Hail, Thou once despised
PASSION OF.
  111 Alas! and did my

CHRIST:
  109 Go to dark Gethsemane
  115 Hark, the voice of love
  113 Lord Jesus, when we
  257 O Christ, what wondrous
  112 O Jesus, sweet the tears
  117 O perfect life of love
  237 Surely Christ thy griefs
  114 When I survey the
PATTERN—See *Example*.
PRECIOUS.
  265 Hail, my ever-blessed.
  293 How sweet the Name of
  370 I need Thee, precious
  288 Jesus, I love thy
  283 Jesus, these eyes have
  289 Jesus, the very thought
  346 My God, the Spring of
  254 My Jesus, I love Thee
  277 O could I speak the
PRESENCE OF.
  129 Always with us, always
  39 Saviour, breathe an
  37 Sun of my soul, Thou
  20 Thou, from whom we
  5 Where two or three with
PRIEST.
  123 Come, let us join in
  120 He lives, the great
  119 I know that my
  222 Join all the glorious
  113 Now to the Lord who
  141 Where high the heavenly
PROPHET.
  123 Come, let us join in
  99 Hark, what mean those
  222 Join all the glorious
  143 Now to the Lord who
REDEEMER.
  124 Behold the glories of the
  119 I know that my
REFUGE.
  335 Jesus, Lover of my soul
  236 Rock of ages, cleft for
  187 What a Friend we have
REIGNING.
  455 Hail to the Lord's
  460 Hasten, Lord, the
  418 Jesus shall reign
  100 Joy to the world, the
  442 Soon may the last glad
  121 The head that once was
  458 When shall the voice of
  95 Ye servants of God
RESURRECTION OF.
  120 He lives, the great
  119 I know that my
  118 The strife is o'er, the
RIGHTEOUSNESS OF.
  268 My hope is built on
  419 No more, my God, I
  213 O Thou that hearest the
  223 Thy works, not mine
ROCK OF AGES.
  437 Glorious things of thee
  268 My hope is built on
  236 Rock of ages, cleft for
SACRIFICE—See *Passion of*.
  111 Alas! and did my

INDEX OF SUBJECTS.

CHRIST:
221 Arise, my soul, arise
115 Hark, the voice of love
116 Not all the blood of
112 O Jesus, sweet the tears
409 Sweet the moments, rich
SAVIOUR, THE.
252 I hear the Saviour say
277 O could I speak the
255 O Saviour, where shall
274 Saviour, happy would
357 Saviour, teach me day
238 Sinners Jesus will
286 The Saviour, O what
Also see *Passion* and *Sacrifice of.*
SECOND COMING OF.
133 At the Name of Jesus
461 Awake, awake, O Zion
455 Hail to the Lord's
486 Hark, ten thousand
450 Jesus, Thy Church with
477 O God, mine inmost
SHEPHERD.
269 I was a wandering sheep
436 Shepherd of tender
350 The King of love my
362 The Lord is my Shepherd
364 The Lord my Shepherd is
358 To Thy pastures fair
SUN OF RIGHTEOUSNESS.
440 O'er the gloomy hills of
SURETY.
221 Arise, my soul, arise
257 O Christ, what burdens
SYMPATHY OF.
101 Behold, where in a
206 The great Physician
141 Where high the heavenly
TEMPTATION OF.
106 My dear Redeemer, and
TRUST IN—See *Trust.*
VICTORIOUS—See *Conqueror.*
WAY, TRUTH, AND LIFE.
135 Thou art the Way; to
WEEPING.
242 Did Christ o'er sinners
CHRISTIANS—See *Saints.*
CHRIST THE LIFE OF.
276 Ask ye what great
272 Christ of all my hopes
258 I bless the Christ of God
263 Jesus, I live to Thee
371 O Lamb of God, still
CONFLICTS OF.
349 As pants the hart for
335 Jesus, Lover of my soul
347 O for a closer walk
CONQUERORS THROUGH CHRIST.
320 Awake, my soul, stretch
317 Go forward, Christian
327 Soldier of Christ, arise
Also see *Warfare.*
DUTIES OF.
312 A charge to keep I have
384 Go, labor on; spend
383 My gracious Lord, I own
385 So let our lips and lives
379 Ye servants of the Lord

CHRISTIANS:
ENCOURAGEMENTS OF.
324 Awake, our souls, away
300 Children of the heavenly
361 How firm a foundation
372 In heavenly love abiding
315 O what, if we are Christ's
322 Stand up, my soul, shake
329 Take, my soul, thy full
362 The Lord is my Shepherd
302 Your harps, ye trembling
EXAMPLE OF.
423 Give me the wings of
385 So let our lips and lives
FELLOWSHIP OF—See *Communion.*
GRACES OF.
355 Blest are the pure in
343 Father, whate'er of
340 O for a heart to praise
385 So let our lips and lives
Also see *Faith, Hope,* and *Love.*
CHRISTIAN ACTIVITY:
CALLS TO.
397 Christian, work for Jesus
384 Go, labor on; spend
382 Laborers of Christ, arise
377 O praise our God to-day
396 Rescue the perishing
318 Stand up, stand up for
400 Work, for the night is
390 Workman of God, O lose
DUTY OF.
312 A charge to keep I have
319 Am I a soldier of the
389 Jesus, Master, whom I
386 Jesus, our best beloved
383 My gracious Lord, I own
385 So let our lips and lives
375 We give Thee but Thine
ENCOURAGEMENT IN.
381 A fitly spoken word
321 Fight the good fight
376 Happy the man who
394 How blessed from the
313 My soul, weigh not thy
380 Sow in the morn thy
CHRISTIAN MINISTRY—See *Ministry.*
CHRISTMAS—See *Angels, Song of,* and *Christ, Advent of.*
CHURCH:
BELOVED OF GOD.
461 Awake, awake, O Zion
437 Glorious things of thee
BELOVED OF SAINTS.
428 I love Thy kingdom,
408 People of the living God
INCREASE OF—See *Missions.*
TRIUMPH OF.
460 Hasten, Lord, the
459 How beauteous, on the
440 O'er the gloomy hills of
447 Though now the nations
UNITY OF.
426 Blest be the dear uniting
427 Blest be the tie that
122 Come, let us join our
425 Happy the souls to Jesus

CHURCH:
430 Let party names no more
424 Let saints below in
CLOSE OF SERVICE.
427 Blest be the tie that
10 Dismiss us with Thy
17 For a season called to
14 Lord, dismiss us with
22 Now may He, who from
48 Now the day is over
18 Part in peace, Christ's
44 Praise the God of our
59 Saviour, again to Thy
47 Sweet Saviour, bless us
20 Thou, from whom we
COMFORTS—See *Afflictions.*
COMMUNION:
OF SAINTS.
426 Blest be the dear
427 Blest be the tie that
122 Come, let us join our
425 Happy the souls to Jesus
428 I love Thy kingdom
430 Let party names no more
424 Let saints below in
102 What grace, O Lord, and
WITH GOD.
3 Far from my thoughts
32 I love to steal awhile
346 My God, the Spring of
374 Nearer, my God, to Thee
25 Our heavenly Father
369 While Thee I seek
WITH CHRIST.
29 From every stormy wind
289 Jesus, the very thought
278 O Love divine, how
409 Sweet the moments, rich
CONFESSION OF FAITH—See *Faith.*
CONFESSION OF SIN—See *Sin.*
CONFIDENCE.
359 Cast thy burden on the
351 Father, I know that all
361 How firm a foundation
253 I lay my sins on Jesus
372 In heavenly love abiding
328 In the cross of Christ
254 My Jesus, I love Thee
362 The Lord is my
368 When sins and fears
CONFORMITY TO CHRIST.
340 O for a heart to praise
Also see *Christ, Example of.*
CONSCIENCE.
116 Not all the blood of
CONSECRATION:
OF POSSESSIONS.
395 O Lord of heaven and
403 Take my life and let it
114 When I survey the
OF SELF.
111 Alas! and did my
418 Lord, I am Thine,
412 My God, accept my
383 My gracious Lord, I own
421 O the bitter shame and
403 Take my life and let it
411 What shall I render to

INDEX OF SUBJECTS. 225

CONSECRATION:
- 114 When I survey tho
- 413 Witness, ye men and
RENEWED.
- 273 Blessed Saviour, Thee I
- 347 O for a closer walk with

To CHRIST.
- 220 I bring my sins to Thee
- 410 I lift my heart to Thee
- 388 Jesus, Master, whose I
- 386 Jesus, our best-beloved
- 407 Lord, in the strength of
- 383 My gracious Lord, I own
- 405 O Jesus, I have promised
- 402 Saviour, Thy dying love
- 422 Thy life was given for

CONSOLATION—See *Afflictions.*

CONSTANCY.
- 312 A charge to keep I have
- 320 Awake, my soul, stretch
- 321 Fight the good fight
- 317 Go forward, Christian
- 313 My soul, weigh not thy

CONTENTMENT.
- 351 Father, I know that all
- 343 Father, whate'er my
- 372 In heavenly love abiding

CONTRITION.
- 111 Alas! and did my
- 212 Did Christ o'er sinners
- 218 God calling yet! shall I
- 112 O Jesus, sweet the tears
- 212 Pass me not, O gracious
- 409 Sweet the moments, rich

CONVERSION.
- 221 Arise, my soul, arise
- 250 Dear Lord, and Master
- 265 Hail, my ever-blessed
- 258 I bless the Christ of God
- 220 I bring my sins to Thee
- 252 I hear the Saviour say
- 249 I heard the voice of
- 333 Jesus, I my cross have
- 246 Just as I am, without
- 266 Lord, with glowing
- 215 Weary of earth and
Also see *Faith.*

COURAGE.
- 319 Am I a soldier of the
- 324 Awake, our souls, away
- 321 Fight the good fight
- 317 Go forward, Christian
- 313 My soul, weigh not thy
- 327 Soldiers of Christ, arise
- 322 Stand up, my soul,
- 318 Stand up, stand up for

COVENANT, ENTERING INTO.
- 418 Lord, I am Thine,
- 417 O happy day, that fixed
- 408 People of the living God
- 416 Thine forever, God of
- 413 Witness, ye men, and

CROSS:
AT THE CROSS.
- 111 Alas! and did my
- 418 Lord, I am Thine,
- 112 O Jesus, sweet the tears

CROSS:
- 420 O the sweet wonders of
- 237 Surely Christ thy griefs
- 409 Sweet the moments, rich
- 234 Thou who didst on
- 239 Weary with my load of
- 114 When I survey the

BANNER OF THE.
- 462 Now be the Gospel
- 314 Rejoice, ye pure in heart
- 463 Uplift the blood-red

BEARING.
- 338 I'm not ashamed to
- 333 Jesus, I my cross have
- 337 Lord, as to Thy dear
- 336 Must Jesus bear the
- 315 O what, if we are
- 332 Take up thy cross, the

GLORYING IN.
- 319 Am I a soldier of the
- 179 I am coming to the cross
- 328 In the cross of Christ
- 333 Jesus, I my cross have
- 336 Must Jesus bear the
- 419 No more, my God, I

POWER OF.
- 138 Dearest of all the names
- 140 O Christ, our King,
- 121 The head that once was

SOLDIER OF.
- 319 Am I a soldier of the
- 317 Go forward, Christian
- 318 Stand up, stand up for

CROWNS OF GLORY.
- 320 Awake, my soul, stretch
- 326 Soldiers, who are
- 322 Stand up, my soul, shake
- 318 Stand up, stand up for

CRUCIFIXION—See *Christ.*

To THE WORLD.
- 333 Jesus, I my cross have
- 114 When I survey the
Also see *Forsaking all for Christ.*

DARKNESS, SPIRITUAL.
- 349 As pants the hart for
- 335 Jesus, Lover of my soul
- 348 Long hath the night of
- 241 Out of the deep I call
- 149 Why should the children
Also see *Declension.*

DAY OF GRACE.
- 197 Behold a Stranger at
- 192 O cease, my wandering
- 240 O where shall rest be

DEATH:
ANTICIPATED.
- 60 Abide with me; fast
- 472 Far from my heavenly
- 473 Forever with the Lord
- 296 Gently, Lord, O gently
- 488 There is an hour of

CONFIDENCE IN.
- 361 How firm a foundation
- 485 The sands of time are

OF SAINTS.
- 474 Asleep in Jesus: blessed
- 475 How blest the righteous
- 471 O for the death of those

DECLENSION, SPIRITUAL.
- 150 Come, Holy Spirit,
- 232 Depth of mercy, can
- 347 O for a closer walk with
- 182 O Jesus, Thou art
- 195 Return, O wanderer

DELAY, DANGER OF.
- 197 Behold a Stranger at
- 208 Child of sin and sorrow
- 211 Delay not, delay not; O
- 198 Life is the time to serve
- 194 Now is the accepted
- 240 O where shall rest be
- 201 Time is earnest; passing
- 200 To-day the Saviour calls

DEPENDENCE:
ON CHRIST.
- 250 Dear Lord and Master
- 220 I bring my sins to Thee
- 253 I lay my sins on Jesus
- 370 I need Thee, precious
- 270 My faith looks up to
- 365 My spirit on Thy care
- 236 Rock of ages, cleft for
- 229 Take me, O my Father
See *Christ All in All.*

ON GOD.
- 359 Cast thy burden on the
- 264 Come, Thou Fount of
- 89 Great God, how infinite
- 43 Vainly through night's

ON GRACE.
- 284 Amazing grace, how
- 264 Come, Thou Fount of
- 259 Grace, 'tis a charming
- 223 Thy works, not mine

DESPONDENCY—See *Christian, Conflicts of.*

DISMISSION—See *Close of Service.*

DOUBTS AND FEARS.
- 354 Give to the winds thy
- 368 When sins and fears

DOXOLOGIES.
- 73 From all that dwell
- 84 Holy, holy, holy, Lord
- 44 Praise the God of our

DUTIES—See *Christian.*

ETERNITY.
- 473 Forever with the Lord
- 89 Great God, how infinite
- 477 O God, mine inmost soul
- 90 O God, our help in ages
- 240 O where shall rest be
- 489 While with ceaseless

EVENING:
- 60 Abide with me; fast
- 34 All praise to Thee, my
- 46 Almighty God, to-night
- 51 At even, ere the sun was
- 55 Father, by Thy love and
- 52 Father of love and
- 36 Great God, to Thee my
- 42 Hear my prayer
- 69 Holy Father, cheer our
- 9 My God, how endless is
- 30 My God, is any hour so
- 56 Now from labor and
- 49 Now God be with us for

INDEX OF SUBJECTS.

EVENING:
  48 Now the day is over
  59 Saviour, again to Thy
  30 Saviour, breathe an
  21 Softly now the light of
  37 Sun of my soul, Thou
  47 Sweet Saviour, bless us
  40 Tarry with me, O my
  20 Thou, from whom we
  43 Vainly through night's
Of LIFE.
  60 Abide with me; fast falls
  69 Holy Father, cheer our
  45 Now when the dusky
Of LORD'S DAY—See *Lord's Day.*
EXAMPLE:
  Of CHRIST—See *Christ.*
  Of CHRISTIANS—See *Christians.*
FAITH:
  ACT OF.
    214 I am trusting Thee, Lord
    220 I bring my sins to Thee
    246 Just as I am, without
    230 Lord, I know Thy
    245 No, not despairingly
    229 Take me, O my Father
  See *Conversion.*
  ASPIRATION OF.
    423 Give me the wings of
    335 Jesus, Lover of my soul
    270 My faith looks up to
    274 Saviour, happy would I
  ASSURANCE OF.
    276 Ask ye what great thing
    258 I bless the Christ of God
    292 I left it all with Jesus
    256 Jesus, I will trust Thee
    254 My Jesus, I love Thee
    226 There is a fountain filled
  See *Assurance.*
  BLESSEDNESS OF.
    249 I heard the voice of
    280 O gift of gifts! O grace
    281 O Jesus, King most
  CONFESSION OF.
    331 Jesus, and shall it ever
    333 Jesus, I my cross have
    417 O happy day that fixed
    408 People of the living God
    413 Witness, ye men and
  See *Covenant.*
  JUSTIFICATION BY.
    116 Not all the blood of
    213 O Thou, that hearest the
    236 Rock of ages, cleft for
  PRAYER OF.
    220 I bring my sins to Thee
    246 Just as I am, without
    213 O Thou that hearest the
  WALKING BY.
    423 Give me the wings of
    309 My feet are worn and
    323 'Tis by the faith of joys
FALL OF MAN—See *Depravity and Sin.*
FAMILY WORSHIP.
  51 At even, ere the sun was
  34 All praise to Thee, my

FAMILY WORSHIP.
  33 Awake, my soul, and
  55 Father, by Thy love and
  52 Father of love and
  38 Forth in Thy name
  36 Great God, to Thee my
  32 I love to steal awhile
  57 In this calm, impressive
  48 Now the day is over
  45 Now when the dusky
  298 O God of Bethel, by
  35 O Jesus, Lord of light
  39 Saviour, breathe an
  436 Shepherd of tender
  21 Softly now the light of
  37 Sun of my soul, Thou
  43 Vainly through night's
  See *Evening, Morning, Praise and Prayer.*
FASTS—See *Humiliation.*
FESTIVALS—See *Advent, National, Resurrection, Thanksgiving* and *Year.*
FOREFATHERS' DAY.
  498 Let children hear the
  501 My country, 'tis of thee
  494 O God, beneath Thy
FORGIVENESS OF SIN—See *Sinner.*
  333 Jesus, I my cross have
  421 O, the bitter shame and
  408 People of the living God
  114 When I survey the
FOUNTAIN:
  Of BLOOD.
    220 I bring my sins to Thee
    226 There is a fountain filled
  Of LIVING WATER.
    189 Come, ye disconsolate
    437 Glorious things of thee
    249 I heard the voice of
    191 The Spirit in our hearts
FRAILTY OF MAN—See *Life.*
FUTURE PUNISHMENT.
  240 O where shall rest be
  196 While life prolongs its
  See *Judgment.*
GETHSEMANE—See *Christ.*
GOD:
  ADORATION OF.
    72 Bless, O my soul, the
    28 God of mercy, God of
    84 Holy, holy, holy Lord
    65 O come, loud anthems
    8 Thee we adore, eternal
    95 Ye servants of God
  ALL IN ALL.
    353 My God, my Life, my
    346 My God, the Spring of
  ATTRIBUTES OF.
    71 High in the heavens
    77 Jehovah reigns; His
  COMMUNION WITH—See *Communion.*
  COMPASSION OF.
    711 God is love; His mercy
    68 God of pity, God of
    80 Praise, my soul, the
    186 There's a wideness in

GOD:
  CREATOR.
    83 Come, sound His praise
    76 Give to our God
    65 O come, loud anthems
  DECREES OF.
    351 Father, I know that all
    341 God moves in a
  ETERNAL.
    86 God eternal, Lord of all
    89 Great God, how infinite
    90 O God, our help in ages
    96 O God, the Rock of ages
  FAITHFULNESS OF.
    359 Cast thy burden on the
    261 How firm a foundation
    345 Through all the
  FATHER.
    429 Behold what wondrous
    339 My God, my Father
  FORBEARANCE OF—See *Long-suffering of.*
  GLORY OF.
    71 High in the heavens
    8 Thee we adore, eternal
  GOODNESS OF.
    72 Bless, O my soul, the
    352 How gentle God's
    93 Jehovah God, Thy
    91 Since all the varying
  GRACE OF.
    72 Bless, O my soul, the
    76 Give to our God
    71 High in the heavens,
    266 Lord, with glowing
  GUIDE.
    297 Guide me, O Thou great
    84 Holy, holy, holy Lord
    298 O God of Bethel, by
  HELPER.
    90 O God, our help in ages
    345 Through all the
  HOLINESS OF.
    84 Holy, holy, holy Lord
    67 Lord, in the morning
    8 Thee we adore, eternal
  IMMUTABLE—See *Unchangeable.*
  INCOMPREHENSIBLE.
    354 Give to the winds thy
    341 God moves in a
  INFINITE—See *Eternal.*
  JUDGE—See *Christ.*
  JUSTICE.
    71 High in the heavens
    77 Jehovah reigns; His
  LONG-SUFFERING OF.
    232 Depth of mercy, can
    218 God calling yet! shall I
  LOVE OF.
    70 God is love; His mercy
    78 Now to the Lord a noble
    88 Sweet the time
  MAJESTY OF.
    77 Jehovah reigns; His
    79 Kingdoms and thrones
    94 O worship the King all
  MERCY OF.
    303 Sweet is Thy mercy
    186 There's a wideness in

INDEX OF SUBJECTS.

GOD:
  MERCIES OF.
    492 Eternal Source of every
    85 Let us with a gladsome
    9 My God, how endless is
    82 O bless the Lord, my
    87 Thank and praise
    92 When all Thy mercies
  OMNIPRESENT.
    372 In heavenly love abiding
    93 Jehovah God, Thy
    369 While Thee I seek
  OMNISCIENCE.
    89 Great God, how infinite
    93 Jehovah, God, Thy
    16 They who seek the
  PITY OF—See *Compassion of.*
  PORTION.
    342 God, my Supporter, and
    346 My God, the Spring of
    374 Nearer, my God, to Thee
  PRAISE OF—See *Praise.*
  PRESENCE OF.
    372 In heavenly love abiding
    61 Welcome, sweet day of
    369 While Thee I seek
  PROVIDENCE OF.
    341 God moves in a
    71 High in the heavens
    93 Jehovah, God, Thy
    85 Let us, with a gladsome
    339 My God, my Father
    91 Since all the varying
    92 When all Thy mercies
    369 While Thee I seek
  REIGNING—See *Sovereign.*
  RECONCILED.
    221 Arise, my soul, arise
  REFUGE.
    366 God is the Refuge of
    96 O God the Rock of ages
    363 Though faint, yet
  SAFETY IN.
    342 God, my Supporter, and
    365 My spirit on Thy care
    90 O God, our help in ages
    345 Through all the changing
  SHEPHERD—See *Christ.*
  SOVEREIGN.
    83 Come, sound His praise
    354 Give to the winds thy
    77 Jehovah reigns; His
    79 Kingdoms and thrones
  SUPREME.
    11 Come, Thou Almighty
    89 Great God, how infinite
  TRUTH OF.
    73 From all that dwell
    71 High in the heavens
    87 Thank and praise
  UNCHANGEABLE.
    89 Great God, how infinite
    90 O God, our help in ages
  WATCHFUL CARE OF.
    354 Give to the winds thy
    352 How gentle God's
    365 My spirit on Thy care
    92 When all Thy mercies
    See *Providence of.*

GOD:
  WILL OF.
    343 Father, whate'er of
    344 I worship Thee, sweet
    91 Since all the varying
  WISDOM OF.
    70 God is love; His mercy
    89 Great God, how infinite
  WORKS OF.
    76 Give to our God
    85 Let us with a gladsome
    94 O worship the King, all
  GOOD WORKS.
    389 Jesus, Master, whom I
    387 O Master, let me walk
    385 So let our lips and lives
  GOSPEL.
    BANNER.
      419 Fling out the banner
      462 Now be the Gospel
      327 Soldiers of the cross
    EXCELLENCY OF.
      172 A glory gilds the sacred
      176 God in the gospel of His
      173 How precious is the
      177 Let everlasting glories
      144 Salvation! O the joyful
    FEAST.
      189 Come, ye disconsolate
      190 From the cross uplifted
    FREENESS OF.
      172 A glory gilds the sacred
      453 Great God, the nations
      191 The Spirit in our hearts
    FULNESS OF.
      189 Come, ye disconsolate
      180 Let every mortal ear
      186 There's a wideness in
    INVITATIONS OF.
      202 Come, said Jesus' sacred
      183 Come unto Me, ye weary
      188 Come, ye sinners, poor
      190 From the cross uplifted
      180 Let every mortal ear
      194 Now is the accepted
      179 The Saviour calls, let
      200 To-day the Saviour calls
      205 Ye dying sons of men
    SPREAD OF.
      440 O'er the gloomy hills of
      144 Salvation! O the joyful
      469 Thou, whose almighty
      463 Uplift the blood-red
      See *Missions.*
    TRIUMPH OF.
      460 Hasten, Lord, the
      457 The morning light is
      See *Kingdom of Christ.*
  GRACE:
    ASPIRATIONS FOR DIVINE—See *Aspirations.*
    CONVERTING.
      264 Come, Thou Fount of
      156 Gracious Spirit, Dove
      157 Holy Ghost, with light
      266 Lord, with glowing heart
    FREE.
      249 I heard the voice of
      179 The Saviour calls, let

GRACE:
    191 The Spirit in our hearts
  FRUITS OF.
    385 So let our lips and lives
  FULNESS OF.
    202 Come, said Jesus' sacred
    189 Come, ye disconsolate
    188 Come, ye sinners, poor
    206 The great Physician
    186 There's a wideness in
  JUSTIFYING.
    236 Rock of ages, cleft for
  MAGNIFIED.
    284 Amazing grace, how
    276 Ask ye what great thing
    260 Awake, and sing the
    290 Awake, my soul, in
    264 Come, Thou Fount of
    23 Come, we that love the
    259 Grace, 'tis a charming
    249 I heard the voice of
    279 I love to tell the story
    269 I was a wandering sheep
    78 Now to the Lord a noble
    262 Raise your triumphant
    409 Sweet the moments, rich
  MIRACLE OF.
    265 Hail, my ever-blessed
  QUICKENING.
    168 Come, Holy Spirit, calm
    150 Come, Holy Spirit
  RENEWING.
    160 Come, Holy Spirit, come
    165 Come, Sacred Spirit
  REVIVING.
    160 Come, Holy Spirit, come
    154 Great Father of each
    161 Lord God, the Holy
  SANCTIFYING.
    166 Come, blessed Spirit
    150 Come, Holy Spirit
    157 Holy Ghost, with light
    151 O Holy Spirit, Fount of
    329 Take, my soul, thy full
    299 O Thou, to whose
  SOVEREIGN.
    259 Grace, 'tis a charming
    227 How sad our state by
  GRACES, CHRISTIAN—See *Christians, Faith, Hope, and Love.*
  GRATITUDE.
    264 Come, Thou Fount of
    258 I bless the Christ of God
    406 Jesus, my Lord, my God
    266 Lord, with glowing heart
    281 O Jesus, King most
    80 Praise, my soul, the
    291 Sing of Jesus, sing
  GRIEVING THE SPIRIT—See *Holy Spirit.*
  GROWTH IN GRACE.
    101 Behold, where in a
    373 More love to Thee
    106 My dear Redeemer, and
    374 Nearer, my God, to Thee
    310 O for a heart to praise
    299 O Thou, to whose
    304 Rise, my soul, and

INDEX OF SUBJECTS.

GROWTH IN GRACE.
 385 So let our lips and lives
GUIDANCE.
 351 Father, I know that all
 372 In heavenly love abiding
 350 The King of love, my
 364 The Lord my Shepherd
 369 While Thee I seek
SOUGHT.
 150 Come, Holy Spirit
 296 Gently, Lord, O gently
 297 Guide me, O Thou great
 306 Lead, kindly Light
 416 Thine forever! God of
GUILT—See *Sin.*
HAPPINESS—See *Joy.*
HARVEST.
 495 Come, ye thankful
 500 Praise to God, immortal
 503 The God of harvest
HEART:
 CHANGE OF—See *Regeneration.*
 CLEAN.
 355 Blest are the pure in
 160 Come, Holy Spirit, come
 157 Holy Ghost, with light
 340 O for a heart to praise
 CONTRITE.
 219 A broken heart, my God
 217 Show pity, Lord, O Lord
 229 Take me, O my Father
 216 With broken heart and
 SURRENDER OF.
 218 God calling yet! shall I
 220 I bring my sins to Thee
 233 Jesus, full of truth and
 229 Take me, O my Father
 VILE—See *Sin.*
HEATHEN.
 441 Arm of the Lord, awake
 454 From Greenland's icy
 90 Hark, what mean those
 443 Look from Thy sphere
HEAVEN:
 ANTICIPATED.
 476 This is not my place of
 308 When I can read my
 BLESSEDNESS OF.
 483 Brief life is here our
 478 There is a land of pure
 HOME.
 472 Far from my heavenly
 473 Forever with the Lord
 484 For thee, O dear, dear
 316 Heirs of unending life
 310 I'm but a stranger here
 479 Jerusalem, my happy
 482 Jerusalem, the golden
 305 Time is winging us away
 LONGED FOR—See *Aspirations.*
 NEARNESS TO.
 470 One sweetly solemn
 302 Your harps, ye trembling
 PRAISE OF.
 423 Give me the wings of
 See *Christ, Lamb of God.*
 PROSPECT OF.
 480 O mother dear
 487 O Paradise, O Paradise

HEAVEN:
 315 O what, if we are Christ's
 329 Take, my soul, thy
 485 The sands of time are
 323 'Tis by the faith of joys
 REST OF.
 483 Brief life is here our
 488 There is an hour of
 476 This is not my place of
 308 When I can read my
 SOCIETY OF.
 483 Brief life is here our
 423 Give me the wings of
HEIRSHIP—See *Adoption.*
HELL—See *Future Punishment.*
HOLINESS—See *God, Heaven, and Saints.*
HOLY SCRIPTURES—See *Word of God.*
HOLY SPIRIT:
 ABSENCE OF.
 150 Come, Holy Spirit
 348 Long hath the night of
 347 O for a closer walk with
 COMFORTER.
 163 Blest Comforter Divine
 146 Come, Holy Ghost, in
 164 Come, O Creator, Spirit
 158 Granted is the Saviour's
 159 Holy Ghost, the Infinite
 157 Holy Ghost, with light
 149 Why should the children
 DESCENT OF.
 158 Granted is the Saviour's
 155 Let songs of praises fill
 161 Lord God, the Holy
 DIVINE.
 165 Come, Sacred Spirit
 158 Granted is the Saviour's
 159 Holy Ghost, the Infinite
 157 Holy Ghost, with light
 161 Lord God, the Holy
 EARNEST OF.
 156 Gracious Spirit, Dove
 154 Great Father of each
 159 Holy Ghost, the Infinite
 152 My soul doth magnify
 149 Why should the children
 ENLIGHTENER.
 166 Come, blessed Spirit
 169 Eternal Spirit, we
 157 Holy Ghost, with light
 153 Spirit Divine, attend our
 GUIDE.
 166 Come, blessed Spirit
 167 Come, Holy Spirit
 164 Come, O Creator, Spirit
 INDWELLING.
 166 Come, blessed Spirit
 164 Come, O Creator, Spirit
 151 O Holy Spirit, Fount of
 329 Take, my soul, thy full
 149 Why should the children
 INFLUENCE OF.
 166 Come, blessed Spirit
 146 Come, Holy Ghost, in
 168 Come, Holy Spirit, calm
 160 Come, Holy Spirit, come
 150 Come, Holy Spirit

HOLY SPIRIT:
 165 Come, Sacred Spirit
 169 Eternal Spirit, we
 145 Love Divine, all
 INVITING.
 191 The Spirit in our hearts
 INVOKED—See *Prayer.*
 163 Blest Comforter Divine
 168 Come, Holy Spirit, calm
 150 Come, Holy Spirit
 154 Great Father of each
 145 Love Divine, all love
 162 O Lord, Thy work
 213 O Thou that hearest the
 PRAYED FOR—See *Prayer.*
 REGENERATING.
 160 Come, Holy Spirit, come
 165 Come, Sacred Spirit
 154 Great Father of each
 155 Let songs of praises fill
 SANCTIFYING.
 168 Come, Holy Spirit, calm
 160 Come, Holy Spirit, come
 167 Come, Holy Spirit
 164 Come, O Creator Spirit
 156 Gracious Spirit, Dove
 157 Holy Ghost, with light
 153 Spirit Divine, attend
 STRIVING.
 218 God calling yet! shall I
 191 The Spirit in our hearts
 WITNESS OF—See *Earnest of.*
HOME MISSIONS—See *Missions.*
HOPE:
 ASPIRATIONS OF.
 429 Behold what wondrous
 472 Far from my heavenly
 328 In the cross of Christ
 335 Jesus, Lover of my soul
 329 Take, my soul, thy full
 See *Heaven, Anticipated.*
 IN AFFLICTION—See *Afflictions.*
 IN CHRIST.
 261 Here I can firmly rest
 338 I'm not ashamed to own
 268 My hope is built on
 302 Your harps, ye trembling
 IN DEATH—See *Death.*
 IN GOD.
 343 Father, whate'er of
 354 Give to the winds thy
 366 God is the Refuge of
 302 Your harps, ye trembling
 OF HEAVEN—See *Heaven.*
HUMILIATION.
 232 Depth of mercy, can
 112 O Jesus, sweet the tears
 212 Pass me not, O gracious
 224 Prostrate, dear Jesus, at
 217 Show pity, Lord, O Lord
 216 With broken heart and
 OF CHRIST—See *Christ.*
HUMILITY—See *Meekness.*
IMMORTALITY.
 473 Forever with the Lord
 240 O where shall rest be
 See *Eternity* and *Heaven.*
IMPORTUNITY—See *Prayer.*

INDEX OF SUBJECTS.

IMPUTATION.
  111 Alas! and did my
  126 Hail, Thou once despised
  252 I hear the Saviour say
  116 Not all the blood of
  257 O Christ, what burdens
  112 O Jesus, sweet the tears
  237 Surely Christ thy griefs
  223 Thy works, not mine
INCARNATION—See *Christ.*
INSPIRATION—See *Word of God.*
INTERCESSION—See *Christ.*
INVITATIONS—See *Gospel, Grace* and *Sinners.*
INVOCATION.
  2 Come, dearest Lord
  11 Come, Thou Almighty
  7 How sweet to leave the
  13 In Thy name, O Lord
  67 Lord, in the morning
  15 Lord, we come before
  54 Safely through another
  5 Where two or three with
See *Prayer* and *Praise.*
ISRAEL.
  464 O that the Lord's
JOINING THE CHURCH—See *Faith, Confession of,* and *Converts Welcomed.*
JOY, SPIRITUAL.
  276 Ask ye what great thing
  290 Awake, my soul, in
  300 Children of the heavenly
  23 Come, we that love the
  244 Fade, fade each earthly
  261 Here I can firmly rest
  249 I heard the voice of Jesus
  406 Jesus, my Lord, my God
  289 Jesus, the very thought
  346 My God, the Spring of
  243 Now I have found a
  282 O for a thousand tongues
  80 Praise, my soul, the
In Hope—See *Sinners.*
JUDGMENT, THE.
  477 O God, mine inmost soul
  196 While life prolongs its
JUSTIFICATION—See *Faith, Justifying.*
KINGDOM OF CHRIST:
Prayed for.
  453 Great God, the nations
  460 Hasten, Lord, the
  445 O Spirit of the living
Progress of.
  467 Christ for the world we
  453 Great God, the nations
  455 Hail to the Lord's
  460 Hasten, Lord, the
  448 Jesus shall reign
  468 Lord of all power and
  440 O'er the gloomy hills of
  457 The morning light is
  458 When shall the voice of
Triumph of.
  448 Jesus shall reign
  464 O that the Lord's
  442 Soon may the last glad

LAMB OF GOD—See *Christ.*
LIFE:
Brevity of.
  305 Time is winging us away
  489 While with ceaseless
Object of.
  198 Life is the time to serve
  313 My soul, weigh not thy
  240 O where shall rest be
  304 Rise, my soul, and
Solemnity of.
  312 A charge to keep I have
  477 O God, mine inmost soul
  240 O where shall rest be
  201 Time is earnest, passing
Uncertainty of.
  470 One sweetly solemn
  40 Tarry with me, O my
  193 To-morrow, Lord, is
  196 While life prolongs its
Vanity of.
  89 Great God, how infinite
  90 O God, our help in ages
LONGINGS—See *Aspirations.*
LOOKING TO JESUS.
  214 I am trusting Thee, Lord
  220 I bring my sins to Thee
  249 I heard the voice of
  246 Just as I am, without
  270 My faith looks up to
  215 Weary of earth, and
LORD'S DAY AND WORSHIP:
Delight in.
  66 Blest day of God, most
  62 How charming is the
  13 In Thy name, O Lord
  85 Let us with a gladsome
Evening.
  60 Abide with me: fast falls
  15 Lord, we come before
Morning.
  58 Again returns the day
  67 Lord, in the morning
  65 O come, loud anthems
  54 Safely through another
Welcomed.
  64 O day of rest and
  63 This is the glorious day
  61 Welcome, sweet day of
See *Invocation* and *Close of Service.*
LORD'S SUPPER.
  404 Lamb of God, whose
  419 No more, my God, I
  371 O Lamb of God, still
  420 O the sweet wonders of
  402 Saviour! Thy dying
  409 Sweet the moments, rich
See *Cross* and *Consecration.*
LOVE:
Of Christ—See *Christ.*
Of God—See *God.*
For Christ.
  273 Blessed Saviour, Thee I
  287 Do not I love Thee, O
  265 Hail, my ever-blessed
  293 How sweet the Name of
  410 I lift my heart to Thee
  279 I love to tell the story

LOVE:
  263 Jesus, I live to Thee
  288 Jesus, I love Thy
  335 Jesus, Lover of my soul
  406 Jesus, my Lord, my God
  289 Jesus, the very thought
  283 Jesus, these eyes have
  271 Jesus, Thy Name I love
  266 Lord, with glowing heart
  373 More love to Thee, O
  254 My Jesus, I love Thee
  277 O could I speak the
  278 O Love Divine, how
  414 One there is above all
  357 Saviour, teach me, day
For God.
  319 As pants the hart for
  353 My God, my Life, my
  346 My God, the Spring of
For Saints.
  426 Blest be the tie that
  425 Happy the souls to Jesus
For the Church.
  428 I love Thy kingdom,
MEDITATION.
  3 Far from my thoughts
  32 I love to steal awhile
  4 My God, permit me not
  409 Sweet the moments, rich
MEEKNESS:
  101 Behold, where in a
  107 How beauteous were the
  106 My dear Redeemer and
MERCY:
Of God—See *God.*
Sought—See *Sinners.*
MERCY-SEAT.
  225 Approach, my soul, the
  29 From every stormy
  62 How charming is the
  303 Sweet is Thy mercy
MINISTRY.
  171 Father of mercies, in
  459 How beauteous are the
  445 O Spirit of the living
  463 Uplift the blood-red
  444 Ye Christian heralds, go
MIRACLES—See *Christ.*
MISSIONS:
Home.
  467 Christ for the world we
  450 Jesus, Thy Church with
  443 Look from Thy sphere
  452 Lord, while for all
  451 On Zion and on Lebanon
  456 Our country's voice is
  439 Saints of God, the dawn
  458 When shall the voice of
Foreign.
  441 Arm of the Lord, awake
  446 Ascend Thy throne,
  467 Christ for the world we
  449 Fling out the banner
  454 From Greenland's icy
  453 Great God, the nations
  466 Hark, what mean those
  450 Jesus, Thy Church with
  462 Now be the Gospel
  445 O Spirit of the living

INDEX OF SUBJECTS.

MISSIONS:
  440 O'er the gloomy hills of
  457 The morning light is
  447 Though now the nations
  458 When shall the voice of
MISSIONARIES:
  459 How beauteous on the
  463 Uplift the blood-red
  444 Ye Christian heralds, go
WORK, CALLS TO.
  449 Fling out the banner
  466 Hark, what mean those
MORNING.
  59 Saviour, again to Thy
  50 As the sun doth daily
  57 In this calm, impressive
  9 My God, how endless is
  45 Now when the dusky
  35 O Jesus, Lord of light
OF LORD'S DAY—See *Lord's Day.*
MORTALITY—See *Death* and *Life.*
NATIONAL.
  502 God bless our native
  498 Let children hear the
  452 Lord, while for all
  501 My country, 'tis of thee
  494 O God, beneath Thy
NATURE.
  492 Eternal Source of every
  499 Lord, in Thy Name Thy
  497 Summer suns are
NEARNESS TO GOD.
  374 Nearer, my God, to
  347 O for a closer walk with
  37 Sun of my soul, Thou
To HEAVEN—See *Heaven.*
NEW YEAR—See *Year.*
OBEDIENCE:
  OF CHRIST—See *Christ.*
  OF THE CHRISTIAN.
  250 Dear Lord and Master,
  376 Happy the man who
  383 My gracious Lord, I
OFFERS OF GRACE — See *Grace.*
OFFICES OF CHRIST — See *Christ.*
OLD AGE.
  60 Abide with me; fast falls
  361 How firm a foundation
  40 Tarry with me, O my
OMNIPOTENCE—See *God.*
OMNIPRESENCE—See *God.*
OMNISCIENCE—See *God.*
OPENING OF SERVICE—See *Invocation.*
ORDINANCES — See *Baptism* and *Lord's Supper.*
ORIGINAL SIN—See *Sin.*
PARDON:
  FOUND—See *Sinners, Rejoicing in Hope,* and *Saved.*
  OFFERED—See *Gospel, Invitations of,* and *Sinners Invited.*
  SOUGHT—See *Sinners, Seeking.*
PARTING—See *Close of Service.*
PASSOVER—See *Christ.*

PASTORS—See *Ministry.*
PATIENCE — See *Afflictions, Resignation under.*
PEACE:
  CHRISTIAN.
  344 I worship Thee, sweet
  372 In heavenly love
  401 Peace, perfect peace, in
  369 While Thee I seek
PRAYER FOR.
  343 Father, whate'er of
  404 Lamb of God, whose
  59 Saviour, again to Thy
NATIONAL.
  502 God bless our native
PENITENTIAL.
  111 Alas! and did my
  251 All that I was, my sin,
  225 Approach, my soul, the
  232 Depth of mercy, can
  242 Did Christ o'er sinners
  233 Jesus, full of truth and
  228 Jesus, Thou art the
  404 Lamb of God, whose
  245 No, not despairingly
  112 O Jesus, sweet the tears
  212 Pass me not, O gracious
  224 Prostrate, dear Jesus, at
  217 Show pity, Lord
  215 Weary of earth and
  216 With broken heart and
PENTECOST.
  158 Granted is the Saviour's
  161 Lord God, the Holy
PERSEVERANCE—See *Saints.*
PESTILENCE.
  39 Saviour, breathe an
PILGRIMS:
  PRAYER OF.
  472 Far from my heavenly
  296 Gently, Lord, O gently
  297 Guide me, O Thou great
  370 I need Thee, precious
  306 Lead, kindly Light
  298 O God of Bethel, by
  299 O Thou to whose all
  391 O very God of very God
  SONG OF.
  300 Children of the heavenly
  23 Come, we that love the
  307 He leadeth me
  310 I'm but a stranger here
  304 Rise, my soul, and
  SPIRIT OF.
  472 Far from my heavenly
  473 Forever with the Lord
  316 Heirs of unending life
  270 My faith looks up to
  304 Rise, my soul, and
  323 'Tis by the faith of joys
  308 When I can read my
  302 Your harps, ye
PILGRIMAGE.
  310 I'm but a stranger here
  309 My feet are worn and
  305 Time is winging us
PRAISE:
  73 From all that dwell
  86 God eternal, Lord of all

PRAISE:
  84 Holy, holy, holy Lord
  1 Songs of praise the
  CALLS TO.
  83 Come, sound His praise
  23 Come, we that love the
  76 Give to our God
  28 God of mercy, God of
  65 O come, loud anthems
  87 Thanks and praise
  To CHRIST.
  139 All hail the power of
  260 Awake, and sing the
  290 Awake, my soul, in
  124 Behold the glories of the
  12 Come, all ye saints of
  123 Come, let us join in
  122 Come, let us join our
  125 Come, let us lift our
  142 Come, let us sing the
  264 Come, Thou Fount of
  131 Crown Him with many
  132 Glory to God on high
  265 Hail, my ever-blessed
  126 Hail, Thou once despised
  258 I bless the Christ of God
  279 I love to tell the story
  288 Jesus, I love Thy
  289 Jesus, the very thought
  100 Joy to the world, the
  177 Let everlasting glories
  266 Lord, with glowing
  285 My Saviour, my
  143 Now to the Lord, who
  140 O Christ, our King
  277 O could I speak the
  282 O for a thousand tongues
  80 Praise, my soul, the
  262 Raise your triumphant
  267 Saviour, blessed Saviour
  436 Shepherd of tender
  291 Sing of Jesus, sing
  286 The Saviour! O what
  147 To Him who for our
  127 Worship, honor, power
  95 Ye servants of God
  To GOD.
  72 Bless, O my soul, the
  83 Come, sound His praise
  491 Eternal Source of every
  76 Give to our God
  89 Great God how infinite
  71 High in the heavens,
  79 Kingdoms and thrones
  85 Let us with a gladsome
  6 My God, my King, Thy
  82 O bless the Lord, my
  87 Thank and praise
  8 Thee we adore, eternal
  92 When all Thy mercies
  To THE HOLY SPIRIT.
  146 Come, Holy Ghost, in
  169 Eternal Spirit, who
  148 To Thee, O Comforter
  To THE TRINITY.
  50 As the sun doth daily
  11 Come, Thou Almighty
  75 Father in Heaven, whose
  81 Glory be to God the

INDEX OF SUBJECTS.

PRAISE.
84 Holy, holy, holy Lord
74 Praises to Him, whose
88 Sweet the time
PRAYER.
29 From every stormy wind
32 I love to steal awhile
30 My God, is any hour so
31 Prayer is the soul's
ENCOURAGEMENT TO.
26 Behold the throne of
19 Come, my soul, thy suit
203 Pilgrim, burdened with
187 What a Friend we have
IMPORTUNITY IN.
15 Lord, we come before
24 Our Lord, who knows
27 Pray, without ceasing
To CHRIST.
406 Jesus, my Lord, my
145 Love Divine, all love
39 Saviour, breathe an
37 Sun of my soul, Thou
47 Sweet Saviour, bless us
40 Tarry with me, O my
To THE HOLY SPIRIT.
146 Come, Holy Ghost, in
160 Come, Holy Spirit, come
150 Come, Holy Spirit
164 Come, O Creator Spirit
165 Come, Sacred Spirit
156 Gracious Spirit, Dove
158 Granted is the Saviour's
154 Great Father of each
159 Holy Ghost, the Infinite
157 Holy Ghost, with light
161 Lord God, the Holy
415 O Spirit of the living
153 Spirit divine, attend our
149 Why should the children
To THE TRINITY.
11 Come, Thou Almighty
55 Father, by Thy love and
212 Pass me not, O gracious
469 Thou, whose Almighty
53 Three in One and One
UNITED.
15 Lord, we come before
24 Our Lord who knows
5 Where two or three with
PROBATION—See *Grace, Day of.*
PROCRASTINATION—See *Delay.*
PROGRESS.
CHRISTIAN — See *Growth in Grace.*
OF CHRIST'S KINGDOM — See *Kingdom.*
PROMISES.
26 Behold the throne of
366 God is the Refuge of
361 How firm a foundation
246 Just as I am, without
177 Let everlasting glories
217 Show pity, Lord, O Lord
PROVIDENCE—See *God.*
PURPOSES OF GOD—See *God, Decrees of.*

RACE, CHRISTIAN.
320 Awake, my soul, stretch
324 Awake, our souls, away
321 Fight the good fight
322 Stand up, my soul, shake
323 'Tis by the faith of joys
REDEMPTION—See *Atonement.*
REFUGE—See *Christ and God.*
REGENERATION:
SOUGHT.
156 Gracious Spirit, Dove
157 Holy Ghost, with light
161 Not all the outward
340 O for a heart to praise
WROUGHT.
160 Come, Holy Spirit, come
169 Eternal Spirit, we
149 Why should the children
REJOICING IN GOD — See *Joy.*
REJOICING IN HOPE—See *Sinners.*
RENOUNCING ALL FOR CHRIST—See *Forsaking all for Christ.*
REPENTANCE — See *Penitential.*
RESIGNATION.
250 Dear Lord and Master
351 Father, I know that all
343 Father, whate'er of
344 I worship Thee, sweet
339 My God, my Father,
91 Since all the varying
369 While Thee I seek,
REST—See *Heaven* and *Weary.*
RESURRECTION:
OF CHRIST—See *Christ.*
OF BELIEVERS.
119 I know that my
471 O for the death of those
REVELATION—See *Word of God.*
REVIVAL:
DESIRED.
349 As pants the hart for
150 Come, Holy Spirit
348 Long hath the night of
PRAYED FOR.
163 Blest Comforter Divine
160 Come, Holy Spirit, come
165 Come, Sacred Spirit
154 Great Father of each
386 Jesus, our best-beloved
162 O Lord, Thy work
212 Pass me not, O gracious
378 Revive Thy work
438 Saviour, visit thy
153 Spirit divine, attend our
REJOICING IN.
158 Granted is the Saviour's
155 Let songs of praises fill
RICHES.
304 Rise, my soul, and
114 When I survey the
RIGHTEOUSNESS OF CHRIST—See *Christ.*
ROCK OF AGES—See *Christ.*
SABBATH—See *Lord's Day.*

SACRAMENTS — See *Baptism* and *Lord's Supper.*
SACRIFICE — See *Atonement and Christ.*
SAFETY OF BELIEVERS— See *Saints.*
SAINTS:
BLESSEDNESS OF.
275 Blessed are the sons of
425 Happy the souls to
COMMUNION OF — See *Communion.*
DEATH OF—See *Death.*
GLORIFIED.
423 Give me the wings of
315 O what, if we are Christ's
PERSEVERANCE OF.
320 Awake, my soul, stretch
321 Fight the good fight
317 Go forward, Christian
311 My soul, be on thy guard
318 Stand up, stand up for
323 'Tis by the faith of joys
SECURITY OF.
366 God is the Refuge of His
361 How firm a foundation
372 In heavenly love abiding
365 My spirit, on Thy care
91 O worship the King
90 O God, our help in ages
364 The Lord my Shepherd
345 Through all the
UNION OF, WITH CHRIST.
275 Blessed are the sons of
426 Blest be the dear uniting
25 Our heavenly Father
UNION OF, WITH EACH OTHER.
427 Blest be the tie that
423 Give me the wings of
425 Happy the souls to Jesus
424 Let saints below in
SALVATION — See *Atonement, Gospel, Grace,* and *Sinners.*
SANCTIFICATION — See *Growth in Grace.*
SATAN.
225 Approach, my soul, the
313 My soul, weigh not thy
308 When I can read my
SAVIOUR—See *Christ.*
SCRIPTURES, HOLY—See *Word of God.*
SEASONS, THE.
492 Eternal Source of every
490 For Thy mercy and Thy
493 Great God, we sing that
499 Lord, in Thy Name Thy
500 Praise to God, immortal
497 Summer suns are
503 The God of harvest
489 While with ceaseless
SECOND BIRTH—See *Regeneration.*
SECOND DEATH—See *Future Punishment.*
SECURITY OF SAINTS—See *Saints.*
SELF-DEDICATION—See *Consecration* and *Covenant.*

INDEX OF SUBJECTS.

SELF-DENIAL.
319 Am I a soldier of the
333 Jesus, I my cross have
336 Must Jesus bear the
332 Take up thy cross, the
114 When I survey the

SICKNESS.
51 At even, ere the sun was
470 One sweetly solemn

SIN:
CONFESSION OF.
251 All that I was, my sin
225 Approach, my soul, the
232 Depth of mercy, can
242 Did Christ o'er sinners
241 Out of the deep I call
212 Pass me not, O gracious
224 Prostrate, dear Jesus, at
217 Show pity, Lord, O Lord
229 Take me. O my Father
216 With broken heart and
HATRED OF.
111 Alas! and did my
347 O for a closer walk with
INDWELLING—See *Holy Spirit.*
51 At even, ere the sun was
233 Jesus, full of truth and
299 O Thou to whose
ORIGINAL.
227 How sad our state by
241 Out of the deep I call

SINNERS:
ANXIOUS.
185 Art thou weary, art thou
477 O God, mine inmost soul
104 O where is He that trod
AWAKENED.
218 God calling yet! shall I
192 O cease, my wandering
BELIEVING.
221 Arise, my soul, arise
269 I was a wandering
333 Jesus, I my cross have
406 Jesus, my Lord, my
246 Just as I am, without
230 Lord, I know Thy grace
270 My faith looks up to
116 Not all the blood of
238 Sinners Jesus will
215 Weary of earth and
239 Weary with my load of
CARELESS.
218 God calling yet! shall I
199 Haste, traveller, haste
204 Sinners, turn, why will
201 Time is earnest, passing
COMING TO CHRIST.
220 I bring my sins to Thee
249 I heard the voice of
233 Jesus, full of truth and
246 Just as I am, without
CONFESSING CHRIST.
383 My gracious Lord, I
408 People of the living
413 Witness, ye men and
CONVICTED OF SIN.
242 Did Christ o'er sinners
241 Out of the deep I call
DELAYING—See *Delay.*

SINNERS:
DIRECTED.
203 Pilgrim, burdened with
237 Surely Christ thy griefs
EXPOSTULATED.
208 Child of sin and sorrow
240 O where shall rest be
195 Return, O wanderer
204 Sinners, turn, why will
184 The King of glory
INVITED.
185 Art thou weary, art thou
197 Behold, a Stranger at
313 Come, said Jesus' sacred
210 Come to the Saviour
183 Come unto me, ye weary
189 Come, ye disconsolate
188 Come, ye sinners, poor
190 From the cross uplifted
218 God calling yet! shall I
207 I have a Saviour, He's
180 Let every mortal ear
194 Now is the accepted
203 Pilgrim, burdened with
195 Return, O wanderer
206 The great Physician
179 The Saviour calls, let
191 The Spirit in our hearts
200 To-day the Saviour calls
205 Ye dying sons of men
PENITENT.
219 A broken heart, my
111 Alas! and did my
251 All that I was, my sin,
242 Did Christ o'er sinners
370 I need Thee, precious
112 O Jesus, sweet the tears
217 Show pity, Lord
PLEADING FOR MERCY.
231 At the door of mercy
232 Depth of mercy, can
235 Holy Father, hear my
247 Jesus, the sinner's
241 Out of the deep I call
212 Pass me not, O gracious
234 Thou who didst on
216 With broken heart and
PRAYER OF ANXIOUS.
225 Approach, my soul, the
75 Father of Heaven, whose
156 Gracious Spirit, Dove
235 Holy Father, hear my
157 Holy Ghost, with light
174 Laden with guilt and
213 O Thou, that hearest the
236 Rock of ages, cleft for
238 Sinners Jesus will
229 Take me, O my Father
239 Weary with my load of
REJOICING IN HOPE.
276 Ask ye what great thing
290 Awake, my soul, in
244 Fade, fade each earthly
258 I bless the Christ of
294 I've found the pearl of
222 Join all the glorious
177 Let everlasting glories
268 My hope is built on
243 Now I have found a

SINNERS:
409 Sweet the moments, rich
329 Take, my soul, thy full
SEEKING.
225 Approach, my soul, the
228 Jesus, Thou art the
192 O cease, my wandering
224 Prostrate, dear Jesus,
216 With broken heart and
248 With tearful eyes I look
SONG OF PRAISE.
139 All hail the power of
112 Come, let us sing the
259 Grace, 'tis a charming
265 Hail, my ever-blessed
258 I bless the Christ of
266 Lord, with glowing
80 Praise, my soul, the
74 Praises to Him whose
226 There is a fountain filled
223 Thy works, not mine
WARNED.
211 Delay not, delay not
240 O where shall rest be
193 To-morrow, Lord, is
196 While life prolongs its
209 Yet there is room
YIELDING.
250 Dear Lord and Master
218 God calling yet! shall I
214 I am trusting Thee
220 I bring my sins to Thee
233 Jesus, full of truth and
418 Lord, I am Thine
229 Take me. O my Father
239 Weary with my load of
SOLDIER, CHRISTIAN—See *Warfare.*
SORROW—See *Afflictions.*
FOR SIN—See *Penitential.*
STEADFASTNESS—See *Saints, Perseverance of.*
SUBMISSION—See *Afflictions* and *Resignation.*
SUPPER, LORD'S—See *Lord's Supper.*
SURRENDER — See *Sinners Yielding.*
SYMPATHY:
OF CHRIST—See *Christ.*
OF CHRISTIANS—See *Communion.*
392 Lord, lead the way the
387 O Master, let me walk
377 O praise our God to-day
375 We give Thee but Thine
TEMPERANCE.
381 A fitly-spoken word
397 Christian, work for
399 Mourn for the thousands
387 O Master, let me walk
396 Rescue the perishing
393 Think gently of the
TEMPTATION.
296 Gently, Lord. O gently
311 My soul, be on thy guard
313 My soul, weigh not thy
27 Pray, without ceasing
398 Yield not to temptation

INDEX OF SUBJECTS.

THANKFULNESS—See *Gratitude.*
THANKSGIVING.
496 Christ, by heavenly
495 Come, ye thankful
492 Eternal Source of every
499 For Thy mercy and
502 God bless our native
498 Let children hear the
85 Let us, with a gladsome
501 My country, 'tis of thee
494 O God, beneath Thy
500 Praise to God, immortal
503 The God of harvest
92 When all Thy mercies
THRONE OF GRACE—See *Mercy-Seat.*
26 Behold the throne of
343 Father, whate'er of
TIME—See *Death, Life,* and *Year.*
TRIALS—See *Afflictions.*
TRIBULATIONS—See *Afflictions.*
TRINITY.
ADORATION OF.
74 Praises to Him whose
75 Father of heaven, whose
81 Glory be to God the
88 Sweet the time
INVOKED.
11 Come, Thou Almighty
469 Thou, whose almighty
53 Three in One and One
PRAISE TO—See *Praise.*
PRAYER TO—See *Prayer.*
WORSHIP OF.
75 Father of heaven, whose
88 Sweet the time
TRUST:
IN CHRIST.
261 Here I can firmly rest
352 How gentle God's
178 I am coming to the cross
214 I am trusting Thee
119 I know that my
292 I left it all with Jesus
338 I'm not ashamed to own
372 In heavenly love
256 Jesus, I will trust Thee
247 Jesus, the sinner's
419 No more, my God, I

TRUST:
243 Now I have found a
103 O Jesus, when I think
315 O what, if we are
274 Saviour, happy would I
368 When sins and fears
IN GOD.
351 Father, I know that all
354 Give to the winds thy
362 The Lord is my
364 The Lord my Shepherd
363 Though faint, yet
358 To Thy pastures fair
369 While Thee I seek
IN PROVIDENCE.
341 God moves in a
361 How firm a foundation
352 How gentle God's
339 My God, my Father
334 O Lord, how happy
92 When all Thy mercies
VANITY OF LIFE—See *Life.*
VICTORY:
OF BELIEVERS—See *Warfare.*
OF CHRIST—See *Christ.*
WARFARE AND VICTORY.
319 Am I a soldier of the
320 Awake, my soul, stretch
325 Christian, seek not yet
321 Fight the good fight
317 Go forward, Christian
311 My soul, be on thy guard
313 My soul, weigh not thy
314 Rejoice, ye pure in
327 Soldiers of Christ, arise
326 Soldiers who are Christ's
322 Stand up, my soul, shake
318 Stand up, stand up for
WARNINGS—See *Sinners, Warned.*
WATCHFULNESS AND PRAYER.
312 A charge to keep I have
325 Christian, seek not yet
311 My soul, be on thy guard
367 They pray the best who
379 Ye servants of the Lord
WAY OF SALVATION—See *Atonement, Grace,* and *Sinners.*
WAY, TRUTH, AND LIFE—See *Christ.*

WEARY, REST FOR THE.
185 Art thou weary, art thou
202 Come, said Jesus' sacred
249 I heard the voice of
192 O cease, my wandering
488 There is an hour of
WORD OF GOD.
172 A glory gilds the sacred
171 Father of mercies, in
176 God, in the Gospel of
366 God is the Refuge of
175 Holy Bible, book divine
173 How precious is the
174 Laden with guilt and
177 Let everlasting glories
WORKING AND GIVING.
384 Go, labor on; spend and
376 Happy the man who
394 How blessed, from the
389 Jesus, Master, whom I
386 Jesus, our best belovéd
382 Laborers of Christ, arise
392 Lord, lead the way the
383 My gracious Lord, I
395 O Lord of heaven and
387 O Master, let me walk
377 O praise our God to-day
380 Sow in the morn thy
375 We give Thee but Thine
400 Work, for the night is
390 Workman of God, O lose
WORLD RENOUNCED—See *Forsaking all for Christ.*
WORSHIP—See *Family Worship, Lord's Day, Praise,* and *Prayer.*
YEAR—See *Seasons.*
BEGINNING OF.
492 Eternal Source of every
499 For Thy mercy and Thy
493 Great God, we sing that
489 While with ceaseless
CLOSE OF.
490 For Thy mercy and Thy
90 O God, our help in ages
491 Thou, who roll'st the
ZEAL.
312 A charge to keep I have
319 Am I a soldier of the
320 Awake, my soul, stretch
287 Do not I love Thee
322 Stand up, my soul

INDEX OF FIRST LINES.

	HYMN		HYMN
A broken heart, my God, my King	219	Behold the throne of grace	26
A charge to keep I have	312	Behold what wondrous grace	429
A fitly spoken word	381	Behold, where, in a mortal form	101
A glory gilds the sacred page	172	Bless, O my soul, the living God	72
A little child the Saviour came	431	Blessed are the sons of God	275
Abide with me: fast falls the eventide	60	Blessed Saviour, Thee I love	273
Again returns the day of holy rest	58	Blest are the pure in heart	355
Alas! and did my Saviour bleed	111	Blest be the dear uniting love	426
All hail the power of Jesus' name	139	Blest be the tie that binds	427
All praise to Thee, my God, this night	34	Blest Comforter Divine	163
All that I was, my sin, my guilt	251	Blest day of God, most calm, most bright	66
Almighty God, to-night	46	Brief life is here our portion	483
Always with us, always with us	129	By cool Siloam's shady rill	433
Am I a soldier of the cross	319		
Amazing grace, how sweet the sound	284	Cast thy burden on the Lord	359
Angels, from the realms of glory	97	Child of sin and sorrow	208
Approach, my soul, the mercy-seat	225	Children of the heavenly King	300
Arise, my soul, arise	221	Christ, above all glory seated	128
Arm of the Lord, awake, awake	441	Christ, by heavenly hosts adored	496
Art thou weary, art thou languid	185	Christ for the world we sing	467
As pants the hart for cooling streams	349	Christ, of all my hopes the ground	272
As the sun doth daily rise	50	Christian, seek not yet repose	325
As with gladness men of old	98	Christian, work for Jesus	397
Ascend Thy throne, Almighty King	446	Come, all ye saints of God	12
Ask ye what great thing I know	276	Come, blessed Spirit, Source of light	166
Asleep in Jesus: blessed sleep	474	Come, dearest Lord, descend and dwell	2
At even, ere the sun was set	51	Come, Holy Ghost, in love	146
At the door of mercy sighing	231	Come, Holy Spirit, calm my mind	168
At the name of Jesus	133	Come, Holy Spirit, come	160
Awake, and sing the song	260	Come, Holy Spirit, Heavenly Dove, With all	150
Awake, awake, O Zion	461		
Awake, my soul, and with the sun	33	Come, Holy Spirit, Heavenly Dove, With peace	167
Awake, my soul, in joyful lays	290		
Awake, my soul, stretch every nerve	320	Come, let us join in songs of praise	123
Awake, our souls, away, our fears	324	Come, let us join our cheerful songs	122
		Come, let us lift our joyful eyes	125
Behold, a Stranger at the door	197	Come, let us sing the song of songs	142
Behold the glories of the Lamb	124	Come, my soul, thy suit prepare	19

234

	HYMN		HYMN
Come, O Creator, Spirit blest	164	Give to our God immortal praise	76
Come, Sacred Spirit, from above	165	Give to the winds thy fears	354
Come, said Jesus' sacred voice	202	Glorious things of thee are spoken	437
Come, sound His praise abroad	83	Glory be to God the Father	81
Come, Thou Almighty King	11	Glory to God on high	132
Come, Thou Fount of every blessing	264	Go forward, Christian soldier	317
Come to the Saviour now	210	Go, labor on; spend and be spent	384
Come unto me, ye weary	183	Go to dark Gethsemane	109
Come, we that love the Lord	23	God bless our native land	502
Come, ye disconsolate, where'er ye	189	God calling yet! shall I not hear	218
Come, ye sinners, poor and wretched	188	God eternal, Lord of all	86
Come, ye thankful people, come	495	God, in the gospel of His Son	176
Crown Him with many crowns	131	God is love; His glory brightens	70
		God is the Refuge of His saints	366
DEAR Lord and Master mine	250	God moves in a mysterious way	311
Dear Saviour, if these lambs should stray	432	God, my Supporter and my Hope	342
Dearest of all the names above	138	God of mercy, God of grace	28
Delay not, delay not; O sinner	211	God of pity, God of grace	68
Depth of mercy, can there be	232	Grace, 'tis a charming sound	259
Did Christ o'er sinners weep	242	Gracious Spirit, Dove divine	156
Dismiss us with Thy blessing, Lord	10	Granted is the Saviour's prayer	158
Do not I love Thee, O my Lord	287	Great Father of each perfect gift	154
		Great God, how infinite art Thou	89
ETERNAL Source of every joy	492	Great God, the nations of the earth	453
Eternal Spirit, we confess	169	Great God, to Thee my evening song	36
		Great God, we sing that mighty hand	493
FADE, fade, each earthly joy	244	Guide me, O thou great Jehovah	297
Far from my heavenly home	472		
Far from my thoughts, vain world, begone	3	HAIL, my ever-blessed Jesus	265
Father, by Thy love and power	55	Hail, Thou once despised Jesus	126
Father, I know that all my life	351	Hail to the Lord's Anointed	455
Father of heaven, whose love profound	75	Happy the man, who knows	376
Father of love and power	52	Happy the souls to Jesus joined	425
Father of mercies, in Thy Word	171	Hark, my soul, it is the Lord	356
Father, whate'er of earthly bliss	343	Hark, ten thousand harps and voices	486
Fight the good fight with all thy might	321	Hark, the voice of love and mercy	115
Fling out the banner; let it float	449	Hark! what mean those holy voices	99
For a season called to part	17	Hark, what mean those lamentations	466
For thee, O dear, dear country	484	Haste, traveller haste! the night comes on	199
For Thy mercy and Thy grace	490	Hasten, Lord, the glorious time	460
Forever with the Lord	473	He leadeth me, O blessed thought	307
Forth in Thy Name, O Lord, I go	38	He lives, the great Redeemer lives	120
From all that dwell below the skies	73	Hear my prayer, O heavenly Father	42
From every stormy wind that blows	29	Heirs of unending life	316
From Greenland's icy mountains	454	Here I can firmly rest	261
From the cross uplifted high	190	High in the heavens, eternal God	71
		Holy Bible, book divine	175
GENTLY, Lord, O gently lead us	296	Holy Father, cheer our way	69
Give me the wings of faith to rise	423	Holy Father, hear my cry	235

INDEX OF FIRST LINES.

First Line	Hymn
Holy Ghost, the Infinite	159
Holy Ghost, with light divine	157
Holy, holy, holy Lord	84
How beauteous on the mountains	459
How beauteous were the marks divine	107
How blessed, from the bonds of sin	394
How blest the righteous when he dies	475
How charming is the place	62
How firm a foundation, ye saints	361
How gentle God's commands	352
How precious is the book divine	173
How sad our state by nature is	227
How sweet the name of Jesus sounds	293
How sweet to leave the world awhile	7
I am coming to the cross	178
I am trusting Thee, Lord Jesus	214
I bless the Christ of God	258
I bring my sins to Thee	220
I have a Saviour, He's pleading in glory	207
I hear the Saviour say	252
I heard the voice of Jesus say	249
"I know that my Redeemer lives"	119
I lay my sins on Jesus	253
I left it all with Jesus long ago	292
I lift my heart to Thee	410
I love Thy kingdom, Lord	428
I love to steal awhile away	32
I love to tell the story	279
I'm but a stranger here	310
I'm not ashamed to own my Lord	338
I need Thee, precious Jesus	370
I've found the pearl of greatest price	294
I was a wandering sheep	269
I worship Thee, sweet Will of God	344
In heavenly love abiding	372
In the cross of Christ I glory	328
In this calm, impressive hour	57
In Thy name, O Lord, assembling	13
It passeth knowledge, that dear love of Thine	295
Jehovah God, Thy gracious power	93
Jehovah reigns; His throne is high	77
Jerusalem, my happy home	479
Jerusalem, the golden	482
Jesus, and shall it ever be	331
Jesus calls us: o'er the tumult	330
Jesus, full of truth and love	233

First Line	Hymn
Jesus, I live to Thee	263
Jesus, I love Thy charming Name	288
Jesus, I my cross have taken	333
Jesus, I will trust Thee	256
Jesus, Lover of my soul	335
Jesus, Master, whom I serve	389
Jesus, Master, whose I am	388
Jesus, my Lord, my God, my All	406
Jesus, our best-beloved Friend	386
Jesus shall reign where'er the sun	448
Jesus, the sinner's Friend, to Thee	247
Jesus, the very thought of Thee	289
Jesus, these eyes have never seen	283
Jesus, Thou art the sinner's Friend	228
Jesus, Thy Church, with longing eyes	450
Jesus, Thy Name I love	271
Join all the glorious names	222
Joy to the world, the Lord is come	100
Just as I am, without one plea	246
Kingdoms and thrones to God belong	79
Laborers of Christ, arise	382
Laden with guilt, and full of fears	174
Lamb of God, whose bleeding love	404
Lead, kindly Light, amid the encircling gloom	306
Let children hear the mighty deeds	498
Let everlasting glories crown	177
Let every mortal ear attend	180
Let party names no more	430
Let saints below in concert sing	424
Let songs of praises fill the sky	155
Let us, with a gladsome mind	85
Life is the time to serve the Lord	198
Long hath the night of sorrow reigned	348
Look from Thy sphere of endless day	443
Look, ye saints, the sight is glorious	134
Lord, as to Thy dear cross we flee	337
Lord, dismiss us with Thy blessing, Bid	130
Lord, dismiss us with Thy blessing, Fill	14
Lord God, the Holy Ghost	161
Lord, I am Thine, entirely Thine	418
Lord, I know Thy grace is nigh me	230
Lord, in the morning Thou shalt hear	67
Lord, in the strength of grace	407
Lord, in Thy Name Thy servants plead	499
Lord Jesus, when we stand afar	113
Lord, lead the way the Saviour went	392

	HYMN		HYMN
Lord of all power and might	468	O bless the Lord, my soul ✓	82
- Lord, we come before Thee now	15	O cease, my wandering soul ✓	192
Lord, while for all mankind we pray	452	O Christ, our King, Creator, Lord	140 -
Lord, with glowing heart I'd praise Thee ✓	266	O Christ, what burdens bowed Thy head	257
- Love Divine, all love excelling	145	O come, loud anthems let us sing	65
		O could I speak the matchless worth	277 -
- Majestic sweetness sits enthroned	137	O day of rest and gladness	64
- May the grace of Christ our Saviour	41	O for a closer walk with God	347 -
- More love to Thee, O Christ	373	O for a heart to praise my God	340 -
- Mourn for the thousands slain	399	O for a thousand tongues to sing	282 -
- Must Jesus bear the cross alone	336	O for the death of those	471 -
- My country, 'tis of thee	501	O gift of gifts! O grace of faith	260 -
- My dear Redeemer, and my Lord	106	O God, mine inmost soul convert	477 -
- My faith looks up to Thee	270	O God, beneath Thy guiding hand	494 -
My feet are worn and weary with the ✓	309	O God of Bethel, by whose hand	298 -
My God, accept my heart this day	412	O God, our help in ages past	90
My God and Father, while I stray	360	O God, the Rock of Ages	96 -
- My God, how endless is Thy love	9	O happy day, that fixed my choice	417 -
My God, is any hour so sweet ✗	30	O Holy Spirit, Fount of love	151
My God, my Father, blissful Name	339	O Jesus, I have promised ✓	405
My God, my King, Thy various praise	6	O Jesus, King most wonderful	281
My God, my Life, my Love ✓	353	O Jesus, Lord of light and grace	35
My God, permit me not to be	4	O Jesus, sweet the tears I shed	112 -
- My God, the Spring of all my joys	316	O Jesus, Thou art standing ✓	182
My gracious Lord, I own Thy right ✓	383	O Jesus, when I think of Thee ✓	103
- My hope is built on nothing less	268	O Lamb of God, still keep me ✓	371
My Jesus, I love Thee	254	O Lord, how happy should we be	334 -
My Saviour, my almighty Friend ✓	285	O Lord of heaven, and earth, and sea ✓	395
- My soul, be on thy guard	311	O Lord, Thy work revive	162 -
My soul doth magnify the Lord	152	O Lord, when we the path retrace	105
- My soul, weigh not thy life	313	O Love divine, how sweet Thou art	278
- My spirit, on Thy care	365	O Master, let me walk with Thee ✓	387
		O mean may seem this house of clay	136
- Nearer, my God, to Thee	374	O mother dear, Jerusalem	480 -
No more, my God, I boast no more	419	O Paradise! O Paradise ✓	487
No, not despairingly	245	O perfect life of love	117
- Not all the blood of beasts	116	O praise our God to-day	377
Not all the outward forms on earth	181	O Saviour, where shall guilty man	255
Now be the Gospel banner ✗	462	O Spirit of the living God ✓	445
· Now begin the heavenly theme	301	O that the Lord's salvation	464
Now from labor and from care ✓	56	O the bitter shame and sorrow ✓	421
Now God be with us, for the night is	49	O the sweet wonders of that cross	420 -
Now I have found a Friend	243	O Thou that hearest prayer	170
- Now is the accepted time	194	O Thou that hear'st the prayer of faith ✓	213
Now may He who from the dead	22	O Thou, to whose all-searching sight	299
~ Now the day is over	48	O very God of very God ✓	391
- Now to the Lord a noble song	78	O what, if we are Christ's ✓	315
Now to the Lord, who makes us know	143	O where is He that trod the sea ✓	104
Now, when the dusky shades of night	45	O where shall rest be found	240 -

INDEX OF FIRST LINES.

	HYMN
- O worship the King, All glorious above...	94
- O'er the gloomy hills of darkness	440
On Zion and on Lebanon	451
- One sweetly solemn thought	470
- One there is above all others	414
Our country's voice is pleading... ✓	456
- Our Heavenly Father calls	25
- Our Lord, who knows full well	24
Out of the deep I call	241
PART in peace, Christ's life was peace	18
- Pass me not, O gracious Father	212
Peace, perfect peace, in this dark world...	401
People of the living God	408
Pilgrim, burdened with thy sin	203
Praise, my soul, the King of heaven ✓	80
Praise the God of our salvation	44
- Praise to God, immortal praise	500
Praises to Him whose love has given ✓	74
Pray, without ceasing, pray ✓	27
- Prayer is the soul's sincere desire	31
Prostrate, dear Jesus, at Thy feet ✓	224
RAISE your triumphant songs	262
Rejoice, ye pure in heart	314
Rescue the perishing	396
- Return, O wanderer, return	195
Revive Thy work, O Lord	378
- Rise, my soul, and stretch thy wings	304
- Rock of ages, cleft for me	236
SAFELY through another week	54
Saints of God, the dawn is brightening...	439
- Salvation, O the joyful sound	144
- Saviour, again to Thy dear Name	59
Saviour, blessed Saviour	267
- Saviour, breathe an evening blessing	39
- Saviour, happy would I be	274
Saviour, sprinkle many nations	465
- Saviour, teach me, day by day	357
- Saviour, Thy dying love	402
- Saviour, visit Thy plantation	438
- Saviour, who Thy flock art feeding	435
- See, Israel's gentle Shepherd stands	434
- Shepherd of tender youth	436
Show pity, Lord, O Lord, forgive	217
Since all the varying scenes of time	91
Sing of Jesus, sing forever	291
Sinners Jesus will receive	238

	HYMN
Sinners, turn, why will ye die	204 -
So let our lips and lives express	385 -
Softly now the light of day	21 -
Soldiers of Christ, arise ✓	327
Soldiers, who are Christ's below	326
Songs of praise the angels sang ✓	1
Soon may the last glad song arise	442 -
Sow in the morn thy seed	380 -
Spirit Divine, attend our prayers	153
Stand up, my soul, shake off thy fears	322 -
Stand up, stand up for Jesus	318 -
Summer suns are glowing ✓	497
Sun of my soul, Thou Saviour dear	37 -
Surely Christ thy griefs hath borne	237
Sweet is Thy mercy, Lord ✓	303
Sweet Saviour, bless us ere we go	47
Sweet the moments, rich in blessing	409 -
Sweet the time, exceeding sweet ✓	88
TAKE me, O my Father, take me	229 -
Take my heart, O Father, take it	415 -
Take my life and let it be ✓	403
Take, my soul, thy full salvation ✓	329
Take up thy cross, the Saviour said	332 -
Tarry with me, O my Saviour	40
Thank and praise Jehovah's name	87
The God of harvest praise ✓	503
The Great Physician now is near	206
The head that once was crowned with	121 -
The King of glory standeth ✓	184
The King of love my Shepherd is ✓	350
The Lord is my Shepherd, no want	362 -
The Lord my Shepherd is	364 -
The morning light is breaking	457 -
The sands of time are sinking	485 -
The Saviour calls, let every ear	179
The Saviour! O what endless charms	286 -
The Spirit in our hearts ✓	191
The strife is o'er, the battle done	118
Thee we adore, eternal Lord	8
There is a fountain filled with blood	226 -
There is a land of pure delight	478 -
There is an hour of peaceful rest	488 -
There's a wideness in God's mercy	186 -
They pray the best who pray and watch ✓	367
They who seek the throne of grace	16 -
Thine for ever! God of love ✓	416
Think gently of the erring one	393
This is not my place of resting	476 -

INDEX OF FIRST LINES.

First Line	HYMN
This is the glorious day	63
Thou art the Way: to Thee alone	135
Thou, from whom we never part	20
Thou, who didst on Calvary bleed	234
Thou who roll'st the year around	491
Thou, whose almighty Word	469
Though faint, yet pursuing, we go on	363
Though now the nations sit beneath	447
Three in One, and One in Three	53
Through all the changing scenes of life	345
Thy life was given for me	422
Thy works, not mine, O Christ	223
Time is earnest, passing by	201
Time is winging us away	305
'Tis by the faith of joys to come	323
'Tis midnight; and on Olive's brow	108
To Him who for our sins was slain	147
To Thee, O Comforter Divine	148
To Thy pastures fair and large	358
To-day the Saviour calls	200
To-morrow, Lord, is Thine	193
Uplift the blood-red banner	463
Vainly through night's weary hours	43
We give Thee but Thine own	375
Weary of earth and laden with my sin	215
Weary with my load of sin	239
Welcome, sweet day of rest	61
What a Friend we have in Jesus	187
What grace, O Lord, and beauty shone	102
What shall I render to my God	411
When all Thy mercies, O my God	92
When I can read my title clear	308
When I survey the wondrous cross	114
When shall the voice of singing	458
When sins and fears prevailing rise	368
Where high the heavenly temple stands	141
Where two or three, with sweet accord	5
While life prolongs its precious light	196
While Thee I seek, protecting Power	369
While with ceaseless course the sun	489
Why should the children of a King	149
With broken heart and contrite sigh	216
With tearful eyes I look around	248
Witness, ye men and angels, now	413
Work, for the night is coming	400
Workman of God, O lose not heart	390
Worship, honor, power, and blessing	127
Ye Christian heralds, go, proclaim	444
Ye dying sons of men	205
Ye servants of God	95
Ye servants of the Lord	379
Yet there is room	209
Yield not to temptation	398
Your harps, ye trembling saints	302
Zion, at thy shining gates	481
Zion's daughter, weep no more	110

www.ingramcontent.com/pod-product-compliance
Lightning Source LLC
Chambersburg PA
CBHW021801230426
43669CB00008B/599